Harris Surname

Ireland: 1600s to 1900s

From Ireland Church Records of Baptism, Marriage and Death

Comprised of Roman Catholic and Church of Ireland Records

From Counties Carlow, Cork, Kerry and Dublin City

Compiled by **Donovan Hurst**

November 8, 2011

Dedication

This work is dedicated to all of those that came before us and shaped our lives to make us the people that we are today.

Table of Contents

Introduction

This is a compilation of individuals who have the surname of Harris that lived in the country of Ireland from the 1600s to the 1900s. I have placed each entry into one of four categories: Families, Individual Births/Baptisms, Individual Burials, and Individual Marriages. If a marriage entry primarily concerns an Individual Harris who is female, then I have placed that entry under the category of Individual Marriages. If a marriage entry primarily concerns an Individual Harris who is male, then I have placed that entry under the category of Families. Images of many of these listings are available at http://churchrecords.irishgenealogy.ie/churchrecords/.

To help guide the reader of this work, the format of this book is as follows:

- Main Family Entry (Husband and Wife) (Father and Mother)

  - Child of Main Family Entry, including Spouse(s) when available

    - Grandchild of Main Family Entry, including Spouse(s) when available

      - Great-Grandchild of Main Family Entry, including Spouse(s) when available

(**Bolded Text**) following any entry includes any additional information such as Residence(s), Occupation(s), Signature(s), etc. when available.

Hurst

Some of the fonts used in this work symbolizes Celtic writing. The traditional letters, numbers, and punctuation marks and their Celtic counterparts are as follows:

Traditional Letters (Uppercase & Lowercase)

A a B b C c D d E f G g H h I i J j K k L l M m N n O o P p Q q R r S s T t U u V v W w X x Y y Z z

Celtic Letters (Uppercase & Lowercase)

A a B b C c D ð E e F f G g H h I i J j K k L l M m

N n O o P p Q q R r S s T t U u V v W w X x Y y Z z

Traditional Numbers

1 2 3 4 5 6 7 8 9 10

Celtic Numbers

1 2 3 4 5 6 7 8 9 10

Traditional Punctuation

. , : ' " & - ( )

Celtic Punctuation

. , : ' " & - ( )

Harris Surname Ireland: 1600s to 1900s

Parish Churches

Carlow (Church of Ireland)

Aghold Parish, Carlow Parish, Cloydagh Parish, Dunleckney Parish, Hacketstown Parish, Staplestown Parish, Tullow Parish, and Wells Parish.

Cork & Ross

(Roman Catholic or RC)

Ardfield & Rathbarry Parish, Aughadown Parish, Ballinhassig Parish, Ballinhassig (Goggins, Ballyheedy, & Ballygarvan) Parish, Bandon Parish, Bantry Parish, Caharagh Parish, Carrigaline & Templebrigid Parish, Castlehaven & Myross Parish, Clonakilty Parish, Clontead Parish, Cork - South Parish, Cork - SS. Peter & Paul Parish, Courcy's Country or Ballinspittal Parish, Desertseges Parish, Douglas Parish, Douglas & Ballygarvan Parrish, Drimoleague Parish, Dunmanway Parish, Enniskeane Parish, Innishannon Parish, Ivelearly Parish, Kilbrittain Parish, Kilmacabea Parish, Kilmeen & Castleventry Parish, Kilmichael Parish, Kilmurry Parish, Kilmurry, Moviddy, Kilbonane, & Cannavee Parish, Kinsale Parish, Lislee, Abbeymahon, & Donoughmore (Barryroe) Parish, Muintervara Parish, Murragh & Templemartin Parish, Rath & the Islands (Cape & Sherkin) Parish, Rossalettiri & Kilkeraunmor (Roscarbery & Lissevard) Parish, Schull East Parish, Schull West Parish, Skibbereen & Rath Parish, Skibbereen (Creagh & Sullon) Parish, Timoleague Parish, Timoleague & Barryroe Parish, and Tracton Abbey Parish.

Dublin (Church of Ireland)

Arbour Hill Barracks Parish, Bethseda Chapel Parish, Chapelizod Parish, Clondalkin Parish, Clontarf Parish, Crumlin Parish, Glasnevin Parish, Grangegorman Parish, Kilmainham Parish, Leeson Park Parish, North Strand Parish, Portobello Barracks Parish, Rathmines Parish, Richmond Barracks Parish, Rotunda Chapel Parish, Royal Hibernian Parish, St. Andrew Parish, St. Anne Parish, St. Audoen Parish, St. Barnabas Parish, St. Bride Parish, St. Catherine Parish, St. George Parish, St. James Parish, St. John Parish, St. Kevin Parish, St. Luke Parish, St. Mark Parish, St. Mary Parish, St. Matthew Parish, St. Michael Parish, St. Michan Parish, St. Nicholas Within Parish, St. Nicholas Without Parish, St. Patrick Parish, St. Paul Parish, St. Peter Parish, St. Stephen Parish, St. Thomas Parish, St. Werburgh Parish, and Taney Parish.

Dublin (Roman Catholic or RC)

Chapelizod Parish, Clondalkin Parish, Harrington Street Parish, Lucan Parish, Palmerstown Parish, Rathfarnham Parish, Rathmines Parish, Saggart Parish, Sandyford Parish, SS. Michael & John Parish, St. Agatha Parish, St. Andrew Parish, St. Audoen Parish, St. Catherine Parish, St. James Parish, St. Joseph Parish, St. Lawrence Parish, St. Mary, Donnybrook Parish, St. Mary, Haddington Road Parish, St. Mary, Pro Cathedral Parish, St. Michan Parish, and St. Nicholas Parish.

Kerry (Church of Ireland)

Ardfert Parish, Ballymacelligott & Ballyseedy Parish, Cahir Parish, Castleisland Parish, Dingle Parish, Dromod & Prior Parish, Kenmare Parish, Kilcolman Parish, Killarney Parish, Killehenney Parish, Killiney Parish, Killorglin Parish, Kilnaughtin Parish, Lisselton Parish, and Tralee Parish.

Kerry (Roman Catholic or RC)

Abbeydorney Parish, Annascaul Parish, Ardfert Parish, Ballybunion Parish, Ballylongford Parish, Ballymacelligott Parish, Boherbue Parish, Caherciveen Parish, Caherdaniel Parish, Castlegregory Parish, Castleisland Parish, Castlemaine Parish, Castletownbere Parish, Causeway Parish, Dingle Parish, Dromod Parish, Dromtariffe Parish, Firies Parish, Glenbeigh/Glencar Parish, Kenmare Parish, Kilgarvan Parish, Killarney Parish, Killeentierna Parish, Killorglin Parish, Listowel Parish, Milltown Parish, Rathmore Parish, Sneem Parish, Spa Parish, Tarbert Parish, Tralee Parish, and Tuosist Parish.

Families

- Abby Harris & Ellen Sullivan

    o Abby Harris – bapt. 10 Jul 1846 (Baptism, Innishannon Parish (RC))

- Abizer Harris & Elizabeth Unknown

    o Elizabeth Harris – bapt. 3 Sep 1827 (Baptism, St. Mary, Pro Cathedral Parish (RC))

Abizer Harris (father):

Residence - Marlboro Street - September 3, 1827

- Abraham Harris & Mary McCarthy

    o Margaret Harris – bapt. 5 Jan 1848 (Baptism, Douglas Parish (RC))

Abraham Harris (father):

Residence - Ballea - January 5, 1848

- Abraham Harris & Mary Anne Desmond – 17 Oct 1875 (Marriage, Kinsale Parish (RC))

    o Elizabeth Harris – b. 1 Oct 1876, bapt. 30 Sep 1876 (Baptism, Kinsale Parish (RC))

    o Mary Bridget Harris – b. 2 Feb 1878, bapt. 3 Feb 1878 (Baptism, Kinsale Parish (RC))

    o Henry Harris – b. 15 Jun 1879, bapt. 15 Jun 1879 (Baptism, Kinsale Parish (RC))

    o Catherine Harris – b. 23 Oct 1880, bapt. 24 Oct 1880 (Baptism, Kinsale Parish (RC))

Abraham Harris (father):

Residence - Market Lane - September 30, 1876

February 3, 1878

June 15, 1879

Hurst

- Abraham Harris & Mary Margaret O'Sullivan

  - John Harris – bapt. 27 Apr 1850 (Baptism, **Douglas Parish (RC)**)

  - Richard Harris – bapt. 30 Jan 1853 (Baptism, **Douglas & Ballygarvan Parish (RC)**)

  - Catherine Harris – bapt. 28 Feb 1854 (Baptism, **Douglas & Ballygarvan Parish (RC)**)

  - Bridget Harris – bapt. 3 Apr 1856 (Baptism, **Douglas & Ballygarvan Parish (RC)**)

  - Mary Harris – bapt. 1 Jul 1858 (Baptism, **Douglas & Ballygarvan Parish (RC)**)

  - James Harris – bapt. 19 Jul 1860 (Baptism, **Douglas & Ballygarvan Parish (RC)**)

  - Ellen Harris – bapt. 24 Nov 1862 (Baptism, **Douglas & Ballygarvan Parish (RC)**)

  - Henry Harris – bapt. 29 Jan 1865 (Baptism, **Douglas & Ballygarvan Parish (RC)**)

  - Bridget Harris – bapt. 27 Apr 1867 (Baptism, **Douglas & Ballygarvan Parish (RC)**)

Abraham Harris (father):
   Residence - Ballea - April 27, 1850

- Abraham Harris & Susan Tierney

  - John Joseph Harris – b. 31 Oct 1876, bapt. 6 Nov 1876 (Baptism, **SS. Michael & John Parish (RC)**)

Abraham Harris (father):
   Residence - 69 Aungier Street - November 6, 1876

- Abraham Harris & Susan Jane Harris

  - Sydney Herbert Nathaniel Harris – b. 21 Aug 1887, bapt. 27 Oct 1887 (Baptism, **Richmond Barracks Parish**)

Abraham Harris (father):
   Residence - Richmond Barracks - August 21, 1887
   Occupation - Corporal 2/13 Coldstream Guards - August 21, 1887

- Alexander Harris & Bridget Unknown

  - Peter Harris – bapt. 28 Aug 1849 (Baptism, **SS. Michael & John Parish (RC)**)

- Amos Harris & Gobinet Rourke – 4 Aug 1834 (Marriage, **Annascaul Parish (RC)**)

Harris Surname Ireland: 1600s to 1900s

- Andrew Harris & Bridget Unknown

  - Mary Harris – bapt. 9 Oct 1832 (Baptism, **St. James Parish** (RC))

- Andrew Harris & Charlotte Unknown

  - Rebecca Harris – bapt. 11 May 1790 (Baptism, **St. Werburgh Parish**)

Andrew Harris (father):

Residence - Hoyne's Court - May 11, 1790

- Andrew Harris & Elizabeth Unknown

  - Gulielmo Harris – bapt. 1821 (Baptism, **St. Andrew Parish** (RC))

- Andrew Harris & Honora Keleher – 25 Sep 1852 (Marriage, **Cork - SS. Peter & Paul Parish** (RC))

- Andrew Harris & Rose MaGarry – 24 Mar 1799 (Marriage, **St. Mary, Pro Cathedral Parish** (RC))

  - Eleanor Harris – bapt. 1801 (Baptism, **St. Andrew Parish** (RC))

- Andrew Harris & Unknown

  - Mary Anne Harris & Charles Augustus Stevens – 29 Aug 1871 (Marriage, **St. Paul Parish**)

Signatures:

Hurst

Mary Anne Harris (daughter):

    Residence - Royal Barracks - August 29, 1871

    Relationship Status at Marriage - minor age

Charles Augustus Stevens, son of Frederick William Stevens (son-in-law):

    Residence - Royal Barracks - August 29, 1871

    Occupation - Sergeant 6th Dragoon Guards - August 29, 1871

Frederick William Stevens (father):

    Occupation - Watch Maker

Andrew Harris (father):

    Occupation - Steward

Wedding Witnesses:

Henrietta Harris

Signature:

- Arthur Harris & Elizabeth Doyle – 7 Feb 1840 (Marriage, **St. Catherine Parish**)

- Arthur Harris, bur. 25 Mar 1678 (Burial, **St. Michan Parish**), & Elizabeth Harris

  - Thomas Harris – bur. 17 Aug 1682 (Burial, **St. Michan Parish**)

The previously transcribed entry in the church register reads as follows:

    "Thomas, son of Anthony Harris, deceased, & his relict Eliz."

- Arthur Harris & Catherine Harris

  - Florence Ruby Harris – b. 22 Oct 1891, bapt. 29 Nov 1891 (Baptism, **Portobello Barracks Parish**)

Arthur Harris (father):

    Residence - Wellington Barracks Dublin - November 29, 1891

    Occupation - Color Sergeant S Staffordshire Regiment - November 29, 1891

Harris Surname Ireland: 1600s to 1900s

- Arthur Harris & Teresa Russell

  - George Patrick Harris – b. 29 Jul 1892, bapt. 8 Aug 1892 (Baptism, St. Mary, Pro Cathedral Parish (RC))

Arthur Harris (father):

Residence - Rotunda Hospital - August 8, 1892

- Arthur Harris & Unknown

  - Henry Harris & Sarah Jackson – 1 Sep 1852 (Marriage, Dingle Parish)

Henry Harris (son):

Residence - Dingle - September 1, 1852

Occupation - Flour Factor - September 1, 1852

Sarah Jackson, daughter of Thomas Jackson (daughter-in-law):

Residence - Dingle - September 1, 1852

Thomas Jackson (father):

Occupation - Chief Officer C Guard

Arthur Harris (father):

Occupation - Architect

- Arthur Harris & Unknown

  - Arthur Harris & Ellen Murray – 9 Aug 1858 (Marriage, St. Andrew Parish (RC))

Arthur Harris (son):

Residence - 36 Upper Mercer Street - August 9, 1858

Ellen Murray, daughter of John Murray (daughter-in-law):

Residence - 36 Upper Mercer Street - August 9, 1858

- Augustine Harris & Catherine Unknown Dixon – 7 Aug 1716 (Marriage, St. Michan Parish)

Augustine Harris (husband):

Occupation - Statuary - August 7, 1716

Catherine Dixon (wife):

Relationship Status at Marriage - widow

Hurst

- B. Harris & Unknown

  - George Bournapark (B o u r n a pa r k) Harris & Mary Anne Dornan (D o r n a n) – 4 Apr 1825

    (Marriage, **St. Audoen Parish (RC)**), 28 Mar 1825 (Marriage, **St. Audoen Parish**)

Signatures:

George Bournapark Harris (husband):

    Residence - London - March 28, 1825

        St. Anne Parish - March 28, 1825

Mary Anne Dornan (wife):

    Residence - St. Audoen Parish - March 28, 1825

- Benjamin Harris & Catherine Hickey – 24 Nov 1827 (Marriage, **Bandon Parish (RC)**)

- Benjamin Harris & Catherine Unknown

  - Elizabeth Harris – bapt. 1753 (Baptism, **St. Andrew Parish (RC)**)

- Benjamin Harris & Elizabeth Harris

  - Ealee Harris – bapt. 18 Jun 1736 (Baptism, **St. Luke Parish**)

Child's name was transcribed as Elace.

The entry from the church register reads as follows:

    "June 18: Ealee Dau of Benjamen and Elisabeth Harris."

- Blaney Harris & Leticia Unknown

  - Sarah Harris – bapt. 12 Dec 1810 (Baptism, **St. Peter Parish**)

Harris Surname Ireland: 1600s to 1900s

- Charles Harris & Anne Unknown

  - Sarah Harris – bapt. 7 Sep 1794 (Baptism, **St. Catherine Parish**)

- Charles Harris & Anne Harris

  - Patrick Joseph Harris – b. 11 Mar 1889, bapt. 12 May 1889 (Baptism, **Bethseda Chapel Parish**)

Charles Harris (father):
  Residence - 107 Lower Dorset Street - May 12, 1889
  Occupation - Carpenter - May 12, 1889

- Charles Harris & Catherine Unknown

  - Charles Harris – bapt. 1795 (Baptism, **St. Andrew Parish** (RC))

- Charles Harris & Catherine Evans

  - James Scivinton Harris – bapt. 23 Nov 1812 (Baptism, **St. James Parish** (RC))

- Charles Harris & Catherine Meyers

  - Francis Joseph Harris – b. 25 Jul 1882, bapt. 16 Aug 1882 (Baptism, **St. Mary, Pro Cathedral Parish** (RC))

Charles Harris (father):
  Residence - 6 Ryder's Row - August 16, 1882

- Charles Harris, b. 1795, bur. 29 Jan 1851 (Burial, **Dunleckney Parish**), & Elizabeth Unknown

  - Abigail Harris – b. 15 May 1818, bapt. 22 May 1818 (Baptism, **Dunleckney Parish**)

  - John Harris – b. 7 Mar 1821, bapt. 7 Mar 1821 (Baptism, **Dunleckney Parish**)

  - John Harris – b. 6 mar 1822, bapt. 10 Mar 1822 (Baptism, **Dunleckney Parish**)

  - Charles Harris – b. 30 Dec 1825, bapt. 15 Jan 1826 (Baptism, **Dunleckney Parish**)

  - Elizabeth Harris – b. 12 May 1831, bapt. 15 May 1831 (Baptism, **Dunleckney Parish**)

Charles Harris (father):

Residence - Long Hills - Before January 29, 1851

Hurst

- Charles Harris & Elizabeth Unknown

  - Lydia Harris – b. 16 Nov 1862, bapt. 25 Jan 1863 (Baptism, St. Catherine Parish)

  - Charles Harris – b. 1862, bapt. 1863 (Baptism, St. Catherine Parish)

Charles Harris (father):

Residence - 25 Brown Street - January 25, 1863

Occupation - Laborer - January 25, 1863

- Charles Harris & Jane Harris

  - Charles Harris – bapt. 6 May 1811 (Baptism, St. Werburgh Parish)

Charles Harris (father):

Residence - Pembroke Court Castle Street - May 6, 1811

- Charles Harris & Judith Unknown

  - Peter Harris – bapt. 30 Jun 1734 (Baptism, St. Luke Parish)

- Charles Harris & Margaret Harris

  - Mary Harris – bapt. 26 Jun 1774 (Baptism, St. Luke Parish)

  - William Harris – bapt. 11 Aug 1776 (Baptism, St. Luke Parish)

  - Anne Harris – bapt. 7 Mar 1779 (Baptism, St. Luke Parish)

Charles Harris (father):

Residence - New Market - June 26, 1774

Skinner's Alley - August 11, 1776

March 7, 1779

Occupation - Worseted Weaver - June 26, 1774

August 11, 1776

March 7, 1779

Harris Surname Ireland: 1600s to 1900s

- Charles Harris & Margaret Mary Unknown

  - Margaret Harris – bapt. 5 Jan 1783 (Baptism, **St. Catherine Parish**)

  - Anne Harris – bapt. 26 Jun 1785 (Baptism, **St. Catherine Parish**)

Charles Harris (father):

Residence - Meath Street - January 5, 1783

June 26, 1785

- Charles Harris & Mary Harris

  - John Harris – bapt. 30 Jan 1833 (Baptism, **St. Mary, Pro Cathedral Parish (RC)**)

- Charles Harris, bur. 26 Nov 1702 (Burial, **St. John Parish**) & Mary Margaret Unknown

  - Witt Harris – bapt. 29 Jun 1690 (Baptism, **St. John Parish**)

  - Thomas Harris – bapt. 22 Feb 1692 (Baptism, **St. John Parish**)

  - Samuel Harris – bapt. 3 Sep 1693 (Baptism, **St. John Parish**)

  - Mary Harris – bapt. 26 Aug 1695 (Baptism, **St. John Parish**)

- Charles Harris & Unknown

  - Frederick Harris & Louisa Anne Hutching – 30 Aug 1874 (Marriage, **Kilmainham Parish**)

Frederick Harris (son):

Residence - Richmond Barracks - August 30, 1874

Occupation - Corporal 46th Regiment - August 30, 1874

Louisa Anne Hutching, daughter of James Hutching (daughter-in-law):

Residence - Richmond Barracks - August 30, 1874

James Hutching (father):

Occupation - Farmer

Charles Harris (father):

Occupation - Coal Merchant

Hurst

- Charles William Harris & Mary Harriet Johnston – 5 Oct 1840 (Marriage, **St. George Parish**)

Signatures:

Charles William Harris (husband):

    Residence - 22 Portland Street, St. George Parish - October 5, 1840

Mary Harriet Johnston (wife):

    Residence - St. George Parish - October 5, 1840

Wedding Witnesses:

William Harris

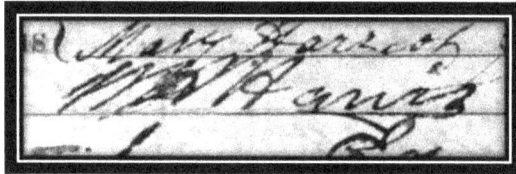

Signature:

- Christopher Harris & Bridget Doyle

  o Thomas Joseph Harris – b. 1 Aug 1886, bapt. 3 Aug 1886 (Baptism, **Harrington Street Parish (RC)**)

Christopher Harris (father):

    Residence - 4 Charlemont Row - August 3, 1886

- Christopher Harris & Jean Unknown

  o James Harris – bapt. 20 Jan 1741 (Baptism, **St. Michan Parish (RC)**)

Christopher Harris (father):

    Residence - Mark Street - January 20, 1741

- Christopher Harris & Mary Harris

  o James Harris – bapt. 1770 (Baptism, **St. Andrew Parish (RC)**)

Harris Surname Ireland: 1600s to 1900s

- Connor Harris & Unknown Harris – b. 1696, bur. 7 Nov 1760 (Burial, **St. Werburgh Parish**)

Unknown Harris (wife):

  Residence - Stephen's Green - Before November 7, 1760

  Cause of Death - decay

- Cornelius (C o r n e l i u s) Harris & Anne Driscoll – 5 Nov 1841 (Marriage, **Lislee, Abbeymahon, & Donoughmore (Barryroe) Parish (RC))** (Marriage, **Timoleague & Barryroe Parish(RC))**

Cornelius Harris (husband):

  Residence - Scatholemann - November 5, 1841

- Daniel Harris & Bridget Dodd – 10 Jan 1848 (Marriage, **St. Andrew Parish (RC)**)

  o John Joseph Harris – b. 20 Oct 1848, bapt. 5 Nov 1848 (Baptism, **St. Peter Parish**)

  o William Harris – b. 9 Nov 1849, bapt. 25 Nov 1849 (Baptism, **St. Peter Parish**)

  o Mary Elizabeth Harris, b. 18 Apr 1851, bapt. 1 Jun 1851 (Baptism, **St. Peter Parish**) & John Joseph Murphy – 8 Feb 1875 (Marriage, **Rathmines Parish (RC)**)

    - Joseph Christopher Murphy – b. Jan 1877, bapt. 26 Jan 1877 (Baptism, **Harrington Street Parish (RC)**)

    - Mary Murphy – b. 3 Feb 1878, bapt. 14 Feb 1878 (Baptism, **Harrington Street Parish (RC)**)

    - Charles John Murphy – b. 30 Jul 1879, bapt. 4 Aug 1879 (Baptism, **Harrington Street Parish (RC)**)

    - Thomas Murphy – b. 23 Jul 1880, bapt. 31 Jul 1880 (Baptism, **Harrington Street Parish (RC)**)

    - Thomas Gerald Patrick Murphy – b. 20 Sep 1881, bapt. 3 Oct 1881 (Baptism, **Harrington Street Parish (RC)**)

Hurst

- Richard Vincent Murphy – b. 16 Jan 1883, bapt. 20 Jan 1883 (Baptism, Harrington Street Parish (RC))

- John Thomas Murphy – b. 23 Feb 1884, bapt. 3 Mar 1884 (Baptism, Harrington Street Parish (RC))

- Eiley Mary Elizabeth Murphy – b. 4 Mar 1887, bapt. 18 Mar 1887 (Baptism, Harrington Street Parish (RC))

Mary Elizabeth Harris (daughter):

Residence - Camden Street - February 8, 1875

John Joseph Murphy, son of Andrew Murphy & Mary Jordan (son-in-law):

Residence - Camden Street - February 8, 1875

1 Camden Street - January 26, 1877

74 Camden Street - February 14, 1878

18 Harcourt Street - August 4, 1879

July 31, 1880

October 3, 1881

January 20, 1883

March 3, 1884

March 18, 1887

- Anne Harris – bapt. 17 Dec 1852 (Baptism, St. Michan Parish (RC))

- Bridget Harris – b. 31 Dec 1853, bapt. 23 Jun 1858 (Baptism, St. Mary Parish)

- Eva Mary Harris – b. 30 Jun 1855, bapt. 8 Apr 1856 (Baptism, St. Mary Parish)

- Daniel Harris – b. 8 Oct 1856, bapt. 23 Jun 1858 (Baptism, St. Mary Parish)

- Daniel Henry Joseph Harris – b. Oct 1856, bapt. 13 Jul 1859 (Baptism, St. Michan Parish (RC))

- Eleanor Harris – b. Aug 1862, bapt. 18 Jan 1863 (Baptism, Rathmines Parish)

- Kathleen Harris – b. 12 Jul 1864, bapt. 30 Aug 1864 (Baptism, St. Peter Parish)

Harris Surname Ireland: 1600s to 1900s

Daniel Harris (father):

Residence - 4 Bannavilla Rathmines - November 5, 1848

June 1, 1851

4 Bannavilla Mount Pleasant Avenue - November 25, 1849

35 Upper Dominick Street - April 8, 1856

June 23, 1858

July 13, 1859

13 Oldmount Pleasant Avenue - January 18, 1863

August 30, 1864

Occupation - Engineer - November 5, 1848

November 25, 1849

Machinist - June 1, 1851

Hotel Keeper - April 8, 1856

Mechanist - June 23, 1858

Mechanical Engineer - January 18, 1863

Billiard Table Maker - August 30, 1864

- Daniel Harris & Bridget Doyle

  o William Harris – bapt. 25 Feb 1850 (Baptism, **St. Nicholas Parish** (RC))

- Daniel Harris & Bridget Unknown

  o Daniel Harris – bapt. 1826 (Baptism, **St. Andrew Parish** (RC))

  o John Harris – bapt. 1826 (Baptism, **St. Andrew Parish** (RC))

- Daniel Harris & Elizabeth Unknown

  o James Harris – bapt. 29 Dec 1811 (Baptism, **St. Peter Parish**)

- Daniel Harris & Eva Hastings

  o David Avonelle Harris – b. 14 Oct 1873, bapt. 14 Oct 1894 (Baptism, **Rathmines Parish** (RC))

  o Robert Aloysius Harris – b. 31 Oct 1875, bapt. 21 May 1896 (Baptism, **Rathmines Parish** (RC))

13

Hurst

Daniel Harris (father):

Residence - Dublin - October 14, 1894

14 Charlemont Mall - May 21, 1896

- Daniel Harris & Mary Cot- - -

  o Mary Harris – bapt. 28 Aug 1796 (Baptism, **Kilmurry Parish (RC)**)

- Daniel Harris & Mary Downs – 19 Nov 1786 (Marriage, **St. Nicholas Parish (RC)**)

- Daniel Harris & Mary Whelan – 7 Apr 1790 (Marriage, **St. Nicholas Parish (RC)**)

- Daniel Harris & Mary Anne Byrne (B y r n e) – 30 Jan 1803 (Marriage, **St. Luke Parish**)

  o Anne Harris – bapt. 19 Feb 1804 (Baptism, **St. Nicholas Parish (RC)**)

Daniel Harris (father):

Residence - St. Luke Parish - January 30, 1803

Mary Anne Byrne (mother):

Residence - St. Luke Parish - January 30, 1803

- David Harris & Anne Harris

  o Anne Harris – bapt. 1762 (Baptism, **St. Andrew Parish (RC)**)

  o John Harris – bapt. 1765 (Baptism, **St. Andrew Parish (RC)**)

  o George Harris – bapt. 1771 (Baptism, **St. Andrew Parish (RC)**)

- David Harris & Honora Beggs

  o Michael Harris – bapt. 7 Oct 1766 (Baptism, **St. Catherine Parish**)

  o James Harris – bapt. 8 Aug 1771 (Baptism, **St. Catherine Parish (RC)**)

- David Harris & Mary Redmond

  o David Harris – bapt. 19 Jun 1846 (Baptism, **St. Catherine Parish (RC)**)

- David Harris & Mary Unknown

  o Elizabeth Harris – d. 22 May 1750 , bur. 22 May 1750 (Burial, **Carlow Parish**)

Harris Surname Ireland: 1600s to 1900s

- David Harris & Unknown

  - David Harris & Margaret Roach – 15 Jan 1885 (Marriage, **Carlow Parish**)

Signatures:

David Harris (son):

    Residence - Oak Park, Painstown Parish - January 15, 1885

    Occupation - Valet - January 15, 1885

Margaret Roach, daughter of John Roach (daughter-in-law):

    Residence - Carlow - January 15, 1885

    Occupation - Servant - January 15, 1885

John Roach (father):

    Occupation - Laborer

Signature:

David Harris (father):

    Occupation - Farm Bailiff

Wedding Witnesses:

John Roach & Mary Roche

Signatures:

Hurst

- David Harris & Mary Waters

  - Bartholomew Harris – bapt. 27 Aug 1820 (Baptism, **Cork - South Parish (RC)**)

- Dennis Harris & Bridget Hannifen – 18 Feb 1890 (Marriage, **Glenbeigh/Glencar Parish (RC)**)

  - Mary Harris – b. 2 Feb 1891, bapt. 3 Feb 1891 (Baptism, **Glenbeigh/Glencar Parish (RC)**)

Dennis Harris (father):

Residence - Coolnaharragill - February 3, 1891

Bridget Hannifen (mother):

Residence - Coolnaharragill - February 18, 1890

- Dennis Harris & Catherine Griffin

  - John Harris – b. 7 Jun 1844, bapt. 7 Jun 1844 (Baptism, **Glenbeigh/Glencar Parish** (RC))

  - Mary Harris – b. 13 Oct 1846, bapt. 13 Oct 1846 (Baptism, **Glenbeigh/Glencar Parish (RC)**)

  - Julia Harris, b. 18 Sep 1852, bapt. 18 Sep 1852 (Baptism, **Glenbeigh/Glencar Parish (RC)**) & Jeremiah Foley – 12 Sep 1891 (Marriage, **Killarney Parish** (RC))

Jeremiah Foley, son of John Foley & Catherine McCrohan (son-in-law).

  - Michael Harris – b. 24 Jun 1856, bapt. 24 Jun 1856 (Baptism, **Glenbeigh/Glencar Parish (RC)**)

Dennis Harris (father):

Residence - Kilnabrack - June 7, 1844

October 13, 1846

Reennanallagane - September 18, 1852

Coolnaharragill - June 24, 1856

Harris Surname Ireland: 1600s to 1900s

- Dennis Harris & Catherine Griffin

  o Bridget Harris – b. 13 Apr 1884, bapt. 13 Apr 1884 (Baptism, **Glenbeigh/Glencar Parish (RC)**)

Dennis Harris (father):

Residence - Reennanallagane - April 13, 1884

- Dennis Harris & Catherine Moriarty

  o Patrick Harris – b. 12 Jul 1856, bapt. 12 Jul 1856 (Baptism, **Glenbeigh/Glencar Parish (RC)**)

Dennis Harris (father):

Residence - Drom - July 12, 1856

- Dennis Harris & Helen Ellen Connor – 22 Feb 1868 (Marriage, **Firies Parish** (RC))

  o Honora Harris – b. 1 Dec 1868, bapt. 1 Dec 1868 (Baptism, **Firies Parish** (RC))

  o Dennis Harris – b. 3 Jul 1870, bapt. 3 Jul 1870 (Baptism, **Firies Parish** (RC))

Dennis Harris (father):

Residence - Farranfore - February 22, 1868

Knockaderry - December 1, 1868

July 3, 1870

- Dennis Harris & Margaret Sugrue

  o Patrick Harris – b. 24 Jan 1844, bapt. 24 Jan 1844 (Baptism, **Glenbeigh/Glencar Parish (RC)**)

  o Michael Harris – b. 1 Oct 1846, bapt. 1 Oct 1846 (Baptism, **Glenbeigh/Glencar Parish (RC)**)

  o Mary Harris – b. 10 Dec 1850, bapt. 10 Dec 1850 (Baptism, **Glenbeigh/Glencar Parish (RC)**)

  o Mary Harris – b. 22 Dec 1856, bapt. 22 Dec 1856 (Baptism, **Glenbeigh/Glencar Parish (RC)**)

Hurst

- Dennis Harris, b. 2 Jun 1859, bapt. 2 Jun 1859 (Baptism, **Glenbeigh/Glencar Parish (RC)**) & Margaret Leen – 30 Jul 1891 (Marriage, **Ballymacelligott Parish** (RC))

    - Dennis Harris – b. 18 Jun 1892, bapt. 19 Jun 1892 (Baptism, **Ballymacelligott Parish** (RC))

    - Margaret Harris – b. 10 Jan 1894, bapt. 12 Jan 1894 (Baptism, **Ballymacelligott Parish** (RC))

    - Helen Harris – b. 27 Jan 1896, bapt. 28 Jan 1896 (Baptism, **Ballymacelligott Parish** (RC))

    - Mary Harris – b. 29 Dec 1896, bapt. 31 Dec 1896 (Baptism, **Ballymacelligott Parish** (RC))

    - Michael Harris – b. 6 Jun 1898, bapt. 6 Jun 1898 (Baptism, **Ballymacelligott Parish** (RC))

    - Joan Harris – b. 5 May 1900, bapt. 7 May 1900 (Baptism, **Ballymacelligott Parish** (RC))

Dennis Harris (son):

Residence - Drom - July 30, 1891

Graffee - June 19, 1892

January 12, 1894

Behenagh - January 28, 1896

June 6, 1898

May 7, 1900

Maghanknockane - 31 Dec 1896

Margaret Leen, daughter of Michael Leen & Ellen Sweeny (daughter-in-law):

Residence - Graffeen - July 30, 1891

- Bridget Harris – b. 18 Jul 1861, bapt. 18 Jul 1861 (Baptism, **Glenbeigh/Glencar Parish** (RC))

Harris Surname Ireland: 1600s to 1900s

Dennis Harris (father):

Residence - Drom - January 24, 1844

October 1, 1846

December 10, 1850

December 22, 1856

June 2, 1859

July 18, 1861

- Dennis Harris & Mary Brosnihan

  o Patrick Harris – b. 25 Mar 1863, bapt. 25 Mar 1863 (Baptism, **Firies Parish** (RC))

  o Michael Harris – b. 28 Oct 1868, bapt. 28 Oct 1868 (Baptism, **Firies Parish** (RC))

Dennis Harris (father):

Residence - Knockaderry - March 25, 1863

October 28, 1868

- Dennis Harris & Mary Roche – 14 Jun 1884 (Marriage, **Glenbeigh/Glencar Parish** (RC))

  o John Harris – b. 16 Apr 1885, bapt. 19 Apr 1885 (Baptism, **Glenbeigh/Glencar Parish** (RC))

  o Dennis Harris – b. 30 Oct 1888, bapt. 1 Nov 1888 (Baptism, **Glenbeigh/Glencar Parish** (RC))

  o Simon Harris – b. 23 May 1891, bapt. 24 May 1891 (Baptism, **Glenbeigh/Glencar Parish** (RC))

  o Bridget Harris – b. 13 Jan 1894, bapt. 21 Jan 1894 (Baptism, **Glenbeigh/Glencar Parish** (RC))

  o Catherine Harris – b. 27 Jan 1898, bapt. 29 Jan 1898 (Baptism, **Glenbeigh/Glencar Parish** (RC))

  o Julia Harris – b. 6 Jul 1900, bapt. 8 Jul 1900 (Baptism, **Glenbeigh/Glencar Parish** (RC))

Hurst

Dennis Harris (father):

    Residence - Reennanallagane - April 16, 1885

                                    November 1, 1888

                                    May 24, 1891

                                    January 21, 1894

                                    January 29, 1898

                                    July 8, 1900

- Dennis Harris & Mary Shea – 1 Jan 1837 (Marriage, **Glenbeigh/Glencar Parish** (RC))

Mary Shea (wife):

    Residence - Kilnabrack - January 1, 1837

- Dennis Harris & Mary Sugrue – 24 Apr 1894 (Marriage, **Glenbeigh/Glencar Parish** (RC))

  - Catherine Harris – b. 20 Mar 1895, bapt. 25 Mar 1895 (Baptism, **Glenbeigh/Glencar Parish** (RC))

  - Michael Harris – b. 27 Aug 1896, bapt. 7 Sep 1896 (Baptism, **Glenbeigh/Glencar Parish** (RC))

  - Helen Harris – b. 1 Dec 1897, bapt. 2 Dec 1897 (Baptism, **Glenbeigh/Glencar Parish** (RC))

Dennis Harris (father):

    Residence - Coolnaharragill - March 25, 1895

                                    September 7, 1896

                                    December 2, 1897

Mary Sugrue (mother):

    Residence - Coolnaharragill - April 24, 1894

Harris Surname Ireland: 1600s to 1900s

- Dennis Harris & Unknown

  - John Harris & Julia Harrington – 6 Mar 1886 (Marriage, **Ardfert Parish** (RC))

    - Mary Harris – b. 28 Nov 1886, bapt. 1 Dec 1886 (Baptism, **Ardfert Parish** (RC))

John Harris (son):

    Residence - East Commons - March 6, 1886

        Skrilough - December 1, 1886

Julia Harrington, daughter of James Harrington (daughter-in-law):

    Residence - Skrilough - March 6, 1886

- Dennis Harris & Unknown

  - Honora Harris & William Carroll – 4 Aug 1894 (Marriage, **Tralee Parish** (RC))

    - Dennis John Carroll – b. 23 Jun 1895, bapt. 30 Jun 1895 (Baptism, **Tralee Parish** (RC))

    - William Carroll – b. 23 Jun 1897, bapt. 27 Jun 1897 (Baptism, **Tralee Parish** (RC))

    - James Carroll – b. 24 Jul 1898, bapt. 26 Jul 1898 (Baptism, **Tralee Parish** (RC))

    - Mary Helen Carroll – b. 6 Jul 1899, bapt. 8 Jul 1899 (Baptism, **Tralee Parish** (RC))

Honor Harris (daughter):

    Residence - Tralee - August 4, 1894

William Carroll, son of James Carroll (son-in-law):

    Residence - Tralee - August 4, 1894

        Steeple View - June 30, 1895

        Brogue Lane - June 27, 1897

          July 26, 1898

          July 8, 1899

- Dionysius Harris & Catherine Unknown

  - Esther Harris & John Owens – 28 Jan 1859 (Marriage, **St. Catherine Parish** (RC))

Esther Harris (daughter):

    Residence - 28 Cole's Alley - January 28, 1859

John Owens, son of Edward Owens & Bridget Unknown (son-in-law):

    Residence - 28 Cole's Alley - January 28, 1859

Hurst

- Edis Harris & Sarah Unknown

  - Mary Harris – bapt. 30 Nov 1740 (Baptism, **St. Catherine Parish**)

- Edward Harris & Anne Crampe – 3 Jun 1809 (Marriage, **Tralee Parish**)

Edward Harris (husband):

   Occupation - Sergeant South Cork Militia - June 3, 1809

Anne Crampe (wife):

   Residence - Tralee - June 3, 1809

- Edward Harris & Anne Harris

  - John Harris – bapt. 1 Dec 1817 (Baptism, **Dingle Parish**)

Edward Harris (father):

   Residence - Ventry - December 1, 1817

- Edward Harris & Elizabeth Ellison

  - William Joseph Harris – b. 5 Dec 1836, bapt. 28 Feb 1898 (Baptism, **Harrington Street Parish (RC)**)

  - John Joseph Harris – b. 26 Aug 1838, bapt. 11 May 1868 (Baptism, **St. Lawrence Parish (RC)**)

Edward Harris (father):

   Residence - 1 Julian Place - May 11, 1868

   21 Gordon's Lane - February 28, 1898

- Edward Harris & Elizabeth Parker

  - Hannah Harris – bapt. Jan 1851 (Baptism, **St. Michan Parish (RC)**)

- Edward Harris & Elizabeth Pegnam – 4 Jun 1833 (Marriage, **St. Michan Parish (RC)**)

- Edward Harris & Elizabeth Short

  o Michael Harris – b. 24 Feb 1861, bapt. 25 Feb 1861 (Baptism, **St. James Parish (RC)**)

  o Catherine Harris – b. 18 Nov 1866, bapt. 21 Nov 1866 (Baptism, **St. Mary, Pro Cathedral Parish (RC)**)

  o Edward Harris – b. 2 Sep 1869, bapt. 15 Sep 1869 (Baptism, **St. Mary, Pro Cathedral Parish (RC)**)

  o Elizabeth Mary Harris – b. 28 Feb 1871, bapt. 6 Mar 1871 (Baptism, **St. Mary, Pro Cathedral Parish (RC)**) & Patrick Sweeny – 28 Apr 1895 (Marriage, **St. Mary, Pro Cathedral Parish (RC)**)

Elizabeth Mary Harris (daughter):
Residence - 64 Lewis Street - April 28, 1895
Patrick Sweeney, son of James Sweeny & Teresa Keily (son-in-law):
Residence - 8 Chancery Place - April 28, 1895

  o John Edward Harris – b. 15 Jul 1875, bapt. 23 Jul 1875 (Baptism, **St. Mary, Pro Cathedral Parish (RC)**)

  o Jane Christine Harris – b. 28 Nov 1877, bapt. 3 Dec 1877 (Baptism, **St. Mary, Pro Cathedral Parish (RC)**) & Christopher Scully – 14 Sep 1899 (Marriage, **St. Mary, Pro Cathedral Parish (RC)**)

    ▪ Edward Patrick Scully – b. 20 Sep 1899, bapt. 29 Sep 1899 (Baptism, **St. Mary, Pro Cathedral Parish (RC)**)

Jane Christine Harris (daughter):
Residence - 64 Jervis Street - September 14, 1899
Christopher Scully, son of Edward Scully & Ellen Farrell (son-in-law):
Residence - 24 Upper Gloucester Street - September 14, 1899
112 Lower Gardiner Street - September 29, 1899

Hurst

- ○ Susan Harris – b. 24 Jan 1883, bapt. 31 Jan 1883 (Baptism, **St. Mary, Pro Cathedral Parish (RC)**)

- ○ Thomas Harris & Margaret Neary – 10 Apr 1893 (Marriage, **St. Mary, Pro Cathedral Parish (RC)**)

  - ▪ Dennis Joseph Harris – b. 1895, bapt. 1895 (Baptism, **St. Andrew Parish (RC)**)

Thomas Harris (son):

Residence - 63 Jervis Street - April 10, 1893

28 Clarence Street - 1895

Margaret Neary, daughter of Michael Neary & Catherine Murphy (daughter-in-law):

Residence - 222 Great Britain Street - April 10, 1893

Edward Harris (father):

Residence - 14 Dolphin's Barn - February 25, 1861

18 Marlboro Street - November 21, 1866

6 Old Abbey Street - September 15, 1869

March 6, 1871

July 23, 1875

December 3, 1877

144 Upper Abbey Street - January 31, 1883

- • Edward Harris & Ellen Caffrey

  - ○ Elizabeth Harris & Michael Corcoran – 23 Apr 1900 (Marriage, **St. Mary, Pro Cathedral Parish (RC)**)

Elizabeth Harris (daughter):

Residence - 4 Lower Rutland Street - April 23, 1900

Michael Corcoran, son of Luke Corcoran & Margaret Unknown (son-in-law):

Residence - 55 Lower Tyrone Street - April 23, 1900

Harris Surname Ireland: 1600s to 1900s

- Edward Harris & Ellen Harris

  o Emily Harris – b. 15 Aug 1872, bapt. 2 Sep 1879 (Baptism, **St. Peter Parish**)

  o Helen Harris – b. 23 Jul 1879, bapt. 2 Sep 1879 (Baptism, **St. Peter Parish**)

  o Thomas Harris – b. 29 Apr 1882, bapt. 4 Jun 1882 (Baptism, **St. Paul Parish**)

Edward Harris (father):

Residence - 10 Peter Street - September 2, 1879

35 Barrack Street - June 4, 1882

Occupation - Cook - September 2, 1879

- Edward Harris & Frances Unknown

  o John Harris – bapt. 24 Oct 1792 (Baptism, **St. Werburgh Parish**)

  o Deborah Harris – bapt. 8 Oct 1793 (Baptism, **St. Werburgh Parish**)

  o Mary Anne Harris – bapt. 30 Aug 1795 (Baptism, **St. Werburgh Parish**)

  o John Harris – bapt. 7 Jul 1801 (Baptism, **St. Werburgh Parish**)

  o Frances Harris – bapt. 27 Nov 1803 (Baptism, **St. Werburgh Parish**)

  o William Harris – bapt. 27 Nov 1803 (Baptism, **St. Werburgh Parish**)

  o Alicia Harris – bapt. 26 Dec 1811 (Baptism, **St. Werburgh Parish**)

Edward Harris (father):

Residence - Orphan's Court Copper Alley - October 24, 1792

October 8, 1793

2 Orphan's Court Copper Alley - July 7, 1801

Exchange Street - November 27, 1803

Fishamble Street - December 26, 1811

Hurst

- Edward Harris & Helen McComb

  o Mary Anne Margaret Harris – b. 1 Jan 1863, bapt. 17 Jul 1883 (Baptism, **St. Audoen Parish**

  (RC))

Edward Harris (father):

Residence - Richmond Barracks - July 17, 1883

- Edward Harris & Honora Walsh – 7 Feb 1895 (Marriage, **Listowel Parish** (RC))

Edward Harris (husband):

Residence - Listowel - February 7, 1895

Honora Walsh (wife):

Residence - Listowel - February 7, 1895

- Edward Harris & Mary Unknown

  o Mary Anne Harris – bapt. 1809 (Baptism, **St. Andrew Parish** (RC))

- Edward Harris & Mary Clarke – 23 Apr 1832 (Marriage, **Rathmines Parish** (RC))

  o Mary Harris – b. 1845, bapt. 1845 (Baptism, **Rathfarnham Parish** (RC))

- Edward Harris & Mary Glasco

  o Thomas Harris – bapt. 13 Dec 1783 (Baptism, **St. Catherine Parish** (RC))

- Edward Harris & Mary Nowlan

  o Elizabeth Harris – bapt. 22 Jul 1781 (Baptism, **St. Nicholas Parish** (RC))

- Edward Harris & Mary Unknown

  o Elizabeth Harris – b. 4 Nov 1749, bapt. 9 Nov 1749 (Baptism, **Carlow Parish**)

  o Anne Harris – bapt. 11 May 1751 (Baptism, **Carlow Parish**)

  o Jane Harris – bapt. 7 Jun 1752 (Baptism, **Carlow Parish**)

- Edward Harris & Mary Unknown

  o John Harris – bapt. 15 Mar 1778 (Baptism, **St. Nicholas Parish** (RC))

Harris Surname Ireland: 1600s to 1900s

- Edward Harris & Mary Unknown

  o Julia Harris – b. 1833, bapt. 1833 (Baptism, *Rathfarnham Parish* (RC))

  o John Harris – b. 1835, bapt. 1835 (Baptism, *Rathfarnham Parish* (RC))

- Edward Harris & Rose Unknown

  o Sarah Jane Harris – b. 16 Sep 1822, bapt. 20 Unclear 1822 (Baptism, *St. Catherine Parish*)

Edward Harris (father):

Residence - Spittalfield - September 16, 1822

- Edward Harris & Sarah Unknown, d. Before 8 Apr 1872

  o Anne Harris, bapt. 12 Sep 1848 (Baptism, *SS. Michael & John Parish* (RC)) & Hugh Reavey – 3 Jul 1870 (Marriage, *St. Michan Parish* (RC))

    ▪ Margaret Mary Reavey, b. 21 Oct 1873, bapt. 31 Oct 1873 (Baptism, *St. Michan Parish* (RC)) & Thomas Delany – 17 Sep 1893 (Marriage, *St. Mary, Pro Cathedral Parish* (RC))

Margaret Mary Reavey (daughter):

Residence - 17 Grenville Street - September 17, 1893

Thomas Delany, son of Cornelius Delany & Mary Gildea (son-in-law):

Residence - 21 Hill Street - September 17, 1893

    ▪ Edward Michael Reavey – b. 26 Sep 1875, bapt. 4 Oct 1875 (Baptism, *St. Michan Parish* (RC))

    ▪ Simon Reavey – b. 25 Jun 1881, bapt. 4 Jul 1881 (Baptism, *St. Mary, Pro Cathedral Parish* (RC))

    ▪ Patrick Joseph Reavey – b. 20 Mar 1884, bapt. 24 Mar 1884 (Baptism, *St. Mary, Pro Cathedral Parish* (RC))

    ▪ Joseph Reavey – b. 18 Sep 1887, bapt. 23 Sep 1887 (Baptism, *St. Mary, Pro Cathedral Parish* (RC))

Hurst

Anne Harris (daughter):

Residence - 6 Henrietta Buildings - July 3, 1870

Hugh Reavey, son of Hugh Reavey & Margaret Unknown (son-in-law):

Residence - 70 Church Street - July 3, 1870

3 Bread Row - October 31, 1873

3 Brady Row Ormond Market - October 4, 1875

5 Britain Court - July 4, 1881

7 Britain Court - March 24, 1884

25 Grenville Street - September 23, 1887

- o Teresa Harris & James Ledwidge – 8 Apr 1872 (Marriage, **St. Michan Parish** (RC))

Teresa Harris (daughter):

Residence - 3 Bread Row - April 8, 1872

James Ledwidge, son of John Ledwidge & Bridget Unknown (son-in-law):

Residence - 22 Aungier Street - April 8, 1872

Edward Harris (father):

Residence - 6 Henrietta Buildings - April 8, 1872

- Edward Harris & The Ladie Waldron – 12 Feb 1626, 12 Jul 1626 (Marriage, **St. John Parish**)

- Edward Harris & Unknown

- o Elizabeth Harris – bapt. 7 Jul 1717 (Baptism, **St. John Parish**)

Edward Harris (father):

Residence - Fishamble Street - July 7, 1717

- Edward Harris & Unknown

- o John Harris – bapt. 1 Dec 1819 (Baptism, **Courcy's Country or Ballinspittal Parish**

  (RC))

The baptismal register is very hard to read, unsure of what is written in the entry.

Harris Surname Ireland: 1600s to 1900s

- Edward Harris & Unknown

  - William Henry Harris & Anne Bowen – 13 Aug 1857 (Marriage, **Clontarf Parish**)

Signatures:

- Elizabeth Anne Harris – b. 31 Aug 1858, bapt. 8 Oct 1858 (Baptism, **Clontarf Parish**)

William Henry Harris (son):

    Residence - Clontarf - August 13, 1857

                October 8, 1858

    Occupation - Coast Guard - August 13, 1857

                October 8, 1858

Anne Bowen, the daughter of George Bowen (daughter-in-law):

    Residence - Clontarf - August 13, 1857

    Occupation - Dressmaker - August 13, 1857

Hurst

- Edward Harris & Unknown

  - Elizabeth Jane Harris & William Holton – 3 Dec 1861 (Marriage, **St. Peter Parish**)

Signatures:

Signatures (Marriage):

Elizabeth Jane Harris (daughter):

   Residence - 1 Prince Arthur Terrace Rathmines - December 3, 1861

William Holton, son of Martin Holton (son-in-law):

   Residence - 4 Bannaville Rathmines - December 3, 1861

   Occupation - Laborer - December 3, 1861

Martin Holton (father):

   Occupation - Farmer

Edward Harris (father):

   Occupation - Laborer

Wedding Witnesses:

Francis Coates & Mary Anne Harris

Signatures:

- o   Mary Anne Harris & Francis Coates – 31 Dec 1861 (Marriage, **St. Peter Parish**)

Signatures:

Signatures (Marriage):

Mary Anne Harris (daughter):

Residence - 7 Anna Ville - December 31, 1861

Francis Coates, son of Richard Aylmer Coates (son-in-law):

Residence - 5 Leinster Road - December 31, 1861

Occupation - Commercial Traveller - December 31, 1861

Hurst

Richard Aylmer Coates (father):

    Occupation - Mercantile Clerk

Edward Harris (father):

    Occupation - Laborer

Wedding Witnesses:

William Holton & Elizabeth Jane Holton

Signatures:

    o   John Harris & Mary Carney – 12 May 1863 (Marriage, **St. Peter Parish**)

Signatures:

John Harris (son):

    Residence - 13 Cuffe Street - May 12, 1863

    Occupation - Laborer - May 12, 1863

Mary Carney, daughter of Peter Carney (daughter-in-law):

    Residence - 14 Cuffe Street - May 12, 1863

Peter Carney (father):

    Occupation - Laborer

Edward Harris (father):

    Occupation - Laborer

Wedding Witnesses:

Catherine Harris & William Harris

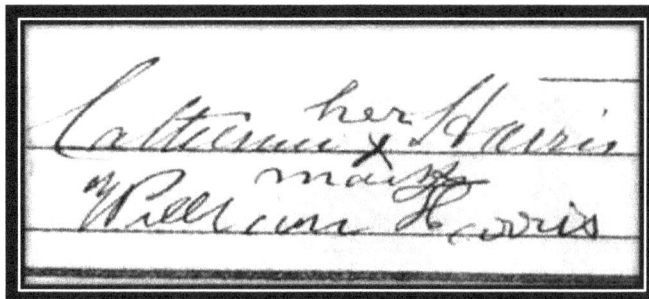

Signatures:

- Edward Harris & Unknown

  - Margaret Harris & William Evans – 23 Dec 1881 (Marriage, **St. Andrew Parish** (RC))

    - William Henry Evans – b. 28 Jul 1870, bapt. 5 Aug 1870 (Baptism, **St. Mary, Pro Cathedral** (RC))

    - John James Evans – b. 1872, bapt. 1872 (Baptism, **St. Andrew Parish** (RC))

    - Margaret Ellen Evans – b. 8 May 1875, bapt. 12 Jul 1875 (Baptism, **St. Michan Parish** (RC))

    - William John Evans – b. 1877, bapt. 1877 (Baptism, **St. Andrew Parish** (RC))

    - Ellen Catherine Evans – b. 1881, bapt. 1881 (Baptism, **St. Andrew Parish** (RC))

Margaret Harris (daughter):

Residence - **79 Townsend Street** - December 23, 1881

William Evans, son of William Evans (son-in-law):

Residence - **1 Cumberland Street** - August 5, 1870

6 Fade Street - 1872

67 Upper Dominick Street - July 12, 1875

28 Wicklow Street - 1877

79 Townsend Street - December 23, 1881

Hurst

- Edwin Octavius Harris & Unknown

  o Louisa Mary Emma Harris & John Magrath Fitzgerald – 30 Jul 1862 (Marriage, **St. Anne Parish**)

Signatures:

Louisa Mary Emma Harris (daughter):

Residence - **25 Molesworth Street - July 30, 1862**

John Magrath Fitzgerald, son of Windham Magrath Fitzgerald (son-in-law):

Residence - **27 South Frederick Street - July 30, 1862**

Occupation - Esquire - July 30, 1862

Windham Magrath Fitzgerald (father):

Occupation - Clerk

Edwin Octavius Harris (father):

Occupation - Barrister at Law

- Felix Harris & Unknown

  o Sarah Harris – bapt. 6 Jan 1769 (Baptism, **St. Peter Parish**)

- Francis Harris & Ellen McCarthy – 24 Jul 1846 (Marriage, **Carrigaline & Templebrigid Parish (RC)**)

  o Margaret Harris – bapt. 18 Aug 1846 (Baptism, **Douglas Parish (RC)**)

Francis Harris (father):

Residence - **Ballygarvan - August 18, 1846**

- Francis Harris & Eleanor Unknown

  o Joan Harris – bapt. Feb 1798 (Baptism, **St. Werburgh Parish**)

Harris Surname Ireland: 1600s to 1900s

- Francis Harris & Mary Hennessy

  o Catherine Harris – bapt. 13 Nov 1842 (Baptism, Cork - South Parish (RC))

- Francis Harris & Mary Unknown

  o Gulielmo Harris – bapt. 27 Nov 1767 (Baptism, St. Nicholas Parish (RC))

- Francis Harris & Unknown

  o Ruth Harris – bur. 17 Jun 1655 (Burial, St. John Parish)

The child's name was incorrectly transcribed as "Knith".

The entry in the church register is as follows:

"Harris Ruth daugh. To Francis bur June 17 - 1655"

  o Lydia Harris – bapt. 25 Apr 1656 (Baptism, St. John Parish)

- Francis Harris & Unknown

  o Ellen Harris & Michael Coffee – 29 Jul 1845 (Marriage, Tralee Parish)

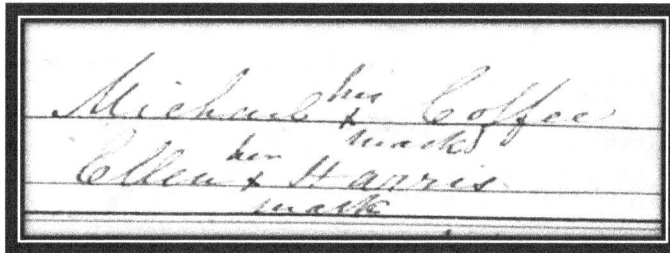

Signatures:

Ellen Harris (daughter):

    Residence - Tralee - July 29, 1845

    Occupation - Servant - July 29, 1845

    Relationship Status at Marriage - widow

Michael Coffee, son of James Coffee (son-in-law):

    Residence - Tralee - July 29, 1845

    Occupation - Laborer - July 29, 1845

    Relationship Status at Marriage - widow

Hurst

James Coffee (father):

   Occupation - Laborer

Francis Harris (father):

   Occupation - Servant

- Frank Harris & Catherine McCarthy

   o Mary Harris – bapt. 1 Apr 1815 (Baptism, **Douglas Parish** (RC))

   o Catherine Harris – bapt. 23 Jun 1818 (Baptism, **Douglas Parish** (RC))

   o Mary Harris – bapt. 8 Aug 1821 (Baptism, **Douglas Parish** (RC))

Frank Harris (father):

   Residence - Rathmacullig - April 1, 1815

             Killanully - June 23, 1818

             August 8, 1821

- Frank Harris & Nanno Griffin

   o Nanno Harris – bapt. 22 May 1845 (Baptism, **Innishannon Parish** (RC))

- Frederick Harris & Anne O'Reilly

   o John Henry Harris – b. 23 Jun 1887, bapt. 24 Jun 1887 (Baptism, **St. Michan Parish** (RC))

   o Mary Ellen Margaret Harris – b. 11 Apr 1889, bapt. 15 Apr 1889 (Baptism, **St. Mary, Pro Cathedral Parish** (RC))

   o Anne Harris – b. 16 Apr 1895, bapt. 22 Apr 1895 (Baptism, **St. Mary, Pro Cathedral Parish** (RC))

   o Francis Harris – b. 5 Jun 1897, bapt. 9 Jun 1897 (Baptism, **St. Mary, Pro Cathedral Parish** (RC))

Frederick Harris (father):

   Residence - 80 Lower Dorset Street - June 24, 1887

             23 Lower Dorset Street - April 15, 1889

             16 Lower Dorset Street - April 22, 1895

             29 Lower Dorset Street - June 9, 1897

Harris Surname Ireland: 1600s to 1900s

- Frederick Harris & Catherine Unknown

  o Frederick Harris – bapt. 8 Sep 1776 (Baptism, **St. Nicholas Parish (RC)**)

- Frederick Harris & Jane Harris

  o Frederick Joseph Harris – b. 1 Dec 1864, bapt. 21 Sep 1886 (Baptism, **St. Michan Parish (RC)**)

Fredrick Harris (father):

Residence - Wyebridge Surrey, England - September 21, 1886

- Frederick Harris & Unknown

  o Frederick Harris – b. 5 Sep 1885, bapt. 11 Sep 1885 (Baptism, **St. Michan Parish (RC)**)

Frederick Harris (father):

Residence - 80 Drumcondra Road - September 11, 1885

- George Harris & Abby Unknown

  o Charles Harris – bapt. 20 Feb 1825 (Baptism, **Tullow Parish**)

- George Harris & Anne Harris

  o Mary Anne Harris – bapt. 10 Jan 1800 (Baptism, **St. Paul Parish**)

- George Harris & Anne Unknown

  o Mary Harris – bapt. 24 Mar Unclear (Baptism, **Aghold Parish**)

- George Harris & Anne Harris

  o Margaret Harris – bapt. 23 Mar 1740 (Baptism, **St. Catherine Parish**)

- George Harris & Bridget Adams

  o Helen Harris – b. 9 Sep 1877, bapt. 25 Sep 1877 (Baptism, **Harrington Street Parish (RC)**)

George Harris (father):

Residence - 5 Upper Kevin Street - September 25, 1877

Hurst

- George Harris & Bridget Burke
  - John Patrick Harris – b. 11 Sep 1882, bapt. 29 Sep 1882 (Baptism, **St. Mary, Pro Cathedral Parish** (RC))

George Harris (father):

    Residence - 30 Fitzgibbon Street - September 29, 1882

- George Harris & Bridget Kavanagh – 15 Jan 1838 (Marriage, **St. Andrew Parish** (RC))

- George Harris & Bridget Unknown
  - George Harris – bapt. 1833 (Baptism, **St. Andrew Parish** (RC))

- George Harris & Eleanor Unknown
  - Mary Anne Harris – bapt. 25 Mar 1764 (Baptism, **St. James Parish**)

- George Harris & Elizabeth Burke
  - James Harris – bapt. 9 Feb 1816 (Baptism, **St. Catherine Parish** (RC))
  - Jane Harris – bapt. 19 Jul 1818 (Baptism, **St. Nicholas Parish** (RC))
  - Elizabeth Harris – bapt. Nov 1823 (Baptism, **St. Nicholas Parish** (RC))

- George Harris & Elizabeth Donohoe
  - Mary Sarah Harris – b. 1902, bapt. 1902 (Baptism, **St. Andrew Parish** (RC))

George Harris (father):

    Residence - Lying in Hospital Holles Street - 1902

- George Harris & Elizabeth Unknown
  - George Harris & Mary Anne O'Neill – 7 Jan 1869 (Marriage, **St. Michan Parish** (RC))

George Harris (son):

    Residence - 36 Whyte's Lane - January 7, 1869

Mary Anne O'Neil, daughter of Daniel O'Neill & Mary Anne Unknown (daughter-in-law):

    Residence - 36 Whyte's Lane - January 7, 1869

Harris Surname Ireland: 1600s to 1900s

- George Harris & Emily Bruce

  o Helen Harris – b. 27 Jan 1872, bapt. 2 Feb 1872 (Baptism, **St. Mary, Pro Cathedral Parish** (RC))

George Harris (father):

Residence - 20 Great Britain Street - February 2, 1872

- George Harris & Esther Unknown

  o Edward Harris – bapt. 13 May 1849 (Baptism, **Rathmines Parish** (RC))

  o Esther Harris – bapt. 27 Mar 1853 (Baptism, **Rathmines Parish** (RC))

- George Harris & Esther Unknown

  o James Harris & Mary Baker – 9 Jun 1867 (Marriage, **St. Nicholas Parish** (RC))

    ▪ George Morgan Harris – b. 1868, bapt. 1868 (Baptism, **St. Andrew Parish** (RC))

James Harris (son):

Residence - 157 Britain Street - June 9, 1867

3 Aungier Street - 1868

Mary Baker, daughter of Morgan Baker & Margaret Unknown (daughter-in-law):

Residence - 39 Bishop Street - June 9, 1867

- George Harris & Esther Unknown

  o William Harris & Hannah Sheehan – 17 Oct 1882 (Marriage, **St. Michan Parish** (RC))

    ▪ George William Harris – b. 8 Jun 1887, bapt. 14 Jun 1887 (Baptism, **St. Michan Parish** (RC))

    ▪ Reginald Kevin Harris – b. 3 Nov 1893, bapt. 7 Nov 1893 (Baptism, **Harrington Street Parish** (RC))

    ▪ Stephen M. A. Harris – b. 1 Dec 1895, bapt. 10 Dec 1895 (Baptism, **Harrington Street Parish** (RC))

    ▪ Charlotte Hannah Harris – b. 4 Feb 1900, bapt. 11 Feb 1900 (Baptism, **St. Mary, Pro Cathedral Parish** (RC))

Hurst

William Harris (son):

Residence - 120 Summer Hill - October 17, 1882

7 Nelson Street - June 14, 1887

103 South Circular Road - November 7, 1893

December 10, 1895

53 Henry Street - February 11, 1900

Hannah Sheehan, daughter of Michael Sheehan & Hannah Unknown (daughter-in-law):

Residence - 29 Unclear Terrace North Circular Road - October 17, 1882

- George Harris & Margaret Harris

  - Elizabeth Harris – b. 28 Oct 1859, bapt. 27 Nov 1859 (Baptism, **St. Peter Parish**)

George Harris (father):

Residence - 13 Wentworth Place - November 27, 1859

Occupation - Soldier - November 27, 1859

- George Harris & Margaret Ward

  - Margaret Harris – b. 12 Jan 1864, bapt. 15 Jan 1864 (Baptism, **St. Michan Parish** (RC))

  - William Harris – b. 13 Jul 1867, bapt. 17 Jul 1867 (Baptism, **St. Michan Parish** (RC))

George Harris (father):

Residence - 10 Anne Street - January 15, 1864

9 North Anne Street - Jul 17, 1867

- George Harris & Mary Harris

  - William Harris – bapt. 22 Sep 1687 (Baptism, **St. Michan Parish**)

George Harris (father):

Occupation - Farrier - September 22, 1687

- George Harris & Mary Harris

  - George Harris – bapt. 18 Apr 1787 (Baptism, **St. Luke Parish**)

George Harris (father):

Residence - New Market - April 18, 1787

Occupation - Printer - April 18, 1787

Harris Surname Ireland: 1600s to 1900s

- George Harris & Mary Unknown

  o Richard Harris – bapt. 23 Nov 1690 (Baptism, **St. Catherine Parish**)

- George Harris & Mary Unknown

  o Anne Harris – bapt. 9 Jul 1826 (Baptism, **St. Nicholas Parish** (RC))

- George Harris & Mary Anne Burke

  o Emily Harris – b. 17 May 1870, bapt. 18 May 1870 (Baptism, **St. Lawrence Parish** (RC))

George Harris (father):

  Residence - 6 Sheriff Street - May 18, 1870

- George Harris & Mary Anne Smyth – 30 Jan 1854 (Marriage, **St. Mary, Pro Cathedral**

  Parish (RC))

  o John Thomas Harris – b. 12 Nov 1854, bapt. 20 Nov 1854 (Baptism, **St. Mary, Pro**

    Cathedral Parish (RC))

  o Mary Anne Harris – b. 31 Aug 1857, bapt. 4 Sep 1857 (Baptism, **St. Mary, Pro Cathedral**

    Parish (RC))

George Harris (The father):

  Residence - 24 Bolton Street - November 20, 1854

  32 Bolton Street - September 4, 1857

- George Harris & Mary Anne Unknown

  o Gulielmo Harris – bapt. 1826 (Baptism, **St. Andrew Parish** (RC))

- George Harris & Mary Anne Unknown

  o Richard Harris – b. 19 Nov 1838, bapt. 3 Feb 1839 (Baptism, **Dunleckney Parish**)

George Harris (father):

  Residence - Knockmill - February 3, 1839

  Occupation - Laborer - February 3, 1839

Hurst

- George Harris & Mary Anne Unknown

  - George Harris – b. 22 Mar 1862, bapt. 6 Apr 1862 (Baptism, **Rathmines Parish (RC)**)

George Harris (father):

Residence - Portobello - April 6, 1862

- George Harris & Mary Magdalen Unknown

  - George Elliot Harris – bapt. 24 Apr 1832 (Baptism, **St. Mary, Pro Cathedral Parish (RC)**)

  - Patrick William Christian Harris – bapt. 18 Dec 1833 (Baptism, **St. Mary, Pro Cathedral Parish (RC)**)

  - John Augustine Harris – bapt. 5 Sep 1837 (Baptism, **St. Mary, Pro Cathedral Parish (RC)**)

- George Harris & Sarah Harris

  - Richard Harris – bapt. 1 Nov 1762 (Baptism, **St. Luke Parish**)

- George Harris & Sarah Harris

  - Anne Elizabeth Harris – b. 10 Jun 1857, bapt. 4 Sep 1857 (Baptism, **St. Mary Parish**)

George Harris (father):

Residence - 30 Abbey Street - September 4, 1857

Occupation - Printer - September 4, 1857

- George Harris & Susanna Unknown

  - John Harris – bapt. 3 Nov 1756 (Baptism, **St. Werburgh Parish**)

George Harris (father):

Residence - Copper Alley - November 3, 1756

- George Harris & Thomaszine Kelly – 23 Jul 1804 (Marriage, **Cork - South Parish (RC)**)

George Harris (husband):

Occupation - Sergt on a Recruiting Party of the 8ᵗʰ Regt Lying - July 23, 1804

Thomaszine Kelly (wife):

Residence - Hanover Street - July 23, 1804

- George Harris & Unknown

  o John Harris & Catherine Weir – 26 Jan 1857 (Marriage, St. Michan Parish)

Signatures:

John Harris (son):

   Residence - Richmond Barracks - January 26, 1857

   Occupation - Sergeant in the 77th Regiment - January 26, 1857

Catherine Weir, daughter of James Weir (daughter-in-law):

   Residence - 26 Church Street - January 26, 1857

James Weir (father):

   Occupation - Painter

George Harris (father):

   Occupation - Basket Maker

- George Harris & Unknown

  o George Harris & Anne Coleman – 4 Apr 1862 (Marriage, St. Catherine Parish)

Signatures:

Hurst

George Harris (son):

Residence - Royal Barracks - April 4, 1862

Occupation - Soldier Coldstream Guards - April 4, 1862

Anne Coleman, daughter of Patrick Coleman (daughter-in-law):

Residence - Cork Street - April 4, 1862

Patrick Coleman (father):

Occupation - Gardener

George Harris (father):

Occupation - Bricklayer

- George Harris & Unknown

  o Owen Harris & Sarah Richards – 5 Mar 1890 (Marriages, **Rathmines Parish**)

Signatures:

Owen Harris (son):

Residence - Ballynafeigh, Co. Down - March 5, 1890

Occupation - Constable R I C - March 5, 1890

Sarah Richards, daughter of Joseph Richards (daughter-in-law):

Residence - 11 Moyne Road - March 5, 1890

Joseph Richards (father):

Occupation - Agent

George Harris (father):

Occupation - Farmer

Wedding Witnesses:

Joseph Vauston Richards & E. Richards

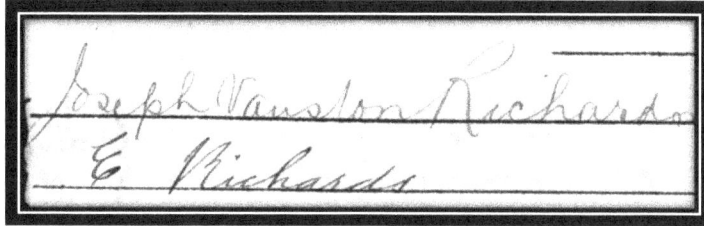

Signatures:

- George Anderson Harris & Elizabeth Molserd

  o   John Henry Harris – b. 21 Mar 1878, bapt. 5 May 1878 (Baptism, **Dromod & Prior Parish**)

George Anderson Harris (father):

   Residence - Ballinskelligs - May 5, 1878

   Occupation - Coast Guard - May 5, 1878

- George Bonaparte Harris & Judith Hackett – 26 Feb 1840 (Marriage, **St. Nicholas Parish** (RC))

  o   Caroline Mary Harris – bapt. 16 Mar 1841 (Baptism, **St. Mary, Pro Cathedral Parish** (RC))

- George C. Harris & Emily Conlon

  o   Eileen Elizabeth Harris – b. 24 Sep 1896, bapt. 7 Oct 1896 (Baptism, **Rathmines Parish** (RC))

George C. Harris (father):

   Residence - 14 Anna Villa - October 7, 1896

Hurst

- George Hemmington Harris & Unknown

  - William Carver Harris & Mary Catherine Hinde – 28 Feb 1861 (Marriage, **St. Peter Parish**)

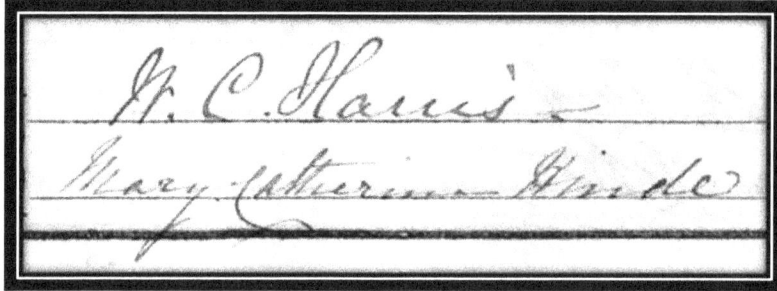

Signatures:

William Carver Harris (son):

    Residence - Kilfergus Union of Glen - February 28, 1861

        Tully Lirgu, Co. Limerick - February 28, 1861

    Occupation - Esquire - February 28, 1861

Mary Catherine Hinde, daughter of Benjamin Hinde (daughter-in-law):

    Residence - 110 Lower Baggot Street - February 28, 1861

        Tarbert, Co. Kerry - February 28, 1861

Benjamin Hinde (father):

    Occupation - Solicitor

George Hemmington Harris (father):

    Occupation - Esquire

Wedding Witnesses:

Richard Hinde

Signature:

Harris Surname Ireland: 1600s to 1900s

- George John Harris & Mary Anne O'Neill

  - Angelina Louisa Harris, b. 6 Dec 1869, bapt. 13 Dec 1869 (Baptism, **St. Lawrence Parish**

    (RC)) & Charles Stevens – 1 Nov 1887 (Marriage, **St. Paul Parish**)

Signatures:

Angelina Louisa Harris (daughter):

    Residence - 32 Queen Street - November 1, 1887

    Relationship Status at Marriage - minor age

Charles Stevens, son of Charles Stevens (son-in-law):

    Residence - Royal Barracks - November 1, 1887

    Occupation - Corporal Royal Highlanders - November 1, 1887

Charles Stevens (father):

    Occupation - Railway Guard

George John Harris (father):

    Residence - 26 Besboro Avenue - December 13, 1869

    Occupation - Soldier

Hurst

- George Spencer Harris & Unknown

  o Elizabeth Charlotte Harris & George Brittain – 17 Jan 1879 (Marriage, St. Paul Parish)

Signatures:

Elizabeth Charlotte Harris (daughter):

    Residence - Arbor Hill - January 17, 1879

George Brittain, son of Henry Brittain (son-in-law):

    Residence - Arbor Hill - January 17, 1879

    Occupation - Trumpeter Royal Scots Greys 2nd Dragoons - January 17, 1879

Henry Brittain (father):

    Occupation - Sexton Military Church

George Spencer Harris (father):

    Occupation - Gun Maker

Wedding Witnesses:

Alfrid Brittain

Signature:

Harris Surname Ireland: 1600s to 1900s

- George Graham McHarris or Harris & Mary Ferguson

    o Georgina Mary McHarris or Harris – b. 19 Apr 1852, bapt. 16 Feb 1879 (Baptism, **Rathmines Parish (RC)**) & John Kehoe – 14 May 1879 (Marriage, **Rathmines Parish (RC)**)

    Georgina Mary McHarris (daughter):

    Residence - Besborough Parade Videra - May 14, 1879

    John Kehoe, son of James Kehoe & Mary Mullaghan (son-in-law):

    Residence - Terranase - May 14, 1879

    George Graham McHarris (father):

    Residence - Starling in Scotia - February 16, 1879

- Gerald Harris & Ellen Lynch

    o James Harris – b. 28 Apr 1825, bapt. 28 Apr 1825 (Baptism, **Dingle Parish** (RC))

    o Ellen Harris – b. 18 Jun 1829, bapt. 18 Jun 1829 (Baptism, **Tralee Parish** (RC))

    o Robert Harris & Elizabeth Forhan – 18 Nov 1860 (Marriage, **Dingle Parish** (RC))

        ▪ William John Harris – b. 15 Oct 1861, bapt. 19 Oct 1861 (Baptism, **Tralee Parish** (RC))

        ▪ Ellen Harris – b. 23 Oct 1862, bapt. 28 Oct 1862 (Baptism, **Tralee Parish** (RC))

        ▪ Mary Elizabeth Harris – b. 8 Sep 1864, bapt. 8 Sep 1864 (Baptism, **Tralee Parish** (RC))

        ▪ Margaret Frances Harris – b. 23 Oct 1869, bapt. 23 Oct 1869 (Baptism, **Tralee Parish** (RC))

        ▪ Josephine Mary Harris – b. 4 May 1874, bapt. 9 May 1874 (Baptism, **Tralee Parish** (RC))

        ▪ Cecelia Mary Bridget Harris – b. 27 Feb 1883, bapt. 10 Mar 1883 (Baptism, **Tralee Parish** (RC))

Hurst

Robert Harris (son):

    Residence - Gaol - November 18, 1860

           Ballymullen - October 19, 1861

                October 28, 1862

                May 9, 1874

                March 10, 1883

        Tralee - October 23, 1869

Elizabeth Forhan, daughter of John Forhan & Margaret Keliher (daughter-in-law):

    Residence - Dingle - November 18, 1860

Gerald Harris (father):

    Residence - Dingle - April 28, 1825

           Derryquay - June 18, 1829

- Gerald Harris & Jane Connor – 29 Jan 1815 (Marriage, **Tralee Parish** (RC))

  - Margaret Harris – b. 22 Nov 1815, bapt. 22 Nov 1815 (Baptism, **Tralee Parish** (RC))

  - Richard Harris – b. 2 Mar 1819, bapt. 2 Mar 1819 (Baptism, **Tralee Parish** (RC))

  - Mary Harris – b. 1 Jan 1821, bapt. 1 Jan 1821 (Baptism, **Tralee Parish** (RC))

  - James Harris – b. 9 Nov 1823, bapt. 9 Nov 1823 (Baptism, **Tralee Parish** (RC))

  - Sarah Harris – b. 16 Dec 1827, bapt. 16 Dec 1827 (Baptism, **Tralee Parish** (RC))

Gerald Harris (father):

    Residence - Curraheen - January 29, 1815

                November 22, 1815

                March 2, 1819

                January 1, 1821

                November 9, 1823

                December 16, 1827

- Gere Harris & Anne Corigan

  - John Harris – bapt. 7 Apr 1846 (Baptism, **St. Catherine Parish** (RC))

Harris Surname Ireland: 1600s to 1900s

- Ginkin Harris & Anne Wood – 8 Feb 1778 (Marriage, **St. Bride Parish**)

Ginkin Harris (husband):

  Occupation - Cabinet Maker - February 8, 1778

- Gulielmo Harris & Anne Eyers

  o Francis Harris – bapt. 20 Jul 1774 (Baptism, **Cork - SS. Peter & Paul Parish** (RC))

- Gulielmo Harris & Anne Unknown

  o Richard Harris – bapt. 1768 (Baptism, **St. Andrew Parish** (RC))

- Gulielmo Harris & Bridget Unknown

  o Mary Harris – b. 1800, bapt. 1800 (Baptism, **St. Andrew Parish** (RC))

  o Robert Harris – b. 1800, bapt. 1800 (Baptism, **St. Andrew Parish** (RC))

- Gulielmo Harris & Catherine Downes

  o Frances Mary Harris – b. 1871, bapt. 18 Dec 1880 (Baptism, **St. Mary, Donnybrook Parish** (RC))

  o James Mary Harris – b. 1871, bapt. 18 Dec 1880 (Baptism, **St. Mary, Donnybrook Parish** (RC))

  o Gulielmo Harris – b. 2 May 1877, bapt. 10 May 1877 (Baptism, **St. Mary, Donnybrook Parish** (RC))

  o Margaret Harris – b. 17 Feb 1880, bapt. 22 Feb 1880 (Baptism, **St. Mary, Donnybrook Parish** (RC))

Gulielmo Harris (father):

  Residence - 10 Church Lane, Donnybrook - May 10, 1877

  Church Lane, Donnybrook - February 22, 1880

  No. 4 Church Lane - December 18, 1880

Hurst

- Gulielmo Harris & Catherine Green

  - Sarah Esther Harris – b. 19 Apr 1867, bapt. 29 Apr 1867 (Baptism, **Harrington Street Parish** (RC))

  - Catherine Harris – b. 12 Jul 1869, bapt. 13 Jul 1869 (Baptism, **Harrington Street Parish** (RC))

Gulielmo Harris (father):

Residence - 44 Cuffe Street - April 29, 1867

July 13, 1869

- Gulielmo Harris & Catherine Unknown

  - Jane Harris – bapt. 1768 (Baptism, **St. Andrew Parish** (RC))

  - Esther Harris – bapt. 1770 (Baptism, **St. Andrew Parish** (RC))

  - Gulielmo Harris – bapt. 1772 (Baptism, **St. Andrew Parish** (RC))

  - Jois Harris – bapt. 1774 (Baptism, **St. Andrew Parish** (RC))

  - Mary Harris – bapt. 1775 (Baptism, **St. Andrew Parish** (RC))

- Gulielmo Harris & Eleanor Marks – 24 Nov 1777 (Marriage, **St. Andrew Parish** (RC))

  - Jane Harris – bapt. 1780 (Baptism, **St. Andrew Parish** (RC))

- Gulielmo Harris & Eleanor Scanlon – 8 Sep 1828 (Marriage, **St. Michan Parish** (RC))

- Gulielmo Harris & Eleanor Unknown

  - Anne Harris – bapt. 1813 (Baptism, **St. Andrew Parish** (RC))

  - Mary Harris – bapt. 1815 (Baptism, **St. Andrew Parish** (RC))

Harris Surname Ireland: 1600s to 1900s

- Gulielmo Harris & Elizabeth Malone

  ○ Mary Harris – b. 30 May 1878, bapt. 13 Jul 1878 (Baptism, **Harrington Street Parish (RC)**)

  ○ Julia F. Harris – b. 11 Sep 1880, bapt. 2 Feb 1881 (Baptism, **Rathmines Parish (RC)**)

  ○ Joseph Harris – b. 23 May 1882, bapt. 13 Jun 1882 (Baptism, **Harrington Street Parish (RC)**)

Gulielmo Harris (father):

Residence - 51 Lower Clanbrassil Street - July 13, 1878

Welworth Road - February 2, 1881

13 Welworth Road - June 13, 1882

- Gulielmo Harris & Honora Collins – 27 Jan 1772 (Marriage, **Timoleague & Barryroe Parish(RC)**)

- Gulielmo Harris & Jane Shea

  ○ Gulielmo George Harris – b. 13 Mar 1864, bapt. 22 Mar 1864 (Baptism, **St. Catherine Parish (RC)**)

Gulielmo Harris (father):

Residence - 39 Coombe - March 22, 1864

- Gulielmo Harris & Jeanne Harris

  ○ John Harris & Mary Anne Rorke – 3 Dec 1863 (Marriage, **St. Mary, Pro Cathedral Parish (RC)**)

    ▪ Thomas Harris – b. 27 Dec 1875, bapt. 3 Jan 1876 (Baptism, **St. Mary, Pro Cathedral Parish (RC)**)

    ▪ Esther Catherine Harris – b. 15 Mar 1878, bapt. 19 Mar 1878 (Baptism, **St. Audoen Parish (RC)**)

    ▪ Rosanna Harris – b. 30 Jun 1880, bapt. 6 Jul 1880 (Baptism, **St. Audoen Parish (RC)**)

    ▪ John Joseph Harris – b. 5 Nov 1882, bapt. 8 Nov 1882 (Baptism, **St. Audoen Parish (RC)**)

Hurst

John Harris (son):

    Residence - 4 Back Lane - December 3, 1863

        5 East Arran Street - January 3, 1875

        33 Nicholas Street - March 19, 1878

        15 Nicholas Street - July 6, 1880

        19 High Street - November 8, 1882

Mary Anne Rorke, daughter of Gulielmo Rorke & Martha Unknown

(daughter-in-law):

    Residence - 22 Little Strand Street - December 3, 1863

- Gulielmo Harris & Margaret Unknown

  - Elizabeth Harris & John Slevin – 24 May 1875 (Marriage, St. Mary, Pro Cathedral

    Parish (RC))

Elizabeth Harris (daughter):

    Residence - Belvidere Court - May 24, 1875

John Slevin, son of John Slevin & Ellen Unknown (son-in-law):

    Residence - Belvidere Court - May 24, 1875

- Gulielmo Harris & Mary Cotter

  - Thomas Harris – bapt. 26 May 1804 (Baptism, Ardfield & Rathbarry Parish (RC))

  - John Harris – bapt. 20 Jun 1810 (Baptism, Ardfield & Rathbarry Parish (RC))

- Gulielmo Harris & Mary Harris

  - Mary Anne Harris & Gulielmo Leary – 22 Aug 1858 (Marriage, St. Mary, Pro Cathedral

    Parish (RC))

Mary Anne Harris (daughter):

    Residence - 2 Moore Lane - August 22, 1858

Gulielmo Leary, son of John Leary & Mary Unknown (son-in-law):

    Residence - 2 McCarni's Court - August 22, 1858

Harris Surname Ireland: 1600s to 1900s

- o Ellen Harris & Timothy Skelly – 15 Aug 1863 (Baptism, **St. Mary, Pro Cathedral Parish (RC)**)

  - ▪ Ellen Skelly – b. 6 Jun 1865, bapt. 7 Jun 1865 (Baptism, **St. Mary, Pro Cathedral Parish (RC)**)

  - ▪ Thomas Skelly – b. 19 Dec 1866, bapt. 21 Dec 1866 (Baptism, **St. Mary, Pro Cathedral Parish (RC)**)

  - ▪ Mary Anne Skelly – b. 1 Jan 1869, bapt. 4 Jan 1869 (Baptism, **St. Mary, Pro Cathedral Parish (RC)**)

Ellen Harris (daughter):
Residence - 4 Cherry Lane - August 15, 1863
Timothy Skelly, son of Michael Skelly & Mary Daly (son-in-law):
Residence - 4 Leary's Court off Farrell Court
off Upper Abbey Street - August 15. 1863
6 Britain Lane - June 7, 1865
December 21, 1866
January 4, 1869

- o Bartholomew Harris & Bridget Brady – 30 Mar 1865 (Marriage, **St. Mary, Pro Cathedral Parish (RC)**)

  - ▪ Mary Harris – b. 2 Jan 1867, bapt. 23 Jan 1867 (Baptism, **St. Mary, Pro Cathedral Parish (RC)**)

  - ▪ Catherine Harris – b. 15 Jan 1869, bapt. 18 Jan 1869 (Baptism, **St. Mary, Pro Cathedral Parish (RC)**) & Michael Langton – 16 Apr 1893 (Marriage, **St. Mary, Pro Cathedral Parish (RC)**)

Catherine Harris (daughter):
Residence - 15 Denmark Place - April 16, 1893
Michael Langton, son of Michael Langton & Sarah Dunn (son-in-law):
Residence - 15 Denmark Place - April 16, 1893

Hurst

- Gulielmo Joseph Harris – b. 3 Apr 1871, bapt. 12 Apr 1871 (Baptism, **St. Mary, Pro Cathedral Parish** (RC))

- James Harris – b. 1 Feb 1881, bapt. 9 Feb 1881 (Baptism, **St. Mary, Pro Cathedral Parish** (RC))

Bartholomew Harris (son):

Residence - 11 Cole's Lane - March 30, 1865

10 Horseman's Row - January 23, 1867

9 Britain Street - January 18, 1869

3 Mason's Market - February 9, 1881

9 Mason's Road - April 12, 1871

Bridget Brady, daughter of James Brady & Anne Unknown (daughter-in-law):

Residence - 11 Cole's Lane - March 30, 1865

- Andrew Harris & Elizabeth Halpin – 20 Jun 1870 (Marriage, **St. Mary, Pro Cathedral Parish** (RC))

  - Peter Harris – b. 1 Nov 1871, bapt. 10 Nov 1871 (Baptism, **St. Mary, Pro Cathedral Parish** (RC))

  - Andrew Harris – b. 25 Feb 1873, bapt. 5 Mar 1873 (Baptism, **St. Mary, Pro Cathedral Parish** (RC))

  - Elizabeth Harris – b. 27 Jun 1874, bapt. 10 Jul 1874 (Baptism, **St. Mary, Pro Cathedral Parish** (RC)) & John Reilly – 28 Apr 1895 (Marriage, **St. Mary, Pro Cathedral Parish** (RC))

    - Bridget Reilly – b. 12 Sep 1897, bapt. 30 Sep 1897 (Baptism, **St. Mary, Pro Cathedral Parish** (RC))

    - Joseph Reilly – b. 16 Aug 1898, bapt. 17 Aug 1898 (Baptism, **St. Mary, Pro Cathedral Parish** (RC))

Harris Surname Ireland: 1600s to 1900s

- Elizabeth Reilly – b. 14 Mar 1900, bapt. 19 Mar 1900 (Baptism, St. Mary, Pro Cathedral Parish (RC))

Elizabeth Harris (daughter):

Residence - 6 Granley Place - April 28, 1895

John Reilly, son of Joseph Reilly & Catherine Lawless (son-in-law):

Residence - 8 Granley Place - April 28, 1895

6 4 Lower Tyrone Street - September 30, 1897

35 Upper Tyrone Street - August 17, 1898

March 19, 1900

- William Harris – b. 26 May 1876, bapt. 5 Jun 1876 (Baptism, St. Mary, Pro Cathedral Parish (RC))

- Mary Anne Harris – b. 16 Nov 1878, bapt. 25 Nov 1878 (Baptism, St. Mary, Pro Cathedral Parish (RC))

- Julia Harris – b. 11 Aug 1881, bapt. 22 Aug 1881 (Baptism, St. Mary, Pro Cathedral Parish (RC))

- Bridget Harris – b. 7 Feb 1885, bapt. 18 Feb 1885 (Baptism, St. Mary, Pro Cathedral Parish (RC))

Andrew Harris (son):

Residence - 2 Graham's Court - November 10, 1871

12 Cole's Lane - June 20, 1870

32 Mabbot Street - March 5, 1873

82 Lower Mecklenburgh Street - July 10, 1874

Henry Place - June 5, 1876

10 Henry Place - November 25, 1878

11 Taaffes Row Denmark Street - August 22, 1881

4 Taaffe Row - February 18, 1885

Hurst

Elizabeth Halpin, daughter of Patrick Halpin & Elizabeth Unknown (daughter-in-law):

Residence - 12 Cole's Lane - June 20, 1870

- o Bridget Harris & Peter Graves – 12 May 1872 (Marriage, St. Mary, Pro Cathedral Parish (RC))

Bridget Harris (daughter):

Residence - 12 Cole's Lane - May 12, 1872

Peter Graves, son of Thomas Graves & Mary Unknown (son-in-law):

Residence - North Strand - May 12, 1872

- • Gulielmo Harris & Mary O'Neill

  - o Catherine Harris – bapt. 14 Nov 1842 (Baptism, St. Michan Parish (RC))

- • Gulielmo Harris & Mary Quinn

  - o Gulielmo Harris & Elizabeth White – 8 Oct 1865 (Marriage, Rathmines Parish (RC))

    - ▪ John Joseph Harris – b. 19 Mar 1867, bapt. 24 Mar 1867 (Baptism, Rathmines Parish (RC))

    - ▪ Mary Harris – b. 12 May 1868, bapt. 17 May 1868 (Baptism, Rathmines Parish (RC))

    - ▪ Gulielmo Harris – b. 17 Oct 1871, bapt. 22 Oct 1871 (Baptism, Rathmines Parish (RC))

    - ▪ Patrick J. Harris – b. 28 Feb 1876, bapt. 5 Mar 1876 (Baptism, Rathmines Parish (RC))

Gulielmo Harris (son):

Residence - Harold's Cross - March 24, 1867

May 17, 1868

October 22, 1871

Greenmount - March 5, 1876

Elizabeth White, daughter of John White & Catherine Brennan (daughter-in-law):

Residence - Harold's Cross - October 8, 1865

Harris Surname Ireland: 1600s to 1900s

- ○ James Harris & Anastasia Anne Mary Quinn – 28 Jun 1869 (Marriage, **Rathmines Parish (RC)**)

  - ▪ Margaret Harris – b. 3 Mar 1870, bapt. 6 Mar 1870 (Baptism, **Rathmines Parish (RC)**)

  - ▪ Mary Harris – b. 3 Mar 1870, bapt. 4 Mar 1870 (Baptism, **Harrington Street Parish (RC)**)

  - ▪ James Harris – b. 7 Sep 1871, bapt. 8 Sep 1871 (Baptism, **Harrington Street Parish (RC)**)

  - ▪ Anastasia Harris – b. 27 May 1874, bapt. 5 Jun 1874 (Baptism, **Harrington Street Parish (RC)**)

James Harris (son):

Residence - Harold's Cross - June 28, 1869

March 6, 1870

6 Long Lane - March 4, 1870

4 Malpas Street - September 8, 1871

Chestnut Place - June 5, 1874

Anastasia Anne Mary Quinn, daughter of Michael Quinn & Catherine Hodgens (daughter-in-law):

Residence - Harold's Cross - June 28, 1869

- • Gulielmo Harris & Mary Reynolds

  - ○ Elizabeth Harris – b. 18 Sep 1859, bapt. 20 Sep 1859 (Baptism, **St. Catherine Parish (RC)**)

Gulielmo Harris (father):

Residence - 18 Rainsford Street - September 20, 1859

Hurst

- Gulielmo Harris & Mary Unknown

  o Frances Harris & Henry Doyle – 6 Sep 1863 (Marriage, **St. Michan Parish** (RC))

Frances Harris (daughter):

  Residence - Temple Henrietta Street - September 6, 1863

Henry Doyle, son of James Doyle & Catherine Unknown (son-in-law):

  Residence - 2 Lisburn Street - September 6, 1863

- Gulielmo Harris & Mary Elizabeth Nolan

  o Henry Gulielmo Harris – b. 27 Jul 1863, bapt. 31 Jul 1863 (Baptism, **St. Mary, Pro Cathedral Parish** (RC))

Gulielmo Harris (father):

  Residence - 140 Great Britain Street - July 31, 1863

- Gulielmo Harris & Sarah Kirby

  o Kathleen Mary Harris – b. 16 Mar 1879, bapt. 15 Apr 1879 (Baptism, **Harrington Street Parish** (RC))

  o Gulielmo Daniel Harris – b. 13 Dec 1880, bapt. 12 May 1882 (Baptism, **Harrington Street Parish** (RC))

Gulielmo Harris (father):

  Residence - 27 Greenville Terrace - April 15, 1879

  15 Liverpool Road South Circular Road - May 12, 1882

- Gulielmo Harris & Unknown

  o Rosanna F. Harris & John G. McGlone – 21 Sep 1891 (Marriage, **St. Agatha Parish** (RC))

Rosanna F. Harris (daughter):

  Residence - 42 Clarence Street - September 21, 1891

John G. McGlone, son of James McGlone (son-in-law):

  Residence - 4 Upper Gloucester Street - September 21, 1891

- Gulielmo O'Hara Harris & Alicia McGlade – 18 Jul 1824 (Marriage, **St. Andrew Parish** (RC))

- Harold Harris & Catherine Finn

  o Ellen Harris – bapt. 3 Feb 1846 (Baptism, **Kinsale Parish** (RC))

Harold Harris (father):

Residence - Ballyngan - February 3, 1846

- Henry Harris & Anne Mary Unknown

  o Mary Ellen Harris – b. 5 Mar 1888, bapt. 22 Mar 1888 (Baptism, **St. Stephen Parish**)

Henry Harris (father):

Residence - 8 East James Street - March 22, 1888

Occupation - Footman - March 22, 1888

- Henry Harris & Catherine Harris

  o Arabella Harris – bapt. 1769 (Baptism, **St. Andrew Parish** (RC))

  o Anne Harris – bapt. 1772 (Baptism, **St. Andrew Parish** (RC))

  o Elizabeth Harris – bapt. 1773 (Baptism, **St. Andrew Parish** (RC))

- Henry Harris & Catherine Delany – 15 Nov 1877 (Marriage, **Innishannon Parish** (RC))

  o William Harris – bapt. 27 Aug 1878 (Baptism, **Innishannon Parish** (RC))

  o John Harris – bapt. 8 Feb 1880 (Baptism, **Innishannon Parish** (RC))

Henry Harris (father):

Residence - Lissagroom - August 27, 1878

Woodlands - February 8, 1880

- Henry Harris & Charlotte Rice – 20 Nov 1844 (Baptism, **Carlow Parish**)

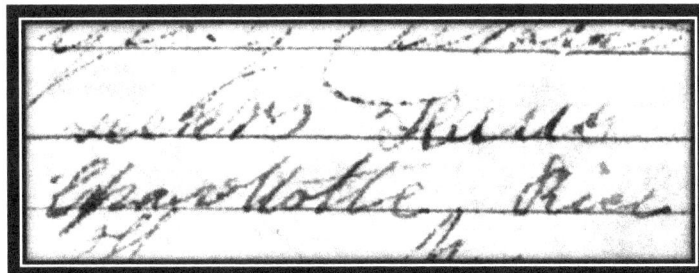

Signatures:

Hurst

Henry Harris (husband):

Residence - Tickeborough, Co. Norfolk - November 20, 1844

Occupation - Private 77ᵗʰ Regiment - November 20, 1844

Charlotte Rice (wife):

Residence - Carlow Parish - November 20, 1844

- Henry Harris & Dorothy Unknown

    o Elizabeth Harris – bapt. 3 Apr 1796 (Baptism, **St. Catherine Parish**)

Henry Harris (father):

Residence - Garden Lane - April 3, 1796

- Henry Harris & Eleanor Unknown

    o Mary Harris – bapt. 12 Jan 1772 (Baptism, **St. Werburgh Parish**)

Henry Harris (father):

Residence - Copper Alley - January 12, 1772

- Henry Harris & Elizabeth Coleman

    o Daniel Harris – bapt. 27 Jan 1833 (Baptism, **Cork - South Parish** (RC))

    o Henry Francis Harris – bapt. 26 Dec 1834 (Baptism, **Cork - South Parish** (RC))

    o Mary Harris – bapt. 21 Feb 1839 (Baptism, **Cork - SS. Peter & Paul Parish** (RC))

    o George Harris – bapt. 20 May 1839 (Baptism, **Cork - SS. Peter & Paul Parish** (RC))

    o Anne Harris – bapt. 6 Sep 1841 (Baptism, **Cork - SS. Peter & Paul Parish** (RC))

    o Elizabeth Harris – bapt. 14 Jan 1845 (Baptism, **Cork - South Parish** (RC))

    o Henry Francis Harris – bapt. 1 May 1847 (Baptism, **Cork - South Parish** (RC))

- Henry Harris & Elizabeth Fitzgerald – 21 Jan 1834 (Marriage, **Ballinhassig Parish** (RC))

    o Richard Harris – bapt. 25 Oct 1834 (Baptism, **Innishannon Parish** (RC))

    o Honora Harris – bapt. 14 Jun 1836 (Baptism, **Innishannon Parish** (RC))

    o Catherine Harris – bapt. 23 Jul 1838 (Baptism, **Innishannon Parish** (RC))

    o Ellen Harris – bapt. 8 Nov 1840 (Baptism, **Innishannon Parish** (RC))

- o John Harris – bapt. 14 May 1842 (Baptism, **Innishannon Parish** (RC))

- o William Harris – bapt. 12 Aug 1845 (Baptism, **Innishannon Parish** (RC))

- o James Harris – bapt. 16 Apr 1848 (Baptism, **Innishannon Parish** (RC))

- o Abraham Harris – bapt. 8 Jan 1851 (Baptism, **Innishannon Parish** (RC))

- Henry Harris & Elizabeth Henderson – 29 Sep 1795 (Marriage, **St. Nicholas Without Parish**)

Elizabeth Henderson (wife):

Residence - New Street - September 29, 1795

- Henry Harris & Elizabeth Unknown

- o Elizabeth Harris – bapt. 26 Jun 1785 (Baptism, **St. Catherine Parish**)

Henry Harris (father):

Residence - Thomas Street - June 26, 1785

- Henry Harris & Elizabeth Unknown

- o Joseph Harris – b. 1803, bapt. 16 Oct 1803 (Baptism, **St. Catherine Parish**)

Henry Harris (father):

Residence - Coombe - October 16, 1803

- Henry Harris & Elizabeth Unknown

- o Joseph Harris, b. 1805, bapt. 27 Oct 1805 (Baptism, **St. Catherine Parish**) & Mary

    Batterton – 14 May 1828 (Marriage, **St. Luke Parish**)

Signatures:

Hurst

Joseph Harris (son):

Residence - St. Catherine Parish - May 14, 1828

Mary Batterton (daughter-in-law):

Residence - St. Luke Parish - May 14, 1828

Henry Harris (father):

Residence - Meath Street - October 27, 1805

Wedding Witnesses:

Henry Harris & Samuel Batterton

Signatures:

- Henry Harris & Jane Harris

  o Henry Harris – bapt. 23 Aug 1730 (Baptism, St. Catherine Parish)

- Henry Harris & Jane Reilly

  o Francis Harris – b. 5 Dec 1887, bapt. 2 Jan 1888 (Baptism, St. Mary, Donnybrook Parish

  (RC))

Henry Harris (father):

Residence - Oak Lawn Roebuck - January 2, 1888

- Henry Harris & Jane Unknown

  o Henry James Harris – b. 5 Jul 1890, bapt. 17 Aug 1890 (Baptism, Taney Parish)

  o Charles William Harris – b. 28 Aug 1892, bapt. 2 Oct 1892 (Baptism, Taney Parish)

Henry Harris (father):

Residence - Bird Avenue - August 17, 1890

Woodly Park - October 2, 1892

Occupation - Gardener - August 17, 1890

October 2, 1892

- Henry Harris & Joan Coleman – 1 Feb 1868 (Marriage, Tracton Abbey Parish (RC))

Harris Surname Ireland: 1600s to 1900s

- Henry Harris & Joan Collins – 23 Feb 1792 (Marriage, **Kilmurry Parish** (RC))

- Henry Harris & Joan Collins – Jun 1793 (Marriage, **Kilmurry Parish** (RC))

- Henry Harris & Margaret Crimmen – 24 Jan 1826 (Marriage, **Innishannon Parish** (RC))

    o Margaret Harris – bapt. 4 Jan 1827 (Baptism, **Innishannon Parish** (RC))

    o John Harris – bapt. 4 Feb 1829 (Baptism, **Innishannon Parish** (RC))

    o Richard Harris – bapt. 18 Jul 1831 (Baptism, **Innishannon Parish** (RC))

    o Henry Harris – bapt. 13 Mar 1834 (Baptism, **Innishannon Parish** (RC))

    o Catherine Harris – bapt. 6 Oct 1836 (Baptism, **Innishannon Parish** (RC))

- Henry Harris & Mary Unknown

    o Mary Anne Eleanor Harris – b. 1812, bapt. 1812 (Baptism, **Clondalkin Parish**)

- Henry Harris & Mary Harris

    o Sarah Jane Harris – b. Aug 1826, bur. 23 Sep 1827 (Burial, **St. Mary Parish**)

Sarah Jane Harris (daughter):

Residence - Britain Street - September 23, 1827

Age at Death - 13 months

    o Sarah Jane Harris – bapt. 24 Jan 1828 (Baptism, **St. Mary Parish**)

    o Mary Maria Harris – bapt. 22 Jul 1829 (Baptism, **St. Mary Parish**)

    o Henry John Harris – bapt. 29 Apr 1831 (Baptism, **St. Mary Parish**)

Henry Harris (father):

Residence - 4 Little Britain Street - January 24, 1828

July 22, 1829

April 29, 1831

Occupation - Gun Maker - January 24, 1828

July 22, 1829

April 29, 1831

Hurst

- Henry Harris & Mary Anne Harris

  o Susanna Harris – b. 20 Sep 1889, bapt. 20 Oct 1889 (Baptism, **St. Anne Parish**)

  o Mabel Jane Harris – b. 14 Apr 1892, bapt. 12 May 1892 (Baptism, **St. Anne Parish**)

  o Richard Henry Harris – b. 11 Dec 1893, bapt. 21 Jan 1894 (Baptism, **St. Anne Parish**)

  o William Harris – b. 28 Jan 1896, bapt. 8 Mar 1896 (Baptism, **St. Anne Parish**)

  o John Robert Harris – b. 17 May 1898, bapt. 19 Jun 1898 (Baptism, **St. Anne Parish**)

  o Margaret Elizabeth Harris – b. 12 Sep 1900, bapt. 2 Oct 1900 (Baptism, **St. Anne Parish**)

Henry Harris (father):

Residence - 9 Leinster Street - October 20, 1889

May 12, 1892

January 21, 1894

March 8, 1896

June 19, 1898

October 2, 1900

Occupation - Groom - October 20, 1889

May 12, 1892

January 21, 1894

March 8, 1896

June 19, 1898

October 2, 1900

Coachman - May 12, 1892

- Henry Harris & Sarah Harris

  o Mary Harris – bapt. 19 Feb 1804 (Baptism, **St. Mary Parish**)

  o Edward Harris – bapt. 10 Nov 1805 (Baptism, **St. Mary Parish**)

  o Mary Anne Harris – bapt. 18 Jan 1807 (Baptism, **St. Mary Parish**)

  o Sarah Harris – bapt. 1 Jan 1816 (Baptism, **St. Mary Parish**)

  o Nathaniel Harris – bapt. 14 Sep 1817 (Baptism, **St. Mary Parish**)

  o Sarah Harris – bapt. 12 Sep 1819 (Baptism, **St. Mary Parish**)

Harris Surname Ireland: 1600s to 1900s

- o Nathaniel Harris – b. 4 Jun 1821, bapt. 1 Jul 1821 (Baptism, **St. Mary Parish**)

- Henry Harris & Sarah Harris

- o Richard Harris – b. 4 Jun 1826, bapt. 9 Jul 1826 (Baptism, **St. George Parish**)

- Henry Harris & Sarah Unknown

- o Elizabeth Harris – bapt. 27 Nov 1808 (Baptism, **St. Werburgh Parish**)

Henry Harris (father):

Residence - Essex Street - November 27, 1808

- Henry Harris & Sarah Harris, bur. 25 Jul 1835 (Burial, **Dingle Parish**)

Henry Harris (husband):

Occupation - Cost Guard

Sarah Harris (wife):

Residence - Minnard Coast Guard Station - July 25, 1835

- Henry Harris & Susanna Bolton – 28 Dec 1677 (Marriage, **St. Michan Parish**)

- o John Harris – bur. 20 Feb 1680 (Burial, **St. Michan Parish**)

- o Peter Harris – bapt. 3 Feb 1681 (Baptism, **St. Michan Parish**), bur. 10 Feb 1681 (Burial, **St. Michan Parish**)

- o Cornelius (C o r n e l i u s) Harris – bapt. 28 Jun 1683 (Baptism, **St. Michan Parish**), bur. 7 Dec 1684 (Burial, **St. Michan Parish**)

- o Stephen Harris – bur. 8 Jan 1684 (Burial, **St. Michan Parish**)

Henry Harris (father):

Occupation - Coachman - February 20, 1680

February 3, 1681

June 28, 1683

January 8, 1684

December 7, 1684

Hurst

- Henry Harris & Unknown

  - George Harris & Elizabeth Lilly – 8 May 1848 (Marriage, **St. George Parish**)

Signatures:

- Mary Anne Harris, b. 22 Mar 1849, bapt. 29 Apr 1849 (Baptism, **St. Mary Parish**) &

  Richard Alexander Connor – 22 Jan 1878 (Marriage, **St. Bride Parish**)

Signatures:

Mary Anne Harris (daughter of George Harris & Elizabeth Lilly):

   Residence - Bride Street - January 22, 1878

Richard Alexander Connor, son of George Connor (son-in-law):

   Residence - South King Street - January 22, 1878

   Occupation - Picture Man - January 22, 1878

George Connor (father):

   Occupation - Wine Worker

George Harris (father):

   Occupation - Gun Maker

Wedding Witnesses:

Bessie Harris

Signature:

- George Harris – b. 16 Jan 1853, bapt. 16 May 1853 (Baptism, St. Peter Parish)

- Elizabeth Charlotte Harris – b. 21 Feb 1855, bapt. 6 Apr 1855 (Baptism, St. Peter Parish)

George Harris (son):

    Residence - 88 Upper Dorset Street - May 8, 1848

        14 Great Britain Street - April 29, 1849

        No 2 Camden Row - May 16, 1853

        April 6, 1855

    Occupation - Gun Maker - May 8, 1848

        April 29, 1849

        May 16, 1853

        April 6, 1855

Elizabeth Lilly, daughter of John Lilly (daughter-in-law):

    Residence - 23 Richmond Place - May 8, 1848

John Lilly (father):

Signature:

    Occupation - Shoemaker

Henry Harris (father):

    Occupation - Gun Maker

Hurst

Wedding Witnesses:

John Lilly

Signature:

    o   Sarah Harris & Henry Fisher – 23 Jul 1851 (Marriage, St. Mary Parish)

Signatures:

Sarah Harris (daughter):

    Residence - 23 Jervis Street - July 23, 1851

Henry Fisher, son of William Fisher (son-in-law):

    Residence - 23 Jervis Street - July 23, 1851

    Occupation - Land Agency Clerk - July 23, 1851

William Fisher (father):

    Occupation - Scripture Reader

Henry Harris (father):

    Occupation - Gun Maker

Wedding Witnesses:

Phobe Harris

Signature:

○ John Henry Harris & Emily Cuddy – 26 Feb 1852 (Marriage, **St. Mary Parish**)

Signatures:

John Henry Harris (son):

Residence - Sandymount - February 26, 1852

Occupation - Gun Maker - February 26, 1852

Emily Cuddy, daughter of William Cuddy (daughter-in-law):

Residence - 13 Denmark Street - February 26, 1852

Occupation - Dress Maker - February 26, 1852

William Cuddy (father):

Occupation - Post Master

Henry Harris (father):

Occupation - Gun Maker

- Henry Harris & Unknown

  ○ Henry James Harris & Emily Anne Ward – 12 Oct 1870 (Marriage, **St. Peter Parish**)

Signatures:

Hurst

Henry James Harris (son):

Residence - Posterdown, Co. Armagh - October 12, 1870

Occupation - Solicitor - October 12, 1870

Emily Anne Ward, daughter of Thomas Henry Ward (daughter-in-law):

Residence - 8 Adelaide Road - October 12, 1870

Thomas Henry Ward (father):

Occupation - Esquire

Henry Harris (father):

Occupation - Solicitor

- Henry Harris & Unknown

  o Mary Anne Harris & William Hatch – 30 Mar 1881 (Marriage, St. Mary Parish)

Signatures:

Mary Anne Harris (daughter):

Residence - 28 Lower Ormond Quay Dublin - March 30, 1881

Duleek - March 30, 1881

William Hatch, son of John Hatch (son-in-law):

Residence - Duleek - March 30, 1881

Occupation - Farmer - March 30, 1881

John Hatch (father):

Occupation - Farmer

Henry Harris (father):

Occupation - Farmer

Harris Surname Ireland: 1600s to 1900s

- Henry Harris & Unknown

  o Mary Harriet Harris & Theophilus Hall – 13 Dec 1900 (Marriage, **St. George Parish**)

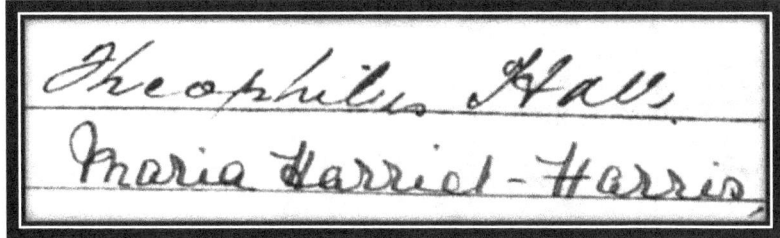

Signatures:

Mary Harriet Harris (daughter):

    Residence - 2 Lower Sherrard Street - December 13, 1900

Theophilus Hall, son of John Hall (son-in-law):

    Residence - 2 Lower Sherrard Street - December 13, 1900

    Occupation - Commercial Traveller - December 13, 1900

John Hall (father):

    Occupation - Merchant

Henry Harris (father):

    Occupation - Gentleman

Wedding Witnesses:

H. R. Harris & H. J. Hall

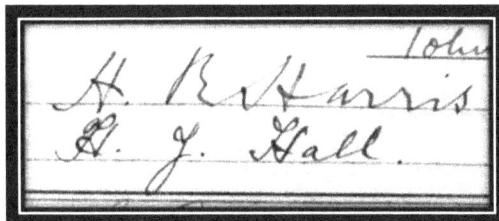

Signatures:

- Henry Harris & Unknown

  o Edward Walter Harris & Catherine Gill – 30 Jan 1894 (Marriage, **Rathmines Parish**)

Signatures:

  ▪ Mary Elizabeth Harris – b. 1894, bapt. 1894 (Baptism, **St. Andrew Parish (RC)**)

Edward Walter Harris (son):

  Residence - Portobello Barracks - January 30, 1894

    32 Holles Street - 1894

  Occupation - Medical Staff Corps - January 30, 1894

Catherine Gill, daughter of Patrick Gill (daughter-in-law):

  Residence - 13 Mount Pleasant Place - January 30, 1894

  Relationship Status at Marriage- minor age

Patrick Gill (father):

  Occupation - Laborer

Henry Harris (father):

  Occupation - Laborer

- Henry Dudley Harris & Elizabeth Harris

  o Arthur Thomas Harris & Margaret Smith – 15 Aug 1893 (Marriage, **St. Peter Parish**)

Signatures:

Harris Surname Ireland: 1600s to 1900s

- Henry Dudley Harris – b. 24 Apr 1894, bapt. 26 Apr 1894 (Baptism, **St. Peter Parish**)

- Margaret Elizabeth Harris – b. 13 Oct 1895, bapt. 10 Dec 1895 (Baptism, **St. Peter Parish**)

- Annie Maud Harris – b. 17 Nov 1897, bapt. 7 Dec 1897 (Baptism, **St. Peter Parish**)

Arthur Thomas Harris (son):

    Residence - Ordnance Stores Montpelier Hill - August 15, 1893

        3 Redmonds Hill - April 26, 1894

        51 Third Avenue Seville Place - December 10, 1895

        30 Wexford Street - December 7, 1897

    Occupation - Joiner - August 15, 1893

        December 10, 1895

        Carpenter - April 26, 1894

        December 7, 1897

Margaret Smith, daughter of Charles Finlay Smith (daughter-in-law):

    Residence - 36 Aungier Street - August 15, 1893

Charles Finlay Smith (father):

    Occupation - Compositor

Henry Dudley Harris (father):

    Occupation - Ordnance Store Dept

Wedding Witnesses:

H. D. Harris & Charlotte Bradfield

Signatures:

Hurst

- Henry Edward Harris & Charlotte Bradfield – 27 Dec 1897 (Marriage, St. Peter Parish)

Signatures:

Henry Edward Harris (son):

    Residence - Ballymacorrett, Co. Down - December 27, 1897

    Occupation - Plumber - December 27, 1897

Charlotte Bradfield, daughter of William Bradfield (daughter-in-law):

    Residence - 50 Aungier Street - December 27, 1897

William Bradfield (father):

    Occupation -Boot Manufacturer

Henry Dudley Harris (father):

    Occupation - Superintendent of Stores Ordnance Dept

Wedding Witnesses:

Harry Bradfield & Martha Bradfield

Signatures:

- Thomas Stephen Harris – b. 21 Jul 1873, bapt. 7 Sep 1873 (Baptism, St. Paul Parish)

- Charles Dudley Harris – b. 14 Oct 1875, bapt. 9 Jan 1876 (Baptism, St. James Parish)

- Edward Cheetham Harris – b. 14 Jan 1878, bapt. 27 Mar 1881 (Baptism, St. Paul Parish)

- Frederick Dudley Harris – b. 16 May 1880, bapt. 27 Mar 1881 (Baptism, St. Paul Parish)

- Emily Selina Harris – b. 10 Mar 1882, bapt. 11 Jun 1882 (Baptism, St. Paul Parish)

- Florence Louisa Harris – b. 11 Jun 1883, bapt. 31 May 1885 (Baptism, **Rotunda Chapel Parish**)

- Violet Elizabeth Harris – b. 2 May 1885, bapt. 31 May 1885 (Baptism, **Rotunda Chapel Parish**)

- Albert Victor Harris – b. 7 Jul 1887, bapt. 14 Sep 1887 (Baptism, **St. Paul Parish**)

- William Dudley Harris – b. 18 Jan 1892, bapt. 24 Jan 1892 (Baptism, **Rotunda Chapel Parish**)

Henry Dudley Harris (father):

Residence - 10 Pembroke Quay - September 7, 1873

13 Pembroke Quay - January 9, 1876

Military Stores North Circular Road - March 27, 1881

Military Stores Montpelier Hill - June 11, 1882

Ordnance Stores Montpelier Hill - September 14, 1887

Montpelier Hill Dublin - May 31, 1885

January 24, 1892

Occupation - Saddler - September 7, 1873

Saddler & Collar Maker - January 9, 1876

Clerk - March 27, 1881

June 11, 1882

Store Orderly - September 14, 1887

Store Holder in Ordnance Department - May 31, 1885

January 24, 1892

Hurst

- Henry Harold Harris & Catherine Sweeny – 23 Feb 1830 (Marriage, **Kinsale Parish** (RC))

  o John Harris – bapt. 2 Jun 1833 (Baptism, **Kinsale Parish** (RC))

  o Mary Harris – bapt. 20 Jul 1836 (Baptism, **Kinsale Parish** (RC))

  o Thomas Harris – bapt. 21 Feb 1839 (Baptism, **Kinsale Parish** (RC))

  o Margaret Harris – bapt. 22 May 1842 (Baptism, **Kinsale Parish** (RC))

Henry Harris (father):

Residence - Ballyregan - February 23, 1830

June 2, 1833

July 20, 1836

May 22, 1842

- Henry James Harris & Unknown

  o Martha Maud Harris & William Henry Townley Tilson – 12 Aug 1893 (Marriage, **St.**

  Werburgh Parish)

Signatures:

Martha Maud Harris (daughter):

Residence - 56 South Richmond Street Dublin - August 12, 1893

William Henry Townley Tilson, son of William Tilson (son-in-law):

Residence - 56 South Richmond Street Dublin - August 12, 1893

Occupation - Esquire - August 12, 1893

William Tilson (father):

Occupation - Secretary

Henry James Harris (father):

Occupation - Solicitor

Harris Surname Ireland: 1600s to 1900s

- Henry Richard Harris & Harriet Hannah Harris

    o Margaret Caroline Harris – bapt. 7 Oct 1866 (Baptism, **Tralee Parish**)

    o Henry John Harris, b. 1877, & Edith Mary Eleanor McCreery – 27 May 1896 (Marriage, **St. Anne Parish**)

Signatures:

Henry John Harris (son):

    Residence - John's Quay Kilkenny - May 27, 1896

    Occupation - Esquire - May 27, 1896

Edith Mary Eleanor McCreery, daughter of Alexander John McCreery (daughter-in-law):

    Residence - John St House, Kilkenny - May 27, 1896

    Occupation - Esquire - May 27, 1896

    Relationship Status at Marriage - minor age

Alexander John McCreery (father):

Signature:

    Occupation - Sub Sherriff City of Aelbeery

Henry Richard Harris (father):

    Residence - Ratass - October 7, 1866

    Occupation - Cashier Bank of Ireland - October 7, 1866

        Bank Clerk

Hurst

Wedding Witnesses:

Alexander John McCreery:

Signature:

- Hopkin Harris & Eleanor Harris

  - Thomas Harris – bapt. 2 Apr 1738 (Baptism, **St. Mark Parish**)

  - Hopkin Harris – bapt. 10 Jul 1740 (Baptism, **St. Mark Parish**)

  - Eleanor Harris – bapt. 17 Feb 1743 (Baptism, **St. Mark Parish**)

  - William Harris – bapt. 9 Sep 1744 (Baptism, **St. Mark Parish**)

  - William Harris – bapt. 12 Feb 1752 (Baptism, **St. Mark Parish**)

Hopkin Harris (father):

Residence - George's Quay - April 2, 1738

July 10, 1740

February 17, 1743

September 9, 1744

February 12, 1752

- Hopkin Harris & Elizabeth Harris

  - Mary Harris – bapt. 18 May 1734 (Baptism, **St. Mark Parish**)

- Hubert Harris & Hannah Fay

  - Hubert Harris – bapt. 15 Sep 1846 (Baptism, **St. Catherine Parish** (RC))

- Hugh Harris & Catherine Barrett – 25 Sep 1791 (Marriage, **St. Michan Parish**)

- Hugh Harris & Elizabeth Unknown

  - Anne Harris – bapt. 27 Aug 1839 (Baptism, **SS. Michael & John Parish** (RC))

Harris Surname Ireland: 1600s to 1900s

- Hugh Harris & Mary Gargan

  o Ellen Harris & Michael Mitchell – 6 Sep 1874 (Marriage, **Harrington Street Parish (RC)**)

Ellen Harris (daughter):

　Residence - 3 West Camden Street Upper - September 6, 1874

Michael Mitchell, son of John Mitchell & Mary Glennie (son-in-law):

　Residence - Unclear - September 6, 1874

- Hugh Harris & Mary Unknown

  o Mary Harris – bapt. 26 Unclear 1841 (Baptism, **SS. Michael & John Parish** (RC))

The church register entry is badly worn and is missing the part that tells the month of the child's baptism.

- Hugh Harris & Mary Unknown

  o James Harris Harris & Elizabeth Burke – 22 Apr 1883 (Marriage, **Chapelizod Parish** (RC))

    ▪ Thomas Harris – bapt. 1883 (Baptism, **Chapelizod Parish** (RC))

    ▪ Edward Harris – bapt. 1885 (Baptism, **Chapelizod Parish** (RC))

James Harris (son):

　Residence - Blanchardstown - April 22, 1883

　　　　Chapelizod - 1883

　　　　New Row - 1885

Elizabeth Burke, daughter of Edward Burke & Bridget Unknown (daughter-in-law):

　Residence - Chapelizod - April 22, 1883

Edward Burke (father):

　Residence - Chapelizod

Hugh Harris (father):

　Residence - Blanchardstown

- Hugh Harris & Unknown

  o Margaret Harris – bapt. 9 Jan 1641 (Baptism, **St. John Parish**)

Hurst

- Hugh Harris & Unknown

Signature:

  o Mary Anne Madeline Harris & Charles Crawford Mayne – 5 Apr 1870 (Marriage, St. George

    Parish)

Signatures:

Mary Anne Madeline Harris (daughter):

  Residence - 3 Mountjoy Place - April 5, 1870

Charles Crawford Mayne, son of Robert Mayne (son-in-law):

  Residence - Westmoreland, England - April 5, 1870

           5 Cavendish Row Dublin - April 5, 1870

  Occupation - Esquire - April 5, 1870

Robert Mayne (father):

  Occupation - M D

Hugh Harris (father):

Signature:

  Occupation - Barrister at Law

Wedding Witnesses:

Hugh Harris & David Stuart

Signatures:

- ○ Margaret Anne Harris & Henry Robert King Irwin – 26 Jun 1873 (Marriage, St. George

  Parish)

Signatures:

Margaret Anne Harris (daughter):

Residence - 3 Mountjoy Square - June 26, 1873

Henry Robert King Irwin, son of Henry Robert King Irwin (son-in-law):

Residence - 45 Upper Rutland Street - June 26, 1873

Occupation - Gentleman - June 26, 1873

Henry Robert King Irwin (father):

Occupation - Esquire

Hugh Harris (father):

Occupation - Barrister at Law

Wedding Witnesses:

Henry Harris & James Francis Mayne

Signatures:

Hurst

- Hugh Harris & Unknown

    o James Harris & Elizabeth Chamley – 28 Feb 1878 (Marriage, **St. Andrew Parish** (RC))

James Harris (son):

Residence - Blanchardstown - February 28, 1878

Elizabeth Chamley, daughter of James Chamley (daughter-in-law):

Residence - 34 Merrion Square - February 28. 1878

- Huston Harris & Mary Roycroft – 4 Jan 1831 (Marriage, **St. James Parish**)

Huston Harris (husband):

Residence - St. James Parish - January 4, 1831

Occupation - Mariner - January 4, 1831

Mary Roycroft (wife):

Residence - St. James Parish - January 4, 1831

- Isaac Harris & Ellen Unknown

    o Mary Harris – bapt. 21 May 1863 (Baptism, **Cork - South Parish** (RC))

- Isaac Harris & Charlotte Unknown

    o Charlotte Harris – b. 15 Dec 1896, bapt. 2 Jan 1897 (Baptism, **St. Stephen Parish**)

    o Eileen Harris – b. 16 Feb 1904, bapt. 24 Mar 1904 (Baptism, **St. Stephen Parish**)

    o Mary Harris – b. 1905, bapt. 1905 (Baptism, **St. Stephen Parish**)

Isaac Harris (father):

Residence - 5 Stephen's Place - January 2, 1897

9 Deuzille Street - March 24, 1904

4 Deuzille Street - 1905

Occupation - Porter - January 2, 1897

Attendant at Pattolovail School T.E.D. - March 24, 1904

Attendant - - - - - - 1905

Harris Surname Ireland: 1600s to 1900s

- Isaac Harris & Unknown

  - Jane Harris & George Wheatley – 9 Jan 1850 (Marriages, **St. Audoen Parish**)

Signatures:

Jane Harris (daughter):

　　Residence - 9 Usher Street - January 9, 1850

　　Occupation - Servant - January 9, 1850

George Wheatley, son of Richard Wheatley (son-in-law):

　　Residence - 9 Usher Street - January 9, 1850

　　Occupation - Laborer - January 9, 1850

Richard Wheatley (father):

　　Occupation - Shoe Maker

Isaac Harris (father):

　　Occupation - Weaver

- James Harris & Anne Harris

  - Robert Harris – bapt. 8 Jun 1752 (Baptism, **St. Mark Parish**)

James Harris (father):

　　Residence - George's Quay - June 8, 1752

- James Harris & Anne Harris

  - Frederick Harris – b. 25 Sep 1881, bapt. 27 Dec 1881(Baptism, **St. Peter Parish**)

  - Charlotte Harris – b. 28 Jul 1885, bapt. 27 Sep 1885 (Baptism, **Bethseda Chapel Parish**)

Hurst

James Harris (father):

> Residence - 2 Brown's Lane off York Street - December 27, 1881

> > 34 Fontenoy Street - September 27, 1885

> Occupation - Smith - December 27, 1881

> > September 27, 1885

- James Harris & Anne Lancashire – 6 Jun 1675 (Marriage, **St. Peter Parish**)

- James Harris & Anne Sanders – 2 Oct 1678 (Marriage, **St. Andrew Parish**)

- James Harris & Bridget Brown – 8 Feb 1812 (Marriage, **Causeway Parish** (RC))

  - Margaret Harris, b. 8 May 1837, bapt. 8 May 1837 (Baptism, **Abbeydorney Parish** (RC))

    & Bartholomew Riordan – 9 May 1862 (Marriage, **Abbeydorney Parish** (RC))

    - Julia Riordan – b. 2 Mar 1856, bapt. 7 Mar 1856 (Baptism, **Ardfert Parish** (RC))

    - Joan Riordan – b. 4 Jul 1869, bapt. 18 Jul 1869 (Baptism, **Ardfert Parish** (RC))

    - Margaret Riordan – b. 20 May 1871, bapt. 4 Jun 1871 (Baptism, **Ardfert Parish** (RC))

    - Mary Riordan – b. 25 Apr 1873, bapt. 27 Apr 1873 (Baptism, **Ardfert Parish** (RC))

    - Thomas Riordan – b. 25 Jan 1875, bapt. 2 Feb 1875 (Baptism, **Ardfert Parish** (RC))

    - Patrick Riordan – b. 12 Mar 1877, bapt. 18 Mar 1877 (Baptism, **Ardfert Parish** (RC))

Margaret Harris (daughter):

> Residence - Ardrahan - May 9, 1862

Bartholomew Riordan, son of William Riordan & Bridget Kirby (son-in-law):

> Residence - Ardfert - May 9, 1862

> > Ballinprior - March 7, 1856

> > > July 18, 1869

> > > June 4, 1871

> > > April 27, 1873

> > > February 2, 1875

> > > March 18, 1877

  - Thomas Harris – b. 23 Mar 1839, bapt. 23 Mar 1839 (Baptism, **Abbeydorney Parish** (RC))

Harris Surname Ireland: 1600s to 1900s

James Harris (father):

> Residence - Abbeydorney - February 8, 1812
>
> Ardrahan - May 8, 1837
>
> March 23, 1839

- James Harris & Bridget Byrne (B y r n e)

  - George Harris – b. 1 May 1895, bapt. 19 Apr 1895 (Baptism, **St. Mary, Pro Cathedral Parish** (RC))

James Harris (father):

> Residence - 54 Mabbot Street - April 19, 1895

- James Harris & Bridget Kennedy

  - Mary Harris – bapt. 27 Mar 1785 (Baptism, **St. Catherine Parish** (RC))

  - John Harris – bapt. 17 Feb 1788 (Baptism, **St. Catherine Parish** (RC))

  - Patrick Harris – bapt. 14 Feb 1790 (Baptism, **St. Catherine Parish** (RC))

- James Harris & Bridget Murphy

  - Mary Harris – bapt. 1 Jun 1846 (Baptism, **St. Nicholas Parish** (RC))

- James Harris & Bridget Riordan

  - John Harris – b. 17 Jul 1881, bapt. 17 Jul 1881 (Baptism, **Glenbeigh/Glencar Parish** (RC))

James Harris (father):

> Residence - Knockboy - July 17, 1881

- James Harris & Bridget Unknown

  - Patrick Harris – bapt. 4 Feb 1840 (Baptism, **St. Catherine Parish** (RC))

- James Harris & Caroline Unknown

  - Peter Harris – bapt. 27 Dec 1756 (Baptism, **St. Werburgh Parish**)

James Harris (father):

> Residence - Skinner's Alley - December 27, 1756

Hurst

- James Harris & Catherine Buoney – 7 Feb 1836 (Marriage, **Glenbeigh/Glencar Parish** (RC))

  - Ellen Harris – b. 11 Jul 1841, bapt. 11 Jul 1841 (Baptism, **Glenbeigh/Glencar Parish** (RC))

  - Mary Harris – b. 21 Jul 1844, bapt. 21 Jul 1844 (Baptism, **Glenbeigh/Glencar Parish** (RC))

  - Simon Harris – b. 1 Apr 1853, bapt. 1 Apr 1853 (Baptism, **Glenbeigh/Glencar Parish** (RC))

James Harris (father):

Residence - Knockbue - July 11, 1841

Coolnaharragill - July 21, 1844

Drom - April 1, 1853

Catherine Buoney (mother):

Residence - Drom - February 7, 1836

- James Harris & Catherine Donnuck

  - Mary Harris & John Coogan – 1 Feb 1874 (Marriage, **Rathmines Parish** (RC))

    - James Coogan – b. 15 Oct 1876, bapt. 22 Oct 1876 (Baptism, **Rathmines Parish** (RC))

    - Mary Catherine Coogan – b. 23 May 1879, bapt. 23 May 1879 (Baptism, **Rathmines Parish** (RC))

Mary Harris (daughter):

Residence - Doyle's Court - February 1, 1874

John Coogan, son of James Coogan & Mary Unknown (son-in-law):

Residence - Doyle's Court - February 1, 1874

Charlemont Avenue - October 22, 1876

May 23, 1879

  - Bridget Harris & Patrick Farrell – 3 Sep 1876 (Marriage, **Rathmines Parish** (RC))

    - Joseph C. Farrell – b. 20 Jun 1878, bapt. 23 Jun 1878 (Baptism, **Rathmines Parish** (RC))

Harris Surname Ireland: 1600s to 1900s

Bridget Harris (daughter):

Residence - Charlemont Avenue - September 3, 1876

Patrick Farrell, son of Maurice Farrell & Mary Byrne (son-in-law):

Residence - Charlemont Avenue - September 3, 1876

June 23, 1878

- James Harris & Catherine Craven

    o Patrick Harris – b. 27 Apr 1895, bapt. 30 Apr 1895 (Baptism, **Harrington Street Parish (RC)**)

    o James Joseph Harris – b. 5 Mar 1897, bapt. 12 Mar 1897 (Baptism, **Harrington Street Parish (RC)**)

    o Joseph Christopher Harris – b. 28 Nov 1899, bapt. 1 Dec 1899 (Baptism, **Harrington Street Parish** (RC))

James Harris (father):

Residence - 7 Charlemont Avenue - April 30, 1895

March 12, 1897

December 1, 1899

- James Harris & Catherine Donovan

    o Mary Harris – bapt. 9 Sep 1855 (Baptism, **Rathmines Parish (RC)**)

- James Harris & Catherine McDonagh – 11 Aug 1845 (Marriage, **Rathfarnham Parish (RC)**)

    o Edward Harris – b. 1846, bapt. 1846 (Baptism, **Rathfarnham Parish (RC)**)

    o Simon Harris – bapt. 2 Sep 1849 (Baptism, **Rathmines Parish (RC)**)

    o Bridget Harris – bapt. 10 Nov 1852 (Baptism, **Rathmines Parish (RC)**)

    o William Harris – b. 15 Jan 1859, bapt. 16 Jan 1859 (Baptism, **Rathmines Parish (RC)**)

    o Gulielmo Harris – b. 15 Jan 1859, bapt. 16 Jan 1859 (Baptism, **Rathmines Parish (RC)**)

    o Catherine Harris –b. 26 Aug 1860, bapt. 4 Sep 1860 (Baptism, **St. Catherine Parish (RC)**)

    o James Harris – b. 16 Feb 1863, bapt. 22 Feb 1863 (Baptism, **Rathmines Parish (RC)**)

Hurst

James Harris (father):

Residence - Harold's Cross - January 16, 1859

February 22, 1863

41 Coombe - September 4, 1860

- James Harris & Catherine Mansfield

  o Alfred James Harris – b. 4 Feb 1875, bapt. 15 Mar 1875 (Baptism, **St. Michan Parish** (RC))

  o John Joseph Harris – b. 1 Aug 1877, bapt. 20 Aug 1877 (Baptism, **St. Michan Parish** (RC))

  o Jane Josephine Harris – b. 17 Mar 1880, bapt. 6 Apr 1880 (Baptism, **St. Michan Parish** (RC))

James Harris (father):

Residence - Linenhall Barracks - March 15, 1875

16 Mountjoy Street - August 20, 1877

51 Bolton Street - April 6, 1880

- James Harris & Catherine Moriarty

  o Dennis Harris – b. 2 Jul 1859, bapt. 2 Jul 1859 (Baptism, **Glenbeigh/Glencar Parish** (RC))

  o Ellen Harris – b. 11 Oct 1862, bapt. 11 Oct 1862 (Baptism, **Glenbeigh/Glencar Parish** (RC))

James Harris (father):

Residence - Drom - July 2, 1859

October 11, 1862

- James Harris & Catherine Riordan – 1 Feb 1867 (Marriage, **Glenbeigh/Glencar Parish** (RC))

  o Mary Harris – b. 28 Jun 1870, bapt. 28 Jun 1870 (Baptism, **Glenbeigh/Glencar Parish** (RC))

  o James Harris – b. 31 Mar 1874, bapt. 31 Mar 1874 (Baptism, **Glenbeigh/Glencar Parish** (RC))

- ○ Joan Harris – b. 20 Sep 1874, bapt. 20 Sep 1874 (Baptism, **Glenbeigh/Glencar Parish (RC)**)

- ○ Catherine Harris – b. 12 Sep 1875, bapt. 12 Sep 1875 (Baptism, **Glenbeigh/Glencar Parish (RC)**)

- ○ Daniel Harris – b. 24 Dec 1877, bapt. 24 Dec 1877 (Baptism, **Glenbeigh/Glencar Parish (RC)**)

- ○ Philip Harris – b. 22 Nov 1880, bapt. 22 Nov 1880 (Baptism, **Glenbeigh/Glencar Parish (RC)**)

- ○ Thomas Harris – b. 5 Dec 1886, bapt. 5 Dec 1886 (Baptism, **Glenbeigh/Glencar Parish (RC)**)

- ○ Margaret Harris – b. 27 Feb 1890, bapt. 27 Feb 1890 (Baptism, **Glenbeigh/Glencar Parish (RC)**)

James Harris (father):

Residence - Kilkeehagh - February 1, 1867

June 28, 1870

March 31, 1874,

September 20, 1874

September 12, 1875

December 24, 1877

November 22, 1880

December 5, 1886

February 27, 1890

- • James Harris & Catherine Riordan – 1 Apr 1868 (Marriage, **Glenbeigh/Glencar Parish (RC)**)

James Harris (husband):

Residence - Kilkeehagh - April 1, 1868

Catherine Riordan (wife):

Residence - Coolnaharragill - April 1, 1868

Hurst

- James Harris & Eleanor Unknown

  - Mary Harris – bapt. 3 May 1761 (Baptism, **St. Catherine Parish** (RC))

- James Harris & Elizabeth Gleeson

  - Frederick Harris & Margaret Shanahan – 3 Nov 1903 (Marriage, **Listowel Parish** (RC))

Frederick Harris (son):

Residence - Tralee - November 3, 1903

Margaret Shanahan, daughter of William Shanahan & Margaret Grogan

(daughter-in-law):

Residence - Listowel - November 3, 1903

- James Harris & Elizabeth Griffin

  - Patrick Harris & Ellen Harmon – 14 Feb 1888 (Marriage, **Abbeydorney Parish** (RC))

    - James Harris – b. 11 Dec 1888, bapt. 15 Dec 1888 (Baptism, **Abbeydorney Parish** (RC))

    - John Harris – b. 22 Feb 1890, bapt. 23 Feb 1890 (Baptism, **Abbeydorney Parish** (RC))

    - Michael Harris – b. 25 Sep 1891, bapt. 26 Sep 1891 (Baptism, **Abbeydorney Parish**

      (RC))

    - Mary Harris – b. 17 Jan 1893, bapt. 21 Jan 1893 (Baptism, **Abbeydorney Parish** (RC))

    - Ellen Harris – b. 4 Jul 1894, bapt. 11 Jul 1894 (Baptism, **Abbeydorney Parish** (RC))

    - Elizabeth Harris – b. 1 Jan 1896, bapt. 1 Jan 1896 (Baptism, **Abbeydorney Parish** (RC))

    - Dennis F. Harris – b. 13 Jul 1897, bapt. 18 Aug 1897 (Baptism, **Abbeydorney Parish**

      (RC))

Patrick Harris (son):

Residence - Ardrahan - February 14, 1888

December 15, 1888

February 23, 1890

September 26, 1891

January 21, 1893

July 11, 1894

Harris Surname Ireland: 1600s to 1900s

Ellen Harmon, daughter of John Harmon & Mary Leary (daughter-in-law):

Residence - Ardrahan - February 14, 1888

- James Harris & Elizabeth Hurly – 5 May 1837 (Marriage, **Cork - South Parish** (RC))

    o Michael Harris – bapt. 21 Feb 1836 (Baptism, **Cork - South Parish** (RC))

    o Margaret Harris – bapt. 9 Feb 1840 (Baptism, **Cork - South Parish** (RC))

    o Thomas Harris – bapt. 11 Feb 1842 (Baptism, **Cork - South Parish** (RC))

    o Elizabeth Harris – bapt. 26 Oct 1844 (Baptism, **Cork - South Parish** (RC))

    o John Harris – bapt. 17 Feb 1847 (Baptism, **Cork - South Parish** (RC))

    o Ellen Harris – bapt. 2 Nov 1851 (Baptism, **Cork - South Parish** (RC))

- James Harris & Elizabeth Kearns – 30 Nov 1850 (Marriage, **Rathfarnham Parish** (RC))

    o Christopher Harris – b. 1855, bapt. 1855 (Baptism, **Rathfarnham Parish** (RC))

- James Harris & Elizabeth Luoney – 10 Sep 1808 (Marriage, **Tralee Parish** (RC))

    o Gerald Harris – b. 23 Aug 1809, bapt. 23 Aug 1809 (Baptism, **Tralee Parish** (RC))

    o Lewis Harris – b. 12 Mar 1811, bapt. 12 Mar 1811 (Baptism, **Tralee Parish** (RC))

    o Sarah Harris – b. 21 Jun 1813, bapt. 21 Jun 1813 (Baptism, **Tralee Parish** (RC))

    o Mary Harris – b. 22 Nov 1815, bapt. 22 Nov 1815 (Baptism, **Tralee Parish** (RC))

    o Richard Harris – b. 13 Dec 1829, bapt. 13 Dec 1829 (Baptism, **Annascaul Parish** (RC))

    o Lovet Harris & Bridget O'Driscoll – 13 Jun 1865 (Marriage, **Tralee Parish** (RC))

        ▪ Margaret Harris – b. 29 Sep 1865, bapt. 1 Oct 1865 (Baptism, **Tralee Parish** (RC))

        ▪ Mary Harris – b. 30 Aug 1868, bapt. 1 Sep 1868 (Baptism, **Tralee Parish** (RC))

        ▪ Bridget Harris – b. 17 Aug 1872, bapt. 20 Aug 1872 (Baptism, **Tralee Parish** (RC))

Hurst

Lovet Harris (son):

    Residence - Derrymore - June 13, 1865, October 1, 1865

        September 1, 1868

        August 20, 1872

Bridget O'Driscoll, daughter of James O'Driscoll & Bridget Ferriter

(daughter-in-law):

    Residence - Derrymore - June 13, 1865

James Harris (father):

    Residence - Derrymore - September 10, 1808

        August 23, 1809

        March 12, 1811

        Glaunrahilly - June 21, 1813

        November 22, 1815

        Killelton - December 13, 1829

- James Harris & Elizabeth Nesbit

  - Ellen Harris – b. 11 Oct 1823, bapt. 11 Oct 1823 (Baptism, **Tralee Parish** (RC))

  - Mary Harris – b. 4 Jul 1826, bapt. 4 Jul 1826 (Baptism, **Tralee Parish** (RC))

  - Anne Harris – b. 14 Apr 1829, bapt. 14 Apr 1829 (Baptism, **Tralee Parish** (RC))

  - William Harris – b. 8 Jan 1832, bapt. 8 Jan 1832 (Baptism, **Tralee Parish** (RC))

  - James Harris – b. 28 Jul 1834, bapt. 28 Jul 1834 (Baptism, **Tralee Parish** (RC))

  - Margaret Harris – b. 18 Mar 1837, bapt. 18 Mar 1837 (Baptism, **Tralee Parish** (RC))

  - Elizabeth Harris – b. 25 Jan 1840, bapt. 25 Jan 1840 (Baptism, **Tralee Parish** (RC))

  - Elizabeth Harris – b. 1 Aug 1841, bapt. 1 Aug 1841 (Baptism, **Tralee Parish** (RC))

  - Jane Harris – b. 3 Mar 1844, bapt. 3 Mar 1844 (Baptism, **Tralee Parish** (RC))

  - Robert Harris – b. 31 May 1846, bapt. 31 May 1846 (Baptism, **Tralee Parish** (RC))

Harris Surname Ireland: 1600s to 1900s

James Harris (father):

Residence - Knockanish - October 11, 1823

July 4, 1826

April 14, 1829

January 8, 1832

July 28, 1834

March 18, 1837

January 25, 1840

August 1, 1841

March 3, 1844

May 31, 1846

- James Harris & Elizabeth Thomas – 11 May 1743 (Marriage, **St. Andrew Parish** (RC))

  - Susanna Harris – b. 1745, bapt. 1745 (Baptism, **St. Andrew Parish** (RC))

  - Robert Harris – b. 1749, bapt. 1749 (Baptism, **St. Andrew Parish** (RC))

  - Martha Harris – b. 1751, bapt. 1751 (Baptism, **St. Andrew Parish** (RC))

- James Harris & Elizabeth Unknown

  - Catherine Harris – bapt. 16 Feb 1715 (Baptism, **St. Werburgh Parish**)

James Harris (father):

Residence - Blind Key - February 16, 1715

- James Harris & Ellen Cuddy – 3 Aug 1841 (Marriage, **Rathfarnham Parish** (RC))

  - Thomas Harris – bapt. 1845 (Baptism, **St. Andrew Parish** (RC))

  - James Harris – bapt. 1851 (Baptism, **St. Andrew Parish** (RC))

  - Mary Harris – b. 1854, bapt. 1854 (Baptism, **St. Andrew Parish** (RC))

  - Mary Anne Harris – b. 1855, bapt. 1855 (Baptism, **St. Andrew Parish** (RC))

- James Harris & Ellen McCarthy

  - Timothy Harris – bapt. 25 Aug 1867 (Baptism, **Cork - South Parish** (RC))

Hurst

- James Harris & Ellen Murphy

  - James Harris – bapt. 19 Dec 1819 (Baptism, **Cork - South Parish** (RC))

- James Harris & Esther Harris

  - John Harris & Elizabeth Kenny – 19 Feb 1865 (Marriage, **Clondalkin Parish** (RC))

    - John Harris – bapt. 1866 (Baptism, **Clondalkin Parish** (RC))

    - Joseph Harris – bapt. 1867 (Baptism, **Clondalkin Parish** (RC))

    - James Harris – bapt. 1869 (Baptism, **Clondalkin Parish** (RC))

John Harris (son):

   Residence - Lucan - February 19, 1865

                                1866

                                1867

                                1869

Elizabeth Kenny, daughter of Nicholas Kenny & Alice Kenny (daughter-in-law):

   Residence - Lucan - February 19, 1865

- James Harris & Esther Sarah Harris

  - James Gibson Harris – b. 12 Jun 1874, bapt. 11 Sep 1874 (Baptism, **St. Mary Parish**)

  - Kathleen Esther Harris – b. 20 Oct 1876, bapt. 5 Sep 1877 (Baptism, **St. Mary Parish**)

James Harris (father)

   Residence - 34 Palace Garden Terrace Kensington, London - September 11, 1874

                  34 Palace Gardens Kensington, London - September 5, 1877

   Occupation - Public Accountant - September 11, 1874

                  Accountant - September 5, 1877

- James Harris & Esther Unknown

  - William Harris – bapt. 18 Aug 1760 (Baptism, **St. Werburgh Parish**)

James Harris (father):

   Residence - Fishamble Street - August 18, 1760

Harris Surname Ireland: 1600s to 1900s

- James Harris & Frances Lawlor – 7 Aug 1831 (Marriage, **St. Mary, Pro Cathedral Parish (RC)**)

- James Harris & Gobinet Buoney – 1 Mar 1829 (Marriage, **Glenbeigh/Glencar Parish (RC)**)

  - Bridget Harris – b. 1 Jan 1830, bapt. 1 Jan 1830 (Baptism, **Glenbeigh/Glencar Parish (RC)**)

  - John Harris – b. 10 Sep 1832, bapt. 10 Sep 1832 (Baptism, **Glenbeigh/Glencar Parish (RC)**)

  - Simon Harris – b. 1 Mar 1835, bapt. 1 Mar 1835 (Baptism, **Glenbeigh/Glencar Parish (RC)**)

James Harris (father):

Residence - Clohane - January 1, 1830

September 10, 1832

March 1, 1835

Gobinet Buoney (mother):

Residence - Clohane - March 1, 1829

- James Harris & Honora Buoney

  - Ellen Harris – b. 24 Nov 1827, bapt. 24 Nov 1827 (Baptism, **Glenbeigh/Glencar Parish (RC)**)

  - Catherine Harris – b. 1 Apr 1830, bapt. 1 Apr 1830 (Baptism, **Glenbeigh/Glencar Parish (RC)**)

  - James Harris – b. 1 Jul 1831, bapt. 1 Jul 1831 (Baptism, **Glenbeigh/Glencar Parish (RC)**)

James Harris (father):

Residence - Ballynakilla - November 24, 1827

Clohane - April 1, 1830

July 1, 1831

Hurst

- James Harris & Isabel Harris

  o Elizabeth Harris – bapt. 7 Jul 1839 (Baptism, **Tralee Parish**)

James Harris (father):

Residence - Tralee - July 7, 1839

Occupation - Private 68th Regiment - July 7, 1839

- James Harris & Jane Higgins

  o James Harris – bapt. 14 Jul 1822 (Baptism, **Cork - South Parish (RC)**)

- James Harris & Jane McCarthy – 15 Jan 1803 (Marriage, **Cork - South Parish** (RC))

James Harris (husband):

Occupation - Mariner - January 15, 1803

- James Harris & Jane Neill

  o James Harris – bapt. 30 Jul 1818 (Baptism, **Desertseges Parish** (RC))

  o Michael Harris – bapt. 28 Oct 1823 (Baptism, **Desertseges Parish** (RC))

- James Harris & Jane O'Murphy – 20 Feb 1844 (Marriage, **Tralee Parish** (RC))

James Harris (husband):

Residence - Derrymore - February 20, 1844

Jane O'Murphy (wife):

Residence - Derrymore - February 20, 1844

- James Harris & Jane O'Shea – 28 Aug 1837 (Marriage, **Tralee Parish** (RC))

  o Mary Harris – b. 11 Feb 1838, bapt. 11 Feb 1838 (Baptism, **Tralee Parish** (RC))

  o Thomas Harris – b. 18 May 1840, bapt. 18 May 1840 (Baptism, **Tralee Parish** (RC))

  o John Harris – b. 6 Jan 1844, bapt. 6 Jan 1844 (Baptism, **Tralee Parish** (RC))

James Harris (father):

Residence - Tralee - August 28, 1837

February 11, 1838

May 18, 1840

January 6, 1844

Jane O'Shea (mother):

Residence - Tralee - August 28, 1837

- James Harris & Joan Murphy – 17 Jan 1807 (Marriage, **Bandon Parish (RC)**)

  - James Harris – bapt. 25 Nov 1809 (Baptism, **Cork - South Parish (RC)**)

- James Harris & Joan Shea – 6 Jun 1837 (Marriage, **Tralee Parish**)

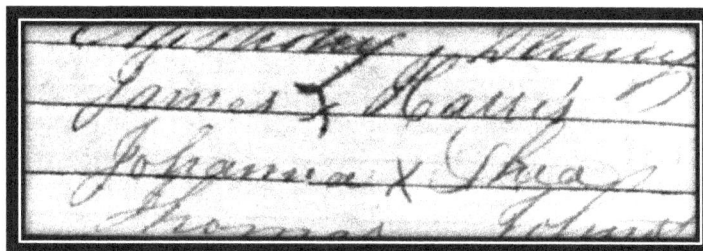

Signatures:

- James Harris & Judith Kennedy – 23 May 1784 (Marriage, **St. Catherine Parish (RC)**)

- James Harris & Margaret Corcoran

  - Jane Harris – bapt. 17 Jun 1836 (Baptism, **St. Catherine Parish (RC)**)

- James Harris & Margaret Daly

  - Margaret Harris – b. 23 Aug 1846, bapt. 23 Aug 1846 (Baptism, **Sneem Parish (RC)**)

James Harris (father):

Residence - Derreenanar - August 23, 1846

- James Harris & Margaret Horgan – 31 Jan 1878 (Marriage, **Ballinhassig (Goggins,**

  Ballyheedy, & Ballygarvan) Parish (RC))

James Harris (husband):

Residence - Ballygar- - - January 31, 1878

Margaret Horgan (wife):

Residence - Farlistown - January 31, 1878

- James Harris & Margaret Lee

  - Julia Harris – bapt. 27 May 1820 (Baptism, **Kinsale Parish (RC)**)

Hurst

- James Harris & Margaret O'Donoghue – 14 Sep 1878 (Marriage, **Ballinhassig (Goggins, Ballyheedy, & Ballygarvan) Parish (RC)**)

  - William Harris – bapt. 12 Nov 1879 (Baptism, **Ballinhassig (Goggins, Ballyheedy, & Ballygarvan) Parish (RC)**)

James Harris (father):

  Residence - Knockavilla - September 14, 1878

Margaret O'Donoghue (mother):

  Residence - Coolatooder - September 14, 1878

- James Harris & Margaret Riordan

  - Simon Harris & Margaret Leyne – 12 Feb 1898 (Marriage, **Killorglin Parish (RC)**)

    - Mary Harris – b. 27 Nov 1898, bapt. 27 Nov 1898 (Baptism, **Killorglin Parish (RC)**)

    - Joan Harris – b. 14 Sep 1901, bapt. 15 Sep 1901 (Baptism, **Killorglin Parish (RC)**)

Simon Harris (son):

  Residence - Glenbeigh - February 12, 1898

  Caragh - November 27, 1898

  Poulbawn - September 15, 1901

Margaret Leyne, daughter of Jeremiah Leyne & Margaret Fenton (daughter-in-law):

  Residence - Caragh Bridge - February 12, 1898

- James Harris & Margaret Sughrue

  - Julia Harris – b. 9 May 1849, bapt. 9 May 1849 (Baptism, **Glenbeigh/Glencar Parish (RC)**)

James Harris (father):

  Residence - Drom - May 9, 1849

- James Harris & Margaret Unknown

  - Margaret Harris – bapt. 30 Jun 1759 (Baptism, **St. Michan Parish (RC)**)

Harris Surname Ireland: 1600s to 1900s

- James Harris & Mary Brian

    o Patrick Harris – bapt. 29 Mar 1852 (Baptism, **St. James Parish** (RC))

James Harris (father):

Residence - Island Bridge - March 29, 1852

- James Harris & Mary Currane – 30 Jan 1864 (Marriage, **Castlegregory Parish** (RC))

    o Michael Harris – b. 22 Nov 1864, bapt. 22 Nov 1864 (Baptism, **Castlegregory Parish** (RC))

    o Deborah Harris – b. 1 Aug 1866, bapt. 4 Aug 1866 (Baptism, **Castlegregory Parish** (RC))

    o Mary Harris, b. 13 Jan 1869, bapt. 20 Jan 1869 (Baptism, **Castlegregory Parish** (RC)) & James Hanlon – 16 Feb 1896 (Marriage, **Castlegregory Parish** (RC))

        ▪ Teresa Hanlon – b. 10 Feb 1898, bapt. 12 Feb 1898 (Baptism, **Castlegregory Parish** (RC))

        ▪ Gerald Hanlon – b. 12 Mar 1899, bapt. 12 Mar 1899 (Baptism, **Castlegregory Parish** (RC))

Mary Harris (daughter):

Residence - Castlegregory - February 16, 1896

James Hanlon, son of Thomas Hanlon (son-in-law):

Residence - Castlegregory - February 16, 1896

February 12, 1898

March 12, 1899

Hurst

- o Margaret Harris, b. 8 Mar 1871, bapt. 8 Mar 1871 (Baptism, **Castlegregory Parish** (RC))

  & Michael Spillane – 27 Feb 1897 (Marriage, **Castlegregory Parish** (RC))

  - ▪ John Spillane – b. 27 Nov 1897, bapt. 28 Nov 1897 (Baptism, **Castlegregory Parish**

    (RC))

  - ▪ Catherine Spillane – b. 11 Feb 1899, bapt. 12 Feb 1899 (Baptism, **Castlegregory Parish**

    (RC))

Margaret Harris (daughter):

 Residence - Cloghaneanode - February 27, 1897

Michael Spillane, son of John Spillane (son-in-law):

 Residence - Glennahoo - February 27, 1897

November 28, 1897

February 12, 1899

- o John Harris – b. 7 Dec 1872, bapt. 10 Dec 1872 (Baptism, **Castlegregory Parish** (RC))

- o Thomas Harris – b. 23 Jun 1875, bapt. 29 Jun 1875 (Baptism, **Castlegregory Parish**

  (RC))

- o James Harris – b. 29 Sep 1877, bapt. 30 Sep 1877 (Baptism, **Castlegregory Parish** (RC))

- o Joan Harris – b. 8 Mar 1880, bapt. 14 Mar 1880 (Baptism, **Castlegregory Parish** (RC))

- o Richard Harris – b. 1 Jun 1882, bapt. 4 Jun 1882 (Baptism, **Castlegregory Parish** (RC))

- o Michael Harris – b. 5 Oct 1884, bapt. 5 Oct 1884 (Baptism, **Castlegregory Parish** (RC))

James Harris (father):

 Residence - Cloghanesheskeen - January 30, 1864

November 22, 1864

December 10, 1872

Cloghaneanode - January 20, 1869

March 8, 1871

June 29, 1875

September 30, 1877

March 14, 1880

Harris Surname Ireland: 1600s to 1900s

June 4, 1882

October 5, 1884

Gurthaghard - August 4, 1866

- James Harris & Mary Flynn – 1 Jan 1831 (Marriage, **Milltown Parish** (RC))

    o Thomas Harris – b. 10 Jan 1834, bapt. 10 Jan 1834 (Baptism, **Milltown Parish** (RC))

    o Ellen Harris – b. 2 Mar 1837, bapt. 2 Mar 1837 (Baptism, **Milltown Parish** (RC))

    o James Harris – b. 17 Mar 1839, bapt. 17 Mar 1839 (Baptism, **Milltown Parish** (RC))

    o John Harris – b. 17 Jul 1842, bapt. 17 Jul 1842 (Baptism, **Milltown Parish** (RC))

    o Ellen Harris – b. 23 Dec 1845, bapt. 23 Dec 1845 (Baptism, **Milltown Parish** (RC))

James Harris (father):

Residence - Castlemaine - January 1, 1831

January 10, 1834

March 2, 1837

July 17, 1842

December 23, 1845

Brackhill - March 17, 1839

- James Harris & Mary Guines

    o James Harris – bapt. 1856 (Baptism, **Clondalkin Parish** (RC))

James Harris (father):

Residence - Esker - 1856

- James Harris & Mary Harmon (H a r m o n)

    o John Harris – b. 27 Mar 1896, bapt. 29 Mar 1896 (Baptism, **Abbeydorney Parish** (RC))

James Harris (The father):

Residence - Ardrahan - March 29, 1896

- James Harris & Mary Harris

    o Mary Anne Harris – bapt. 22 Feb 1831 (Baptism, **St. Mary, Pro Cathedral Parish** (RC))

- James Harris & Mary Johnston – 24 Jul 1784 (Marriage, **St. Paul Parish**)

Hurst

- James Harris & Mary Leary

  o James Harris – bapt. 12 Apr 1820 (Baptism, **Cork - South Parish** (RC))

- James Harris & Mary Lyne

  o John Harris – b. 19 Jul 1833, bapt. 19 Jul 1833 (Baptism, **Firies Parish** (RC))

James Harris (father):

Residence - Ballynoe - July 19, 1833

- James Harris & Mary McDermott (M c D e r m o t t)

  o James Harris – bapt. 29 Oct 1828 (Baptism, **St. Catherine Parish** (RC))

- James Harris & Mary Riordan – 6 Feb 1872 (Marriage, **Glenbeigh/Glencar Parish** (RC))

  o Simon Harris – b. 21 Nov 1872, bapt. 21 Nov 1872 (Baptism, **Glenbeigh/Glencar Parish** (RC))

  o Dennis Harris – b. 16 Aug 1874, bapt. 16 Aug 1874 (Baptism, **Glenbeigh/Glencar Parish** (RC))

  o Bridget Harris – b. 13 Aug 1875, bapt. 13 Aug 1875 (Baptism, **Glenbeigh/Glencar Parish** (RC))

  o John Harris – b. 4 Oct 1876, bapt. 4 Oct 1876 (Baptism, **Glenbeigh/Glencar Parish** (RC))

  o James Harris – b. 19 Nov 1881, bapt. 19 Nov 1881 (Baptism, **Glenbeigh/Glencar Parish** (RC))

  o Patrick Harris – b. 19 Nov 1882, bapt. 19 Nov 1882 (Baptism, **Glenbeigh/Glencar Parish** (RC))

  o Gobinet Harris – b. 24 Dec 1883, bapt. 24 Dec 1883 (Baptism, **Glenbeigh/Glencar Parish** (RC))

  o Catherine Harris – b. 4 Dec 1884, bapt. 9 Dec 1884 (Baptism, **Glenbeigh/Glencar Parish** (RC))

Harris Surname Ireland: 1600s to 1900s

- o Dennis Harris – b. 15 Jul 1888, bapt. 15 Jul 1888 (Baptism, **Glenbeigh/Glencar Parish (RC)**)

- o Margaret Harris – b. 17 Mar 1892, bapt. 20 Mar 1892 (Baptism, **Glenbeigh/Glencar Parish (RC)**)

James Harris (father):

Residence - Knockboy - August 16, 1874

Drom - November 21, 1872

October 4, 1876

November 19, 1882

December 9, 1884

Upper Drom - March 20, 1892

Kilkeehagh - August 13, 1875

December 23, 1883

Boherbee - July 15, 1888

Mary Riordan (mother):

Residence - Glenbeigh - February 6, 1872

- James Harris & Mary Sullivan

  - o Mary Harris – b. 1 Feb 1797, bapt. 1 Feb 1797 (Baptism, **Tralee Parish (RC)**)

James Harris (father):

Residence - Tralee - February 1, 1797

- James Harris & Mary Unknown

  - o Bridget Harris – bapt. 24 May 1778 (Baptism, **St. Nicholas Parish (RC)**)

- James Harris & Mary Unknown

  - o Jane Harris – bapt. 18 Feb 1827 (Baptism, **St. Michan Parish (RC)**)

- James Harris & Mary Unknown

  - o Joseph Harris – b. 1849, bapt. 1849 (Baptism, **St. Andrew Parish (RC)**)

Hurst

- James Harris & Mary Wallis

  o Margaret Harris – b. 11 Feb 1808, bapt. 11 Feb 1808 (Baptism, **Tralee Parish** (RC))

  o John Harris – b. 9 Aug 1810, bapt. 9 Aug 1810 (Baptism, **Tralee Parish** (RC))

James Harris (The father):

Residence - Spa - February 11, 1808

Barn - August 9, 1810

- James Harris & Mary Walsh

  o Catherine Harris – bapt. 9 Jun 1829 (Baptism, **Kinsale Parish** (RC))

- James Harris & Mary A. Unknown

  o Thomas Harris – bapt. 1850 (Baptism, **St. Mary, Haddington Road Parish** (RC))

- James Harris & Mary Anne Harris

  o Mary Anne Harris – b. 6 Sep 1847, bapt. 19 Sep 1847 (Baptism, **St. Mark Parish**)

  o Emma Harris – b. 8 Mar 1853, bapt. 20 Mar 1853 (Baptism, **St. Mark Parish**)

  o John Harris – b. 9 Jan 1856, bapt. 20 Jan 1856 (Baptism, **St. Mark Parish**)

James Harris (father):

Residence - 74 Sir John's Quay - September 19, 1847

Sir John's Quay - March 20, 1853

69 Sir John's Quay - January 20, 1856

Occupation - Revenue Officer - September 19, 1847

March 20, 1853

January 20, 1856

- James Harris & Mary Anne Scully – 24 Jan 1843 (Marriage, **St. Andrew Parish** (RC))

  o James Harris – bapt. 1844 (Baptism, **St. Andrew Parish** (RC))

  o Catherine Harris – bapt. 1846 (Baptism, **St. Andrew Parish** (RC))

  o Mary Anne Harris – bapt. 1847 (Baptism, **St. Andrew Parish** (RC))

  o Patrick Harris – bapt. 1848 (Baptism, **St. Andrew Parish** (RC))

- o Mary Anne Harris – b. 1850, bapt. 1850 (Baptism, **St. Andrew Parish** (RC))

- o Bridget Harris – bapt. 1851 (Baptism, **St. Andrew Parish** (RC))

- o Emma Amelia Harris – b. 1853, bapt. 1853 (Baptism, **St. Andrew Parish** (RC))

- o John Harris – b. 1856, bapt. 1856 (Baptism, **St. Andrew Parish** (RC))

- James Harris & Mary Margaret Leary

  - o Michael Harris, b. 13 May 1861, bapt. 14 May 1861 (Baptism, **Ardfert Parish** (RC)), &

    Mary O'Sullivan – 18 Feb 1896 (Marriage, **Castlemaine Parish** (RC))

    - ▪ Mary Harris – b. 25 Jul 1898, bapt. 31 Jul 1898 (Baptism, **Abbeydorney Parish** (RC))

    - ▪ James Harris – b. 29 Jul 1900, bapt. 4 Aug 1900 (Baptism, **Abbeydorney Parish** (RC))

Michael Harris (son):

Residence - Abbeydorney - February 18, 1896

Ardrahan - July 31, 1898

Mary O'Sullivan, daughter of Patrick O'Sullivan & Elizabeth Reilly

(daughter-in-law):

Residence - Gurrane - February 18, 1896

- o Patrick Harris – b. 18 Apr 1864, bapt. 24 Apr 1864 (Baptism, **Ardfert Parish** (RC))

- o James Harris – b. 21 Jul 1867, bapt. 27 Jul 1867 (Baptism, **Ardfert Parish** (RC))

- o James Harris – b. 9 Apr 1870, bapt. 10 Apr 1870 (Baptism, **Ardfert Parish** (RC))

- o Bridget Harris – b. 23 Jan 1874, bapt. 25 Jan 1874 (Baptism, **Ardfert Parish** (RC))

James Harris (father):

Residence - Lerrig - May 14, 1861

Ballyrobert - April 24, 1864

July 27, 1867

April 10, 1870

January 25, 1874

Hurst

- James Harris & Mary Margaret McCarthy – 29 Aug 1837 (Marriage, **Kinsale Parish** (RC))

  - Mary Anne Harris – bapt. 11 Jun 1838 (Baptism, **Kinsale Parish** (RC))

  - Catherine Harris – bapt. 5 Dec 1839 (Baptism, **Kinsale Parish** (RC))

  - Margaret Harris – bapt. 17 Oct 1841 (Baptism, **Kinsale Parish** (RC))

  - Michael Harris – bapt. 11 Aug 1843 (Baptism, **Kinsale Parish** (RC))

  - Mary Anne Harris – bapt. 25 Jun 1848 (Baptism, **Kinsale Parish** (RC))

  - Jane Harris – bapt. 31 May 1850 (Baptism, **Kinsale Parish** (RC))

James Harris (father):

Residence - Blind Gate - August 29, 1837

December 5, 1839

October 17, 1841

August 11, 1843

June 25, 1848

May 31, 1850

Rose Abbey - June 11, 1838

- James Harris & Nancy Barrett

  - Ansty Harris – bapt. 31 May 1802 (Baptism, **Cork - South Parish** (RC))

- James Harris & Honora Elliard

  - Deborah Harris – bapt. 20 Jan 1837 (Baptism, **Cork - SS. Peter & Paul Parish** (RC))

- James Harris & Rose Walsh – 24 Nov1844 (Marriage, **Rathmines Parish** (RC))

  - Catherine Harris – bapt. 1848 (Baptism, **St. Andrew Parish** (RC))

- James Harris & Rose Harris

  - Elizabeth Harris – bapt. 2 Jul 1780 (Baptism, **St. Mary Parish**)

  - Bridget Harris – bapt. 21 Nov 1784 (Baptism, **St. Catherine Parish** (RC))

James Harris (father):

Residence - Liffey Street - July 2, 1780

Harris Surname Ireland: 1600s to 1900s

- James Harris & Rose Unknown

    o Eleanor Harris – bapt. 19 Feb 1825 (Baptism, **St. Nicholas Parish (RC)**)

- James Harris & Unknown

    o Elizabeth Harris – bapt. 9 Sep 1669 (Baptism, **St. John Parish**)

    o Elizabeth Harris – bapt. 10 Mar 1672 (Baptism, **St. John Parish**)

- James Harris & Unknown

    o Thomas Harris – bapt. 4 Apr 1686 (Baptism, **St. Michan Parish**)

James Harris (father):

   Occupation - Seaman - April 4, 1686

- James Harris & Unknown

    o Augustus Harris & Catherine Butter – 4 Apr 1864 (Marriage, **St. Paul Parish**)

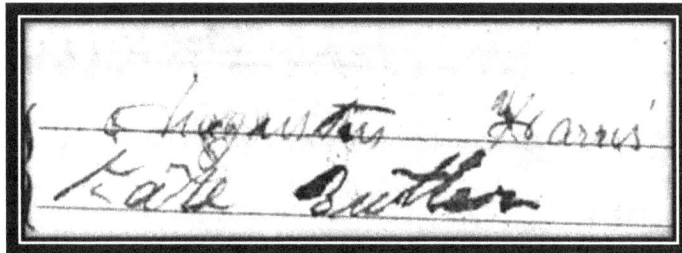

Signatures:

Augustus Harris (son):

   Residence - Royal Barracks - April 4, 1864

   Occupation - Private 4th Hussars - April 4, 1864

Catherine Butter, daughter of Patrick Butter (daughter-in-law):

   Residence - Royal Barracks - April 4, 1864

Patrick Butter (father):

   Occupation - Trademan

James Harris (father):

   Occupation - Laborer

Hurst

- James Harris & Unknown

  o John Harris & Catherine Murphy – 18 Feb 1868 (Marriage, **Caherciveen Parish (RC)**)

John Harris (son):

    Residence - Glenbeigh - February 18, 1868

Catherine Murphy, daughter of Michael Murphy (daughter-in-law):

    Residence - Filemore - February 18, 1868

- James Harris & Unknown

  o John Harris & Ellen Gough Aston – 23 Dec 1879 (Marriage, **St. Catherine Parish**)

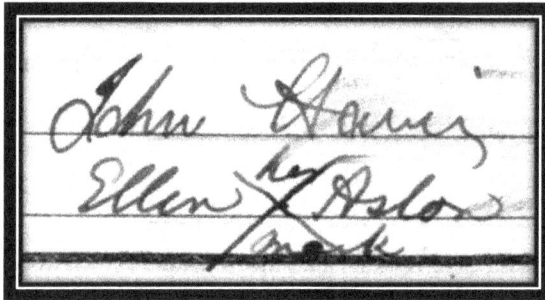

Signatures:

John Harris (son):

    Residence - 13 Chamber Street - December 23, 1879

        Ballencollis - December 23, 1879

    Occupation - Soldier in the Royal Horse Artillery - December 23, 1879

Ellen Gough, daughter of John Gough (daughter-in-law):

    Residence - 23 Chamber Street - December 23, 1879

        Lucan - December 23, 1879

    Relationship Status at Marriage- widow

John Gough (father):

Signature:

  Occupation - Laborer

James Harris (father):

  Occupation - Currier

Wedding Witnesses:

John Gough:

Signature:

- James Harris & Unknown

  o Ellen Harris & John Linehan – 2 Sep 1880 (Marriage, Cork - South Parish (RC))

Ellen Harris (daughter):

  Residence - Haggart Lane - September 2, 1880

John Linehan, son of William Linehan (son-in-law):

  Residence - Vagus - September 2, 1880

Hurst

- James Harris & Unknown

    o Margaret Harris & William Patrick Connolly – 4 Nov 1884 (Marriage, St. Michan Parish)

Signatures:

Margaret Harris (daughter):

   Residence - Philltown, Co. Kilkenny - November 4, 1884

William Patrick Connolly, son of Patrick Connolly (son-in-law):

   Residence - Angel Hotel Dublin - November 4, 1884

                     Philltown, Co. Kilkenny - November 4, 1884

   Occupation - Clergyman - November 4, 1884

Patrick Connolly (father):

   Occupation - Gentleman Farmer

James Harris (father):

   Occupation - Agent

Wedding Witnesses:

Ellie Harris

Signature:

- James Harris & Unknown

Signature:

  o James Harris & Lavinia Sophia Euster, b. 1866 – 4 Aug 1885 (Marriage, **St. Thomas Parish**)

Signatures:

  ▪ James William Harris – b. 16 Mar 1886, bapt. 13 Jun 1886 (Baptism, **St. Werburgh**

  Parish)

James Harris (son):

  Residence - 106 Lower Gardiner Street - August 4, 1885

  49 Fishamble Street - June 13, 1886

  Occupation - Smith - August 4, 1885

  Blacksmith - June 13, 1886

Sophia Lavinia Euster, daughter of William C. Euster (daughter-in-law):

  Residence - 106 Lower Gardiner Street - August 4, 1885

William C. Euster (father):

Signature:

  Occupation - Linesman Electric Light Department

Hurst

James Harris (father):

    Occupation - Smith

Wedding Witnesses:

W. Euster & Elizabeth Middleton

Signatures:

    ○   Thomas Harris & Sarah Agnes McConnell – 6 Sep 1887 (Marriage, St. Mary Parish)

Signatures:

Thomas Harris (son):

    Residence - 2 Proud's Lane off York Street - September 6, 1887

    Occupation - House Carpenter - September 6, 1887

Sarah Agnes McConnell, daughter of William McConnell (daughter-in-law):

    Residence - 50 Fontenoy Street - September 6, 1887

William McConnell (father):

    Occupation - Mercantile Clerk

James Harris (father):

Signature:

    Occupation - Smith

Harris Surname Ireland: 1600s to 1900s

Wedding Witnesses:

John Willey & James Harris

Signatures:

○ John Harris & Emma Sandys Kincaid – 29 Feb 1892 (Marriage, **St. Mark Parish**)

Signatures:

- John Herbert Harris – b. 15 May 1892, bapt. 15 Jun 1892 (Baptism, **St. James Parish**)

- Frederick James Harris – b. 12 Aug 1893, bapt. 24 Sep 1893 (Baptism, **St. James Parish**)

- William Edwin Harris – b. 20 Apr 1896, bapt. 17 May 1896 (Baptism, **St. James Parish**)

- Samuel Robert Harris – b. 25 May 1898, bapt. 3 Jul 1898 (Baptism, **St. James Parish**)

- Emma Sandys Harris – b. 15 Dec 1899, bapt. 7 Jan 1900 (Baptism, **St. James Parish**)

- George Henry Harris – b. 21 Oct 1901, bapt. 1 Dec 1901 (Baptism, **St. James Parish**)

Hurst

John Harris (son):

    Residence - Millmount House Dolphin's Barn - February 29, 1892

        17 Washington Street South Circular Road - September 24, 1893

        5 Thornville Dolphin's Barn South Circular Road - May 17, 1896

                July 3, 1898

                January 7, 1900

                December 1, 1901

                June 15, 1892

    Occupation - Carpenter - February 29, 1892

        June 15, 1892

        September 24, 1893

        House Carpenter/Carpenter - May 17, 1896

        July 3, 1898

        January 7, 1900

        December 1, 1901

Emma Sandys Kincaid, daughter of Thomas Kincaid (daughter-in-law):

    Residence - 12 Howard Street - February 29, 1892

    Occupation - Counter Woman - February 29, 1892

Thomas J. Kincaid (father):

Signature:

    Occupation - Bootmaker

James Harris (father):

    Occupation - Foreman

Wedding Witnesses:

Thomas J. Kincaid & Jessie Jackson

Signatures:

- Thomas Harris & Elizabeth Tyrrell – 16 Nov 1892 (Marriage, **St. George Parish**)

Signatures:

Thomas Harris (son):

Residence - Millmount House Dolphin's Barn - November 16, 1892

Occupation - Builder - November 16, 1892

Elizabeth Tyrrell, daughter of George F. Tyrrell (daughter-in-law):

Residence - 14 St. Ignatius Road - November 16, 1892

George F. Tyrrell (father):

Signature:

Occupation - Builder

Hurst

James Harris (father):

    Occupation - Iron Founder

Wedding Witnesses:

George F. Tyrrell

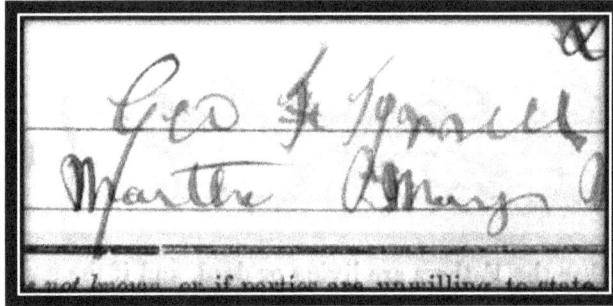

Signature:

- James Harris & Unknown

  - Thomas Harris & Catherine McCarthy – 19 May 1877 (Marriage, **Ardfert Parish** (RC))

    - Bridget Harris – b. 10 Feb 1878, bapt. 13 Feb 1878 (Baptism, **Ardfert Parish** (RC))

    - Mary Harris – b. 28 Sep 1879, bapt. 4 Oct 1879 (Baptism, **Ardfert Parish** (RC))

    - James Harris – b. 2 Sep 1881, bapt. 4 Sep 1881 (Baptism, **Ardfert Parish** (RC))

    - Patrick Harris – b. 20 Aug 1883, bapt. 22 Aug 1883 (Baptism, **Ardfert Parish** (RC))

    - Thomas Harris – b. 20 Oct 1884, bapt. 22 Oct 1884 (Baptism, **Ardfert Parish** (RC))

    - Catherine Harris – b. 12 Aug 1887, bapt. 14 Aug 1887 (Baptism, **Ardfert Parish** (RC))

    - Julia Harris – b. 6 Oct 1891, bapt. 7 Oct 1891 (Baptism, **Ardfert Parish** (RC))

    - John Harris – b. 21 Dec 1893, bapt. 23 Dec 1893 (Baptism, **Ardfert Parish** (RC))

    - Catherine Harris – b. 30 Aug 1897, bapt. 1 Sep 1897 (Baptism, **Ardfert Parish** (RC))

    - Elizabeth Harris – b. 23 Oct 1898, bapt. 26 Oct 1898 (Baptism, **Ardfert Parish** (RC))

Thomas Harris (son):

    Residence - Ballymacquin - May 19, 1877

        Banna - February 13, 1878

           October 4, 1879

           September 4, 1881

August 22, 1883

October 22, 1884

December 23, 1893

September 1, 1897

October 26, 1898

Banna North - August 14, 1887

October 7, 1891

Catherine McCarthy, daughter of Patrick McCarthy (daughter-in-law):

Residence - Banna - May 19, 1877

- James Harris & Wilhelmina Harris

  o Thomas Victor Harris – b. 17 Aug 1899, bapt. 27 Aug 1899 (Baptism, Rotunda Chapel Parish)

James Harris (father):

Residence - 6 Lord Edward Street - August 27, 1899

Occupation - Superintendent Working Boy's House - August 27, 1899

- James Beveridge Harris & Elizabeth Malony – 12 Nov 1829 (Marriage, St. Peter Parish)

James Beveridge Harris (husband):

Residence - Plumstead, Kent - November 12, 1829

Elizabeth Malony (wife):

Residence - Upper Mount Street - November 12, 1829

Occupation - Spinster - November 12, 1829

Hurst

- James Fitz Harris & Unknown

  - Mary Fitz Harris & Charles Goodie – 28 Dec 1896 (Marriage, **St. Mark Parish**)

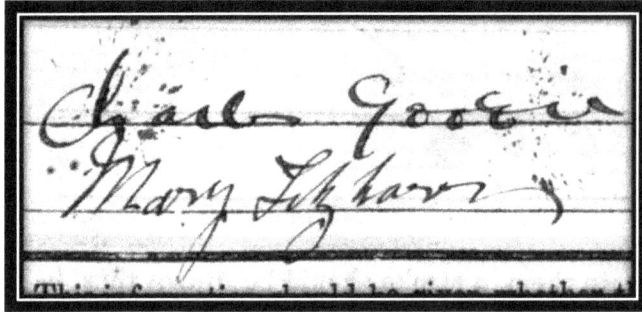

Signatures:

Mary Fitz Harris (daughter):

    Residence - 3 Warrington Lane - December 28, 1896

Charles Goodie, son of Elisha Goodie (son-in-law):

    Residence - 132 Great Brunswick Street - December 28, 1896

    Occupation - Draper - December 28, 1896

Elisha Goodie (father):

    Occupation - Miller

James Fitz Harris (father):

    Occupation - Painter

- Jason Harris & Elizabeth Unknown

  - Eleanor Harris – bapt. 25 Dec 1808 (Baptism, **St. Audoen Parish (RC)**)

- Jeremiah Harris & Elizabeth Owens

  - Elizabeth Harris – bapt. 13 Apr 1857 (Baptism, **Kinsale Parish (RC)**)

Jeremiah Harris (father):

    Residence - Scilly - April 13, 1857

- Jerry Harris & Margaret Dulea

  - Margaret Harris – bapt. 14 Jul 1822 (Baptism, **Cork - South Parish (RC)**)

- Joais Harris & Bridget Unknown

  - Joais Harris – bapt. 1759 (Baptism, **St. Andrew Parish (RC)**)

- John Harris & Alice Boxter

  o Mary Harris – bapt. 31 Mar 1818 (Baptism, **St. Nicholas Parish (RC)**)

- John Harris & Alice Unknown

  o Grace Harris – b. 1758, bapt. 1758 (Baptism, **SS. Michael & John Parish (RC)**)

- John Harris & Anne Carthor

  o John Harris – b. 3 Nov 1856, bapt. 6 Nov 1856 (Baptism, **St. James Parish (RC)**)

John Harris (father):

Residence - Nashes Court - November 6, 1856

- John Harris & Anne Coleman – 10 Nov 1844 (Marriage, **St. Mary, Haddington Road Parish (RC)**)

  o Catherine Harris – bapt. 1846 (Baptism, **St. Mary, Haddington Road Parish (RC)**)

  o Michael Harris – bapt. 1849 (Baptism, **St. Mary, Haddington Road Parish (RC)**)

  o Teresa Harris – b. 1855, bapt. 1855 (Baptism, **St. Andrew Parish (RC)**)

  o John Harris – b. 1859, bapt. 1860 (Baptism, **St. Andrew Parish (RC)**)

  o Timothy Harris – b. 1863, bapt. 1863 (Baptism, **St. Andrew Parish (RC)**)

John Harris (father):

Residence - 4 Moss Street - 1860

18 Upper Mercer Street - 1863

- John Harris & Anne Cullen

  o Elizabeth Harris – bapt. 13 Jun 1850 (Baptism, **St. James Parish (RC)**)

- John Harris & Anne Harris

  o Mary Harris – bapt. 30 Jul 1721 (Baptism, **St. Paul Parish**)

- John Harris & Anne Harris

  o Anne Harris – bapt. 26 Nov 1727 (Baptism, **St. Mary Parish**)

Hurst

- John Harris & Anne Harris

  o William Harris – bapt. 27 Apr 1735 (Baptism, **St. Luke Parish**)

- John Harris & Anne Harris

  o John Harris – b. 1811, bapt. 14 Apr 1811 (Baptism, **St. James Parish**)

- John Harris & Anne Harris

  o John Harris – b. 26 Jan 1897, bapt. 25 Apr 1897 (Baptism, **St. Barnabas Parish**)

John Harris (father):

Residence - 3 Lower Sheriff Street - April 25, 1897

Occupation - Signalman - April 25, 1897

- John Harris & Anne Hamilton – 25 Jun 1855 (Marriage, **St. Catherine Parish (RC)**)

- John Harris & Anne Riordan

  o John Harris – b. 21 Jan 1891, bapt. 25 Jan 1891 (Baptism, **Milltown Parish (RC)**)

John Harris (father):

Residence - Rathpook - January 25, 1891

- John Harris & Anne Unknown

  o Frances Harris – b. 20 Aug 1705, bapt. 28 Aug 1705 (Baptism, **St. Werburgh Parish**)

John Harris (father):

Residence - Crane Lane - August 28, 1705

- John Harris & Anne Unknown

  o Mary Harris – bapt. 25 Mar 1759 (Baptism, **St. Catherine Parish**)

- John Harris & Anne Unknown

  o Mary Margaret Harris – bapt. 1851 (Baptism, **St. Mary, Haddington Road Parish (RC)**)

- John Harris & Anne Unknown

  o Michael Harris & Mary McBride – 4 May 1873 (Marriage, **St. Andrew Parish (RC)**)

    ▪ John Harris – b. 1875, bapt. 1875 (Baptism, **St. Mary, Haddington Road Parish (RC)**)

      & Jane Thompson – 15 Jan 1899 (Marriage, **St. Mary, Pro Cathedral Parish (RC)**)

Harris Surname Ireland: 1600s to 1900s

John Harris (son of Michael Harris & Mary McBride):

    Residence - 18 North Cumberland Street - January 15, 1899

Jane Thompson, daughter of Henry Thompson & Louisa Curran (daughter-in-law):

    Residence - 7 Lower Gardiner Street - January 15, 1899

Michael Harris (son):

    Residence - 14 Erne Place - May 4, 1873

Mary McBride, daughter of Patrick McBride & Elizabeth Unknown (daughter-in-law):

    Residence - 18 Harmony Row - May 4, 1873

- John Harris & Bridget Brennan – 28 Nov 1885 (Marriage, **Caherdaniel Parish** (RC))

John Harris (husband):

    Residence - Derrynane - November 28, 1885

- John Harris & Bridget Murphy – 26 Feb 1805 (Marriage, **Cork - South Parish** (RC))

  - Jane Harris – bapt. 17 Jun 1806 (Baptism, **Cork - South Parish** (RC))

  - Thomas Harris – bapt. 4 Aug 1808 (Baptism, **Cork - South Parish** (RC))

John Harris (father):

    Residence - Pouladuff - February 26, 1805

           Bandon Road - June 17, 1806

           Cat Lane - August 4, 1808

Bridget Murphy (mother):

    Residence - Pouladuff - February 26, 1805

- John Harris & Bridget Unknown

  - Thomas Harris – bapt. 26 Jul 1685 (Baptism, **St. Peter Parish**)

- John Harris & Catherine Coolleen

  - Catherine Harris – bapt. 1845 (Baptism, **St. Mary, Haddington Road Parish** (RC))

Hurst

- John Harris & Catherine Cullen – 16 Jan 1807 (Marriage, **St. Mary, Pro Cathedral Parish (RC)**)

  - Mary Anne Harris – bapt. 28 May 1814 (Baptism, **St. Nicholas Parish** (RC))

  - Peter Harris – bapt. 8 Jul 1816 (Baptism, **St. Nicholas Parish** (RC))

  - Elizabeth Frances Harris – bapt. 23 Nov 1818 (Baptism, **St. Nicholas Parish** (RC))

- John Harris & Catherine Daly – 15 Jan 1857 (Marriage, **Killeentierna Parish** (RC))

  - Joan Harris – b. 1 Sep 1858, bapt. 1 Sep 1858 (Baptism, **Castleisland Parish** (RC))

John Harris (father):

Residence - Kilsarkan - January 15, 1857

Dromultan - September 1, 1858

- John Harris & Catherine Doyle

  - Margaret Harris & Patrick Coyle – 16 May 1886 (Marriage, **St. Mary, Donnybrook Parish** (RC))

    - Mary Margaret Coyle & Thomas Emlyn Smith – 11 Jan 1911 (Baptism, **Harrington Street Parish** (RC))

Mary Margaret Coyle (daughter):

Residence - 14 Clanbrassil Lane - January 11, 1911

Thomas Emlyn Smith, son of Thomas Smith & Naomi Unknown (son-in-law):

Residence - Curragh Camp, Co. Kildare - January 11, 1911

Margaret Harris (daughter):

Residence - 9 Ailesbury Road Donnybrook - May 16, 1886

Patrick Coyle, son of Dennis Coyle & Catherine Phelan (son-in-law):

Residence - 24 Usher's Poland Dublin - May 16, 1886

Harris Surname Ireland: 1600s to 1900s

- John Harris & Catherine Hawkins

    o William Harris – b. 5 Dec 1806, bapt. 8 Dec 1806 (Baptism, St. Catherine Parish (RC))

    o Margaret Harris – b. 11 Oct 1814, bapt. 17 Oct 1814 (Baptism, St. Catherine Parish (RC))

    o Mary Harris – bapt. 29 Sep 1818 (Baptism, St. Catherine Parish (RC))

    o Michael Harris – bapt. 29 Sep 1818 (Baptism, St. Catherine Parish (RC))

- John Harris & Catherine Land

    o John Harris – b. 6 Jul 1877, bapt. 9 Jul 1877 (Baptism, St. Mary, Pro Cathedral Parish (RC))

    o Jane Harris – b. 10 Sep 1878, bapt. 13 Sep 1878 (Baptism, St. Mary, Pro Cathedral Parish (RC))

    o Matthew Harris, b. 12 Jun 1880, bapt. 18 Jun 1880 (Baptism, St. Mary, Pro Cathedral Parish (RC)) & Christine Downing – 8 May 1904 (Marriage, St. Mary, Pro Cathedral Parish (RC))

Matthew Harris (son):
    Residence - 4 Empress Place - May 8, 1904
Christine Downing, Daughter of William Downing & Mary Lambert
(daughter-in-law):
    Residence - 51 Lower Tyrone Street - May 8, 1904

    o Anne Esther Harris – b. 29 Mar 1882, bapt. 3 Apr 1882 (Baptism, St. Mary, Pro Cathedral Parish (RC))

    o Edward Joseph Harris – b. 7 Mar 1884, bapt. 10 Mar 1884 (Baptism, St. Mary, Pro Cathedral Parish (RC))

    o Elizabeth Harris – b. 19 Jan 1886, bapt. 22 Jan 1886 (Baptism, St. Mary, Pro Cathedral Parish (RC))

Hurst

- ○ James Harris – b. 17 Nov 1887, bapt. 21 Nov 1887 (Baptism, **St. Mary, Pro Cathedral Parish** (RC))

- ○ Christopher John Harris – b. 20 Dec 1888, bapt. 21 Dec 1888 (Baptism, **St. Mary, Pro Cathedral Parish** (RC))

- ○ Patrick Joseph Harris – b. 5 Mar 1891, bapt. 9 Mar 1891 (Baptism, **St. Mary, Pro Cathedral Parish** (RC))

- ○ Julia Harris – b. 13 Mar 1893, bapt. 15 Mar 1893 (Baptism, **St. Mary, Pro Cathedral Parish** (RC))

- ○ Mary Jane Harris – b. 18 Jun 1897, bapt. 21 Jun 1897 (Baptism, **St. Mary, Pro Cathedral Parish** (RC))

John Harris (father):

Residence - 2 Beaver Street - July 9, 1877

June 18, 1880

3 Beaver Street - September 13, 1878

44 Montgomery Street - November 21, 1887

46 Montgomery Street - April 3, 1882

47 Lower Tyrone Street - March 15, 1893

June 21, 1897

57 Lower Tyrone Street - March 9, 1891

50 Lower Mecklenburgh Street - March 10, 1884

January 22, 1886

51 Mecklenburgh Street - December 21, 1888

- • John Harris & Catherine Murphy

- ○ Mary Harris – b. 18 Jul 1869, bapt. 18 Jul 1869 (Baptism, **Glenbeigh/Glencar Parish** (RC))

- ○ John Harris – b. 25 Jul 1880, bapt. 25 Jul 1880 (Baptism, **Glenbeigh/Glencar Parish** (RC))

Harris Surname Ireland: 1600s to 1900s

John Harris (father):

    Residence - Kilkeehagh - July 18, 1869

        Drom - July 25, 1880

- John Harris & Catherine Pollard

  - Elizabeth Harris – bapt. Apr 1853 (Baptism, **St. Michan Parish (RC)**)

- John Harris & Catherine Quinn

  - John Harris – bapt. 19 Apr 1810 (Baptism, **St. James Parish (RC)**)

- John Harris & Catherine Riordan

  - John Harris – b. 3 Mar 1872, bapt. 3 Mar 1872 (Baptism, **Glenbeigh/Glencar Parish (RC)**)

  - John Harris – b. 12 Apr 1874, bapt. 12 Apr 1874 (Baptism, **Glenbeigh/Glencar Parish (RC)**)

  - Mary Harris – b. 28 Dec 1877, bapt. 28 Dec 1877 (Baptism, **Glenbeigh/Glencar Parish (RC)**)

  - Michael Harris – b. 13 Sep 1879, bapt. 13 Sep 1879 (Baptism, **Glenbeigh/Glencar Parish (RC)**)

John Harris (father):

    Residence - Kilkeehagh - March 3, 1872

        April 12, 1874

        December 28, 1877

        September 13, 1879

- John Harris & Catherine Unknown

  - Catherine Harris – bapt. 24 Jul 1755 (Baptism, **St. Nicholas Without Parish**)

John Harris (father):

    Residence - Patrick's Close - July 24, 1755

Hurst

- John Harris & Catherine Unknown

  - Anne Harris – bapt. 5 Oct 1806 (Baptism, **St. Werburgh Parish**)

John Harris (father):

Residence - Little Ship Street - October 5, 1806

- John Harris & Catherine Unknown

  - Patrick Harris – bapt. 22 Mar 1810 (Baptism, **St. Nicholas Parish** (RC))

- John Harris & Dorothea Unknown

  - Joas Harris – bapt. 1751 (Baptism, **St. Andrew Parish** (RC))

- John Harris & Eleanor Harris

  - Mary Anne Harris – bapt. 5 Sep 1802 (Baptism, **St. Mary Parish**)

- John Harris & Eleanor McCarthy

  - Anne Harris – bapt. 8 May 1794 (Baptism, **Cork - South Parish** (RC))

- John Harris & Elizabeth Connor – 28 Feb 1835 (Marriage, **Murragh & Templemartin Parish** (RC))

  - Mary Harris – bapt. 11 Nov 1836 (Baptism, **Murragh & Templemartin Parish** (RC))

  - William Harris – bapt. 16 Apr 1839 (Baptism, **Murragh & Templemartin Parish** (RC))

  - Thomas Harris – bapt. 12 Sep 1841 (Baptism, **Murragh & Templemartin Parish** (RC))

  - John Harris – bapt. 4 Sep 1845 (Baptism, **Murragh & Templemartin Parish** (RC))

- John Harris & Elizabeth Finch – 18 Sep 1781 (Marriage, **Clondalkin Parish** (RC))

- John Harris & Elizabeth Gordon

  - Joseph Samuel Harris – b. 21 Apr 1881, bapt. 19 Mar 1901 (Baptism, **Harrington Street Parish** (RC))

John Harris (father):

Residence - 10 Camden Buildings - March 19, 1901

Harris Surname Ireland: 1600s to 1900s

- John Harris & Elizabeth Green

  - Mary Harris – b. 21 Feb 1856, bapt. 19 Mar 1856 (Baptism, **St. Nicholas Parish (RC)**)

John Harris (father):

Residence - 12 Canon Street - March 19, 1856

- John Harris & Elizabeth Griffin

  - William Harris & Catherine Fay – 2 Jul 1892 (Marriage, **St. Mary, Pro Cathedral Parish (RC)**)

    - Mary Elizabeth Harris – b. 19 Aug 1892, bapt. 31 Aug 1892 (Baptism, **St. Mary, Pro Cathedral Parish (RC)**)

    - John James Harris – b. 20 Apr 1895, bapt. 8 May 1895 (Baptism, **St. Mary, Pro Cathedral Parish (RC)**)

    - Michael William Harris – b. 5 Sep 1897, bapt. 13 Sep 1897 (Baptism, **St. Mary, Pro Cathedral Parish (RC)**)

William Harris (son):

Residence - 30 Mabbot Street - July 2, 1892

May 8, 1895

33 Gloucester Place - August 31, 1892

36 Mabbot Street - September 13, 1897

Catherine Fay, daughter of James Fay & Mary Loftus (daughter-in-law):

Residence - 33 Upper Gloucester Place - July 2, 1892

- John Harris & Elizabeth Harris

  - William Harris – bapt. 3 Jan 1734 (Baptism, **St. Catherine Parish**)

- John Harris & Elizabeth Harris

  - Robert Harris – bapt. 11 Jul 1742 (Baptism, **St. Catherine Parish**)

- John Harris & Elizabeth Harris

  - Margaret Harris – bapt. 10 Dec 1745 (Baptism, **St. Luke Parish**)

Hurst

- John Harris & Elizabeth Harris

  o Catherine Harris – bapt. 19 Dec 1756 (Baptism, **St. Mark Parish**)

John Harris (father):

Residence - Fleet Lane - December 19, 1756

- John Harris & Elizabeth Harris

  o Elizabeth Harris – bapt. 17 May 1784 (Baptism, **St. Mary Parish**)

John Harris (father):

Residence - Co. Wicklow - May 17, 1784

- John Harris & Elizabeth Harris

  o Patience Harris – bapt. 7 Jan 1822 (Baptism, **St. Paul Parish**)

- John Harris & Elizabeth Harris – 27 Oct 1846 (Marriage, **St. James Parish** (RC))

  o Edward Harris – bapt. 11 Dec 1848 (Baptism, **St. James Parish** (RC))

  o John Harris – bapt. 2 Jun 1851 (Baptism, **St. James Parish** (RC))

- John Harris & Elizabeth Harris

  o Anne Harris – b. 6 Feb 1854, bapt. 2 Mar 1854 (Baptism, **Clontarf Parish**)

John Harris (father):

Residence - Sheds Clontarf - March 2, 1854

Occupation - Coast Guard - March 2, 1854

- John Harris & Elizabeth Harris

  o Jessie McKindy Harris – b. 26 Jul 1892, bapt. 26 Aug 1892 (Baptism, **St. Catherine Parish**)

John Harris (father):

Residence - 29 Emerald Square - August 26, 1892

Occupation - Painter - August 26, 1892

Harris Surname Ireland: 1600s to 1900s

- John Harris & Elizabeth Harry

  o Patrick Harris & Teresa Redmond – 28 Oct 1900 (Marriage, **St. Mary, Pro Cathedral Parish** (RC))

Patrick Harris (son):

  Residence - **32 Mabbot Street** - October 28, 1900

Teresa Redmond, daughter of Edward Redmond & Mary Jane Unknown (daughter-in-law):

  Residence - **19 Lower Gardiner Street** - October 28, 1900

- John Harris & Elizabeth Kearns (K e a r n s)

  o Elizabeth Harris & Michael Keogh – 2 Feb 1890 (Baptism, **Harrington Street Parish** (RC))

Elizabeth Harris (daughter):

  Residence - **4 Camden Place** - February 2, 1890

Michael Keogh, son of Owen Keogh & Catherine Duffey (son-in-law):

  Residence - **53 Coombe** - February 2, 1890

  o Thomas Harris – b. 1852, bapt. 1852 (Baptism, **Rathfarnham Parish** (RC))

- John Harris & Elizabeth Tangee or Tansey – 27 Jul 1857 (Marriage, **St. Andrew Parish** (RC))

  o George Harris – b. 1858, bapt. 1858 (Baptism, **St. Andrew Parish** (RC))

  o Mary Harris – b. 1863, bapt. 1863 (Baptism, **St. Andrew Parish** (RC))

  o John Michael Harris – b. 1865, bapt. 1865 (Baptism, **St. Andrew Parish** (RC)) & Bridget Ryan – 28 Apr 1888 (Marriage, **St. Mary, Pro Cathedral Parish** (RC))

    ▪ James Harris – b. 9 Dec 1889, bapt. 10 Dec 1889 (Baptism, **St. Mary, Pro Cathedral Parish** (RC))

    ▪ John Harris – b. 27 Jun 1892, bapt. 1 Jul 1892 (Baptism, **St. Mary, Pro Cathedral Parish** (RC))

Hurst

- Patrick Harris – b. 9 Jul 1898, bapt. 18 Jul 1898 (Baptism, **St. Mary, Pro Cathedral Parish** (RC))

John Harris (son):

Residence - 54 Mabbot Street - April 28, 1888

49 Lower Tyrone Street - December 10, 1889

30 Mabbot Street - July 1, 1892

32 Mabbot Street - July 18, 1898

Bridget Ryan, daughter of James Ryan & Mary Murphy (daughter-in-law):

Residence - 54 Mabbot Street - April 28, 1888

- o Thomas Harris – b. 1867, bapt. 1867 (Baptism, **St. Andrew Parish** (RC))

- o Bridget Harris – b. 1870, bapt. 1870 (Baptism, **St. Andrew Parish** (RC))

- o William Harris – b. 1872, bapt. 1872 (Baptism, **St. Andrew Parish** (RC))

- o James Harris – b. 1874, bapt. 1874 (Baptism, **St. Andrew Parish** (RC))

- o Sarah Harris – b. 1876, bapt. 1876 (Baptism, **St. Andrew Parish** (RC)) & Nicholas Duffy – 10 Jan 1897 (Marriage, **St. Mary, Pro Cathedral Parish** (RC))

  - Owen Duffy – b. 7 Aug 1897, bapt. 9 Aug 1897 (Baptism, **St. Mary, Pro Cathedral Parish** (RC))

  - Elizabeth Duffy – b. 12 Apr 1899, bapt. 14 Apr 1899 (Baptism, **St. Mary, Pro Cathedral Parish** (RC))

Sarah Harris (daughter):

Residence - 39 Mabbot Street - January 10, 1897

Nicholas Duffy, son of Eugene Duffy & Mary Boylan (son-in-law):

Residence - 22 Mabbot Street - January 10, 1897

32 Mabbot Street - August 9, 1897

April 14, 1899

- o Patrick Harris – b. 1880, bapt. 1880 (Baptism, **St. Andrew Parish** (RC))

Harris Surname Ireland: 1600s to 1900s

John Harris (father):

Residence - 26 Moss Street - 1858

8 Moss Street - 1863

Stocking Lane - 1865

19 Moss Street - 1872

1876

1880

47 Moss Street - 1874

57 Poolbeg Street - 1867

47 Townsend Street - 1870

54 Mabbot Street - April 28, 1888

- John Harris & Elizabeth Unknown

  o James Harris & Bridget McGacoran – 19 Jul 1896 (Marriage, St. Mary, Pro Cathedral Parish (RC))

James Harris (son):

Residence - 33 Mabbot Street - July 19, 1896

Bridget McGacoran, daughter of George McGacoran & Bridget O'Connell (daughter-in-law):

Residence - 12 Mabbot Street - July 19, 1896

- John Harris & Ellen Donega

  o Michael Harris – bapt. 23 Sep 1824 (Baptism, St. Catherine Parish (RC))

- John Harris & Ellen Donovan

  o Thomas Harris – b. 8 Aug 1825, bapt. 8 Aug 1825 (Baptism, Tralee Parish (RC))

  o John Harris – b. 4 Jul 1828, bapt. 4 Jul 1828 (Baptism, Tralee Parish (RC))

  o Ellen Harris – b. 15 Jan 1830, bapt. 15 Jan 1830 (Baptism, Tralee Parish (RC))

  o Catherine Harris – b. 1 May 1831, bapt. 1 May 1831 (Baptism, Tralee Parish (RC))

  o Mary Harris – b. 15 Sep 1836, bapt. 15 Sep 1836 (Baptism, Tralee Parish (RC))

  o Agnes Harris – b. 6 Jul 1840, bapt. 6 Jul 1840 (Baptism, Castlegregory Parish (RC))

Hurst

John Harris (father):

Residence - Tralee - August 8, 1825

July 4, 1828

January 15, 1830

May 1, 1831

September 15, 1836

Ballyquin - July 6, 1840

- John Harris & Ellen Harris
  - Mary Harris – bapt. 14 Dec 1830 (Baptism, **St. Mary, Pro Cathedral Parish** (RC))

- John Harris & Ellen Lawlor
  - Edward Harris – b. 24 Jan 1830, bapt. 24 Jan 1830 (Baptism, **Tralee Parish** (RC))

John Harris (father):

Residence - Derrymore - January 24, 1830

- John Harris & Ellen Murphy
  - Ellen Harris – bapt. 14 Jun 1846 (Baptism, **Cork - SS. Peter & Paul Parish** (RC))

- John Harris & Esther Unknown
  - Jane Harris – bapt. 23 Aug 1761 (Baptism, **St. Werburgh Parish**)

John Harris (father):

Residence - Garden Lane - August 23, 1761

- John Harris & Frances Harris
  - John Harris – bapt. 20 Oct 1737 (Baptism, **St. Catherine Parish**)

- John Harris & Frances Moore
  - Joseph Harris – bapt. 11 May 1817 (Baptism, **Bandon Parish** (RC))

- John Harris & Hannah Harris
  - Anne Harris – bapt. 13 Mar 1740 (Baptism, **St. Mark Parish**)

John Harris (father):

Residence - Pole Begg Street - March 13, 1740

Harris Surname Ireland: 1600s to 1900s

- John Harris & Hannah Harris

  o Anne Esther Harris – b. 29 Apr 1888, bapt. 12 May 1888 (Baptism, **St. George Parish**)

John Harris (father):

  Residence - 37 Great Charles Street - May 12, 1888

  Occupation - Clerk - May 12, 1888

- John Harris & Hannah Reilly

  o Mary Harris – bapt. 8 May 1848 (Baptism, **St. James Parish** (RC))

- John Harris & Hannah Unknown

  o Mary Anne Esther Harris – b. 22 Apr 1848, bapt. 30 Apr 1848 (Baptism, **St. James Parish**)

John Harris (father):

  Residence - Bow Bridge - April 30, 1848

  Occupation - Private 44th Regiment - April 30, 1848

- John Harris & Helen Donovan

  o Mary Harris – b. 25 Jun 1813, bapt. 25 Jun 1813 (Baptism, **Tralee Parish** (RC))

John Harris (father):

  Residence - Tralee - June 25, 1813

- John Harris & Hester Harris

  o John Harrill Harris, b. 2 Feb 1851, bapt. 26 Apr 1886 (Baptism, **St. Anne Parish**) & Hannah Lowrey – 28 Apr 1886 (Marriage, **St. Anne Parish**)

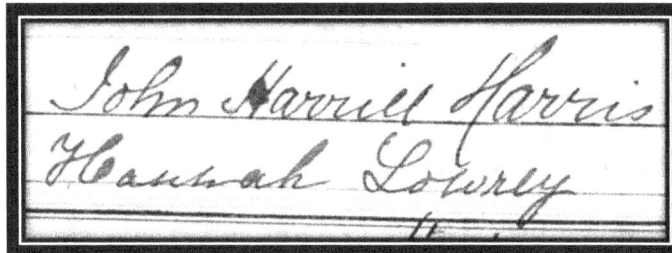

Signatures:

135

Hurst

John Harrill Harris (son):

   Residence - 30 Upper Sackville Street - April 28, 1886

   Occupation - Clerk - April 28, 1886

Hannah Lowrey, daughter of Daniel Lowrey (daughter-in-law):

   Residence - 32 South Anne Street Dublin - April 28, 1886

Daniel Lowrey (father):

Signature:

   Occupation - Comedian

John Harris (father):

   Residence - 30 Upper Sackville Street - February 2, 1851

   Occupation - Clerk - February 2, 1851

          Missionary

Wedding Witnesses:

Daniel Lowrey

Signature:

Harris Surname Ireland: 1600s to 1900s

- John Harris & Honora Foley

  - Margaret Harris – b. 9 Aug 1832, bapt. 9 Aug 1832 (Baptism, **Dromtariffe Parish** (RC))

  - Honora Harris – b. 24 Jan 1835, bapt. 24 Jan 1835 (Baptism, **Dromtariffe Parish** (RC))

  - Joan Harris – b. 3 Apr 1837, bapt. 3 Apr 1837 (Baptism, **Dromtariffe Parish** (RC))

  - Julia Harris – b. 14 Apr 1839, bapt. 14 Apr 1839 (Baptism, **Dromtariffe Parish** (RC))

  - Agnes Harris – b. 3 May 1842, bapt. 3 May 1842 (Baptism, **Dromtariffe Parish** (RC))

  - Ellen Harris – b. 29 Dec 1844, bapt. 29 Dec 1844 (Baptism, **Dromtariffe Parish** (RC))

John Harris (father):

Residence - Drominagh - August 9, 1832

January 24, 1835

April 3, 1837

Dromuck - April 14, 1839

Dromskehy - May 3, 1842

Lisnacon - December 29, 1844

- John Harris & Jane Harris

  - Anne Harris – bapt. 20 Jan 1793 (Baptism, **St. Mary Parish**)

John Harris (father):

Residence - Henry Street - January 20, 1793

- John Harris & Jane Meehan

  - Samuel S. Harris & Mary Jane Davis – 10 Sep 1884 (Marriage, **St. Mary, Pro Cathedral Parish** (RC))

Samuel S. Harris (son):

Residence - Co. Roscommon - September 10, 1884

Mary Jane Davis, daughter of Paul Davis & Catherine Oram (daughter-in-law):

Residence - Co. Roscommon - September 10, 1884

Hurst

- John Harris & Jane Unknown

  - Jane Harris – b. Oct 1847, bapt. 24 Feb 1848 (Baptism, **Carlow Parish**)

  - Charles Harris – b. 25 Dec 1849, bapt. 7 Feb 1850 (Baptism, **Dunleckney Parish**)

John Harris (father):

Residence - Carlow - February 24, 1848

     Curracutt - February 7, 1850

Occupation - Process Servant - February 24, 1848

     Process Server, Dunleckney Parish - February 7, 1850

- John Harris & Jane Harris, bur. 31 Jul 1643 (Burial, **St. Michan Parish**)

- John Harris & Joan Lynch – 16 Sep 1831 (Marriage, **Cork - South Parish** (RC))

  - James Harris – bapt. 19 Nov 1832 (Baptism, **Cork - South Parish** (RC))

  - Michael Harris – bapt. 15 Dec 1835 (Baptism, **Cork - South Parish** (RC))

  - John Harris – bapt. 13 May 1838 (Baptism, **Cork - South Parish** (RC))

  - Timothy Harris – bapt. 11 Sep 1842 (Baptism, **Cork - South Parish** (RC))

  - Michael Harris – bapt. 19 Feb 1853 (Baptism, **Cork - South Parish** (RC))

- John Harris & Joan Murphy

  - John Harris – b. 22 Jun 1846, bapt. 22 Jun 1846 (Baptism, **Tralee Parish** (RC))

John Harris (father):

Residence - Curraheen - June 22, 1846

- John Harris & Joan Sullivan

  - Joan Harris – b. 21 Jul 1900, bapt. 25 Jul 1900 (Baptism, **Glenbeigh/Glencar Parish**

    (RC))

John Harris (father):

Residence - Droumbrain - July 25, 1900

- John Harris & Lillie Harris

  - Norman (N o r m a n) Beamish Harris – b. 8 Nov 1892, bapt. 13 Nov 1892 (Baptism, **Rotunda**

    Chapel Parish)

Harris Surname Ireland: 1600s to 1900s

John Harris (father):

Residence - **2 Washington Street South Circular Road** - November 13, 1892

Occupation - Clerk - November 13, 1892

- John Harris & Margaret Bacon – 18 Jun 1816 (Marriage, **St. Mark Parish**)

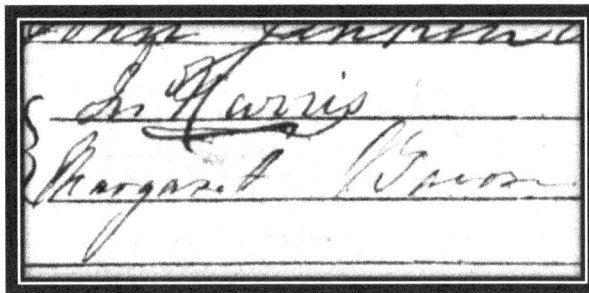

Signatures:

○ Frances Harris – bapt. 2 Apr 1817 (Baptism, **St. Mark Parish**)

Wedding Witnesses:

Francis Bacon

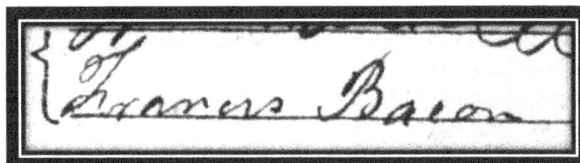

Signature:

- John Harris & Margaret Brien

  ○ Sarah Harris – b. 8 Jun 1880, bapt. 5 Jul 1880 (Baptism, **St. Nicholas Parish** (RC))

John Harris (father):

Residence - **28 Plunket Street** - July 5, 1880

- John Harris & Margaret Connor

  ○ Richard Harris – b. 17 Aug 1823, bapt. 17 Aug 1823 (Baptism, **Tralee Parish** (RC))

  ○ James Harris – b. 24 Jun 1825, bapt. 24 Jun 1825 (Baptism, **Tralee Parish** (RC))

John Harris (father):

Residence - **Derrymore** - August 17, 1823

June 24, 1825

Hurst

- John Harris & Margaret Deleigh – 4 Feb 1837 (Marriage, **Ballinhassig Parish** (RC))

- John Harris & Margaret Flinn

  - Mary Anne Harris – bapt. 14 Jul 1834 (Baptism, **St. Nicholas Parish** (RC))

- John Harris & Margaret Harris

  - Margaret Harris – bapt. 2 Apr 1817 (Baptism, **St. Mary Parish**)

- John Harris & Margaret Harris

  - Elizabeth Harris – b. 22 Jul 1827, bapt. 15 Aug 1827 (Baptism, **St. Mark Parish**)

  - Adelaide Harris – b. 27 Jul 1840, bapt. 16 Sep 1840 (Baptism, **St. Mark Parish**) & Charles Bolton Geoghegan – 26 Mar 1864 (Marriage, **St. Peter Parish**)

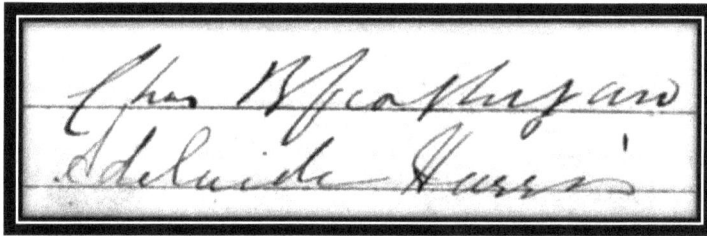

Signatures:

Adelaide Harris (daughter):

Residence - 124 Upper Rathmines - March 26, 1864

Charles Bolton Geoghegan, son of William Moore Geoghegan (son-in-law):

Residence - 124 Upper Rathmines - March 26, 1864

Occupation - Esquire - March 26, 1864

William Moore Geoghegan (father):

Occupation - Merchant

John Harris (father):

Residence - 8 Hanare Street - August 15, 1827

Creighton Street - September 16, 1840

Occupation - Commission Agent

Merchant - August 15, 1827

September 16, 1840

Harris Surname Ireland: 1600s to 1900s

- John Harris & Margaret Harris

  o Ellen Harris – b. Mar 1843, bapt. 3 May 1843 (Baptism, **St. Catherine Parish**)

John Harris (father):

Residence - Earl Street - May 3, 1843

Occupation - Merchant - May 3, 1843

- John Harris & Margaret Harris

  o Benjamin McCoy Harris – b. 17 Apr 1858, bapt. 25 Apr 1858 (Baptism, **Kilnaughtin**

  Parish)

John Harris (father):

Residence - Tarbert - April 25, 1858

Occupation - Late Master Gunner Royal Artillery - April 25, 1858

- John Harris & Margaret Harris

  o Henry Harris – b. 18 Jan 1859, bapt. 30 Jan 1859 (Baptism, **St. Peter Parish**)

John Harris (father):

Residence - Rathmines - January 30, 1859

Occupation - Laborer - January 30, 1859

Hurst

- John Harris & Margaret Harris

Signatures:

    o   Elizabeth Harris & Edward D'Arcy McCrea – 1 Mar 1856 (Marriage, **St. Anne Parish**)

Signatures:

    ▪ John Harris McCrea & Jeannette Eleanor Seale – 11 Apr 1894 (Marriage, **St. Anne Parish**)

Signatures:

John Harris McCrea (son of Elizabeth Harris & Edward D'Arcy McCrea):

    Residence - 51 William Street Dublin - April 11, 1894

    Occupation - Shirt Manufacturer - April 11, 1894

Jeannette Eleanor Seale, daughter of William Henry Seale (daughter-in-law):

    Residence - Mount Aventine Foxrock, Co. Dublin - April 11, 1894

William Henry Seale (father):

Signature:

    Occupation - Merchant

Edward D'Arcy McCrea (father):

    Occupation - Manufacturer

Wedding Witnesses:

William Henry Seale

Signature:

Elizabeth Harris (daughter):

    Residence - 23 Dawson Street - March 1, 1856

Edward D'Arcy McCrea, son of John McCrea (son-in-law):

Signature:

    Residence - 51 William Street - March 1, 1856

    Occupation - Merchant - March 1, 1856

        Manufacturer

Hurst

John McCrea (father):

    Occupation - Esquire

John Harris (father):

    Occupation - Assistant Secretary King's Inn

Wedding Witnesses:

John Harris & John Pitt Harris

Signatures:

    o   Margaret Harris & Thomas Wilson – 3 Jun 1856 (Marriage, **St. Anne Parish**)

Signatures:

Margaret Harris (daughter):

    Residence - 12 Stephen's Green North - June 3, 1856

Thomas Wilson, son of Joseph Wilson (son-in-law):

    Residence - Islington - June 3, 1856

    Occupation - Esquire - June 3, 1856

Harris Surname Ireland: 1600s to 1900s

Joseph Wilson (father):

    Occupation - Esquire

John Harris (father):

Signature:

    Occupation - Assistant Secretary King's Inn

Wedding Witnesses:

John Wilson

Signature:

    o   John Pitt Harris, bapt. 16 Nov 1828 (Baptism, **St. Mary Parish**), & Margaret Anne Curry –

       27 Jun 1860 (Marriage, **St. Peter Parish**)

Signature:

Signatures (Marriage):

Hurst

John Pitt Harris (son):

Residence - 49 Camden Street - June 27, 1860

Occupation - Esquire M D - June 27, 1860

Margaret Anne Curry, daughter of James Curry (daughter-in-law):

Residence - 13 Mount Pleasant Avenue - June 27, 1860

James Curry (father):

Occupation - Esquire

John Harris (father):

Occupation - Secretary to Benchers King's Inn

- o Rebecca Harris – bapt. 28 May 1830 (Baptism, St. Mary Parish)

- o Harriet Harris – bapt. 30 Nov 1831 (Baptism, St. Mary Parish)

- o Louisa Harris – bapt. 30 Nov 1831 (Baptism, St. Mary Parish)

John Harris (father):

Residence - King's Inns Henrietta Street - November 19, 1828

May 28, 1830

November 30, 1831

Occupation - Servant - November 19, 1828

May 28, 1830

November 30, 1831

- • John Harris & Margaret Harris

- o Henry James Harris – b. 5 Mar 1895, bapt. 19 May 1895 (Baptism, St. Peter Parish)

- o Mary Margaret Harris – b. 27 Aug 1897, bapt. 3 Oct 1897 (Baptism, St. George Parish)

John Harris (father):

Residence - 17 Cuffe Street - May 19, 1895

2 Hill Street - October 3, 1897

Occupation - Laborer - May 19, 1895

October 3, 1897

Harris Surname Ireland: 1600s to 1900s

- John Harris & Margaret Hyde – 1 Jul 1822 (Marriage, **Cork - South Parish** (RC))

Margaret Hyde (wife):

   Residence - Blue B Lane - July 1, 1822

- John Harris & Margaret McCoy

   o   Margaret Harris – bapt. Unclear (Baptism, **Ballylongford Parish** (RC))

John Harris (father):

   Residence - Tarbert - Unclear

- John Harris & Margaret Newman

   o   Mary Anne Harris – b. 9 Nov 1868, bapt. 12 Nov 1868 (Baptism, **Cork - SS. Peter & Paul Parish** (RC))

- John Harris & Margaret O'Brien

   o   Catherine Harris – b. 9 Jan 1854, bapt. 29 Mar 1857 (Baptism, **Rathmines Parish** (RC))

   o   Julia Harris – b. 28 Mar 1868, bapt. 3 Apr 1868 (Baptism, **Harrington Street Parish** (RC))

John Harris (father):

   Residence - 31 Kevin Street - April 3, 1868

- John Harris & Margaret O'Neill

   o   Catherine Harris & James Kavanagh – 16 Sep 1878 (Marriage, **Rathmines Parish** (RC))

      ▪   Charles Kavanagh – b. 9 Jul 1879, bapt. 13 Jul 1879 (Baptism, **Rathmines Parish** (RC))

      ▪   John Kavanagh – b. 11 Nov 1880, bapt. 19 Dec 1880 (Baptism, **Rathmines Parish** (RC))

      ▪   Margaret Mary Kavanagh – b. 24 Mar 1883, bapt. 1 Apr 1883 (Baptism, **Rathmines Parish** (RC))

      ▪   Anne Kavanagh – b. 24 Nov 1884, bapt. 24 Nov 1884 (Baptism, **Rathmines Parish** (RC))

      ▪   Catherine Mary Kavanagh – b. 2 Jul 1886, bapt. 14 Jul 1886 (Baptism, **Rathmines Parish** (RC))

Hurst

- Florence Kavanagh – b. 9 Aug 1890, bapt. 13 Aug 1890 (Baptism, **Rathmines Parish (RC)**)

- Josephine Agnes Kavanagh – b. 4 Mar 1893, bapt. 8 Mar 1893 (Baptism, **Rathmines Parish (RC)**)

- Elizabeth Kavanagh – b. 25 Sep 1895, bapt. 29 Sep 1895 (Baptism, **Rathmines Parish (RC)**)

Catherine Harris (daughter):

Residence - Rathmines - September 16, 1878

James Kavengh, son of Charles Kavengh & Catherine Whelan (son-in-law):

Residence - Rathmines - September 16, 1878

July 13, 1879

Mount Pleasant Ave - December 19, 1880

6 Mount Pleasant Place - August 13, 1890

March 8, 1893

September 29, 1895

5 Swanville Rathmines - April 1, 1883

November 24, 1884

Swanville Place - July 14, 1886

- John Harris & Margaret Unknown

  - Joseph Harris – b. 30 Jul 1822, bapt. 6 Aug 1822 (Baptism, **St. Catherine Parish**)

John Harris (father):

Residence - Coombe - August 6, 1822

- John Harris & Margaret Unknown

  - Elizabeth Harris – b. 12 Jan 1825, bapt. 16 Jan 1825 (Baptism, **St. Peter Parish**)

  - Anne Harris – b. 8 Dec 1825, bapt. 11 Dec 1825 (Baptism, **St. Peter Parish**)

  - Margaret Harris – b. 8 Dec 1825, bapt. 11 Dec 1825 (Baptism, **St. Peter Parish**)

- John Harris & Margaret Unknown

  o Catherine Harris – b. 6 Feb 1834, bapt. 21 Feb 1834 (Baptism, **St. Peter Parish**)

John Harris (father):

Residence - No 87 Charlotte Street - February 21, 1834

- John Harris & Margaret Unknown

  o Catherine Harris – b. 9 Jan 1854, bapt. 29 Mar 1857 (Baptism, **Rathmines Parish (RC)**)

John Harris (father):

Residence - Church Lane - March 29, 1857

- John Harris & Mary Auree

  o Michael Harris – b. 1866, bapt. 1866 (Baptism, **St. Mary, Haddington Road Parish (RC)**)

- John Harris & Mary Barnane (B a r n a n e) – 7 Mar 1848 (Marriage, **Kinsale Parish (RC)**)

John Harris (husband):

Residence - Blind Gate - March 7, 1848

- John Harris & Mary Barnes (B a r n e s)

  o Patrick Harris – b. 1883, bapt. 1883 (Baptism, **St. Andrew Parish (RC)**)

John Harris (father):

Residence - 49 Townsend Street - 1883

- John Harris & Mary Brien – 2 Feb 1788 (Marriage, **Kilmurry Parish (RC)**)

- John Harris & Mary Brown

  o Margaret Harris – bapt. Jul 1789 (Baptism, **Kilmurry Parish (RC)**)

  o Julia Harris – bapt. Jul 1791 (Baptism, **Kilmurry Parish (RC)**)

- John Harris & Mary Caffrey – 24 Jun 1792 (Marriage, **St. Michan Parish (RC)**)

  o Catherine Harris – bapt. 30 Jul 1800 (Baptism, **St. Michan Parish (RC)**)

  o James Harris – bapt. 9 Dec 1802 (Baptism, **St. Michan Parish (RC)**)

  o Elizabeth Harris – bapt. 16 Sep 1804 (Baptism, **St. Michan Parish (RC)**)

Hurst

- John Harris & Mary Connell

  - Ellen Harris – bapt. 24 Apr 1839 (Baptism, **Douglas Parish** (RC))

John Harris (father):

Residence - Tullig - April 24, 1839

- John Harris & Mary Dunn – 21 Sep 1821 (Marriage, **St. Mary Parish**)

  - Henry Harris – bapt. 9 May 1831 (Baptism, **Kinsale Parish** (RC))

John Harris (father):

Residence - Fort - May 9, 1831

- John Harris & Mary Farquhar

  - John Harris – bapt. 17 Dec 1852 (Baptism, **St. Michan Parish** (RC))

- John Harris & Mary Ferrall

  - Patrick Harris – bapt. 16 Feb 1770 (Baptism, **St. Catherine Parish** (RC))

- John Harris & Mary Griffin – 23 Sep 1866 (Marriage, **Annascaul Parish** (RC))

  - John Harris – b. 17 Jun 1867, bapt. 17 Jun 1867 (Baptism, **Annascaul Parish** (RC))

  - Anne Harris – b. 25 Apr 1869, bapt. 25 Apr 1869 (Baptism, **Annascaul Parish** (RC))

  - Rose Anne Harris – b. 16 Jul 1871, bapt. 16 Jul 1871 (Baptism, **Annascaul Parish** (RC))

John Harris (father):

Residence - Derrygorman - September 23, 1866

April 25, 1869

Glenmore - June 17, 1867

Cloomveen - July 16, 1871

- John Harris & Mary Harris

  - John Harris – bapt. 14 May 1716 (Baptism, **St. Luke Parish**)

John Harris (father):

Residence - New Roe - May 14, 1716

Harris Surname Ireland: 1600s to 1900s

- John Harris & Mary Harris

  o Thomas Harris – bapt. 25 Mar 1717 (Baptism, **St. Catherine Parish**)

- John Harris & Mary Harris – 8 Nov 1873 (Marriage **Cork - South Parish** (RC))

- John Harris & Mary Kearny (K e a r n y)

  o John Harris – b. 1 Jul 1895, bapt. 10 Jul 1895 (Baptism, **St. Mary, Pro Cathedral Parish**

  (RC))

John Harris (father):

Residence - 2 Jervis Street - July 10, 1895

- John Harris & Mary Leary

  o Mary Harris – b. 15 Feb 1835, bapt. 15 Feb 1835 (Baptism, **Tralee Parish** (RC))

  o Sarah Harris – b. 16 May 1841, bapt. 16 May 1841 (Baptism, **Tralee Parish** (RC))

John Harris (father):

Residence - Tralee - February 15, 1835

May 16, 1841

- John Harris & Mary Mahony – 19 Sep 1830 (Marriage, **Dunmanway Parish** (RC))

  o James Harris – bapt. 16 May 1831 (Baptism, **Dunmanway Parish** (RC))

  o Joan Harris – bapt. 23 Oct 1833 (Baptism, **Dunmanway Parish** (RC))

  o Terence Harris – bapt. 30 Jun 1836 (Baptism, **Dunmanway Parish** (RC))

  o Abigail Harris – bapt. 19 Jun 1839 (Baptism, **Dunmanway Parish** (RC))

  o James Harris – bapt. 24 Jan 1842 (Baptism, **Dunmanway Parish** (RC))

  o Mary Harris – bapt. 8 Aug 1844 (Baptism, **Dunmanway Parish** (RC))

  o John Harris – bapt. 22 Feb 1847 (Baptism, **Dunmanway Parish** (RC))

Hurst

John Harris (father):

> Residence - Chapel Cross - September 19, 1830

> > October 23, 1833

> > June 30, 1836

> > June 19, 1839

> > January 24, 1842

> > August 8, 1844

> Kilbarry - February 22, 1847

Mary Mahony (mother):

> Residence - Chapel Cross - September 19, 1830

- John Harris & Mary Martin

  o John Harris – bapt. 23 Apr 1831 (Baptism, **Innishannon Parish** (RC))

- John Harris & Mary Murphy

  o John Harris – bapt. 1 Jun 1800 (Baptism, **Cork - SS. Peter & Paul Parish** (RC))

John Harris (father):

> Residence - Hughe's Lane - June 1, 1800

- John Harris & Mary Riordan

  o Ellen Harris – b. 29 Jun 1872, bapt. 29 Jun 1872 (Baptism, **Glenbeigh/Glencar Parish** (RC))

  o Jane Harris – b. 18 Dec 1884, bapt. 20 Dec 1884 (Baptism, **Glenbeigh/Glencar Parish** (RC))

  o Simon Harris – b. 29 Sep 1889, bapt. 5 Oct 1889 (Baptism, **Glenbeigh/Glencar Parish** (RC))

John Harris (father):

> Residence - Kilkeehagh - June 29, 1872

> > December 20, 1884

> > October 5, 1889

Harris Surname Ireland: 1600s to 1900s

- John Harris & Mary Sekarie – 15 Sep 1628, 15 Dec 1628 (Marriage, **St. John Parish**)

- John Harris & Mary Sheehan

  o Daniel Harris – bapt. 4 Jun 1843 (Baptism, **Courcy's Country or Ballinspittal Parish (RC)**)

  o Sally Harris – bapt. 4 Jun 1843 (Baptism, **Courcy's Country or Ballinspittal Parish (RC)**)

  o Mary Harris – bapt. 1 Sep 1844 (Baptism, **Courcy's Country or Ballinspittal Parish (RC)**)

- John Harris & Mary Sugrue

  o Ellen Harris – b. 21 May 1892, bapt. 22 May 1892 (Baptism, **Glenbeigh/Glencar Parish (RC)**)

John Harris (father):
  Residence - Drom - May 22, 1892

- John Harris & Mary Sweeny – 7 Feb 1826 (Marriage, **Kilmurry, Moviddy, Kilbonane, & Cannavee Parish** (RC))

  o Michael Harris – bapt. 21 Feb 1827 (Baptism, **Cork - South Parish** (RC))

  o Mary Anne Harris – bapt. 3 Aug 1830 (Baptism, **Cork - South Parish** (RC))

- John Harris & Mary Toole

  o Eleanor Harris – b. 3 Aug 1866, bapt. 5 Aug 1866 (Baptism, **Rathmines Parish** (RC))

  o John J. Harris – b. 22 Jun 1870, bapt. 26 Jun 1870 (Baptism, **Rathmines Parish** (RC))

  o Margaret Harris – b. 11 Feb 1872, bapt. 13 Feb 1872 (Baptism, **Harrington Street Parish (RC)**)

  o John Harris – b. 2 Oct 1876, bapt. 8 Oct 1876 (Baptism, **Rathmines Parish** (RC))

  o Alicia Harris – b. 4 Nov 1878, bapt. 10 Nov 1878 (Baptism, **Rathmines Parish** (RC))

  o Mary Harris & Martin Beehan – 17 Aug 1884 (Marriage, **Rathmines Parish** (RC))

Hurst

- Mary Joseph Beehan – b. 8 Jul 1885, bapt. 12 Jul 1885 (Baptism, *Rathmines Parish (RC)*)

- James Beehan – b. 22 Jul 1886, bapt. 25 Jul 1886 (Baptism, *Rathmines Parish (RC)*)

- Margaret Beehan – b. 11 Nov 1887, bapt. 13 Nov 1887 (Baptism, *Rathmines Parish (RC)*)

- John Isidore Beehan – b. 4 Apr 1889, bapt. 7 Apr 1889 (Baptism, *Rathmines Parish (RC)*)

- Martin Beehan – b. 28 Nov 1890, bapt. 30 Nov 1890 (Baptism, *Rathmines Parish (RC)*)

- John Beehan – b. 22 Sep 1892, bapt. 25 Sep 1892 (Baptism, *Rathmines Parish (RC)*)

- Christopher Beehan – b. 25 Dec 1893, bapt. 27 Dec 1893 (Baptism, *Rathmines Parish (RC)*)

- Michael Beehan – b. 14 Sep 1896, bapt. 16 Sep 1896 (Baptism, *Rathmines Parish (RC)*)

- Ellen Beehan – b. 20 Nov 1898, bapt. 20 Nov 1898 (Baptism, *Rathmines Parish (RC)*)

- William Christopher Beehan – b. 18 Dec 1899, bapt. 20 Dec 1899 (Baptism, *Rathmines Parish (RC)*)

Mary Harris (daughter):

Residence - *7 Limekiln Lane Harold's Cross - August 17, 1884*

Martin Beehan, son of James Beehan & Elizabeth Gerety (son-in-law):

Residence - 11 Limekiln Lane Harold's Cross - August 17, 1884

2 Limekiln Lane Harold's Cross - November 30, 1890

November 20, 1898

December 20, 1899

2 Greenmount Harold's Cross - September 25, 1892

December 27, 1893

Harold's Cross - July 12, 1885

November 13, 1887

Harris Surname Ireland: 1600s to 1900s

Factory Lane - July 25, 1886

3 Factory Lane Harold's Cross - April 7, 1889

22 Limekiln Terrace Greenmount - September 16, 1896

- Ellen Harris & Thomas Maguire – 18 Aug 1895 (Marriage, **Rathmines Parish** (RC))

Ellen Harris (daughter):

Residence - 7 Limekiln Lane - August 18, 1895

Thomas Maguire, son of Terence Maguire & Harriett Reid (son-in-law):

Residence - 3 Pleasant Place - August 18, 1895

- Margaret Harris & Michael Keegan – 19 Apr 1896 (Marriage, **Rathmines Parish** (RC))

Margaret Harris (daughter):

Residence - 7 Greenmount Lane - April 19, 1896

Michael Keegan, son of John Keegan & Mary O'Hara (son-in-law):

Residence - 10 Mapes Street - April 19, 1896

John Harris (father):

Residence - Harold's Cross - August 5, 1866

June 27, 1870

October 8, 1876

Kill Lane - November 10, 1878

4 Malpas Street - February 13, 1872

- John Harris & Mary Tuohy

  - Michael Harris – b. 8 Feb 1870, bapt. 18 Feb 1870 (Baptism, **St. Mary, Pro Cathedral Parish** (RC))

John Harris (father):

Residence - Britain Court - February 18, 1870

- John Harris & Mary Unknown

  - Jane Harris – bapt. 11 Oct 1697 (Baptism, **St. John Parish**)

John Harris (father):

Residence - Wood Key - October 11, 1697

- John Harris & Mary Unknown

  - Mary Harris – bapt. 17 Apr 1754 (Baptism, **St. Catherine Parish**)

- John Harris & Mary Unknown

  - Sarah Harris – bapt. 27 Dec 1762 (Baptism, **St. Catherine Parish** (RC))

- John Harris & Mary Unknown

  - Anne Harris – bapt. 15 Dec 1799 (Baptism, **St. Werburgh Parish**)

John Harris (father):

Residence - Hoey's Court - December 15, 1799

- John Harris & Mary Unknown

  - Ellen Harris – bapt. 1830 (Baptism, **Palmerstown Parish** (RC))

- John Harris & Mary Unknown

  - James Harris – b. 13 Jun 1839, bapt. 19 Apr 1840 (Baptism, **St. Catherine Parish**)

John Harris (father):

Residence - Dolphin's Barn - April 19, 1840

- John Harris & Mary Unknown

  - John Harris – bapt. 28 Jul 1840 (Baptism, **St. Catherine Parish** (RC))

- John Harris & Mary Unknown

  - John Harris – bapt. 1846 (Baptism, **St. Andrew Parish** (RC))

  - Bridget Harris – b. 1851, bapt. 1851 (Baptism, **St. Andrew Parish** (RC))

- John Harris & Mary Unknown

  - Margaret Harris – b. 3 Aug 1874, bapt. 9 Aug 1874 (Baptism, **Cork - South Parish** (RC))

  - John Harris – b. 3 Jan 1876, bapt. 9 Jan 1876 (Baptism, **Cork - South Parish** (RC))

  - Hannah Harris – b. 11 Jan 1878, bapt. 13 Jan 1878 (Baptism, **Cork - South Parish** (RC))

John Harris (father):

Residence - 30 Three Hatchet Lane - January 13, 1878

Harris Surname Ireland: 1600s to 1900s

- John Harris & Mary Unknown

  o John Harris & Dora Gosson – 21 Feb 1860 (Marriage, **St. Michan Parish (RC)**)

John Harris (son):

Residence - 62 Mary's Lane - February 21, 1860

Dora Gosson, daughter of Lawrence Gosson & Jeanne Unknown (daughter-in-law):

Residence - 62 Mary's Lane - February 21, 1860

- John Harris & Mary Unknown

  o Bridget Harris & Terence Kelly – 19 Jan 1879 (Marriage, **St. Andrew Parish (RC)**)

    ▪ Rose Anne Kelly – b. 20 Oct 1879, bapt. 22 Oct 1879 (Baptism, **St. Michan Parish (RC)**)

Bridget Harris (daughter):

Residence - 6 Upper Fitzwilliam Lane - January 19, 1879

Terence Kelly, son of Terence Kelly & Rose Unknown (son-in-law):

Residence - 102 Lower Dorset Street - January 19, 1879

October 22, 1879

- John Harris & Mary Walsh – 12 Nov 1860 (Marriage, **St. Mary, Haddington Road Parish (RC)**)

- John Harris & Mary Anne Reynolds – 23 Jul 1832 (Marriage, **St. Michan Parish (RC)**)

- John Harris & Mary Maryanne Rourke

  o William Thomas Harris – b. 8 Dec 1864, bapt. 27 Dec 1864 (Baptism, **SS. Michael & John Parish (RC)**)

  o Joan Harris – b. 19 Oct 1866, bapt. 1 Nov 1866 (Baptism, **SS. Michael & John Parish (RC)**)

  o Mary Martha Harris – b. 19 Oct 1866, bapt. 1 Nov 1866 (Baptism, **SS. Michael & John Parish (RC)**)

  o William Thomas Harris – b. 15 Feb 1868, bapt. 24 Feb 1868 (Baptism, **SS. Michael & John Parish (RC)**)

- o Mary Jane Harris – b. 3 May 1870, bapt. 9 May 1870 (Baptism, **SS. Michael & John Parish (RC)**)

- o Mary Anne Harris – b. 15 Aug 1872, bapt. 26 Aug 1872 (Baptism, **SS. Michael & John Parish (RC)**)

John Harris (father):

Residence - 11 Werburgh Street - December 27, 1864

59 Back Lane - November 1, 1866

42 Castle Street - February 24, 1868

54 Fishamble Street - May 9, 1870

11 Nicholas Street - August 26, 1872

- John Harris & Honora Cooney

  - o John Harris – bapt. 3 Apr 1862 (Baptism, **Douglas & Ballygarvan Parrish (RC)**)

- John Harris & Rachel Harris

  - o Jane Harris – bapt. 8 Jan 1735 (Baptism, **St. Catherine Parish**)

- John Harris & Rebecca Hughes

  - o Dorah Harris & Edward Farrell – 21 Jun 1881 (Marriage, **St. Nicholas Parish (RC)**)

Dorah Harris (daughter):

Residence - 2 MacClean's Lane - June 21, 1881

Edward Farrell, son of John Farrell & Margaret Hogan (son-in-law):

Residence - 2 MacClean's Lane - June 21, 1881

- John Harris & Rebecca Richards – 10 Aug 1833 (Marriage, **St. Paul Parish**)

- John Harris & Robertha Lopdell

  - o Elizabeth Harris & John Murray – 17 May 1891 (Marriage, **St. Mary, Pro Cathedral Parish (RC)**)

    - ▪ Elizabeth Mary Murray – b. 5 Aug 1891, bapt. 28 Aug 1891 (Baptism, **St. Mary, Pro Cathedral Parish (RC)**)

- Walter Raymond Murray – b. 1 Nov 1895, bapt. 12 Nov 1895 (Baptism, **Harrington Street Parish (RC)**)

- Valentine John Murray – b. 13 Feb 1900, bapt. 23 Feb 1900 (Baptism, **Harrington Street Parish (RC)**)

Elizabeth Harris (daughter):

Residence - 39 Lower Abbey Street - May 17, 1891

John Murray, son of John Murray & Margaret Flynn (son-in-law):

Residence - 39 Lower Abbey Street - May 17, 1891

August 28, 1891

47 Raymond Street - November 12, 1895

55 Raymond Street South Circular Road - February 23, 1900

- John Harris & Rosanna Gaynor

  o Rachel Harris – b. 7 Sep 1883, bapt. 19 Sep 1883 (Baptism, **St. Mary, Pro Cathedral Parish (RC)**)

John Harris (father):

Residence - 28 Great Britain Street - September 19, 1883

- John Harris & Rosanna Harris, b. 1779, bur. 6 Jul 1853 (Burial, **St. Werburgh Parish**)

  o Mary Anne Harris – b. 4 Feb 1824, bapt. 15 Feb 1824 (Baptism, **St. Werburgh Parish**)

Rosanna Harris (mother):

Residence - 21 Werburgh Street - July 6, 1853

- John Harris & Rubertha Adams

  o William Harris & Christine Brien – 12 Feb 1900 (Marriage, **St. Mary, Pro Cathedral Parish (RC)**)

William Harris (son):

Residence - 27 Upper Temple Street - February 12, 1900

Christine Brien, daughter of Michael Brien & Elizabeth Boland (daughter-in-law):

Residence - 24 Bolton Street - February 12, 1900

Hurst

- John Harris & Sarah Harris

  - Peter Harris & Mary McGarrick – 9 Sep 1877 (Marriage, **Harrington Street Parish (RC)**)

Peter Harris (son):

    Residence - 5 Pleasant Place - September 9, 1877

Mary McGarrick, daughter of John McGarrick & Catherine Unknown (daughter-in-law):

    Residence - 57 Lower Camden Street - September 9, 1877

- John Harris, d. Before 30 Aug 1827, & Sarah Unknown (**Aghold Parish**)

  - Susan Harris – bapt. 6 Sep 1818 (Baptism, **Aghold Parish**)

  - Thomas Harris – bapt. 9 Nov 1823 (Baptism, **Aghold Parish**)

John Harris (father):

    Residence - Coolkenno

He died before August 30 1827, when his wife Sarah remarried to Michael Durdon.

- John Harris & Sarah Unknown

  - Catherine Harris – b. 1857, bapt. 1857 (Baptism, **St. Andrew Parish (RC)**)

- John Harris & Sarah Unknown

  - Patrick Harris & Catherine Hacket – 2 Aug 1858 (Marriage, **St. Andrew Parish (RC)**)

Patrick Harris (son):

    Residence - Black Rock - August 2, 1858

Catherine Hacket, daughter of Christopher Hacket & Margaret Unknown (daughter-in-law):

    Residence - 2 Merrion Square South - August 2, 1858

- John Harris & Susan Unknown

  - Samuel Robert Harris – b. 16 Jan 1866, bapt. 11 Feb 1866 (Baptism, **St. James Parish**)

John Harris (father):

    Residence - Constabulary Depot Phoenix PK - February 11, 1866

    Occupation - Head of Constabulary - February 11, 1866

Harris Surname Ireland: 1600s to 1900s

- John Harrise Harris & Unknown

  - Elizabeth Harris – bapt. 29 Sep 1625 (Baptism, **St. John Parish**)

  - John Harris – bapt. 12 Nov 1626 (Baptism, **St. John Parish**)

  - Marie Harris – bapt. 13 Mar 1627 (Baptism, **St. John Parish**)

  - Elizabeth Harris – bapt. 24 Oct 1631 (Baptism, **St. John Parish**)

  - William Harris – bapt. 16 Nov 1637 (Baptism, **St. John Parish**)

  - Mary Harris – bapt. 11 Dec 1637 (Baptism, **St. John Parish**)

  - Marie Harris – bapt. 12 Dec 1637 (Baptism, **St. John Parish**)

  - Richard Harris – bapt. 26 May 1639 (Baptism, **St. John Parish**)

  - Sarah Harris – bapt. 10 Dec 1641 (Baptism, **St. John Parish**)

- John Harris & Unknown

  - Nicholas Harris – bur. 16 Jul 1703 (Burial, **St. John Parish**)

  - John Harris – bur. 13 Jun 1704 (Burial, **St. John Parish**)

- John Harris & Unknown, bur. 8 Jan 1726 (Baptism, **St. Patrick Parish**)

The entry in the church register reads as follows:

"Jan 8 1726. [Blank] Harris late wife of Mr. John Harris interrd in the churchyard."

- John Harris & Unknown

  - Joseph Harris – bur. 4 Mar 1707 (Burial, **St. Werburgh Parish**)

Joseph Harris (son):

    Age at Death - infant

    Place of Burial - churchyard

John Harris (father):

    Residence - Cren Leane - March 4, 1707

- John Harris & Unknown

  - Margaret Harris – bapt. 24 May 1726 (Baptism, **St. Audoen Parish**)

Hurst

- John Harris & Unknown

  - Sarah Harris & Benjamin Colville – 6 Jul 1846 (Marriage, St. Peter Parish)

Signatures:

  - Elizabeth Colville – b. 7 Sep 1849, bapt. 28 May 1867 (Baptism, St. Nicholas Parish

    (RC))

Elizabeth Colville (daughter):

    Residence - 79 Bride Street - May 28, 1867

Sarah Harris (daughter):

    Residence - 45 Cuffe Street - July 6, 1846

    Occupation - Servant - July 6, 1846

Benjamin Colville, son of Isaac Colville (son-in-law):

    Residence - 45 Cuffe Street - July 6, 1846

    Occupation - Servant - July 6, 1846

    Relationship Status at Marriage - under age

Isaac Colville (father):

    Occupation - Hatter

John Harris (father):

    Occupation - Butcher

Wedding Witnesses:

Joseph Harris

Signature:

- John Harris & Unknown

  o John Harris & Margaret Rowe – 14 Aug 1848 (Marriage, St. Andrew Parish)

Signatures:

John Harris (son):

   Residence - 6 Trinity Place - August 14, 1848

   Occupation - Tailor - August 14, 1848

Margaret Rowe, daughter of James Rowe (daughter-in-law):

   Residence - 6 Trinity Place - August 14, 1848

   Occupation - Servant - August 14, 1848

James Rowe (father):

   Occupation - Tailor

John Harris (father):

   Occupation - Farmer

Hurst

- John Harris & Unknown

  - John Harris & Julia Nicol – 1 Jul 1848 (Marriage, **St. Mark Parish**)

Signatures:

John Harris (son):

    Residence - 4 Mark Street - July 1, 1848

    Occupation - Gentleman - July 1, 1848

Julia Nicol, daughter of Henry Nicol (daughter-in-law):

    Residence - 3 Hawkins Street - July 1, 1848

Henry Nicol (father):

    Occupation - Printer

John Harris (father):

    Occupation - Gentleman

Wedding Witnesses:

Agnes Nicol

Signature:

Harris Surname Ireland: 1600s to 1900s

- John Harris & Unknown

  - Anne Harris & Thomas Harcombe, d. Before 11 Oct 1856 – 26 Jan 1854 (Marriage, **St. Paul Parish**)

Signatures:

Anne Harris (daughter):

  Residence - Royal Barracks - January 26, 1854

  Occupation - Servant - January 26, 1854

Thomas Harcombe, son of John Harcombe (son-in-law):

  Residence - Royal Barracks - January 26, 1854

  Occupation - Corporal 2nd Dragoon Guards - January 26, 1854

John Harcombe (father):

  Occupation - Veterinary Surgeon

John Harris (father):

  Occupation - Farmer

  - Anne Harris Harcombe & James Gillespie – 11 Oct 1856 (Marriage, **St. Mary Parish**)

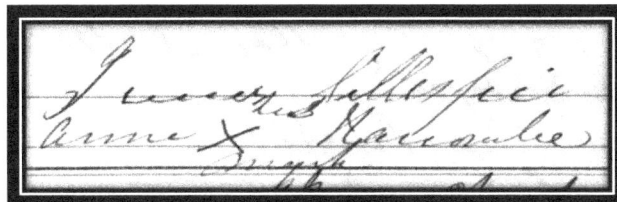

Signatures:

Hurst

Anne Harris Harcombe (daughter):

   Residence - 139 Great Britain Street - October 11, 1856

James Gillespie, son of James Gillespie (son-in-law):

   Residence - Royal Barracks - October 11, 1856

   Occupation - Sergeant 2nd Dragoon Guards - October 11, 1856

James Gillespie (father):

   Occupation - Farmer

John Harris (father):

   Occupation - Veterinary Surgeon

Probably written down incorrectly, since John Harris was employed as a Farmer and John Harcombe was employed as a Veterinary Surgeon.

- John Harris & Unknown

   o   Joseph Harris & Anne Willis – 26 Oct 1854 (Marriage, **St. Anne Parish**)

Signatures:

Joseph Harris (son):

   Residence - 43 South King Street - October 26, 1854

   Occupation - Servant - October 26, 1854

Anne Willis, daughter of Edward Willis (daughter-in-law):

   Residence - 43 South King Street - October 26, 1854

   Occupation - Servant - October 26, 1854

Edward Willis (father):

   Occupation - Clerk

John Harris (father):

   Occupation - Laborer

Harris Surname Ireland: 1600s to 1900s

- John Harris & Unknown

  - Bridget Harris & Daniel Dempsey – 5 Feb 1855 (Marriage, **St. Peter Parish**)

Signatures:

  - Patrick Dempsey – bapt. 24 Jun 1855 (Baptism, **Rathmines Parish** (RC))

  - John Daniel Dempsey – bapt. 1 Nov 1857 (Baptism, **Rathmines Parish** (RC))

  - Eleanor Josephine Dempsey – b. 8 Jun 1859, bapt. 12 Jun 1859 (Baptism, **Rathmines Parish** (RC))

  - Daniel Dempsey – b. 5 Feb 1864, bapt. 14 Feb 1864 (Baptism, **Rathmines Parish** (RC))

Bridget Harris (daughter):

  Residence - Milltown - February 5, 1855

  Occupation - Servant - February 5, 1855

Daniel Dempsey, son of Patrick Dempsey (son-in-law):

  Residence - Milltown - February 5, 1855

  Rathmines - June 12, 1859

  February 14, 1864

  Occupation -Laborer - February 5, 1855

Patrick Dempsey (father):

  Occupation - Dairyman

John Harris (father):

  Occupation - Gardener

Hurst

- John Harris & Unknown

  - Elizabeth Harris & James Wood – 24 Feb 1857 (Marriage, **St. Peter Parish**)

Signatures:

Elizabeth Harris (daughter):

   Residence - 7 Merrion Square North - February 24, 1857

James Wood, son of John Wood (son-in-law):

   Residence - Currie Parish, Co. Monaghan - February 24, 1857

   Occupation - Land Steward - February 24, 1857

John Wood (father):

   Occupation - Farmer

John Harris (father):

   Occupation - Caretaker

- John Harris & Unknown

  - Robert Harris & Elizabeth Warham – 7 Jan 1858 (Marriage, **St. Catherine Parish**)

Signatures:

Robert Harris (son):

   Residence - 11 Crumlin Road - January 7, 1858

   Occupation - Gentleman - January 7, 1858

Elizabeth Warham, daughter of William Warham (daughter-in-law):

    Residence - 18 Grand Canal Harbor - January 7, 1858

    Relationship Status at Marriage - minor age

William Warham (father):

Signature:

    Occupation - Gentleman

John Harris (father):

    Occupation - Gentleman

Wedding Witnesses:

William Warham

Signature:

    o   Susan Harris & Richard Heaslips – 19 Jul 1861 (Marriage, **Crumlin Parish**)

Susan Harris (daughter):

    Residence - 34 Harold's Cross - July 19, 1861

Richard Heaslips, son of Robert Heaslips (son-in-law):

    Residence - Village of Crumlin - July 19, 1861

    Occupation - School Master - July 19, 1861

Robert Heaslips (father):

    Occupation - Farmer

John Harris (father):

    Occupation - Gentleman

Hurst

- John Harris & Unknown

Signature:

- ○ Fanny Harris & Thomas Dodd – 5 Sep 1859 (Marriage, **St. Thomas Parish**)

Signatures:

Fanny Harris (daughter):

    Residence - **25 Upper Mecklenburgh Street** - September 5, 1859

Thomas Dodd, son of Thomas Dodd (son-in-law):

    Residence - **25 Upper Mecklenburgh Street** - September 5, 1859

    Occupation - Carpenter - September 5, 1859

Thomas Dodd (father):

    Occupation - Farmer

John Harris (father):

Signature:

    Occupation - Farmer

Harris Surname Ireland: 1600s to 1900s

Wedding Witnesses:

John Harris

Signature:

- o Joseph Harris & Esther Thompson – 31 Oct 1859 (Marriage, **St. Peter Parish**)

Signatures:

- ▪ Hannah Harris – b. 30 Nov 1863, bapt. 28 Feb 1864 (Baptism, **St. Peter Parish**)

- ▪ Joseph Harris – b. 31 Mar 1866, bapt. 2 Jul 1866 (Baptism, **St. Peter Parish**), & Anne

  Henry – 17 Jun 1889 (Marriage, **St. George Parish**)

Signatures:

- • Anne Harris – b. 15 Apr 1890, Bapt. 14 May 1890 (Baptism, **St. George Parish**)

Hurst

Joseph Harris (son of Joseph Harris & Esther Thompson):

Residence - 17 Russell Street - June 17, 1889

May 14, 1890

Occupation - Upholsterer - June 17, 1889

May 14, 1890

Anne Henry, daughter of Robert Henry (daughter-in-law):

Residence - Moorland Row Dundalk Coy Louth - June 17, 1889

Robert Henry (father):

Occupation - Farmer

Joseph Harris (father):

Occupation - Butler

Wedding Witnesses:

Hannah Harris

Signature:

Joseph Harris (son of John Harris & Unknown):

Residence - 25 Lower Mount Street - October 31, 1859

7 Turners Cottages Ball's Bridge - February 28, 1864

July 2, 1866

Occupation - Servant - October 31, 1859

Butler - February 28, 1864

July 2, 1866

Esther Thompson, daughter of William Thompson (daughter-in-law):

Residence - 25 Lower Mount Street - October 31, 1859

William Thompson (father):

Occupation - Farmer

John Harris (father):

Occupation - Farmer

Wedding Witnesses:

Bessie Thompson

Signature:

- John Harris & Unknown

    o James Harris & Mary Anne Hogg – 30 Jul 1861 (Marriage, **St. Peter Parish**)

Signatures:

James Harris (son):

    Residence - 9 Haddington Road - July 30, 1861

    Occupation - Plumber - July 30, 1861

Mary Anne Hogg, daughter of Solomon Hogg (daughter-in-law)

    Residence - 7 Merrion Square - July 30, 1861

Solomon Hogg (father):

    Occupation - Tradesman

John Harris (father):

    Occupation - Engine Fitter

Hurst

- John Harris & Unknown

  - Joseph Harris & Jane Edwards – 11 Apr 1863 (Marriage, **St. Paul Parish**)

Signatures:

Joseph Harris (son):

   Residence - Royal Barracks - April 11, 1863

   Occupation - Private in 10th Regiment - April 11, 1863

Jane Edwards, daughter of Thomas Edwards (daughter-in-law):

   Residence - Royal Barracks - April 11, 1863

Thomas Edwards (father):

   Occupation - Miner

John Harris (father):

   Occupation - Boot Closer

- John Harris & Unknown

  - Michael Harris & Mary Dunne – 12 May 1869 (Marriage, **St. Andrew Parish (RC)**)

Michael Harris (son):

   Residence - Brady's Cottages - May 12, 1869

Mary Dunne, daughter of Thomas Dunne (daughter-in-law):

   Residence - 23 George's Quay - May 12, 1869

- John Harris & Unknown

  o John Harris & Sarah Jane Belford – 9 Jan 1872 (Marriage, **St. Mary Parish**)

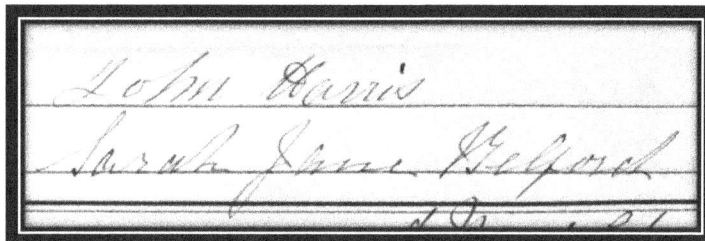

Signatures:

John Harris (son):

  Residence - Aughawant Ballinalee, Co. Longford - January 9, 1872

  Occupation - Farmer - January 9, 1872

Sarah Jane Belford, daughter of John Belford (daughter-in-law):

  Residence - 17 Middle Mountjoy Street - January 9, 1872

  Relationship Status at Marriage - minor age

John Belford (father):

  Occupation - Farmer

John Harris (father):

  Occupation - Farmer

Wedding Witnesses:

Alex Harris & George Arthur Belford

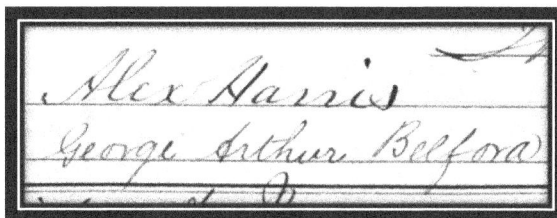

Signatures:

Hurst

- John Harris & Unknown

  - William Harris & Mary Anne Harrison Humphreys – 21 Aug 1872 (Marriage, **St. Anne Parish**)

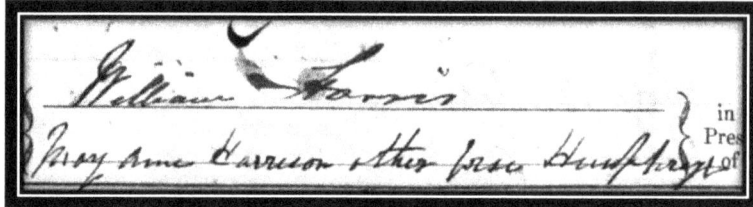

Signatures:

William Harris (son):

    Residence - 40 Wicklow Street - August 2, 1872

                Cork Barracks - August 2, 1872

    Occupation - Sergeant 43rd Regiment - August 2, 1872

Mary Anne Harrison Humphreys, daughter of William Harrison Humphreys (daughter-in-law):

    Residence - 40 Wicklow Street - August 21, 1872

William Harrison Humphreys (father):

    Occupation - Glover

John Harris (father):

    Occupation - Commercial Traveller

Wedding Witnesses:

Elizabeth Humphreys

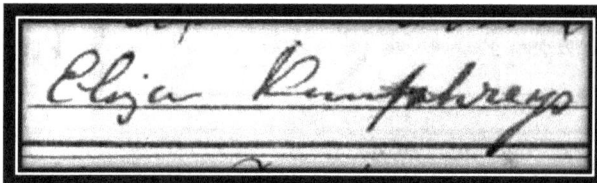

Signature:

- John Harris & Unknown

  o James Harris & Esther Sarah Gibson – 12 Aug 1873 (Marriage, Clontarf Parish)

Signatures:

James Harris (son):

    Residence - 34 Palace Garden Terrace Kensington London - August 12, 1873

    Occupation - Public Accountant - August 12, 1873

Esther Sarah Gibson, daughter of H. James Gibson (daughter-in-law):

    Residence - Amardun Castle Avenue Clontarf - August 12, 1873

    Relationship Status at Marriage - minor age

H. James Gibson (father):

    Occupation - Esquire

John Harris (father):

    Occupation - Esquire

Wedding Witnesses:

Henry Gibson

Signature:

- John Harris & Unknown

  - Elizabeth Frances Harris & George Edward Kendrick – 10 Sep 1874 (Marriage, **St. Peter Parish**)

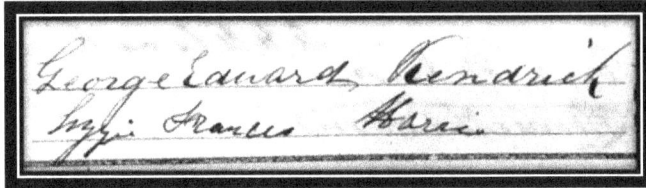

Signatures:

Elizabeth Frances Harris (daughter):

    Residence - 6 Hume Street - September 10, 1874

George Edward Kendrick, son of Samuel Kendrick (son-in-law):

    Residence - 103 Seville Place - September 10, 1874

    Occupation - Custom House Officer - September 10, 1874

Samuel Kendrick (father):

    Occupation - Farmer

John Harris (father):

    Occupation - Tailor

- John Harris & Unknown

  - Patrick Harris & Mary Moore – 20 Feb 1879 (Marriage, **St. James Parish** (RC))

Patrick Harris (son):

    Residence - 103 Thomas Street - February 20, 1879

Mary Moore, daughter of John Moore (daughter-in-law):

    Residence - 118 James Street - February 20, 1879

- John Harris & Unknown

  - Elizabeth Harris & Thomas Kearney (K e a r n e y) – 12 Sep 1880 (Marriage, **St. Andrew Parish** (RC))

Thomas Kearney, son of James Kearney (son-in-law).

Harris Surname Ireland: 1600s to 1900s

- John Harris & Unknown

  o Lawrence Harris & Bridget Molloy – 16 May 1881 (Marriage, **St. Andrew Parish** (RC))

    ▪ Lawrence Harris – b. 1882, bapt. 1882 (Baptism, **St. Andrew Parish** (RC))

    ▪ Mary Harris – b. 1884, bapt. 1884 (Baptism, **St. Andrew Parish** (RC))

    ▪ George Harris – b. 1888, bapt. 1888 (Baptism, **St. Andrew Parish** (RC))

Lawrence Harris (son):

Residence - 47 Townsend Street - May 16, 1881

McGuinness's Place - 1882

13 Tooles Court - 1884

35 South Gloucester Street - 1888

Bridget Molloy, daughter of Peter Molloy (daughter-in-law):

Residence - 5 McGuinness Place - May 16, 1881

- John Harris & Unknown

  o Timothy Harris & Mary Fowler – 29 Aug 1887 (Marriage, **St. Andrew Parish** (RC))

    ▪ Anne Elizabeth Harris – b. 1889, bapt. 1889 (Baptism, **St. Andrew Parish** (RC))

Timothy Harris (son):

Residence - 5 Wentworth Place - August 29, 1887

1889

Mary Fowler, daughter of Matthew Fowler (daughter-in-law):

Residence - 5 Wentworth Place - August 29, 1887

Hurst

- John Harris & Unknown

  - John Harris & Margaret Cooke – 21 Nov 1887 (Marriage, **St. Peter Parish**)

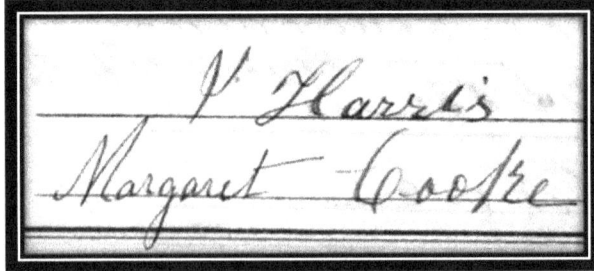

Signatures:

- Robert John Harris – b. 30 Jul 1887, bapt. 15 Dec 1887 (Baptism, **St. Peter Parish**)

John Harris (son):

Residence - Portobello Barracks - November 21, 1887

December 15, 1887

Occupation - Gunner Royal Horse Artillery - November 21, 1887

December 15, 1887

Margaret Cooke, daughter of Robert Cooke (daughter-in-law):

Residence - 13 Digges Street - November 21, 1887

Robert Cooke (father):

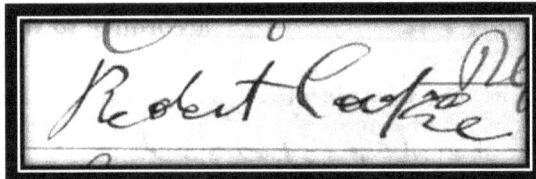

Signature:

Occupation - Gardener

John Harris (father):

Occupation - Laborer

Wedding Witnesses:

Robert Cooke

Signature:

- John Harris & Unknown

  o   Jane Harris & William McKeane – 21 Mar 1892 (Marriage, **St. Luke Parish**)

Signatures:

Jane Harris (daughter):

   Residence - 15 Belview Thomas Street - March 21, 1892

William McKeane, son of James McKeane (son-in-law):

   Residence - 50 Swift's Square Back Lane - March 21, 1892

   Occupation - Groom - March 21, 1892

James McKeane (father):

   Occupation - Laborer

John Harris (father):

   Occupation - Farmer

Hurst

- John Harris & Unknown

  - Esther Harris & John Meade – 12 Nov 1892 (Marriage, **Lucan Parish** (RC))

    - Mary Helen Meade – b. 1893, bapt. 1893 (Baptism, **Lucan Parish** (RC))

    - John Meade – b. 1895, bapt. 1895 (Baptism, **Lucan Parish** (RC))

Esther Harris (daughter):

    Residence - Mount Joseph - November 12, 1892

John Meade, son of Robert Meade (son-in-law):

    Residence - Grange - 1893

            12th Lock - 1895

  - John Harris & Jane Gannon – 1 Feb 1893 (Marriage, **Lucan Parish** (RC))

    - Mary Elizabeth Harris – b. 1894, bapt. 1894 (Baptism, **Lucan Parish** (RC))

    - Kathleen Mary Gannon Harris – b. 1896, bapt. 1896 (Baptism, **Lucan Parish** (RC))

    - Anastasia Monol Harris – b. 1899, bapt. 1899 (Baptism, **Lucan Parish** (RC))

John Harris (son):

    Residence - Mount Joseph - February 1, 1893

           Old Spa Lucan - 1894

               1896

               1899

Jane Gannon, daughter of Lawrence Gannon (daughter-in-law):

    Residence - Lucan - February 1, 1893

- John Harris & Unknown

Signatures:

- o Anne Harris & William Mitchell Matthews – 14 Oct 1896 (Marriage, **St. Thomas Parish**)

Signatures:

Anne Harris (daughter):

    Residence - 17 Talbot Street City of Dublin - October 14, 1896

William Mitchell Matthews, son of Henry Matthews (son-in-law):

    Residence - 10 Frankfort Place Upper Rathmines Dublin - October 14, 1896

    Occupation - Clerk (Bank) - October 14, 1896

Henry Matthews (father):

    Occupation - Cloth Manufacturer

John Harris (father):

Signature:

    Occupation - Merchant Tailor

Hurst

Wedding Witnesses:

W. J. Harris

Signature:

- o William James Harris & Frances Georgina Ball – 4 Nov 1896 (Marriage, **St. Thomas**

  Parish)

Signature:

Signatures (Marriage):

- ▪ John Charles Harris – b. 9 Nov 1898, bapt. 8 Dec 1898 (Baptism, **St. Thomas Parish**)

William James Harris (son):

  Residence - 17 Talbot Street Dublin - November 4, 1896

  December 8, 1898

  Occupation - Merchant Tailor - November 4, 1896

  December 8, 1898

Harris Surname Ireland: 1600s to 1900s

Frances Georgina Ball, daughter of James Charles Ball (daughter-in-law):

Residence - Ellesmere St. Lawrence Road Clontarf - November 4, 1896

James Charles Ball (father):

Signature:

Occupation - Accountant

John Harris (father):

Signature:

Occupation - Merchant Tailor

Wedding Witnesses:

James C. Ball & John Harris

Signatures:

Hurst

- John Edward Harris & Sophia Disney Harris

Signature:

     ○ Mary Ellen Harris & William Jack Jackson – 29 Aug 1871 (Marriage, **St. Thomas Parish**)

Signatures:

Mary Ellen Harris (daughter):

    Residence - 5 Commons Street - August 29, 1871

    Relationship Status at Marriage - minor age

William Jack Jackson, son of John Jackson (son-in-law):

    Residence - 5 Commons Street - August 29, 1871

John Edward Harris (father):

Signature:

    Occupation - Schoolteacher

Harris Surname Ireland: 1600s to 1900s

Wedding Witnesses:

John Edward Harris

Signature:

- Elizabeth Mary Harris – b. 30 Sep 1849, bapt. 7 Oct 1849 (Baptism, **St. Luke Parish**), bur. 17 Oct 1849 (Burial, **St. Luke Parish**)

Elizabeth Mary Harris (daughter):

Residence - School House Coombe - October 17, 1849

Age at Death - 2 weeks

- Sophia Luisea Harris – b. 27 Oct 1850, bapt. 24 Nov 1850 (Baptism, **St. Luke Parish**)

John Edward Harris (father):

Residence - Coombe - October 7, 1849

School House 108 Coombe - November 24, 1850

Occupation - School Master - October 7, 1849

Teacher - November 24, 1850

- John Eyre Harris & Mary Harris

  - Frances Mary Evelyn Harris – b. 31 Mar 1881, bapt. 18 May 1881 (Baptism, **St. George Parish**)

John Eyre Harris (father):

Residence - 11 North Great Georges Street - May 18, 1881

Occupation - House & Land Agent - May 18, 1881

- John H. Harris & Cecelia Dolly

  - Mary Harris – b. 3 Feb 1888, bapt. 5 Feb 1888 (Baptism, **Tralee Parish** (RC))

John H. Harris (father):

Residence - Tralee - February 5, 1888

Hurst

- John H. Harris & Hannah Unknown

  - Catherine Edith Harris – b. 29 Nov 1895, bapt. 25 Dec 1895 (Baptism, **St. Kevin Parish**)

  - Dorothy Violet Harris – b. 6 Jun 1897, bapt. 4 Jul 1897 (Baptism, **St. Kevin Parish**)

John H. Harris (father):

Residence - 42 South Circular Road - December 25, 1895

July 4, 1897

Occupation - Commercial Traveller - December 25, 1895

July 4, 1897

- John Fitzharris & Mary Doyle

  - Catherine Fitzharris – b. 1872, bapt. 1872 (Baptism, **St. Andrew Parish (RC)**)

John Fitzharris (father):

Residence - Boyne Street - 1872

- Jonathan Harris & Ruth Unknown

  - Mary Harris – bapt. 28 Dec 1697 (Baptism, **St. Peter Parish**)

Jonathan Harris (father):

Residence - Butter Lane - December 28, 1697

- Jonathan Harris & Sarah Harris

  - William Harris – bapt. 15 Feb 1807 (Baptism, **St. Werburgh Parish**)

Jonathan Harris (father):

Residence - Werburgh Street - February 15, 1807

- Jonathon Harris & Mary Unknown

  - Philip Harris – bapt. 4 May 1701 (Baptism, **St. Nicholas Without Parish**)

Jonathon Harris (father):

Residence - Theakers Alley near Nicholas Gate - May 4, 1701

Harris Surname Ireland: 1600s to 1900s

- Jonathon Harris & Sarah Unknown

  o William Harris – bapt. 10 Apr 1803 (Baptism, **St. Catherine Parish**)

  o Richard Harris – b. 1805, bapt. 9 Jun 1805 (Baptism, **St. Catherine Parish**)

Jonathan Harris (father):

Residence - Cork Street - April 10, 1803

June 9, 1805

- Joseph Harris & Anne Unknown

  o Joseph Harris & Margaret Dwyer – 2 Feb 1873 (Marriage, **St. Michan Parish (RC)**)

    ▪ Mary Anne Harris, b. 6 Mar 1875, bapt. 15 Mar 1875 (Baptism, **St. Michan Parish (RC)**)

      & Joseph Ronan – 1 Apr 1894 (Marriage, **St. Mary, Pro Cathedral Parish (RC)**)

Mary Anne Harris (daughter):

Residence - 37 North Strand Street - April 1, 1894

Joseph Ronan, son of George Ronan & Mary O'Brien (son-in-law):

Residence - 35 Bride Street - April 1, 1894

    ▪ Edward Harris – b. 24 Oct 1880, bapt. 3 Nov 1880 (Baptism, **St. Mary, Pro Cathedral Parish (RC)**)

    ▪ Joseph Harris – b. 10 Jan 1883, bapt. 17 Jan 1883 (Baptism, **St. Michan Parish (RC)**)

Joseph Harris (father):

Residence - 19 Charles Street - February 2, 1873

March 15, 1875

34 Little Strand Street - November 3, 1880

5 Ormond Place - January 17, 1883

Margaret Dwyer, daughter of John Dwyer & Mary Unknown (daughter-in-law):

Residence - 19 Charles Street - February 2, 1873

Hurst

- Joseph Harris & Bridget Tully

  o Patrick Joseph Harris – b. 1 Mar 1884, bapt. 12 Mar 1884 (Baptism, **St. Michan Parish**

    (RC))

  o Mary Harris – b. 8 Jun 1885, bapt. 15 Jun 1885 (Baptism, **St. Michan Parish** (RC))

Joseph Harris (father):

Residence - 40 Upper Church Street - March 12, 1884

31 Mary's Lane - June 15, 1885

- Joseph Harris & Catherine Richardson

  o Joseph Harris – b. 4 Oct 1822, bapt. 21 Oct 1822 (Baptism, **St. Catherine Parish** (RC))

- Joseph Harris & Catherine Agnes Normine (N o r m i n e)

  o Albert Edward Harris – b. 28 Aug 1881, bapt. 23 Oct 1881 (Baptism, **St. James Parish**

    (RC))

Joseph Harris (father):

Residence - Island Bridge Barracks - October 23, 1881

- Joseph Harris & Catherine Ellen Driscol

  o Joseph Harris – bapt. 15 Dec 1816 (Baptism, **Skibbereen (Creagh & Sullon) Parish**

    (RC))

  o Catherine Harris – bapt. 2 Jul 1820 (Baptism, **Skibbereen (Creagh & Sullon) Parish**

    (RC))

Joseph Harris (father):

Residence - Battimore - December 15, 1816

July 2, 1820

- Joseph Harris & Eleanor Byrne (B y r n e) – 17 Nov 1751 (Marriage, **St. Andrew Parish**)

Harris Surname Ireland: 1600s to 1900s

- Joseph Harris & Elizabeth Harris

  o Margaret Harris & George Quigley – 16 Nov 1860 (Marriage, **St. Mary, Pro Cathedral Parish (RC)**)

Margaret Harris (daughter):

    Residence - 109 Summerhill - November 16, 1860

George Quigley, son of Gulielmo Quigley & Rose Unknown (son-in-law):

    Residence - Black-Horse Lane - November 16, 1860

- Joseph Harris & Elizabeth Unknown

  o Thomas Harris & Bridget Lynam – 1 Oct 1871 (Marriage, **St. Michan Parish (RC)**)

Thomas Harris (son):

    Residence - 14 Usher's Quay - October 1, 1871

Bridget Lynam, daughter of Bartholomew Lynam & Margaret Unknown (daughter-in-law):

    Residence - 39 Beresford Street - October 1, 1871

- Joseph Harris & Elizabeth Unknown

  o Elizabeth Harris & John Byrne (B y r n e) – 4 May 1873 (Marriage, **St. Michan Parish (RC)**)

    ▪ Catherine Byrne – b. 6 Jan 1878, bapt. 9 Jan 1878 (Baptism, **St. Michan Parish (RC)**)

Elizabeth Harris (daughter):

    Residence - 4 Catherine Villa Canal - May 4, 1873

John Byrne, son of John Byrne & Catherine Unknown (son-in-law):

    Residence - Swords Pickerstown - May 4, 1873

        18 Phibsborough Road - January 9, 1878

  o Mary Harris & Michael Joseph Wade – 11 May 1873 (Marriage, **St. Michan Parish (RC)**)

Mary Harris (daughter):

    Residence - 4 Catherine Villa Canal - May 11, 1873

Michael Joseph Wade, son of Daniel Wade & Anne Unknown (son-in-law):

    Residence - 4 Monks Cottages Sheriff Street - May 11, 1873

Hurst

- Joseph Harris & Elizabeth Unknown

  - Margaret Harris & Arthur Haden – 18 Oct 1891 (Marriage, **St. Mary, Haddington Road Parish** (RC))

Margaret Harris (daughter):

  Residence - 5 St Mary's Road - October 18, 1891

Arthur Haden, son of John Haden & Mary Unknown (son-in-law):

  Residence - Lancaster - October 18, 1891

- Joseph Harris & Hannah Waynhurst – 25 May 1658 (Marriage, **St. Michael Parish**)

- Joseph Harris & Hester Harris

  - Joseph Richard Harris – b. 27 Jul 1861, bapt. 19 Mar 1862 (Baptism, **St. Peter Parish**)

Joseph Harris (father):

  Residence - 25 Grattan Court - March 19, 1862

  Occupation - Servant - March 19, 1862

- Joseph Harris & Joan Hut

  - Ellen Harris – bapt. 7 Mar 1810 (Baptism, **Bandon Parish** (RC))

- Joseph Harris & Julia Farrell – 25 Oct 1841 (Marriage, **Palmerstown Parish** (RC))

  - Michael Harris – bapt. 1842 (Baptism, **Palmerstown Parish** (RC))

  - Bernard Harris – bapt. 1844 (Baptism, **Palmerstown Parish** (RC))

  - William Patrick Harris – bapt. 19 Mar 1851 (Baptism, **St. Michan Parish** (RC))

  - John Harris – bapt. 3 Nov 1853 (Baptism, **SS. Michael & John Parish** (RC))

  - Catherine Harris – b. 27 Jul 1856, bapt. 1 Aug 1856 (Baptism, **SS. Michael & John Parish** (RC))

  - John Harris – b. 8 Mar 1858, bapt. 16 Mar 1858 (Baptism, **SS. Michael & John Parish** (RC))

  - Andrew Harris – b. 16 May 1860, bapt. 22 May 1860 (Baptism, **SS. Michael & John Parish** (RC))

Harris Surname Ireland: 1600s to 1900s

- o Patrick Harris – b. 8 Mar 1862, bapt. 18 Mar 1862 (Baptism, **SS. Michael & John Parish** (RC))

Joseph Harris (father):

Residence - 11 Cooke Street - August 1, 1856

March 16, 1858

May 22, 1860

March 18, 1862

- Joseph Harris & Margaret Unknown

  - o Mary Harris – b. 25 Aug 1828, bapt. 31 Aug 1828 (Baptism, **St. Peter Parish**)

Joseph Harris (father):

Residence - 10 Lower Kevin Street - August 31, 1828

- Joseph Harris & Mary Doyle

  - o Elizabeth Sarah Harris – b. 1902, bapt. 1902 (Baptism, **St. Andrew Parish** (RC))

Joseph Harris (father):

Residence - 11 Holles Street - 1902

- Joseph Harris & Mary Hanlon

  - o Teresa Harris – b. 3 Mar 1855, bapt. 7 Mar 1855 (Baptism, **St. Mary, Pro Cathedral Parish** (RC))

Joseph Harris (father):

Residence - 8 Liffey Street - March 7, 1855

- Joseph Harris & Mary Unknown

  - o Ellen Harris & Thomas McCarthy – 4 Nov 1860 (Marriage, **St. Nicholas Parish** (RC))

Ellen Harris (daughter):

Residence - 10 Peter's Row - November 4, 1860

Thomas McCarthy, son of Michael McCarthy & Bridget Unknown (son-in-law):

Residence - Beggars Bush Barracks - November 4, 1860

- Joseph Harris & Sarah Ellis – 9 Oct 1693 (Marriage, **St. Bride Parish**)

Hurst

- Joseph Harris & Sarah Unknown

  o Mary Harris – bapt. 14 Sep 1707 (Baptism, **St. Werburgh Parish**)

  o Peter Harris – bapt. 11 Dec 1711 (Baptism, **St. Werburgh Parish**)

Joseph Harris (father):

Residence - Copper Alley - September 14, 1707

December 11, 1711

- Joseph Harris & Unknown

  o Anne Harris – bapt. 6 Feb 1699 (Baptism, **St. Catherine Parish**)

- Joseph Harris & Unknown

  o John Harris & Mary Anne Wade – 15 Jan 1856 (Marriage, **St. Bride Parish**)

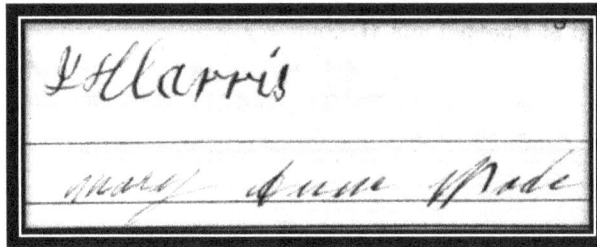

Signatures:

John Harris (son):

Residence - Ship Street Barracks - January 15, 1856

Occupation - Bugle Major South Mays Militia - January 15, 1856

Mary Anne Wade, daughter of George Wade (daughter-in-law):

Residence - 10 Harcourt Street - January 15, 1856

Occupation - Housekeeper - January 15, 1856

George Wade (father):

Occupation - Mechanic

Joseph Harris (father):

Occupation - Mechanic

Harris Surname Ireland: 1600s to 1900s

- Joseph Harris & Unknown

    o   Thomas Harris & Elizabeth Williams – 19 Jul 1861 (Marriage, **St. Mark Parish**)

Signatures:

Thomas Harris (son):

   Residence - 1 Molesworth Place, St Anne Parish - July 19, 1861

   Occupation - Servant - July 19, 1861

Elizabeth Williams, daughter of William Williams (daughter-in-law):

   Residence - 43 Dengille Street, St Mark Parish - July 19, 1861

William Williams (father):

   Occupation - Stone Mason

Joseph Harris (father):

   Occupation - Farm Bailiff

- Joseph Harris & Unknown

    o   Kathleen Harris & John Jones – 10 Jun 1869 (Marriage, **St. Thomas Parish**)

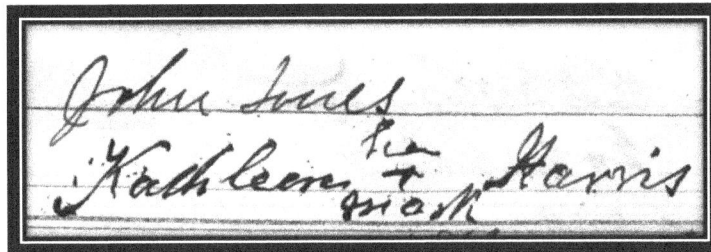

Signatures:

Kathleen Harris (daughter):

   Residence - Summer House Chapelizod Cobra Co Dublin - June 10, 1869

Hurst

John Jones, son of Henry Jones (son-in-law):

    Residence - Aldboro Barrack - June 10, 1869

    Occupation - Soldier - June 10, 1869

Henry Jones (father):

    Occupation - Factory

Joseph Harris (father):

    Occupation - Farmer

- Joseph Harris & Unknown

  - Samuel Musgrave Harris & Anne Heron – 29 Nov 1869 (Marriage, **St. Stephen Parish**)

Signatures:

    ▪ Ethel Musgrave Harris – b. 21 Jul 1870, bapt. 9 Nov 1870 (Baptism, **Rathmines Parish**)

    ▪ Arthur Rupert Harris – b. 16 Oct 1884, bapt. 24 Dec 1884 (Baptism, **Rathmines Parish**)

Samuel Musgrave Harris (son):

    Residence - 50A Leinster Road Rathmines - November 29, 1869

                2 Westway Terrace Brighton Road - November 9, 1870

                23 Leinster Road - December 24, 1884

    Occupation - Clerk in Holy Orders - November 29, 1869

                              November 9, 1870

                              December 24, 1884

Anne Heron, daughter of William Heron (daughter-in-law):

    Residence - 34 Upper Baggot Street - November 29, 1869

William Heron (father):

    Occupation - Surgeon

Joseph Harris (father):

    Occupation - Esquire

Harris Surname Ireland: 1600s to 1900s

- ○ Stewart Hall Harris & Martha Grant – 5 Apr 1870 (Marriage, **St. Peter Parish**)

Signatures:

Stewart Hall Harris (son):

    Residence - 98 Kingsland Park - April 5, 1870

    Occupation - Surgeon - April 5, 1870

Martha Grant, daughter of Robert Grant (daughter-in-law):

    Residence - 98 Kingsland Park - April 5, 1870

Robert Grant (father):

    Occupation - Surgeon

Joseph Harris (father):

    Occupation - Esquire

- • Joseph Dominick Harris & Mary Elizabeth Telford – 10 May 1852 (Marriage, **St. Mary, Pro Cathedral Parish (RC)**)

  - ○ Samuel Harris – b. 9 Dec 1854, bapt. 27 Dec 1854 (Baptism, **St. Mary, Pro Cathedral Parish (RC)**)

  - ○ Gulielmo Patrick Harris – b. 13 Apr 1857, bapt. 4 May 1857 (Baptism, **St. Mary, Pro Cathedral Parish (RC)**)

  - ○ Deborah Bridget Harris – b. 3 May 1859, bapt. 21 May 1859 (Baptism, **St. Mary, Pro Cathedral Parish (RC)**)

Hurst

- o Mary Elizabeth Harris – b. 20 Jan 1862, bapt. 24 Jan 1862 (Baptism, **St. Mary, Pro Cathedral Parish** (RC)) & Michael Feeling – 12 Sep 1870 (Marriage, **St. Mary, Pro Cathedral Parish** (RC))

  - ▪ Mary Elizabeth Feeling – b. 13 Aug 1871, bapt. 16 Aug 1871 (Baptism, **St. Mary, Pro Cathedral Parish** (RC))

Mary Elizabeth Harris (daughter):
  Residence - 150 Upper Abbey Street - September 12, 1870
Michael Feeling, son of Thomas Feeling & Catherine Unknown (son-in-law):
  Residence - 18 Abbey Street - September 12, 1870
          18 Upper Abbey Street - August 16, 1871

- o Agnes Harris – b. 20 Jan 1864, bapt. 22 Jan 1864 (Baptism, **St. Mary, Pro Cathedral Parish** (RC))

- o Teresa Emerentia Harris – b. 23 Jan 1868, bapt. 3 Feb 1868 (Baptism, **St. Mary, Pro Cathedral Parish** (RC))

- o John Joseph Harris – b. 20 Jan 1870, bapt. 16 Feb 1870 (Baptism, **St. Mary, Pro Cathedral Parish** (RC))

- o Monica Rebecca Harris – b. 8 May 1871, bapt. 8 May 1871 (Baptism, **St. Mary, Pro Cathedral Parish** (RC))

- o Thomas D. Harris, b. 20 Aug 1873, bapt. 29 Aug 1873 (Baptism, **St. Mary, Pro Cathedral Parish** (RC)) & Mary Smith – 14 Sep 1902 (Marriage, **St. Mary, Pro Cathedral Parish** (RC))

Thomas Harris (son):
  Residence - 50 Bryton Street Liverpool - September 14, 1902
Mary Smith, daughter of John Smith & Bridget Clarke (daughter-in-law):
  Residence - 56 Mary Street - September 14, 1902

Harris Surname Ireland: 1600s to 1900s

Joseph Dominick Harris (father):

Residence -143 Abbey Street - February 16, 1870

145 Abbey Street - December 27, 1854

146 Abbey Street - May 21, 1859

150 Upper Abbey Street - May 4, 1857

February 3, 1868

14 Lower Abbey Street - August 29, 1873

Abbey Street - January 24, 1862

January 22, 1864

660 Abbey Street - May 5, 1871

- Joseph Edward Harris & Elizabeth Rock – 21 Apr 1829 (Marriage, St. George Parish)

Signatures:

- o Caroline Elizabeth Harris – b. 21 Mar 1830, bapt. 18 Apr 1830 (Baptism, St. George Parish)

- o Frances Harris – b. 14 Sep 1831, bapt. 7 Oct 1831 (Baptism, St. George Parish)

- o William Harris – b. 1 May 1833, bapt. 5 Jun 1833 (Baptism, St. George Parish)

- o Frederick Harris – bapt. 26 Apr 1835 (Baptism, St. Mary Parish)

- o Joseph Harris – bapt. 19 Feb 1837 (Baptism, St. Mary Parish)

Hurst

- ○ Stewart Harris – b. 10 Jul 1839, bapt. 23 Aug 1839 (Baptism, **St. George Parish**), & Mary

    Fulham Rogers – 20 Mar 1861 (Marriage, **St. Thomas Parish**)

Signatures:

Stewart Harris (son):

    Residence - Poller's Alley - March 20, 1861

    Occupation - Coachmaker - March 20, 1861

Mary Fulham, daughter of Patrick Fulham (daughter-in-law):

    Residence - 2 Poller's Alley - March 20, 1861

    Relationship Status at Marriage - widow

Patrick Fulham (father):

    Occupation - Painter

Joseph Edward Harris (father):

    Occupation - Clerk

- ○ Charles Harris – b. 6 Aug 1841, bapt. 6 Aug 1841 (Baptism, **St. George Parish**)

Joseph Harris (father):

    Residence - Great Britain Street - April 21, 1829

        No 11 Daniel Place - April 18, 1830

            October 7, 1831

        No 1 Portland Place - June 5, 1833

          6 Wellington Place - April 26, 1835

            February 19, 1837

        No 3 Villa Bank - August 23, 1839

            August 6, 1841

Occupation - Gentleman - April 21, 1829

April 18, 1830

October 7, 1831

June 5, 1833

February 19, 1837

August 23, 1839

August 6, 1841

Clerk - April 26, 1835

Elizabeth Rock (mother):

Residence - St. George Parish - April 21, 1829

- Joseph Edward Harris & Unknown

  o Anne Harris Cremer & Arthur Carroll, b. 1853 – 1 Feb 1873 (Marriage, **St. Peter Parish**)

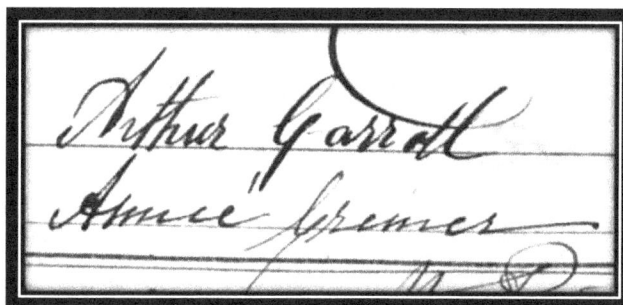

Signatures:

Anne Harris (daughter):

Residence - Gardra terrace - February 1, 1873

Relationship Status at Marriage - widow

Arthur Carroll, son of W. H. Carroll (son-in-law):

Residence - 34 Upper Clanbrassil Street - February 1, 1873

Occupation - Esquire - February 1, 1873

W. H. Carroll (father):

Occupation - Solicitor

Joseph Edward Harris (father):

Occupation - Solicitor

Hurst

- Josh Harris & Catherine Unknown

  - Anne Harris – bapt. 30 Apr 1794 (Baptism, **St. Catherine Parish**)

Josh Harris (father):

  Residence - Marrowbone Lane - April 30, 1794

- Josh Harris & Elizabeth Harris

  - William Harris – bapt. Unknown (Baptism, **St. Catherine Parish**)

Josh Harris (father):

  Residence - Vicar Street

- Josh Harris & Ruth Unknown

  - Henry Harris – bapt. 13 Aug 1775 (Baptism, **St. Catherine Parish**)

  - Mary Harris – bapt. 16 Nov 1777 (Baptism, **St. Catherine Parish**)

Josh Harris (father):

  Residence - Skinner's Alley - August 13, 1775

    Elbow Lane - November 16, 1777

- Josiah Rees Harris & Unknown

  - David Harris & Mary Anne Jennett – 13 Apr 1863 (Marriage, **St. Paul Parish**)

Signatures:

David Harris (son):

  Residence - Arbour Hill Barracks - April 13, 1863

  Occupation - Corporal Military Train Arbour Hill - April 13, 1863

Harris Surname Ireland: 1600s to 1900s

Mary Anne Jennett, daughter of Thomas Jennett (daughter-in-law):

Residence - 6 Temple Street West - April 13, 1863

Relationship Status at Marriage - under age

Thomas Jennett (father):

Occupation - Carrier

Josiah Rees Harris (father):

Occupation - Tailor

- J. S. Harris & Bridget Leary

  o J. S. Harris – bapt. 27 Nov 1856 (Baptism, **Clonakilty Parish** (RC))

- Lawrence Harris & Elizabeth Kavanagh

  o John Harris – b. 1886, bapt. 1886 (Baptism, **St. Andrew Parish** (RC))

Lawrence Harris (father):

Residence - Moors Street - 1886

- Lawrence Harris & Elizabeth Unknown

  o Thomas William Harris – b. 1889, bapt. 1889 (Baptism, **Royal Hibernian Parish**)

Lawrence Harris (father):

Occupation - SERGT R. H. M. S. - 1889

- Lawrence Harris & Julia Gonan

  o Bridget Harris & John Brady – 24 May 1875 (Marriage, **St. Mary, Pro Cathedral Parish** (RC))

Bridget Harris (daughter):

Residence - 28 Mabbot Street - May 24, 1875

John Brady, son of Patrick Brady & Mary Unknown (son-in-law):

Residence - 28 Mabbot Street - May 24, 1875

Hurst

- Lawrence John Harris & Mary Harris

  o Catherine Harris – bapt. 10 Jun 1849 (Baptism, **Skibbereen (Creagh & Sullon) Parish (RC)**)

  o John Harris – bapt. 10 Jun 1849 (Baptism, **Skibbereen (Creagh & Sullon) Parish (RC)**)

- Leonard Harris & Anne Unknown

  o Mary Harris – bapt. 16 Feb 1766 (Baptism, **St. Catherine Parish**)

  o Elizabeth Harris – bapt. 22 Nov 1767 (Baptism, **St. Catherine Parish**)

Leonard Harris (father):

Residence - Marrowbone Lane - February 16, 1766

November 22, 1767

- Lovet Harris & Julia O'Donohue – 27 Jul 1775 (Marriage, **Tralee Parish (RC)**)

Lovet Harris (husband):

Residence - Tralee - July 27, 1775

- Lovet Harris & Mary Connor

  o Sarah Harris – b. 25 Apr 1774, bapt. 25 Apr 1774 (Baptism, **Tralee Parish (RC)**)

Lovet Harris (father):

Residence - Derrymore Annac - April 25, 1774

- Luke Fitzharris & Catherine Woods – 25 Jul 1841 (Marriage, **SS. Michael & John Parish (RC)**)

- Luke Harris & Diana Harris

  o John Harris – bapt. 26 May 1776 (Baptism, **St. Mark Parish**)

Luke Harris (father):

Residence - City Quay - May 26, 1776

- Marry Harris & Mary Callaghan

  o Catherine Harris – bapt. 6 Apr 1847 (Baptism, **Douglas Parish (RC)**)

Marry Harris (father):

Residence - Ballygarvan - April 6, 1847

The father's name is hard to read in the Baptismal Register, it could be Henry.

Harris Surname Ireland: 1600s to 1900s

- Matthew Harris & Anne Unknown

  - Elizabeth Harris – b. 9 Jun 1834, bapt. 15 Jun 1834 (Baptism, **Ballymacelligott & Ballyseedy Parish**)

- Matthew Harris & Eleanor Unknown

  - Thomas Harris – bapt. 1765 (Baptism, **St. Andrew Parish** (RC))

- Matthew Harris & Honora Barrett – 1 Aug 1826 (Marriage, **St. James Parish**) (Marriage, **St. Paul Parish**)

Matthew Harris (husband):

Residence - St. James Parish - 1826

Honora Barrett (wife):

Residence - St. James Parish - 1826

- Matthew Harris & Margaret Unknown

  - James Harris – bapt. 5 Oct 1704 (Baptism, **St. Catherine Parish**)

- Maurice Harris & Esther Unknown

  - Harriet Harris – b. 1855, bapt. 1855 (Baptism, **St. Andrew Parish** (RC))

- Maurice Harris & Kathleen Hynes

  - Kathleen Harris – b. 11 Sep 1892, bapt. 12 Sep 1892 (Baptism, **Rathmines Parish** (RC))

Maurice Harris (father):

Residence - 152 Leinster Road - September 12, 1892

- Michael Harris & Anne Mulligan

  - Joseph Harris & Anne Trarney (T r a r n e y) – 2 Aug 1893 (Marriage, **St. Mary, Pro Cathedral Parish** (RC))

Joseph Harris (son):

Residence - Cloncurry - August 2, 1893

Anne Trarney, daughter of Thomas Trarney & Mary Mooney (daughter-in-law):

Residence - Downings - August 2, 1893

Hurst

- Michael Harris & Anne Murphy – 13 Feb 1866 (Marriage, **Kilmichael Parish** (RC))

  o Mary Harris – bapt. 20 Nov 1866 (Baptism, **Kilmichael Parish** (RC))

  o Honora Harris – bapt. 7 May 1868 (Baptism, **Kilmichael Parish** (RC))

  o Ellen Harris – bapt. 28 Apr 1870 (Baptism, **Kilmichael Parish** (RC))

  o John Harris – bapt. 25 Oct 1871 (Baptism, **Kilmichael Parish** (RC))

Michael Harris (father):

Residence - Clashbredane - November 20, 1866

May 7, 1868

April 28, 1870

October 25, 1871

- Michael Harris & Anne Slattery – 7 Feb 1844 (Marriage, **SS. Michael & John Parish** (RC))

- Michael Harris & Anne Unknown

  o John Harris – bapt. 5 Oct 1845 (Baptism, **St. Mary, Pro Cathedral Parish** (RC))

  o Patrick Harris – bapt. 9 Mar 1851 (Baptism, **St. Mary, Pro Cathedral Parish** (RC))

- Michael Harris & Anne Unknown

  o Ellen Harris – b. 1850, bapt. 1850 (Baptism, **St. Andrew Parish** (RC))

- Michael Harris & Bridget Dill

  o Michael Harris – bapt. Jul 1835 (Baptism, **Cork - South Parish** (RC))

- Michael Harris & Bridget Donovan – Aug 1834 (Marriage, **Cork - South Parish** (RC))

- Michael Harris & Catherine Connell

  o Michael Harris – bapt. 13 Feb 1825 (Baptism, **Kinsale Parish** (RC))

- Michael Harris & Catherine Murphy

  o Margaret Harris & Patrick Skelly – 5 May 1901 (Marriage, **St. Mary, Pro Cathedral Parish** (RC))

Harris Surname Ireland: 1600s to 1900s

Margaret Harris (daughter):

> Residence - 222 Great Britain Street - May 5, 1901

Patrick Skelly, son of Thomas Skelly & Margaret Gore (son-in-law):

> Residence - 31 Upper Dorset Street - May 5, 1901

- Michael Harris & Catherine Riordan – 12 Feb 1861 (Marriage, **Ardfert Parish** (RC))

    - Julia Harris, b. 5 Apr 1865, bapt. 9 Apr 1865 (Baptism, **Abbeydorney Parish** (RC)) & Thomas Shaughnessy – 12 Jan 1889 (Marriage, **Abbeydorney Parish** (RC))

        - Margaret Shaughnessy – b. 14 Nov 1889, bapt. 17 Nov 1889 (Baptism, **Ardfert Parish** (RC))

        - Mary Shaughnessy – b. 5 Sep 1891, bapt. 14 Sep 1891 (Baptism, **Ardfert Parish** (RC))

        - Thomas Shaughnessy – b. 8 Jun 1893, bapt. 11 Jun 1893 (Baptism, **Ardfert Parish** (RC))

        - Patrick Shaughnessy – b. 3 May 1895, bapt. 10 May 1895 (Baptism, **Ardfert Parish** (RC))

        - Catherine Shaughnessy – b. 22 Dec 1896, bapt. 27 Dec 1896 (Baptism, **Ardfert Parish** (RC))

        - Michael Shaughnessy – b. 9 Aug 1898, bapt. 14 Aug 1898 (Baptism, **Ardfert Parish** (RC))

Julia Harris (daughter):

> Residence - Ardrahan - January 12, 1889

Thomas Shaughnessy, son of Thomas Shaughnessy & Margaret Regan (son-in-law):

> Residence - Kilmoyley - January 12, 1889
>
> > Baltovin - November 17, 1889
> >
> > > September 14, 1891
> > >
> > > June 11, 1893
> > >
> > > March 10, 1895
> > >
> > > December 27, 1896
> > >
> > > August 14, 1898

Hurst

- o Margaret Harris – b. 24 Apr 1867, bapt. 26 Apr 1867 (Baptism, **Abbeydorney Parish (RC)**) & Patrick Sullivan – 9 Jan 1889 (Marriage, **Abbeydorney Parish** (RC))

  - ▪ Bridget Sullivan – b. 22 Feb 1889, bapt. 24 Feb 1889 (Baptism, **Ardfert Parish** (RC))

  - ▪ Catherine Sullivan – b. 31 Mar 1890, bapt. 6 Apr 1890 (Baptism, **Ardfert Parish** (RC))

Margaret Harris (daughter):

Residence - Ardrahan - January 9, 1889

Patrick Sullivan, son of Patrick Sullivan & Bridget Browne (son-in-law):

Residence - Lerrig - January 9, 1889

Kilcooly - February 24, 1889

April 6, 1890

- o Thomas Harris – b. 28 May 1869, bapt. 30 May 1869 (Baptism, **Abbeydorney Parish** (RC))

- o Mary Harris – b. 25 Mar 1871, bapt. 30 Mar 1871 (Baptism, **Abbeydorney Parish** (RC))

- o Catherine Harris – b. 28 Jul 1873, bapt. 2 Aug 1873 (Baptism, **Abbeydorney Parish** (RC))

- o William Harris – b. 23 Dec 1875, bapt. 2 Jan 1876 (Baptism, **Abbeydorney Parish** (RC))

- o Patrick Harris – b. 25 May 1878, bapt. 28 May 1878 (Baptism, **Abbeydorney Parish** (RC))

- o Bridget Harris – b. 15 Jun 1882, bapt. 25 Jun 1882 (Baptism, **Abbeydorney Parish** (RC))

Michael Harris (father):

Residence - Ardrahan - February 12, 1861

April 9, 1865

April 26, 1867

May 30, 1869

March 30, 1871

August 2, 1873

January 2, 1876

May 28, 1878

Catherine Riordan (mother):

Residence - Ballinprior - February 12, 1861

Harris Surname Ireland: 1600s to 1900s

- Michael Harris & Catherine Woodlock

  o William Harris – b. 11 Apr 1841, bapt. 11 Apr 1841 (Baptism, **Tralee Parish** (RC))

Michael Harris (father):

Residence - Tralee - April 11, 1841

- Michael Harris & Elizabeth Locke – 1 Mar 1832 (Marriage, **St. Nicholas Parish** (RC))

  o John Peter Harris – bapt. 1835 (Baptism, **St. Andrew Parish** (RC))

  o Patrick Harris – bapt. 1836 (Baptism, **St. Andrew Parish** (RC))

  o Walter Harris – bapt. 1838 (Baptism, **St. Andrew Parish** (RC)) & Anne Mahoney – 6 Feb

    1874 (Marriage, **St. Catherine Parish** (RC))

Walter Harris (son):

Residence - 87 Camden Street - February 6, 1874

Anne Mahoney, daughter of Francis Mahoney & Mary Unknown (daughter-in-law):

Residence - 3 New Row - February 6, 1874

  o Lawrence Harris – bapt. 1840 (Baptism, **St. Andrew Parish** (RC))

  o Richard Joseph Harris – bapt. 1841 (Baptism, **St. Andrew Parish** (RC))

- Michael Harris & Ellen McElligott

  o Mary Harris – b. 21 Feb 1861, bapt. 23 Feb 1861 (Baptism, **Dingle Parish** (RC))

  o Thomas Harris & Mary Flaherty – 25 Jan 1885 (Marriage, **Dingle Parish** (RC))

Thomas Harris (son):

Residence - Goat Street - January 25, 1885

Mary Flaherty, daughter of Timothy Flaherty & Joan Griffin (daughter-in-law):

Residence - Middle Street - January 25, 1885

Michael Harris (father):

Residence - Dingle - February 23, 1861

- Michael Harris & Honora Mahony – 25 Nov 1856 (Marriage, **Cork - South Parish** (RC))

Hurst

- Michael Harris & Honora Sullivan

  - Grace Harris – bapt. 22 Mar 1857 (Baptism, **Drimoleague Parish (RC)**)

- Michael Harris & Honora Mary Riordan – 26 Jan 1826 (Marriage, **Kilmichael Parish (RC)**)

  - John Harris – bapt. 27 Dec 1827 (Baptism, **Kilmichael Parish (RC)**)

  - Mary Harris – bapt. 29 Dec 1831 (Baptism, **Kilmichael Parish (RC)**)

  - Owen Eugene Harris, bapt. 4 Dec 1834 (Baptism, **Kilmichael Parish (RC)**), & Ellen Herrick

    – 26 Feb 1867 (Marriage, **Kilmichael Parish (RC)**)

    - Michael Harris – bapt. 2 May 1871 (Baptism, **Kilmichael Parish (RC)**)

    - John Harris – bapt. 1 Mar 1874 (Baptism, **Kilmichael Parish (RC)**)

    - Honora Harris – bapt. 6 May 1876 (Baptism, **Kilmichael Parish (RC)**)

    - Daniel Harris – bapt. 16 Dec 1878 (Baptism, **Kilmichael Parish (RC)**)

Owen Harris (son):

Residence - Baullrack - May 2, 1871

Cooldorragha - March 1, 1874

Moneycusker - May 6, 1876

December 16, 1878

  - Mary Harris – bapt. 9 Sep 1837 (Baptism, **Kilmichael Parish (RC)**)

  - Michael Harris – bapt. 11 Oct 1840 (Baptism, **Kilmichael Parish (RC)**)

  - William Harris – bapt. 22 Jan 1844 (Baptism, **Kilmichael Parish (RC)**)

  - Thomas Harris – bapt. 29 Jun 1846 (Baptism, **Kilmichael Parish (RC)**)

Michael Harris (father):

Residence - Cooldorragha - December 27, 1827

September 9, 1837

October 11, 1840

Carrigboy - January 22, 1844

June 29, 1846

Harris Surname Ireland: 1600s to 1900s

- Michael Harris & Jane Ellen Farrell

  - Mary Jane Harris – b. 8 Oct 1889, bapt. 14 Oct 1889 (Baptism, **St. Mary, Pro Cathedral Parish** (RC))

  - Sarah Catherine Harris – b. 7 Jul 1891, bapt. 17 Jul 1891 (Baptism, **St. Mary, Pro Cathedral Parish** (RC))

  - Edward Joseph Harris – b. 26 Mar 1894, bapt. 2 Apr 1894 (Baptism, **St. Mary, Pro Cathedral Parish** (RC))

Michael Harris (father):

Residence - 30 Lower Gardiner Street - October 14, 1889

154 Britain Street - July 17, 1891

31 Stafford Street - April 2, 1894

- Michael Harris & Joan Mullins

  - Julia Harris – b. 15 Oct 1846, bapt. 15 Oct 1846 (Baptism, **Tralee Parish** (RC))

Michael Harris (father):

Residence - Rathass - October 15, 1846

- Michael Harris & Julia Murphy – 28 Jul 1861 (Marriage, **Cork - South Parish** (RC))

  - Elizabeth Harris – bapt. 13 Jan 1863 (Baptism, **Cork - South Parish** (RC))

  - Mary Bridget Harris – bapt. 3 Oct 1865 (Baptism, **Cork - South Parish** (RC))

  - Jeremiah Harris – b. 4 May 1879, bapt. 5 May 1879 (Baptism, **Cork - South Parish** (RC))

  - Julia Harris – b. 4 May 1879, bapt. 5 May 1879 (Baptism, **Cork - South Parish** (RC))

Michael Harris (father):

Residence - Tower Street - May 5, 1879

- Michael Harris & Margaret Unknown

  - John Harris – bapt. 1835 (Baptism, **St. Andrew Parish** (RC))

Hurst

- Michael Harris & Martha Thunder – 3 Nov 1842 (Marriage, **St. Mary, Pro Cathedral Parish (RC)**)

  - Michael James Harris – b. 27 Jun 1857, bapt. 1 Jul 1857 (Baptism, **St. Mary, Pro Cathedral Parish (RC)**)

  - James Harris – b. 21 Jun 1859, bapt. 24 Jun 1859 (Baptism, **St. Michan Parish (RC)**)

  - Richard Harris – b. 3 Jan 1862, bapt. 13 Jan 1862 (Baptism, **St. Michan Parish (RC)**)

Michael Harris (father):

Residence - 9 Mabbot Street - July 1, 1857

3 Buthlers Court - June 24, 1859

2 Walsh's Row - January 13, 1862

- Michael Harris & Mary Dolane

  - Bridget Harris – b. 7 Aug 1829, bapt. 7 Aug 1829 (Baptism, **Listowel Parish (RC)**)

  - Joan Harris – b. 7 Aug 1829, bapt. 7 Aug 1829 (Baptism, **Listowel Parish (RC)**)

Michael Harris (father):

Residence - Finuge - August 7, 1829

- Michael Harris & Mary Dunne

  - Mary Anne Harris – b. 13 Sep 1870, bapt. 21 Sep 1870 (Baptism, **St. Lawrence Parish (RC)**)

Michael Harris (father):

Residence - 6 Church Place - September 21, 1870

- Michael Harris & Mary Joy

  - Michael Harris – b. 20 May 1831, bapt. 20 May 1831 (Baptism, **Tralee Parish (RC)**)

Michael Harris (father):

Residence - Tralee - May 20, 1831

Harris Surname Ireland: 1600s to 1900s

- Michael Harris & Mary McAuliffe

  ○ Michael Harris – bapt. 9 Jun 1795 (Baptism, **Cork - SS. Peter & Paul Parish** (RC))

  ○ Catherine Harris – bapt. 3 Oct 1796 (Baptism, **Cork - SS. Peter & Paul Parish** (RC))

  ○ Rose Harris – bapt. Nov 1797 (Baptism, **Cork - SS. Peter & Paul Parish** (RC))

Michael Harris (father):

Residence - Castle Street - June 9, 1795

November 1797

- Michael Harris, d. Before 28 Nov 1876, & Mary McCarthy (1st Marriage) – 7 Oct 1854 (Marriage, **Kinsale Parish** (RC))

  ○ Catherine Harris – bapt. 28 Jun 1857 (Baptism, **Kinsale Parish** (RC))

  ○ Richard Harris – bapt. 20 Aug 1858 (Baptism, **Kinsale Parish** (RC))

  ○ Michael Harris – b. 15 Jun 1861, bapt. 16 Jun 1861 (Baptism, **Kinsale Parish** (RC))

  ○ John Harris – b. 7 Jan 1864, bapt. 7 Jan 1864 (Baptism, **Kinsale Parish** (RC))

  ○ Patrick Maurice Harris – b. 18 Mar 1867, bapt. 19 Mar 1867 (Baptism, **Kinsale Parish** (RC))

Michael Harris (father):

Residence - Fisher Street - August 20, 1858

Friar's Street - June 16, 1861

January 7, 1864

March 19, 1867

Mary McCarthy Harris remarried to George Roberts on November 28, 1876.

- Mary McCarthy Harris (2nd Marriage) & George Roberts – 28 Nov 1876 (Marriage, **Kinsale Parish** (RC))

  ○ Mary Anne Roberts – b. 13 Sep 1878, bapt. 13 Sep 1878 (Baptism, **Kinsale Parish** (RC))

George Roberts (father):

Residence - Friar's Street - September 13, 1878

Hurst

- Michael Harris & Mary Noonan

  - Ellen Harris – b. 19 Jan 1841, bapt. 19 Jan 1841 (Baptism, **Listowel Parish** (RC))

Michael Harris (father):

Residence - Islandganniv - January 19, 1841

- Michael Harris & Mary Parker

  - Ellen Harris – bapt. 29 Apr 1811 (Baptism, **Cork - South Parish** (RC))

Michael Harris (father):

Residence - Three Hatchet Lane - April 29, 1811

- Michael Harris & Mary Shea – 1 Feb 1848 (Marriage, **Glenbeigh/Glencar Parish** (RC))

  - John Harris – b. 19 Aug 1849, bapt. 19 Aug 1849 (Baptism, **Glenbeigh/Glencar Parish**

    (RC))

Michael Harris (father):

Residence - Reennanallagane - August 19, 1849

Mary Shea (mother):

Residence - Reennanallagane - February 1, 1848

- Michael Harris & Mary Anne Monks

  - Lawrence Harris – bapt. 1835 (Baptism, **St. Mary, Haddington Road Parish** (RC))

- Michael Harris & Sarah Hawkes

  - John Harris – bapt. 19 Mar 1846 (Baptism, **Kenmare Parish**)

John Harris was an illegitimate son of Michael Harris & Sarah Hawkes.

- Michael Harris & Unknown

  o Elizabeth Harris Gore & John Kennedy – 1 Jul 1845 (Marriage, **St. Peter Parish**)

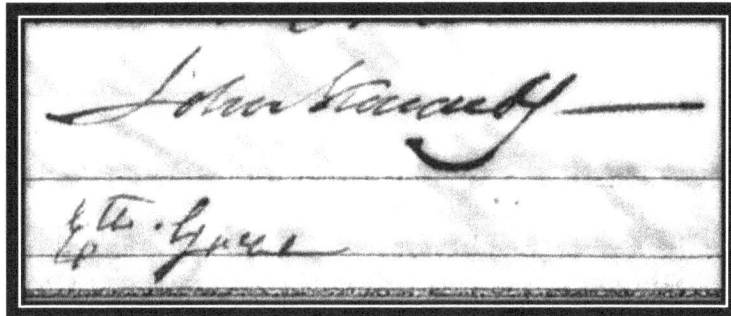

Signatures:

Elizabeth Harris (daughter):

    Residence - Fitzwilliam Square, Dublin - July 1, 1845

    Relationship Status at Marriage - widow

John Kennedy, son of John Kennedy (son-in-law):

    Residence - Sackville Street, Dublin - July 1, 1845

    Occupation - Gentleman - July 1, 1845

    Relationship Status at Marriage - widow

John Kennedy (father):

    Occupation - Gentleman

Michael Harris (father):

    Occupation - Solicitor

- Michael Harris & Unknown

  o Margaret Harris & Miles Kinsella – 19 Jul 1891 (Marriage, **St. Andrew Parish (RC)**)

Margaret Harris (daughter):

    Residence - 32 Glosten Street - July 19, 1891

Miles Kinsella, son of James Kinsella (son-in-law):

    Residence - 122 Townsend Street - July 19, 1891

Hurst

- Michael Harris & Unknown

    - Mary Harris & James Moriarty – 29 Apr 1894 (Marriage, **Tralee Parish** (RC))

        - Margaret Mary Moriarty – b. 21 Mar 1895, bapt. 24 Mar 1895 (Baptism, **Tralee Parish**

            (RC))

        - Helen Moriarty – b. 20 May 1896, bapt. 26 May 1896 (Baptism, **Tralee Parish** (RC))

        - Bridget Moriarty – b. 20 Jan 1899, bapt. 22 Jan 1899 (Baptism, **Tralee Parish** (RC))

Mary Harris (daughter):

  Residence - Tralee - April 29, 1894

James Moriarty, son of Thomas Moriarty (son-in-law):

  Residence - Tralee - April 29, 1894

  Abbey Street - March 24, 1895

  Mary Street - May 26, 1896

  January 22, 1899

- Michael Harris & Unknown

    - Michael Harris & Jane Harnett – 7 Jul 1900 (Marriage, **Abbeydorney Parish** (RC))

Michael Harris (son):

  Residence - Ardrahan - July 7, 1900

Jane Harnett, daughter of Daniel Harnett (daughter-in-law):

  Residence - Ardrahan - July 7, 1900

- Miles Harris & Anne Sullivan

    - Cotte Harris – bapt. 21 Nov 1819 (Baptism, **Courcy's Country or Ballinspittal Parish**

        (RC))

Harris Surname Ireland: 1600s to 1900s

- Morris Harris & Unknown

  o Elizabeth Harris & William Sinclair – 8 Sep 1875 (Marriage, **St. Stephen Parish**)

Signatures:

Elizabeth Harris (daughter):

   Residence - 152 Leinster Road Rathmines - September 8, 1875

William Sinclair, son of John Sinclair (son-in-law):

   Residence - 30 Lower Pembroke Street - September 8, 1875

   Occupation - Esquire - September 8, 1875

John Sinclair (father):

   Occupation - Master House Painter

Morris Harris (father):

   Occupation - Merchant

- Mortimer Harris & Fanny Anne Harris

  o Wintour Mortimer Harris – b. 27 Apr 1856, bapt. 28 May 1856 (Baptism, **St. Peter Parish**)

Mortimer Harris (father):

   Residence - 9 Peter Place - May 28, 1856

   Occupation - Esquire - May 28, 1856

- Nathan Harris & Elizabeth Unknown

  o Einemmol Harris – bapt. 30 Apr 1702 (Baptism, **St. Catherine Parish**)

Hurst

- Nathaniel Harris & Anne Unknown

  o Hugh Harris – bapt. 21 Dec 1806 (Baptism, **St. Werburgh Parish**)

Nathaniel Harris (father):

Residence - High Street - December 21, 1806

- Nathaniel Harris & Eleanor Unknown

  o Elizabeth Harris – bapt. 26 Dec 1743 (Baptism, **St. Nicholas Parish** (RC))

- Nathaniel Harris & Elizabeth Harris

  o Sarah Harris – bur. 22 Nov 1716 (Burial, **St. Luke Parish**)

Sarah Harris (daughter):

Cause of Death - measles

  o Samuel Harris – bur. 25 Nov 1716 (Burial, **St. Luke Parish**)

Samuel Harris (son):

Cause of Death - fever

  o John Harris – bapt. 2 Apr 1723 (Baptism, **St. Luke Parish**)

  o John Harris – bapt. 26 Apr 1724 (Baptism, **St. Luke Parish**)

  o Henry Harris – bapt. 11 Feb 1730 (Baptism, **St. Luke Parish**)

Nathaniel Harris (father):

Residence - Mill Street - November 22, 1716

Truk Street - April 26, 1724

Occupation - Weaver - November 22, 1716

April 2, 1723

April 26, 1724

Harris Surname Ireland: 1600s to 1900s

- Nathaniel Harris & Elizabeth Unknown

    o Thomas Harris – bapt. 29 Mar 1751 (Baptism, **Aghold Parish**)

    o Thomas Harris – bapt. 20 Jun 1753 (Baptism, **Aghold Parish**)

    o Elizabeth Harris – bapt. May 1758 (Baptism, **Aghold Parish**)

    o Margaret Harris – bapt. May 1760 (Baptism, **Aghold Parish**)

    o Mary Harris – bapt. 20 Dec 1762 (Baptism, **Aghold Parish**)

    o Jane Harris – bapt. 18 Aug Unclear (Baptism, **Aghold Parish**)

- Nathaniel Harris & Juliana Donovan

    o Ellen Harris – bapt. 15 Feb 1818 (Baptism, **Lislee, Abbeymahon, & Donoughmore (Barryroe) Parish (RC)**)

Nathaniel Harris (father):
Residence - Grange - February 15, 1818

- Nathaniel Harris & Margaret Curfy – 31 Dec 1741 (Marriage, **St. Andrew Parish**)

- Nathaniel Harris & Mary Unknown

    o William Harris – bapt. 11 Jul 1749 (Baptism, **St. Nicholas Without Parish**)

Nathaniel Harris (father):
Residence - Walker's Alley - July 11, 1749

- Nathaniel Harris & Sarah Pretchard – 18 Sep 1871 (Marriage, **St. Michael Parish**)

- Nicholas Harris & Juliana Rierdon

    o Margaret Harris – bapt. 6 Oct 1786 (Baptism, **Cork - SS. Peter & Paul Parish (RC)**)

    o Anne Harris – bapt. 18 Dec 1787 (Baptism, **Cork - SS. Peter & Paul Parish (RC)**)

Hurst

- Nicholas Harris & Mary Harris

  o John Harris – bapt. 22 May 1707 (Baptism, **St. John Parish**), bur. 29 May 1707 (Burial, **St. John Parish**)

Nicholas Harris (father):

Residence - Fishamble Street - May 22, 1707

- Obidia Harris & Elizabeth Unknown

  o Susan Harris – bapt. 21 Jul 1821 (Baptism, **St. Mary, Pro Cathedral Parish (RC)**)

Obidia Harris (father):

Residence - Thomas Lane - July 21, 1821

- Patrick Harris & Alicia McClean

  o John Harris – bapt. 30 Aug 1800 (Baptism, **St. Michan Parish (RC)**)

- Patrick Harris & Anne Lafferty – 1 Jun 1824 (Marriage, **St. Andrew Parish (RC)**)

  o James Harris – bapt. 1827 (Baptism, **St. Andrew Parish (RC)**)

  o Bridget Harris – bapt. 1829 (Baptism, **St. Andrew Parish (RC)**)

- Patrick Harris & Anne Mahony

  o Teresa Harris – b. 6 Oct 1870, bapt. 9 Oct 1870 (Baptism, **Tarbert Parish (RC)**)

  o Francis Harris – b. 7 Mar 1872, bapt. 10 Mar 1872 (Baptism, **Tarbert Parish (RC)**)

  o Gerald Harris – b. 6 Dec 1873, bapt. 20 Dec 1873 (Baptism, **Tarbert Parish (RC)**)

  o Henrietta Harris – b. 10 Jun 1875, bapt. 11 Jun 1875 (Baptism, **Tarbert Parish (RC)**)

  o Walter Harris – b. 11 Aug 1876, bapt. 3 Sep 1876 (Baptism, **Tarbert Parish (RC)**)

Patrick Harris (father):

Residence - Tarbert Island - October 9, 1870

March 10, 1872

December 20, 1873

June 11, 1875

September 3, 1876

Harris Surname Ireland: 1600s to 1900s

- Patrick Harris & Anne Murphy

  o Mary Harris – bapt. 29 Oct 1780 (Baptism, **St. James Parish (RC)**)

  o Michael Harris – bapt. 29 Oct 1780 (Baptism, **St. James Parish (RC)**)

- Patrick Harris & Anne Neill

  o Julia Harris – b. 11 May 1868, bapt. 30 May 1868 (Baptism, **Ardfert Parish (RC)**)

Patrick Harris (father):

Residence - Ballinprior - May 30, 1868

- Patrick Harris & Anne Sayers – 26 Nov 1802 (Marriage, **St James Parish**)

- Patrick Harris & Bridget Cugan – 27 Nov 1819 (Marriage, **Clondalkin Parish (RC)**)

- Patrick Harris & Bridget Donovan – 4 Jun 1801 (Marriage, **Cork - SS. Peter & Paul Parish (RC)**)

- Patrick Harris & Eleanor Unknown

  o Mary Harris – bapt. 12 Sep 1760 (Baptism, **St. James Parish (RC)**)

  o James Harris – b. 1766, bapt. 13 Sep 1766 (Baptism, **St. Catherine Parish (RC)**)

- Patrick Harris & Frances Unknown

  o Michael Harris – bapt. 29 Sep 1745 (Baptism, **St. Mary, Pro Cathedral Parish (RC)**)

  o Mary Harris – bapt. 26 Jul 1747 (Baptism, **St. Mary, Pro Cathedral Parish (RC)**)

  o Catherine Harris – bapt. 15 Sep 1748 (Baptism, **St. Mary, Pro Cathedral Parish (RC)**)

  o Thomas Harris – bapt. 27 May 1752 (Baptism, **St. Mary, Pro Cathedral Parish (RC)**)

- Patrick Harris & Joan Harris

  o Agnes Harris – b. 5 Apr 1880, bapt. 12 Apr 1880 (Baptism, **St. Mary, Haddington Road Parish (RC)**)

Patrick Harris (father):

Residence - Irishtown Road - April 12, 1880

Hurst

- Patrick Harris & Margaret Barry

  o Michael Harris – b. 1778, bapt. 1778 (Baptism, **Rathfarnham Parish** (RC))

- Patrick Harris & Mary Harris

  o Daniel Harris – b. 10 Nov 1871, bapt. 10 Nov 1871 (Baptism, **Glenbeigh/Glencar Parish** (RC))

Patrick Harris (father):

Residence - Coolnaharragill - November 10, 1871

- Patrick Harris & Mary Kearey – 17 Mar 1846 (Marriage, **St. Andrew Parish** (RC))

- Patrick Harris & Mary Meale

  o James Harris – b. 14 Jul 1871, bapt. 18 Jul 1871 (Baptism, **Ardfert Parish** (RC))

Patrick Harris (father):

Residence - Kilcooley - July 18, 1871

- Patrick Harris & Mary O'Sullivan – 30 Nov 1833 (Marriage, **Tralee Parish** (RC))

Patrick Harris (husband):

Residence - Tallivideen - November 30, 1833

Mary O'Sullivan (wife):

Residence - Tallivideen - November 30, 1833

- Patrick Harris & Mary Pillan – 14 May 1854 (Marriage, **Rathfarnham Parish** (RC))

- Patrick Harris & Mary Riordan

  o Patrick Harris – b. 18 Sep 1870, bapt. 18 Sep 1870 (Baptism, **Glenbeigh/Glencar Parish** (RC))

Patrick Harris (father):

Residence - Kilkeehagh - September 18, 1870

- Patrick Harris & Mary Unknown

  o William Harris – bapt. 14 Mar 1807 (Baptism, **St. Mary, Pro Cathedral Parish** (RC))

Harris Surname Ireland: 1600s to 1900s

- Patrick Harris & Mary Unknown

  - Michael Harris – bapt. 1840 (Baptism, **St. Andrew Parish** (RC))

  - Catherine Mary Harris – bapt. 1841 (Baptism, **St. Andrew Parish** (RC))

  - Joseph Harris – bapt. 1843 (Baptism, **St. Andrew Parish** (RC))

  - Mary Harris – bapt. 1844 (Baptism, **St. Andrew Parish** (RC))

  - Charles Harris – bapt. 1846 (Baptism, **St. Andrew Parish** (RC))

- Patrick Harris & Rose Unknown

  - James Harris – bapt. 1752 (Baptism, **St. Andrew Parish** (RC))

- Patrick Harris & Unknown

  - Anne Harris – bapt. 17 Jan 1725 (Baptism, **St. John Parish**)

- Peter Harris & Anne Russell

  - Mary Harris – b. 1770, bapt. 1770 (Baptism, **SS. Michael & John Parish** (RC))

Peter Harris (father):

Residence - Copper Alley, Graham's - 1770

- Peter Harris & Anne Unknown

  - Mary Isabel Harris – bapt. 13 Sep 1786 (Baptism, **St. Werburgh Parish**)

Peter Harris (father):

Residence - Castle - September 13, 1786

- Peter Harris & Eleanor Unknown

  - Jane Harris – bapt. 18 Jul 1767 (Baptism, **St. Peter Parish**)

Hurst

- Peter Harris & Grace Harris

    o Esther Harris – bapt. 23 Apr 1827 (Baptism, **St. Mary, Pro Cathedral Parish (RC)**)

    o Julia Harris & Francis Monks – 8 Oct 1861 (Marriage, **St. Mary, Pro Cathedral Parish**

    (RC))

Julia Harris (daughter):

  Residence - 75 Talbot Street - October 8, 1861

Francis Monks, son of Thomas Monks & Eleanor Unknown (son-in-law):

  Residence - 75 Talbot Street - October 8, 1861

Peter Harris (father):

  Residence - Purden Street - April 23, 1827

- Peter Harris & Isabel Perrott – 4 Oct 1818 (Marriage, **St. Mark Parish**)

Signatures:

Wedding Witnesses:

Henry Harris

Signature:

Harris Surname Ireland: 1600s to 1900s

- Peter Harris & Joan Callaghan – 27 Nov 1843 (Marriage, **Dromtariffe Parish** (RC))

  - James Harris – b. 10 Mar 1843, bapt. 10 Mar 1843 (Baptism, **Dromtariffe Parish** (RC))

  - Patrick Harris – b. 29 Mar 1846, bapt. 29 Mar 1846 (Baptism, **Dromtariffe Parish** (RC))

Peter Harris (father):

    Residence - Dysert - March 10, 1843

        Lisnacon - March 29, 1846

Joan Callaghan (mother):

    Residence - Lisnacon - November 27, 1843

- Peter Harris & June Unknown

  - Peter Harris – bapt. 10 Jul 1763 (Baptism, **St. Peter Parish**)

- Peter Harris & Unknown

  - Anne Harris – bur. 23 Sep 1674 (Burial, **St. John Parish**)

- Peter Harris & Unknown

  - Bridget Harris & John Browne – 5 Feb 1888 (Marriage, **St. Andrew Parish** (RC))

Bridget Harris (daughter):

    Residence - 1 Sir John's Quay - February 5, 1888

John Browne, son of Thomas Browne (son-in-law):

    Residence - 6 Gray Street - February 5, 1888

- Philip Harris & Catherine Mary Sullivan

  - John Harris – b. 28 May 1842, bapt. 28 May 1842 (Baptism, **Glenbeigh/Glencar Parish** (RC))

  - Mary Harris – b. 23 Aug 1845, bapt. 23 Aug 1845 (Baptism, **Glenbeigh/Glencar Parish** (RC))

  - Catherine Harris – b. 1 Aug 1849, bapt. 1 Aug 1849 (Baptism, **Glenbeigh/Glencar Parish** (RC))

- o Ellen Harris – b. 29 Mar 1853, bapt. 29 Mar 1853 (Baptism, **Glenbeigh/Glencar Parish (RC)**)

- o Daniel Harris – b. 2 Apr 1856, bapt. 2 Apr 1856 (Baptism, **Glenbeigh/Glencar Parish (RC)**)

- o Joan Harris – b. 1 Apr 1859, bapt. 1 Apr 1859 (Baptism, **Glenbeigh/Glencar Parish (RC)**)

Philip Harris (father):

Residence - Drom - May 28, 1842

August 23, 1845

Kilkeehagh - August 1, 1849

April 2, 1856

April 1, 1859

Kilnabrack - March 29, 1853

- • Philip Harris & Margaret Griffin – 16 Feb 1873 (Marriage, **Glenbeigh/Glencar Parish (RC)**)

- o Catherine Harris – b. 8 Feb 1874, bapt. 8 Feb 1874 (Baptism, **Glenbeigh/Glencar Parish (RC)**)

- o James Harris – b. 5 Oct 1875, bapt. 5 Oct 1875 (Baptism, **Glenbeigh/Glencar Parish (RC)**)

- o John Harris – b. 29 Jan 1878, bapt. 29 Jan 1878 (Baptism, **Glenbeigh/Glencar Parish (RC)**)

- o John Harris – b. 20 Apr 1879, bapt. 20 Apr 1879 (Baptism, **Glenbeigh/Glencar Parish (RC)**)

- o Patrick Harris – b. 7 Apr 1881, bapt. 7 Apr 1881 (Baptism, **Glenbeigh/Glencar Parish (RC)**)

- o Dennis Harris – b. 6 Jul 1885, bapt. 11 Jul 1885 (Baptism, **Glenbeigh/Glencar Parish (RC)**)

- o Philip Harris – b. 7 Dec 1890, bapt. 10 Dec 1890 (Baptism, **Glenbeigh/Glencar Parish (RC)**)

- o Margaret Harris – b. 15 Mar 1894, bapt. 17 Mar 1894 (Baptism, **Glenbeigh/Glencar Parish (RC)**)

Philip Harris (father):

Residence - Drom - February 16, 1873

October 5, 1875

April 7, 1881

Coolnaharragill - February 8, 1874

July 11, 1885

December 10, 1890

Knockboy - January 29, 1878

April 20, 1879

Knockbee Upper - March 17, 1894

Mary Griffin (mother):

Residence - Letter - February 16, 1873

- Philip Harris & Mary Atwood – 23 Nov 1693 (Marriage, **St. Andrew Parish**)

- Philip Harris & Mary Cluvane

- o Mary Harris – b. 1 Dec 1826, bapt. 1 Dec 1826 (Baptism, **Glenbeigh/Glencar Parish (RC)**)

Philip Harris (father):

Residence - Keel. - December 1, 1826

- Philip Harris & Mary Unknown

- o David Harris – bapt. 10 Nov 1754 (Baptism, **St. Catherine Parish (RC)**)

- Philip Harris & Unknown, bur. 1 Mar 1680 (Burial, **St. Nicholas Within Parish**)

Hurst

- Ralph Harris & Ellen Donovan

  - Michael Harris – bapt. 24 Mar 1845 (Baptism, **Dunmanway Parish** (RC))

Ralph Harris (father):

Residence - Dunmanway - March 24, 1845

- Ralph Harris (1st Marriage) & Ellen Mahony, d. Before 30 May 1837

  - Mary Harris – bapt. 16 May 1822 (Baptism, **Rossalettiri & Kilkeraunmor (Roscarbery & Lissevard) Parish** (RC))

  - Patrick Harris – bapt. 7 Mar 1826 (Baptism, **Rossalettiri & Kilkeraunmor (Roscarbery & Lissevard) Parish** (RC))

  - Ellen Harris – bapt. 23 Sep 1830 (Baptism, **Rossalettiri & Kilkeraunmor (Roscarbery & Lissevard) Parish** (RC))

  - Margaret Harris – bapt. 1 May 1836 (Baptism, **Rossalettiri & Kilkeraunmor (Roscarbery & Lissevard) Parish** (RC))

Ralph Harris (father):

Residence - Ch Rock - May 16, 1822

September 23, 1830

May 1, 1836

Rock of Ross - March 7, 1826

Ralph Harris remarried to Margaret Hurly on May 30, 1837.

- Ralph Harris (2nd Marriage) & Margaret Hurly – 30 May 1837 (Marriage, **Rossalettiri & Kilkeraunmor (Roscarbery & Lissevard) Parish** (RC))

Ralph Harris (husband):

Residence - Rock - May 30, 1837

Margaret Hurly (wife):

Residence - Rock - May 30, 1837

Harris Surname Ireland: 1600s to 1900s

- Richard Harris & Alice Unknown

  o Henry Harris – b. 1816, bur. 22 Dec 1833 (Burial, **Dingle Parish**)

Henry Harris (son):

Residence - Dingle - Before December 22, 1833

  o Samuel Harris – bapt. 11 Jun 1826 (Baptism, **Dingle Parish**)

Richard Harris (father):

Occupation - Cost Guard - June 11, 1826

- Richard Harris & Anne Garrett – 13 May 1844 (Marriage, **St. George Parish**)

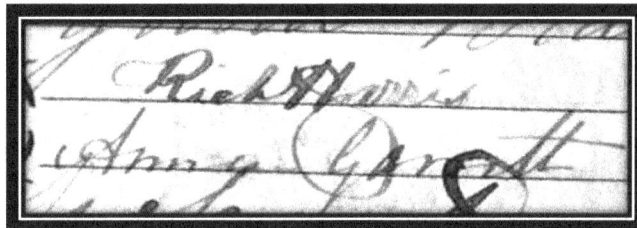

Signatures:

  o Isabel Anne Harris – b. 4 Mar 1845, bapt. 3 Apr 1845 (Baptism, **St. George Parish**)

Richard Harris (father):

Residence - 67 Harcourt Street Dublin, St Peters Parish -May 13, 1844

Lower Dorset Street - April 3, 1845

Occupation - Esquire - May 13, 1844

April 3, 1845

Anne Garrett (mother):

Residence - 10 Upper Gardiner Street, St George Parish - May 13, 1844

Wedding Witnesses:

George Garrett

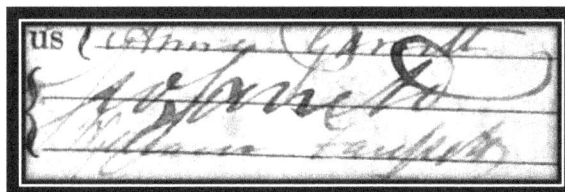

Signature:

Hurst

- Richard Harris & Anne Harris

  - David Harris – bapt. 27 Aug 1786 (Baptism, **St. Paul Parish**)

  - Elizabeth Harris – bapt. 5 Oct 1788 (Baptism, **St. Paul Parish**)

  - Anne Harris – bapt. 18 Apr 1790 (Baptism, **St. Paul Parish**)

- Richard Harris & Anne Harris

  - Catherine Harris – b. 15 Mar 1869, bapt. 25 Apr 1869 (Baptism, **St. Mark Parish**)

Richard Harris (father):

Residence - 3 Erne Place - April 25, 1869

Occupation - Laborer - April 25, 1869

- Richard Harris & Anne Unknown

  - Nathaniel Harris – bapt. 7 Nov 1773 (Baptism, **St. Paul Parish**)

- Richard Harris & Anne Unknown

  - Anne Harris – bapt. 20 Sep 1795 (Baptism, **St. Catherine Parish**)

- Richard Harris & Bridget Brien

  - Elizabeth Harris – bapt. 13 Jul 1777 (Baptism, **St. Catherine Parish (RC)**)

  - Bridget Harris – bapt. 28 Oct 1781 (Baptism, **St. Catherine Parish (RC)**)

  - William Harris – bapt. 21 Mar 1784 (Baptism, **St. Catherine Parish (RC)**)

  - Mary Harris – bapt. 13 Mar 1785 (Baptism, **St. Catherine Parish (RC)**)

  - Anne Harris – bapt. 5 Oct 1788 (Baptism, **St. Catherine Parish (RC)**)

- Richard Harris & Bridget Unknown

  - Mary Harris – bapt. 25 Jun 1751 (Baptism, **St. Werburgh Parish**)

Richard Harris (father):

Residence - Castle Street - June 25, 1751

- Richard Harris & Calia Barry

  - Richard Harris – bapt. 1824 (Baptism, **Sandyford Parish (RC)**)

Harris Surname Ireland: 1600s to 1900s

- Richard Harris & Catherine Daly – 22 Nov 1862 (Marriage, **Cork - SS. Peter & Paul Parish (RC)**)

  ○ John Paul Harris – b. 27 Jun 1866, bapt. 8 Jul 1866 (Baptism, **Cork - SS. Peter & Paul Parish (RC)**)

Richard Harris (father):

Residence - Brown Street - November 22, 1862

- Richard Harris & Catherine Harris

  ○ Anne Harris – bapt. 8 Feb 1830 (Baptism, **St. Mary, Pro Cathedral Parish (RC)**)

Richard Harris (father):

Residence - Leacy Lane - February 8, 1830

- Richard Harris & Catherine Heffernan (H e f f e r n a n)

  ○ Samuel Harris – b. 31 Jul 1883, bapt. 10 Aug 1883 (Baptism, **Tralee Parish**)

  ○ Mary Louisa Harris – b. 27 Aug 1884, bapt. 27 Nov 1884 (Baptism, **Tralee Parish**)

  ○ Richard Frederick Harris – b. 9 Jun 1887, bapt. 22 Jul 1887 (Baptism, **Dingle Parish**)

  ○ Michael Reginald Heffernan Harris – b. 4 Oct 1888, bapt. 2 Nov 1888 (Baptism, **Dingle Parish**)

  ○ Helen Jane Harris – b. 4 Apr 1890, bapt. 14 Apr 1890 (Baptism, **Castleisland Parish (RC)**)

Richard Harris (father):

Residence - Tralee - August 10, 1883

November 27, 1884

Dingle - July 22, 1887

November 2, 1888

Castleisland - April 14, 1890

Occupation - Sub Constable - August 10, 1883

Constable R J C - November 27, 1884

S R I Constabulary - July 22, 1887

November 2, 1888

Hurst

- Richard Harris & Catherine Herbert – 3 Jul 1825 (Marriage, **St. Andrew Parish** (RC))

  - Catherine Harris – bapt. 1832 (Baptism, **St. Andrew Parish** (RC))

  - Patrick Harris – bapt. 1834 (Baptism, **St. Andrew Parish** (RC))

  - Thomas Harris – bapt. 1836 (Baptism, **St. Andrew Parish** (RC))

- Richard Harris & Catherine Lewis – 1 Feb 1877 (Marriage, **Kinsale Parish** (RC))

  - William Harris – b. 28 Dec 1877, bapt. 30 Dec 1877 (Baptism, **Kinsale Parish** (RC))

  - Catherine Harris – b. 12 Dec 1878, bapt. 12 Dec 1878 (Baptism, **Kinsale Parish** (RC))

  - Hannah Harris – b. 3 Dec 1879, bapt. 4 Dec 1879 (Baptism, **Kinsale Parish** (RC))

Richard Harris (father):

Residence - Guard Well - December 30, 1877

December 12, 1878

- Richard Harris & Catherine Mee

  - Elizabeth Harris – bapt. 22 Sep 1805 (Baptism, **St. Michan Parish** (RC))

- Richard Harris & Catherine Sullivan – 26 May 1825 (Marriage, **Castlemaine Parish** (RC))

  - Sarah Harris – b. 25 Oct 1830, bapt. 25 Oct 1830 (Baptism, **Annascaul Parish** (RC))

  - Catherine Harris – b. 22 Dec 1833, bapt. 22 Dec 1833 (Baptism, **Annascaul Parish** (RC))

Richard Harris (father):

Residence - Lack - October 25, 1830

December 22, 1833

Catherine Sullivan (mother):

Residence - Whitegate - May 26, 1825

- Richard Harris & Catherine Unknown

  - Helen Jane Harris – b. 4 Apr 1890, bapt. 15 May 1890 (Baptism, **Ballymacelligott & Ballyseedy Parish**) (Baptism, **Castleisland Parish**)

  - Kathleen A. Harris – b. 1 Sep 1894, bapt. 7 Oct 1894 (Baptism, **Ballymacelligott & Ballyseedy Parish**)

Harris Surname Ireland: 1600s to 1900s

Richard Harris (father):

Residence - Castleisland - May 15, 1890

Occupation - Sergeant of Police - May 15, 1890

Sergeant in R.I.C. - October 7, 1894

- Richard Harris & Cecilia Bing

  - Owen Harris – b. 1826, bapt. 1826 (Baptism, **Rathfarnham Parish** (RC))

  - Honora Harris – b. 1834, bapt. 1834 (Baptism, **Rathfarnham Parish** (RC))

  - Patrick Harris – b. 1836, bapt. 1836 (Baptism, **Rathfarnham Parish** (RC))

  - Joseph Harris – b. 1841, bapt. 1841 (Baptism, **Rathfarnham Parish** (RC))

- Richard Harris & Cecelia Unknown

  - Hannah Harris & Thomas Shortall – 28 Nov 1869 (Marriage, **St. Nicholas Parish** (RC))

    - Mary Joan Shortall – b. 16 Jul 1871, bapt. 25 Jul 1871 (Baptism, **Harrington Street Parish** (RC))

Hannah Harris (daughter):

Residence - Bishop Place - November 28, 1869

Thomas Shortall, son of Thomas Shortall & Hannah Unknown (son-in-law):

Residence - 4 Bishop Place - November 28, 1869

36 Charlotte Street - July 25, 1871

Hurst

- Richard Harris & Dorothea Stone, b. 1802, bur. 27 Apr 1837 (Burial, **Tullow Parish**) – 28 Apr 1829 (Marriage, **Tullow Parish**)

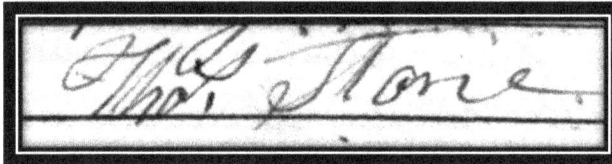

Signatures:

Richard Harris (husband):

    Residence - Hacketstown - April 28, 1829

Dorothea Stone (wife):

    Residence - Tullow - April 28, 1829

        Hacketstown - April 27, 1837

Wedding Witnesses:

Thomas Stone

Signature:

- Richard Harris & Dorothy Mors – 13 Feb 1669 (Marriage, **St. Peter Parish**)

- Richard Harris & Elizabeth Harris

    o George Harris – bapt. 10 Feb 1719 (Baptism, **St. Luke Parish**)

Richard Harris (father):

    Residence - Skinner's Alley - February 10, 1719

    Occupation - Weaver - February 10, 1719

Harris Surname Ireland: 1600s to 1900s

- Richard Harris & Elizabeth Harris

  o Arthur Thomas Patrick Harris – b. 3 Mar 1896, bapt. 15 Mar 1896 (Baptism, **St. Paul Parish**)

Richard Harris (father):

Residence - 39 Oxmantown Road - March 15, 1896

Occupation - Plasterer - March 15, 1896

- Richard Harris & Ellen Evans

  o Margaret Harris – b. 25 Feb 1819, bapt. 25 Feb 1819 (Baptism, **Tralee Parish** (RC))

  o Mary Harris – b. 13 Jan 1825, bapt. 13 Jan 1825 (Baptism, **Tralee Parish** (RC))

  o James Harris – b. 25 May 1828, bapt. 25 May 1828 (Baptism, **Tralee Parish** (RC))

  o Sarah Harris – b. 14 Aug 1831, bapt. 14 Aug 1831 (Baptism, **Tralee Parish** (RC))

  o Ellen Harris – b. 30 Jun 1834, bapt. 30 Jun 1834 (Baptism, **Tralee Parish** (RC))

Richard Harris (father):

Residence - Derrymore - February 25, 1819

January 13, 1825

May 25, 1828

August 14, 1831

June 30, 1834

- Richard Harris & Ellen Leahy

  o Richard Harris – bapt. 6 Jan 1816 (Baptism, **Cork - South Parish** (RC))

- Richard Harris & Ellen Sheehan – 1 Jul 1789 (Marriage, **Tralee Parish** (RC))

Richard Harris (husband):

Residence - Ballyvelly - July 1, 1789

- Richard Harris & Frances Geary

  o Julia Harris – bapt. 5 Jun 1843 (Baptism, **Cork - SS. Peter & Paul Parish** (RC))

- Richard Harris & Honora Flynn

  o Honora Harris – bapt. 11 Apr 1826 (Baptism, **Innishannon Parish** (RC))

Hurst

- Richard Harris & Isabel Unknown

  o Catherine Harris – bapt. 28 Oct 1760 (Baptism, **St. Catherine Parish**)

  o Sarah Harris – bapt. 12 Jan 1772 (Baptism, **St. Catherine Parish**)

Richard Harris (father):

Residence - Thomas Court - January 12, 1772

- Richard Harris & Joan Buckley – 19 Apr 1836 (Marriage, **Kilmichael Parish (RC)**)

  o Nell Harris – bapt. 23 Mar 1837 (Baptism, **Kilmichael Parish (RC)**)

  o Jane Harris – bapt. 17 Oct 1839 (Baptism, **Kilmichael Parish (RC)**)

  o James Harris – bapt. 13 Sep 1842 (Baptism, **Kilmichael Parish (RC)**)

  o Catherine Harris – bapt. 13 Sep 1842 (Baptism, **Kilmichael Parish (RC)**)

  o Thomas Harris – bapt. 10 Aug 1846 (Baptism, **Kilmichael Parish (RC)**)

  o John Harris – bapt. 4 Jun 1854 (Baptism, **Kilmichael Parish (RC)**)

  o Mary Harris – bapt. 4 Jun 1854 (Baptism, **Kilmichael Parish (RC)**)

Richard Harris (father):

Residence - Annefield - March 23, 1837

Inchinashingane - September 13, 1842

August 10, 1846

June 4, 1854

- Richard Harris & Joan O'Sullivan – 14 Nov 1856 (Marriage, **Douglas & Ballygarvan Parrish (RC)**)

  o Margaret Harris – bapt. 22 Sep 1857 (Baptism, **Douglas & Ballygarvan Parrish (RC)**)

  o Henry Harris – bapt. 24 May 1860 (Baptism, **Douglas & Ballygarvan Parrish (RC)**)

  o Daniel Harris – bapt. 3 Aug 1862 (Baptism, **Douglas & Ballygarvan Parrish (RC)**)

  o William Harris – bapt. 9 May 1864 (Baptism, **Douglas & Ballygarvan Parrish (RC)**)

  o James Harris – bapt. 29 Mar 1868 (Baptism, **Cork - South Parish (RC)**)

  o Mary Harris – Bapt. 29 Mar 1868 (Baptism, **Cork - South Parish (RC)**)

Harris Surname Ireland: 1600s to 1900s

- Richard Harris & Judith Eves

  o William Harris – bapt. 7 Sep 1744 (Baptism, **St. Catherine Parish** (RC))

  o Bridget Harris – bapt. 19 Apr 1747 (Baptism, **St. Catherine Parish** (RC))

- Richard Harris & Julia Malone – 6 Nov 1802 (Marriage, **St. Andrew Parish** (RC))

- Richard Harris & Margaret McAuliffe

  o Margaret Harris – bapt. 21 Feb 1804 (Baptism, **Cork - South Parish** (RC))

Richard Harris (father):

Residence - Lying in Hospital - February 21, 1804

- Richard Harris & Margaret Waters

  o Mary Harris – bapt. Jul 1824 (Baptism, **Ballinhassig Parish** (RC))

- Richard Harris & Martha Harris, bur. 26 May 1672 (Burial, **St. Michan Parish**)

Richard Harris (husband):

Occupation - Graser - May 26, 1672

Innkeeper - May 26, 1672

- Richard Harris & Mary Cotter – 24 May 1862 (Marriage, **Cork - South Parish** (RC))

  o Elizabeth Harris – bapt. 14 Jun 1863 (Baptism, **Cork - South Parish** (RC))

  o Bridget Harris – bapt. 11 Dec 1864 (Baptism, **Cork - South Parish** (RC))

  o Mary Harris – bapt. 19 Dec 1866 (Baptism, **Cork - South Parish** (RC))

  o Honora Harris – bapt. 22 Nov 1868 (Baptism, **Cork - South Parish** (RC))

  o Catherine Harris – bapt. 2 May 1872 (Baptism, **Cork - South Parish** (RC))

  o Ellen Harris – bapt. 9 Aug 1874 (Baptism, **Cork - South Parish** (RC))

  o Henry Harris – b. 7 Oct 1877, bapt. 14 Oct 1877 (Baptism, **Cork - South Parish** (RC))

  o Julia Harris – b. 1 Jul 1880, bapt. 4 Jul 1880 (Baptism, **Cork - South Parish** (RC))

Richard Harris (father):

Residence - 106 Quary Road - July 4, 1880

Hurst

- Richard Harris & Mary Boylan – 6 Nov 1774 (Marriage, **St. Michan Parish (RC)**)

- Richard Harris & Mary Harris

  - John Topham Harris – b. 23 Jun 1822, bapt. 21 Jul 1822 (Baptism, **St. Mary Parish**)

  - Richard Edward Harris – b. 29 Apr 1824, bapt. 16 May 1824 (Baptism, **St. Mary Parish**)

  - Harriet Teresa Harris – bapt. 1 Jan 1828 (Baptism, **St. Mary Parish**)

Richard Harris (father):

Residence - 32 Stafford Street - May 16, 1824

40 Mary Street - January 1, 1828

- Richard Harris & Mary Harris

  - Catherine Harris – bapt. Dec 1828 (Baptism, **St. Mary, Pro Cathedral Parish (RC)**)

Richard Harris (father):

Residence - Britain Street - Dec 1828

- Richard Harris, b. 1786, bur. 10 Jan 1839 (Burial, **Dingle Parish**) & Mary Lucas (1st Marriage) –

  9 Dec 1832 (Marriage, **Dingle Parish**)

Signatures:

  - Mary Harris – bapt. 11 Feb 1835 (Baptism, **Dingle Parish**)

  - Rebecca Harris – bapt. 23 Oct 1836 (Baptism, **Dingle Parish**)

  - Elizabeth Harris – bapt. 25 Nov 1838 (Baptism, **Dingle Parish**)

Harris Surname Ireland: 1600s to 1900s

Richard Harris (father):

    Residence - Dingle - December 9, 1832

                    February 11, 1835

                    October 23, 1836

                    November 25, 1838

                    January 10, 1839

    Occupation - Coast Guard - February 11, 1835

                    October 23, 1836

                    November 25, 1838

                    January 10, 1839

Mary McLucas, daughter of William Lucas (mother):

    Residence - Dingle - December 9, 1832

- Mary Lucas Harris (2nd Marriage) & John Snooks – 5 Aug 1846 (Marriage, **Dingle Parish**)

Mary Lucas Harris (wife):

    Residence - Dingle - August 5, 1846

    Occupation - Shopkeeper - August 5, 1846

John Snooks, son of John Snooks (husband):

    Residence - Dingle - August 5, 1846

    Occupation - Seaman - August 5, 1846

John Snooks (father):

    Occupation - Shipwright

William Lucas (father):

    Occupation - Farmer

Hurst

- Richard Harris & Mary Mahony – 16 Feb 1858 (Marriage, **Kilmurry, Moviddy, Kilbonane, & Cannavee Parish** (RC))

  o Mary Harris – bapt. 22 Feb 1859 (Baptism, **Murragh & Templemartin Parish** (RC))

  o William Harris – bapt. 7 Jun 1860 (Baptism, **Murragh & Templemartin Parish** (RC))

  o John Harris – bapt. 7 Feb 1862 (Baptism, **Murragh & Templemartin Parish** (RC))

Richard Harris (father):

Residence - Knockadooma - February 22, 1859

June 7, 1860

February 7, 1862

- Richard Harris & Mary Toole – 10 Feb 1807 (Marriage, **St. Catherine Parish** (RC))

- Richard Harris & Mary Unknown

  o Bridget Harris – b. 1792, bapt. 1792 (Baptism, **SS. Michael & John Parish** (RC))

- Richard Harris & Mary Unknown

  o Mary Harris – b. 1 Jun 1826, bapt. 4 Jun 1826 (Baptism, **St. George Parish**)

- Richard Harris & Mary Unknown

  o Mary Harris & William O'Brien – 29 Sep 1857 (Marriage, **St. Peter Parish**)

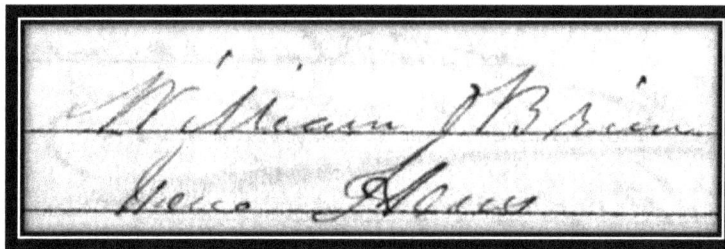

Signatures:

Mary Harris (daughter):

Residence - 34 Camden Street - September 29, 1857

William O'Brien, son of Martin O'Brien (son-in-law):

Residence - Besboro Avenue, St. Thomas Parish - September 29, 1857

Occupation - Officer in the Customs - September 29, 1857

Harris Surname Ireland: 1600s to 1900s

Martin O'Brien (father):

    Occupation - Merchant

Richard Harris (father):

    Occupation - Auctioneer

- o Charles Henry Harris – b. 19 Apr 1835, bapt. 5 Jul 1835 (Baptism, **St. Peter Parish**)

- o Emma Harris – b. 20 Sep 1839, bapt. 30 Oct 1839 (Baptism, **St. Peter Parish**)

- o Albert Harris – b. 6 Jul 1843, bapt. 30 Jul 1843 (Baptism, **St. Peter Parish**)

- o Joseph Harris – b. 14 Dec 1845, bapt. 15 Mar 1846 (Baptism, **St. Peter Parish**)

Richard Harris (father):

    Residence - Ranelagh - July 5, 1835

        Mount Pleasant Avenue - October 30, 1839

        Cullenswood North - July 30, 1843

        3 Stephen's Green North St Anne - March 15, 1846

    Occupation - Auctioneer - July 30, 1843

        March 15, 1846

- Richard Harris & Mary Anne Harris

  - o George Harris – bapt. 23 Jun 1733 (Baptism, **St. Mary Parish**)

- Richard Harris & Mary Anne Unknown

  - o Mary Anne Harris – bapt. Jul 1828 (Baptism, **St. Mary, Pro Cathedral Parish (RC)**)

Richard Harris (father):

    Residence - Liffey Street - July 1828

- Richard Harris & Rebecca McGill

  - o Mary Harris – bapt. 29 Aug 1806 (Baptism, **SS. Michael & John Parish (RC)**)

  - o Richard Harris – bapt. 29 Aug 1806 (Baptism, **SS. Michael & John Parish (RC)**)

  - o Mary Anne Harris – bapt. 2 Aug 1808 (Baptism, **SS. Michael & John Parish (RC)**)

Hurst

- Richard Harris & Rebecca Unknown

  - Rebecca Harris – bapt. 15 Aug 1731 (Baptism, **St. Peter Parish**)

- Richard Harris & Sarah Harris

  - Elizabeth Harris – bur. 11 May 1682 (Burial, **St. Michan Parish**)

Richard Harris (father):

> Occupation - Glasier - May 11, 1682

- Richard Harris & Sarah Jackson – 23 Mar 1838 (Marriage, **Carlow Parish**)

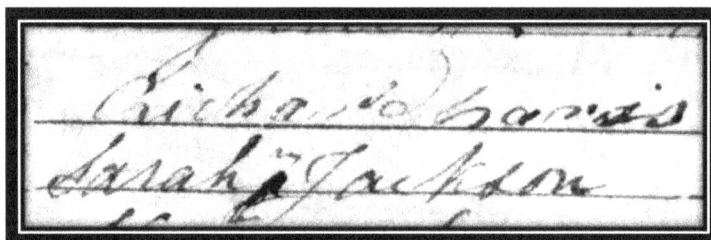

Signatures:

Richard Harris (husband):

> Residence - Hacketstown - March 23, 1838

Sarah Jackson (wife):

> Residence - Carlow Parish - March 23, 1838

Wedding Witnesses:

Thomas Jackson & Isaac Jackson

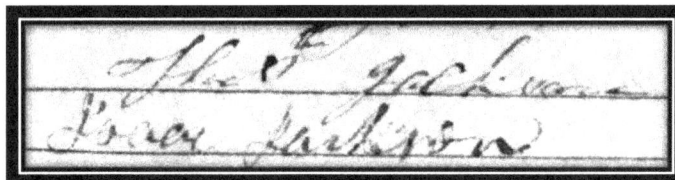

Signatures:

- Richard Harris & Susan Unknown

  - Sophia Harris – b. 3 Feb 1844, bapt. 6 Mar 1844 (Baptism, **St. Peter Parish**)

Richard Harris (father):

> Residence - Fitzwilliam Lane - March 6, 1844

> Occupation - Carpenter - March 6, 1844

- Richard Harris & Unknown

    o Mary Anne Harris & Walter Bowles – 14 May 1870 (Marriage, **St. Stephen Parish**)

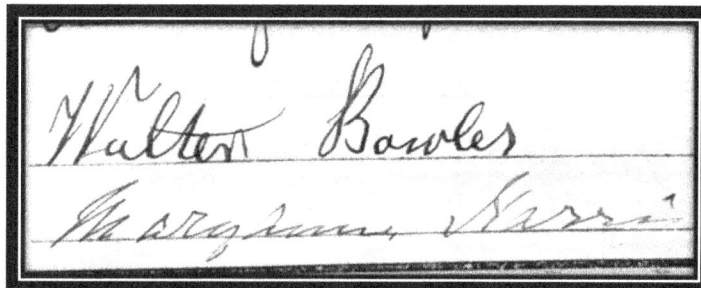

Signatures:

Mary Anne Harris (daughter):

　　Residence - 14 South Cumberland Street - May 14, 1870

Walter Bowles, son of Walter Bowles (son-in-law):

　　Residence - 18 East James Street - May 14, 1870

　　Occupation - Plumber - May 14, 1870

Walter Bowles (father):

　　Occupation - Gardener

Richard Harris (father):

　　Occupation - Soldier

Wedding Witnesses:

Elizabeth Boles

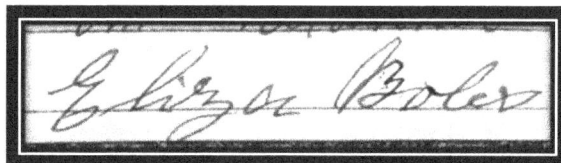

Signature:

Hurst

- Richard Harris & Unknown

  - Elizabeth Harris & Thomas Black – 11 May 1874 (Marriage, **St. Mark Parish**)

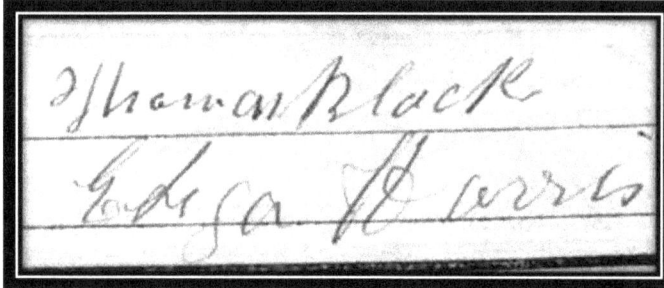

Signatures:

Elizabeth Harris (daughter):

   Residence - South Cumberland Street - May 11, 1874

Thomas Black, son of John Black (son-in-law):

   Residence - 24 South Cumberland Street - May 11, 1874

   Occupation - Coachman - May 11, 1874

John Black (father):

   Occupation - Steward

Richard Harris (father):

   Occupation - Pensioner

- Richard Harris & Unknown

  - Richard Harris & Alice Bradshaw – 22 Sep 1883 (Marriage, St. George Parish)

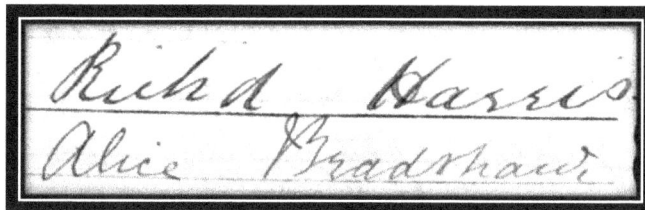

Signatures:

Richard Harris (son):

  Residence - 6 Rutland Square - September 22, 1883

  Occupation - Coachman - September 22, 1883

Alice Bradshaw, daughter of George Bradshaw (daughter-in-law):

  Residence - 6 Belview Buildings James Street - September 22, 1883

           Cliff Rathfarnam - September 22, 1883

  Relationship Status at Marriage - minor age

George Bradshaw (father):

  Occupation - Coachman

Richard Harris (father):

  Occupation - Gardiner

Hurst

- Richard Harris & Unknown

  - George Harris & Ellen McEnroe – 10 Oct 1894 (Marriage, **St. Werburgh Parish**)

Signatures:

- Michael George Harris – b. 16 Dec 1894, bapt. 31 Dec 1894 (Baptism, **St. Mary, Pro**

    Cathedral Parish (RC))

George Harris (son):

  Residence - Chatham Row - October 10, 1894

       95 Talbot Street - December 31, 1894

  Occupation - Fireman - October 10, 1894

Ellen McEnroe, daughter of Michael McEnroe (daughter-in-law):

  Residence - Werburgh Street - October 10, 1894

Michael McEnroe (father):

  Occupation - Dealer

Richard Harris (father):

  Occupation - Farmer

Wedding Witnesses:

Anne McEnroe

Signature:

Harris Surname Ireland: 1600s to 1900s

- Richard Charles Harris & Georgina Alice Harris

  o Ellen Caroline Harris – b. 9 Nov 1884, bapt. 7 Dec 1884 (Baptism, **St. Mary Parish**)

  o Georgina Alice Harris – b. 5 Jul 1886, bapt. 5 Sep 1886 (Baptism, **St. Mary Parish**)

Richard Charles Harris (father):

Residence - 78 Upper Dorset Street - December 7, 1884

15 Shamrock Street - September 5, 1886

Occupation - Servant - December 7, 1884

Coach (Probably abbreviated for Coachman) - September 5, 1886

- Richard Nathaniel Harris & Mary Harris

  o Mary Harris – bapt. 26 Mar 1828 (Baptism, **St. Mary Parish**)

Richard Nathaniel Harris (father):

Residence - 18 Upper Ormond Quay - March 26, 1828

Occupation - Book Seller - March 26, 1828

- Richard West Harris & Unknown

  o Thomas Harris – bur. 30 Dec 1706 (Burial, **St. Mary Parish**)

- Robert Harris & Anne Harris

  o John Harris – bapt. 9 Sep 1762 (Baptism, **St. Mary Parish**)

- Robert Harris & Catherine O'Hurley – 5 Feb 1831 (Marriage, **Tralee Parish** (RC))

- Robert Harris & Eleanor Harris, bur. 3 Jan 1692 (Burial, **St. Michan Parish**)

Robert Harris (husband):

Occupation - Cooper - January 3, 1692

- Robert Harris & Elioa Unknown

  o Esther Harris – bapt. 1756 (Baptism, **St. Andrew Parish** (RC))

- Robert Harris & Elizabeth Barstow – 11 Jul 1631 (Marriage, **St. John Parish**)

Hurst

- Robert Harris & Elizabeth Forhan

    o Robert William Harris – b. 31 May 1867, bapt. 1 Jun 1867 (Baptism, **Tralee Parish** (RC))

    o Gerald Fitzgerald Harris – b. 20 Sep 1871, bapt. 24 Sep 1871 (Baptism, **Tralee Parish** (RC))

    o John James Harris – b. 20 Jul 1875, bapt. 24 Jul 1875 (Baptism, **Tralee Parish** (RC))

Robert Harris (father):

Residence - Tralee - June 1, 1867

Ballymullen - September 24, 1871

July 24, 1875

- Robert Harris & Elizabeth Harris

    o Bernard Henry Harris – b. 20 Aug 1880, bapt. 8 Sep 1880 (Baptism, **Tralee Parish** (RC))

Robert Harris (father):

Residence - Tralee - September 8, 1880

- Robert Harris & Elizabeth Unknown

    o Jane Harris – bapt. 12 Nov 1702 (Baptism, **Carlow Parish**)

- Robert Harris & Elizabeth Unknown

    o Elizabeth Harris – b. 7 Nov 1858, bapt. 3 Jun 1859 (Baptism, **St. Catherine Parish**)

    o John Harris – b. 9 May 1861, bapt. 2 Oct 1861 (Baptism, **St. Catherine Parish**)

Robert Harris (father):

Residence - Grand Canal Harbor - June 3, 1859

October 2, 1861

Occupation - Gentleman - June 3, 1859

October 2, 1861

- Robert Harris & Ellen Murphy – 1 Nov 1845 (Marriage, **Cork - South Parish** (RC))

    o Henry Harris – bapt. 4 Feb 1842 (Baptism, **Cork - South Parish** (RC))

    o Dennis Harris – bapt. 8 Sep 1844 (Baptism, **Cork - SS. Peter & Paul Parish** (RC))

- Robert Harris & Eleanor Gregory – 1 Oct 1676 (Marriage, **St. Michan Parish**)

Harris Surname Ireland: 1600s to 1900s

- Robert Harris & Fanny St. George – 8 Jul 1841 (Marriage, **St. Peter Parish**)

Robert Harris (husband):

    Residence - Merrion Square - July 8, 1841

    Occupation - Reverend Clerk - July 8, 1841

Fanny St. George (wife):

    Residence - Merrion Square - July 8, 1841

- Robert Harris & Jane Unknown

  - Christopher Harris – b. 1856, bapt. 1856 (Baptism, **St. Andrew Parish** (RC))

- Robert Harris & Jeanne Devitt

  - Henry Harris – b. 12 Sep 1860, bapt. 28 Sep 1860 (Baptism, **St. Mary, Pro Cathedral Parish** (RC))

Robert Harris (father):

    Residence - 18 Grenville Street - September 28, 1860

- Robert Harris & Jeanne Ritchey

  - Gulielmo Robert Harris, b. 1835, bapt. 17 Mar 1860 (Baptism, **St. Mary, Pro Cathedral Parish** (RC)) & Rosanna Gaynor – 2 Jul 1860 (Marriage, **St. Mary, Pro Cathedral Parish** (RC))

    - Margaret Harris – b. 11 Aug 1864, bapt. 15 Aug 1864 (Baptism, **St. Lawrence Parish** (RC))

    - Rose Anne Harris – b. 20 Feb 1869, bapt. 3 Mar 1869 (Baptism, **St. Lawrence Parish** (RC))

    - Elizabeth Harris – b. 12 Nov 1872, bapt. 27 Nov 1872 (Baptism, **St. Lawrence Parish** (RC))

    - Margaret Jane Harris – b. 9 Oct 1874, bapt. 16 Oct 1874 (Baptism, **St. Mary, Pro Cathedral Parish** (RC))

Hurst

- Gulielmo Patrick Harris – b. 2 Apr 1876, bapt. 5 Apr 1876 (Baptism, **St. Mary, Pro Cathedral Parish** (RC))

Gulielmo Harris (son):

Residence - 3 Talbot Lane - March 17, 1860

July 2, 1860

84 Common Street - August 15, 1864

31 Common Street - March 3, 1869

30 Common Street - November 27, 1872

147 Upper Mecklenburgh Street - October 16, 1874

47 Upper Mecklenburgh Street - April 5, 1876

Rosanna Gaynor, daughter of James Gaynor & Margaret Unknown (daughter-in-law):

Residence - 3 Talbot Lane - July 2, 1860

- Robert Harris & Julia Harris

  o Robert Saville Harris Harris – b. 10 Dec 1877, bapt. 17 Feb 1878 (Baptism, **St. Peter Parish**)

  o Frederick Harris – b. 26 Nov 1878, bapt. 24 Jul 1879 (Baptism, **St. Peter Parish**)

  o Victor Harris – b. 8 Feb 1880, bapt. 23 Dec 1880 (Baptism, **St. Peter Parish**)

  o Helen Louisa Harris – b. 11 Aug 1881, bapt. 6 Apr 1882 (Baptism, **St. Peter Parish**)

  o Walter Harris – b. 29 Dec 1882, bapt. 5 Jun 1884 (Baptism, **St. Peter Parish**)

  o Julia Harris – b. 24 Mar 1884, bapt. 29 May 1884 (Baptism, **St. Peter Parish**)

  o Eva Harris – b. 9 Sep 1885, bapt. 25 Mar 1886 (Baptism, **St. Peter Parish**)

Robert Harris (father):

Residence - 34 Lombard Street West - February 17, 1878

July 24, 1879

86 Upper Leeson Street - December 23, 1880

May 29, 1884

June 5, 1884

April 6, 1882

Harris Surname Ireland: 1600s to 1900s

66 Marlborough Road - March 25, 1886

Occupation - Commercial Traveller - February 17, 1878

July 24, 1879

December 23, 1880

April 6, 1882

May 29, 1884

June 5, 1884

March 25, 1884

- Robert Harris & Margaret Harrington

  - Elizabeth Harris – b. 28 Dec 1845, bapt. 28 Dec 1845 (Baptism, Tralee Parish (RC))

  - Patrick Harris – b. 24 Dec 1848, bapt. 24 Dec 1848 (Baptism, Tralee Parish (RC))

  - Ellen Harris – b. 5 May 1850, bapt. 5 May 1850 (Baptism, Tralee Parish (RC))

  - Patrick Harris – b. 18 Mar 1852, bapt. 18 Mar 1852 (Baptism, Tralee Parish (RC))

  - Mary Harris – b. 14 Jul 1854, bapt. 14 Jul 1854 (Baptism, Tralee Parish (RC))

  - Robert Harris – b. 10 Feb 1857, bapt. 12 Feb 1857 (Baptism, Tralee Parish (RC))

  - John Harris – b. 9 Jun 1859, bapt. 11 Jun 1859 (Baptism, Tralee Parish (RC))

  - Margaret Harris – b. 24 Apr 1863, bapt. 26 Apr 1863 (Baptism, Tralee Parish (RC))

Robert Harris (father):

Residence - Curragraigue - December 28, 1845

December 24, 1848

May 5, 1850

July 14, 1854

February 12, 1857

April 26, 1863

Tralee - March 18, 1852

Blennerville - June 11, 1859

- Robert Harris & Margaret Unknown

  - Peter Harris – bapt. 2 Jul 1763 (Baptism, St. Michan Parish (RC))

Hurst

- Robert Harris & Mary Dessie – 20 Sep 1730 (Marriage, **St. Michan Parish**)

Robert Harris (husband):

Occupation - VICTR - September 20, 1730

- Robert Harris & Mary Harrington

  - Nancy Harris – bapt. 27 Sep 1821 (Baptism, **Kilmurry Parish (RC)**)

  - Anne Harris – bapt. 18 Apr 1828 (Baptism, **Kilmurry, Moviddy, Kilbonane, & Cannavee Parish** (RC))

  - William Harris – bapt. 16 Aug 1836 (Baptism, **Murragh & Templemartin Parish** (RC))

Robert Harris (father):

Residence - Ballinyilla - September 27, 1821

Rafylane - April 18, 1828

- Robert Harris & Mary Moore

  - William Harris – b. 17 May 1847, bapt. 17 May 1847 (Baptism, **Tralee Parish** (RC))

Robert Harris (father):

Residence - Curragraigue - May 17, 1847

- Robert Harris & Mary Smyth – Oct 1815 (Marriage, **St. Michan Parish** (RC))

  - Mary Harris – bapt. 17 Nov 1817 (Baptism, **St. Michan Parish** (RC))

- Robert Harris & Mary Tuomy

  - Andrew Harris – bapt. 1834 (Baptism, **Saggart Parish** (RC))

- Robert Harris & Mary Unknown

  - John Henry Harris – b. 15 Jun 1891, bapt. 22 Jul 1891 (Baptism, **Taney Parish**)

Robert Harris (father):

Residence - Roebuck - July 22, 1891

Occupation - Yard Man - July 22, 1891

- Robert Harris & Mary Anne Harris

  - Robert Harris – b. 3 Aug 1895, bapt. 25 Aug 1895 (Baptism, **St. George Parish**)

  - Thomas Harris – b. 20 Dec 1896, bapt. 7 Feb 1897 (Baptism, **St. George Parish**)

Harris Surname Ireland: 1600s to 1900s

Robert Harris (father):

Residence - 108 Lower Dorset Street - August 25, 1896

51 Upper Dorset Street - February 7, 1897

Occupation - Van Man - August 25, 1896

Van Driver - February 7, 1897

- Robert Harris & Mary J. Gannon

  - Catherine Harris – b. 9 Oct 1876, bapt. 10 Oct 1876 (Baptism, **Harrington Street Parish (RC)**)

Robert Harris (father):

Residence - 94 Lower Clanbrassil Street - October 10, 1876

- Robert Harris & Sarah Handcock – 27 Jun 1802 (Marriage, **St. James Parish**)

  - Francis Harris – b. 1805, bapt. 12 May 1805 (Baptism, **St. Catherine Parish**)

  - Sarah Harris – b. 1806, bapt. 21 Dec 1806 (Baptism, **St. Catherine Parish**)

  - Richard Harris – b. 1810, bapt. 25 Nov 1810 (Baptism, **St. Catherine Parish**)

Robert Harris (father):

Residence - 65 Thomas Street - May 12, 1805

12 Earl Street - December 21, 1806

- Robert Harris & Sarah Harris

  - William Harris – bapt. 5 Jun 1803 (Baptism, **St. Paul Parish**)

- Robert Harris & Sarah Unknown

  - Elizabeth Harris – bapt. 27 Jun 1790 (Baptism, **St. Werburgh Parish**)

Hurst

- Robert Harris & Unknown

    o Elizabeth Harris & Thomas Whitton – 3 May 1851 (Marriage, **St. Peter Parish**)

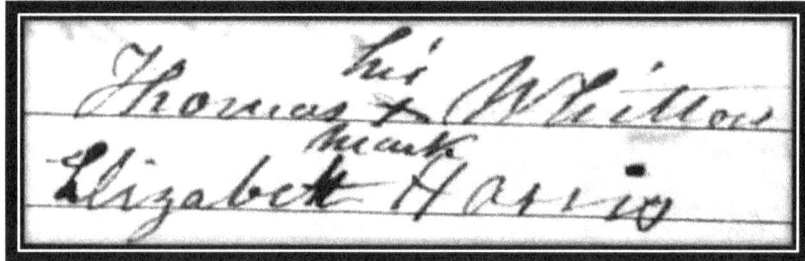

Signatures:

Elizabeth Harris (daughter):

    Residence - 100 Upper Leeson Street - May 3, 1851

Thomas Whitton, son of Thomas Whitton (son-in-law):

    Residence - 100 Upper Leeson Street - May 3, 1851

    Occupation - Farmer - May 3, 1851

Thomas Whitton (father):

    Occupation - Farmer

Robert Harris (father):

    Occupation - Carpenter

Harris Surname Ireland: 1600s to 1900s

- Robert Harris & Unknown

  o Hannah Harris & James H. Gray – 19 Mar 1856 (Marriage, **St. Thomas Parish**)

Signatures:

Hannah Harris (daughter):

　　Residence - Northumberland Buildings - March 19, 1856

James Gray, son of James Gray (son-in-law):

　　Residence - 36 Mabbot Street - March 19, 1856

　　Occupation - Traveller - March 19, 1856

James Gray (father):

　　Occupation - Musician

Robert Harris (father):

　　Occupation - Farmer

Wedding Witnesses:

Thomas Harris

Signature:

Hurst

- Robert Harris & Unknown

  - Hannah Harris & William Duncan – 8 Aug 1863 (Marriage, **St. George Parish**)

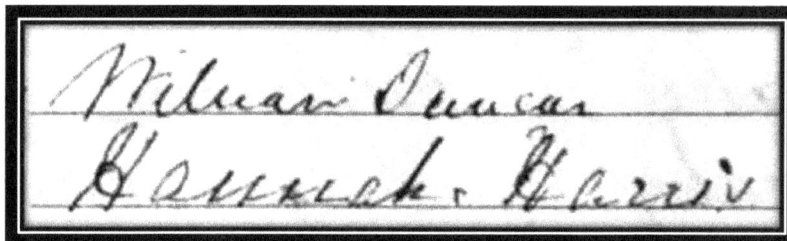

Signatures:

Hannah Harris (daughter):

    Residence - 23 Portland Street - August 8, 1863

William Duncan, son of William Duncan (son-in-law):

    Residence - 34 Westmoreland Street - August 8, 1863

          Liverpool - August 8, 1863

    Occupation - Esquire - August 8, 1863

William Duncan (father):

    Occupation - Merchant

Robert Harris (father):

    Occupation - Esquire

- Robert Harris & Unknown

  - Robert Harris & Elizabeth Jordan – 11 Apr 1878 (Marriage, **St. James Parish (RC)**)

    - Mary Christine Harris – b. 1884, bapt. 1884 (Baptism, **Saggart Parish (RC)**)

Robert Harris (son):

    Residence - Richmond Barracks - April 11, 1878

          The Slade - 1884

Elizabeth Jordan, daughter of Ralph Jordan (daughter-in-law):

    Residence - Golden Bridge - April 11, 1878

- Robert Harris & Unknown

  o Catherine Harris & George Woodhouse Round – 2 Jun 1891 (Marriage, **Leeson Park Parish**)

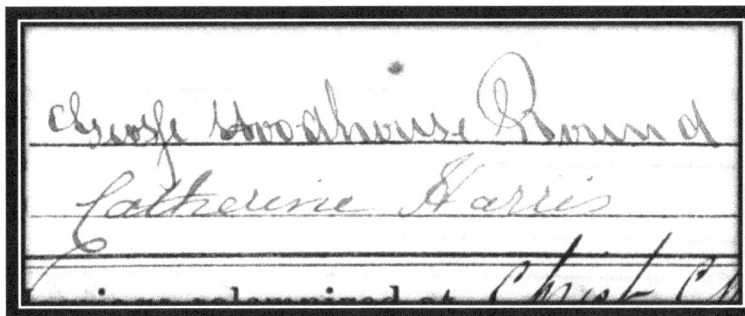

Signatures:

Catherine Harris (daughter):

   Residence - 10 McGowan Terrace Ranelagh - June 2, 1891

George Woodhouse Round, son of John Round (son-in-law):

   Residence - Rathdrum, Co. Wicklow - June 2, 1891

   Occupation - Carpenter - June 2, 1891

   Relationship Status at Marriage - widow

John Round (father):

   Occupation - Builders

Robert Harris (father):

   Occupation - Clerk

Wedding Witnesses:

John Harris

Signature:

Hurst

- Robert Harris & Unknown

  - Susanna Harris & George Watson – 29 Sep 1895 (Marriage, **St. Agatha Parish (RC)**)

Susanna Harris (daughter):

  Residence - 18 Belvedere Avenue - September 29, 1895

George Watson, son of George Watson (son-in-law):

  Residence - 38 Summerhill - September 29, 1895

- Robert Caleb Harris & Mary Anne Harris

  - Mary Anne Harris – b. 15 May 1899, bapt. 16 Jul 1899 (Baptism, **Glasnevin Parish**)

Robert Caleb Harris (father):

  Residence - Santry Village - July 16, 1899

  Occupation - Laborer - July 16, 1899

- Robert Russell Harris & Sabina Unknown

Signatures:

- Emily Harris & Henry Wingfield Figgis – 4 Apr 1871 (Marriage, **St. Peter Parish**)

Signatures:

Harris Surname Ireland: 1600s to 1900s

Emily Harris (daughter):

Residence - 28 Livester Road - April 4, 1871

Henry Wingfield Figgis, son of Edmund Johnstone Figgis (son-in-law):

Residence - 2 Palmerstown Park - April 4, 1871

Occupation - Merchant - April 4, 1871

Edmund Johnstone Figgis (father):

Signature:

Occupation - Merchant

Robert Russell Harris (father):

Occupation - Colonel in the Army

Wedding Witnesses:

Edmund Johnstone Figgis & R. R. Harris

Signatures:

Hurst

o   George Frederick Harris & Susanna Featherstonhaugh Boyce – 15 Jan 1873 (Marriage, St.

Peter Parish)

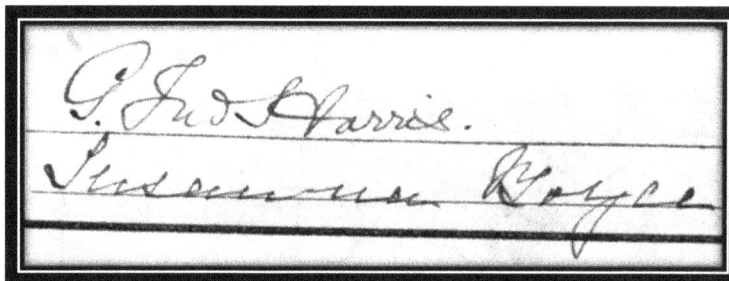

Signatures:

George Fredrick Harris (son):

Residence - United SE- Club Stephen's Green - January 15, 1873

Occupation - Captain 20th Regiment - January 15, 1873

Susanna Featherstonhaugh Boyce, daughter of William Featherstonhaugh

(daughter-in-law):

Residence - 100 Stephen's Green - January 15, 1873

Relationship Status at Marriage - widow

William Featherstonhaugh (father):

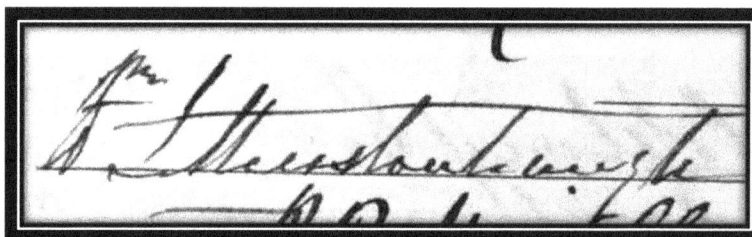

Signature:

Occupation - I P

Robert Russell Harris (father):

Occupation - Colonel in the army

Harris Surname Ireland: 1600s to 1900s

Wedding Witnesses:

William Featherstonhaugh & R. R. Harris

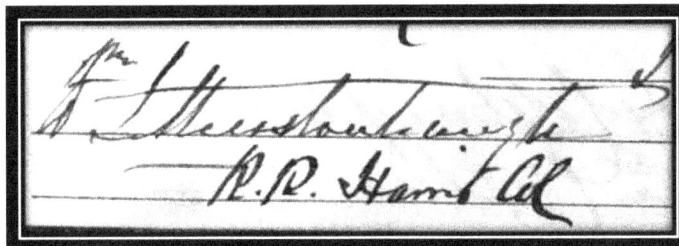

Signatures:

- o Gertrude Harris – b. 15 Jul 1850, bapt. 14 Aug 1850 (Baptism, **St. Stephen Parish**)

- o Chilcott Douglas Harris – b. 17 Oct 1853, bapt. 15 Nov 1853 (Baptism, **St. Stephen Parish**)

Robert Russell Harris (father):

Residence - 3 Haddington Road - August 14, 1850

Shadding Fort Road - November 15, 1853

Occupation - Staff Captain - August 14, 1850

Major in the Staff - August 14, 1850

Military Rank - Colonel

Captain - August 14, 1850

Major - August 14, 1850

- • Rodolph Gleuber Harris & Anne Howard – 25 Feb 1779 (Marriage, **St. Anne Parish**)

- o John Vesey Harris – bapt. 22 Apr 1780 (Baptism, **St. Mary Parish**)

- o John Vesey Harris – bapt. 7 May 1781 (Baptism, **St. Mary Parish**) & Elizabeth Curtis – 23 Feb 1805 (Marriage, **St. Mary Parish**)

Elizabeth Curtis (daughter-in-law):

Relationship Status at Marriage - widow

- o Jane Catherine Harris – bapt. 19 Aug 1782 (Baptism, **St. Mary Parish**)

- o Rodolph Glanber Harris – bapt. 19 Aug 1783 (Baptism, **St. Mary Parish**)

Hurst

- Roger Harris, bur. 30 Aug 1693 (Burial, **St. Nicholas Within Parish**) & Alice Harris

  - Catherine Harris – bur. 17 Sep 1685 (Burial, **St. Michan Parish**)

  - Jane Harris – bur. 25 May 1688 (Burial, **St. Nicholas Within Parish**)

- Roland Henry Harris & Unknown

  - Henry Charles Harris & Mabel Catherine O'Brien – 25 Mar 1889 (Marriage, **St. Peter Parish**)

Signatures:

Henry Charles Harris (son):

   Residence - Portobello Barracks - March 25, 1889

   Occupation - Private Anny Service Corps - March 25, 1889

Mabel Catherine O'Brien, daughter of James O'Brien (daughter-in-law):

   Residence - 106 Harold's Cross Cottages - March 25, 1889

James O'Brien (father):

   Occupation - Farmer

Roland Henry Harris (father):

   Occupation - Hosier

- Samson Harris & Mary Unknown

  - Sarah Harris – bapt. 23 Apr 1706 (Baptism, **St. Catherine Parish**)

- Samuel Harris & Anne O'Neill – 11 Jul 1829 (Marriage, **St. James Parish**)

Samuel Harris (husband):

   Occupation - 1st Grenadier Guards - July 11, 1829

Harris Surname Ireland: 1600s to 1900s

- Samuel Harris & Bridget Kelly

    o Elizabeth Harris – bapt. 3 Oct 1825 (Baptism, **Innishannon Parish** (RC))

- Samuel Harris & Elizabeth Evans

    o Hannah Harris – bapt. 1863 (Baptism, **St. Andrew Parish** (RC))

Samuel Harris (father):

Residence - 1 Bamfield Lane - 1863

- Samuel Harris & Margaret Horgan

    o Thomas Harris – bapt. 9 Mar 1833 (Baptism, **Cork - South Parish** (RC))

    o John Harris – bapt. Mar 1834 (Baptism, **Cork - South Parish** (RC))

- Samuel Harris & Margaret Unknown

    o Samuel Harris – bapt. 17 May 1705 (Baptism, **St. Catherine Parish**)

- Samuel Harris & Rebecca Devicas – Feb 1719 (Marriage, **St. Werburgh Parish**)

    o Peter Harris – bapt. 11 Jan 1719 (Baptism, **St. Nicholas Within Parish**)

    o Charles Harris – bapt. 14 Jul 1721 (Baptism, **St. Nicholas Within Parish**)

    o Unknown Child Harris – bur. 29 May 1723 (Burial, **St. Nicholas Within Parish**)

This child could be either Peter or Charles.

    o John Harris – bapt. 13 Jul 1723 (Baptism, **St. Nicholas Within Parish**)

    o Samuel Harris – bapt. 17 Dec 1724 (Baptism, **St. Nicholas Within Parish**)

Hurst

- Samuel Harris & Unknown

  o William Harris & Elizabeth Gentleman – 17 Jul 1855 (Marriage, **Ardfert Parish**) (Marriage,

    Tralee Parish)

Signatures:

William Harris (son):

    Residence - Tralee - July 17, 1855

    Occupation - Butcher - July 17, 1855

Elizabeth Gentleman, daughter of Nicholas B. Gentleman (daughter-in-law):

    Residence - Ardfert - July 17, 1855

Nicholas B. Gentleman (father):

Signature:

    Occupation - Butcher

Samuel Harris (father):

    Occupation - Pensioner

Wedding Witnesses:

Nich. B. Gentleman & Nicholas Gentleman Junior

Signatures:

- Samuel Harris & Unknown

    o Martha Harris & John Maloney – 7 Jun 1868 (Marriage, **Grangegorman Parish**)

Signatures:

Martha Harris (daughter):

   Residence - 69 Manor Street - June 7, 1868

   Occupation - Servant - June 7, 1868

John Maloney, son of Thomas Maloney (son-in-law):

   Residence - Beer Somond Circular Terrace Road - June 7, 1868

   Occupation - Servant - June 7, 1868

Thomas Maloney (father):

   Occupation - Laborer

Samuel Harris (father):

   Occupation - Farmer

Hurst

Wedding Witnesses:

Richard Harris

Signature:

- Samuel Harris & Unknown

    o Samuel Harris & Mary White Brownrigg – 22 Jul 1863 (Marriage, **St. Anne Parish**)

Signatures:

Samuel Harris (son):

    Residence - Hiberman Hotel Dublin - July 22, 1863

        6 Thomas Street Waterford - July 22, 1863

    Occupation - Merchant - July 22, 1863

Mary White Brownrigg, daughter of George Brownrigg (daughter-in-law):

    Residence - 26 Molesworth Street - July 22, 1863

George Brownrigg (father):

    Occupation - Accountant

Samuel Harris (father):

    Occupation - Merchant

Harris Surname Ireland: 1600s to 1900s

- Samuel H. Harris & Catherine Harris

  o Richard Harris & Anne O'Kelly – 22 Nov 1864 (Marriage, **St. Mary, Pro Cathedral Parish** (RC))

Richard Harris (son):

Residence - Limerick - November 22, 1864

Anne O'Kelly, daughter of John O'Kelly & Anne Unknown (daughter-in-law):

Residence - Clare - November 22, 1864

- Simon Harris & Anne Sullivan – 1 May 1897 (Marriage, **Glenbeigh/Glencar Parish** (RC))

Anne Sullivan (wife):

Residence - Reennanallagane - May 1, 1897

- Simon Harris & Bridget Mangane

  o Bridget Harris – b. 1 Aug 1831, bapt. 1 Aug 1831 (Baptism, **Glenbeigh/Glencar Parish** (RC))

  o Simon Harris – b. 1 Dec 1833, bapt. 1 Dec 1833 (Baptism, **Glenbeigh/Glencar Parish** (RC))

Simon Harris (father):

Residence - Drom - August 1, 1831

December 1, 1833

- Simon Harris & Mary Burke – 3 Mar 1878 (Marriage, **Glenbeigh/Glencar Parish** (RC))

  o Catherine Harris – b. 23 Oct 1877, bapt. 23 Oct 1877 (Baptism, **Glenbeigh/Glencar Parish** (RC))

  o Catherine Harris – b. 25 Sep 1881, bapt. 25 Sep 1881 (Baptism, **Glenbeigh/Glencar Parish** (RC))

Hurst

Simon Harris (father):

Residence - Boherbee - October 23, 1877

Drom - September 25, 1881

Mary Burke (mother):

Residence - Drom - March 3, 1878

- Simon Harris & Mary Clifford – 14 Feb 1870 (Marriage, **Glenbeigh/Glencar Parish** (RC))

  - Julia Harris – b. 1 Feb 1873, bapt. 1 Feb 1873 (Baptism, **Glenbeigh/Glencar Parish** (RC))

  - John Harris – b. 31 May 1874, bapt. 31 May 1874 (Baptism, **Glenbeigh/Glencar Parish** (RC))

  - Catherine Harris – b. 22 Sep 1877, bapt. 22 Sep 1877 (Baptism, **Glenbeigh/Glencar Parish** (RC))

  - Simon Harris – b. 27 Sep 1880, bapt. 27 Sep 1880 (Baptism, **Glenbeigh/Glencar Parish** (RC))

  - Bridget Harris – b. 17 Apr 1884, bapt. 17 Apr 1884 (Baptism, **Glenbeigh/Glencar Parish** (RC))

Simon Harris (father):

Residence - Reennanallagane - February 1, 1873

May 31, 1874

September 22, 1877

September 27, 1880

April 17, 1884

Mary Clifford (mother):

Residence - Glenbeigh - February 14, 1870

- Simon Harris & Mary Lawler

  - John Harris – b. 1809, bapt. 1809 (Baptism, **Rathfarnham Parish** (RC))

  - William Harris – b. 1814, bapt. 1814 (Baptism, **Rathfarnham Parish** (RC))

Harris Surname Ireland: 1600s to 1900s

- Simon Harris & Mary Unknown

  - Anne Harris – b. 1828, bapt. 1828 (Baptism, *Rathfarnham Parish* (RC))

  - Simon Harris – b. 1834, bapt. 1834 (Baptism, *Rathfarnham Parish* (RC))

- Simon Harris & Rebecca Labore – 11 Sep 1731 (Marriage, *St. Andrew Parish*)

- Simon Harris, bur. 28 Sep 1674 (Burial, *St. John Parish*) & Unknown

  - Peter Harris – bapt. 3 Jul 1664 (Baptism, *St. John Parish*), bur. 5 Jul 1664 (Burial, *St. John Parish*)

- Simon Harris & Unknown

  - Julia Harris – b. 1 Feb 1825, bapt. 1 Feb 1825 (Baptism, *Glenbeigh/Glencar Parish* (RC))

Simon Harris (father):

Residence - Drom - February 1, 1825

- Solomon Harris & Catherine Day – 13 Jul 1849 (Marriage, *Cork - South Parish* (RC))

  - Francis Henry Harris – bapt. 1860 (Baptism, *St. Mary, Haddington Road Parish* (RC))

- Standish John Thornhill Harris & Catherine Harris

  - Anne Harris – b. 8 Aug 1891, bapt. 18 Oct 1891 (Baptism, *Arbour Hill Barracks Parish*)

  - Kathleen Mary Harris – b. 1 Jul 1893, bapt. 23 Sep 1893 (Baptism, *Arbour Hill Barracks Parish*)

  - Standish Richard Bateman Harris – b. 10 Jul 1895, bapt. 25 Aug 1895 (Baptism, *Arbour Hill Barracks Parish*)

  - John Standish Harris – b. 19 Feb 1897, bapt. 14 Mar 1897 (Baptism, *St. Andrew Parish*)

  - Mary Speering Harris – b. 10 Jul 1899, bapt. 6 Aug 1899 (Baptism, *St. Andrew Parish*)

Hurst

Standish John Thornhill Harris (father):

Residence - Linen Hall Barracks - October 18, 1891

September 23, 1893

Married Quarters Linen Hall Barracks - August 25, 1895

1 College Green - March 14, 1897

Foster Place - August 6, 1899

Occupation - Sergt Dublin City Artillery - October 18, 1891

September 23, 1893

Company Sergeant Major Dublin City Artillery - August 25, 1895

House Keeper - March 14, 1897

Caretaker - August 6, 1899

- Stephen Harris & Elizabeth O'Neill – 27 Nov 1843 (Marriage, **St. Nicholas Parish** (RC))

    o Gulielmo Harris – b. 26 May 1860, bapt. 4 Jun 1860 (Baptism, **St. Agatha Parish** (RC))

    (Baptism, **St. Lawrence Parish** (RC))

    o Elizabeth Harris – b. 24 Feb 1864, bapt. 29 Feb 1864 (Baptism, **St. Michan Parish** (RC))

    o Ellen Harris – b. 16 Jul 1865, bapt. 24 Jul 1865 (Baptism, **St. Michan Parish** (RC))

Stephen Harris (father):

Residence - 1 Aldboro Place - June 4, 1860

12 Lurgan Street - February 29, 1864

July 24, 1865

- Stephen Harris & Unknown

    o Joyce Harris – bur. 2 Mar 1703 (Burial, **St. Werburgh Parish**)

Joyce Harris (daughter):

Age at Death - infant

Place of Burial - church yard - March 2, 1703

Stephen Harris (father):

Residence - Damas Street - March 2, 1703

Harris Surname Ireland: 1600s to 1900s

- Thomas Harris & Abigail Murphy – 20 Jan 1789 (Marriage, **Cork - South Parish** (RC))

Thomas Harris (father):

Residence - Innishannon - January 20, 1789

Abigail Murphy (mother):

Residence - May Pole Road Cross - January 20, 1789

- Thomas Harris & Anne Harris

  o Elizabeth Harris – bur. 24 Sep 1671 (Burial, **St. Michan Parish**)

Thomas Harris (father):

Occupation - Carpenter

- Thomas Harris & Anne Harris

  o Samuel Harris – bapt. 12 Sep 1739 (Baptism, **St. Mark Parish**)

Thomas Harris (father):

Residence - Lazer's Hill - September 12, 1739

- Thomas Harris & Anne Johnson – 7 Jul 1758 (Marriage, **St. Catherine Parish**)

- Thomas Harris & Anne McEvoy

  o Thomas Harris – bapt. 2 Apr 1809 (Baptism, **St. Catherine Parish** (RC))

- Thomas Harris & Anne Murry

  o Patience Harris – bapt. 8 May 1743 (Baptism, **St. Catherine Parish** (RC))

  o Edward Harris – bapt. 13 Apr 1746 (Baptism, **St. Catherine Parish** (RC))

- Thomas Harris & Anne Harris

  o Thomas Harris – b. 11 Aug 1857, bapt. 9 Sep 1857 (Baptism, **St. Mary Parish**)

Thomas Harris (father):

Residence - 72 Upper Dominick Street - September 9, 1857

Occupation - Servant - September 9, 1857

Hurst

- Thomas Harris & Anne Redmond – 4 Jan 1825 (Marriage, **Rathfarnham Parish** (RC))

  o John Harris – b. 1829, bapt. 1829 (Baptism, **Rathfarnham Parish** (RC))

  o Mary Harris – b. 1831, bapt. 1831 (Baptism, **Rathfarnham Parish** (RC))

  o Thomas Harris – b. 1836, bapt. 1836 (Baptism, **Rathfarnham Parish** (RC))

  o Christopher Harris – b. 1839, bapt. 1839 (Baptism, **Rathfarnham Parish** (RC))

  o James Harris – b. 1844, bapt. 1844 (Baptism, **Rathfarnham Parish** (RC))

  o Henry Harris – b. 1845, bapt. 1845 (Baptism, **Rathfarnham Parish** (RC))

- Thomas Harris & Anne Unknown

  o James Harris – bapt. 13 Jan 1755 (Baptism, **St. Catherine Parish**)

- Thomas Harris & Anne Unknown

  o Benjamin Harris – b. 20 Mar 1878, bapt. 21 Jul 1878 (Baptism, **Hacketstown Parish**)

Thomas Harris (father):

Residence - Ballykillane - July 21, 1878

Occupation - Farmer - July 21, 1878

- Thomas Harris & Bridget Callaghan – 5 Oct 1839 (Marriage, **Bandon Parish** (RC))

- Thomas Harris & Bridget Farrell – 3 Feb 1843 (Marriage, **St. Andrew Parish** (RC))

  o Ellen Harris – bapt. 1845 (Baptism, **St. Andrew Parish** (RC))

  o Thomas Harris – bapt. 1853 (Baptism, **St. Andrew Parish** (RC))

- Thomas Harris & Bridget Harris

  o Joseph Harris – bapt. 24 Jul 1842 (Baptism, **St. Mary Parish**)

Thomas Harris (father):

Residence - St. Luke's Parish - July 24, 1842

Occupation - Shoemaker - July 24, 1842

- Thomas Harris & Bridget Rourke

  o William Harris – b. 1783, bapt. 1783 (Baptism, **Rathfarnham Parish** (RC))

  o William Harris – b. 1786, bapt. 1786 (Baptism, **Rathfarnham Parish** (RC))

Harris Surname Ireland: 1600s to 1900s

- Thomas Harris & Bridget Unknown

  o Thomas Harris Harris – b. 21 Nov 1824, bapt. 27 Dec 1824 (Baptism, **St. Peter Parish**)

- Thomas Harris & Bridget Unknown

  o Elizabeth Harris & John Holland – 16 May 1867 (Marriage, **St. Michan Parish (RC)**)

    ▪ Thomas Henry Holland – b. 3 Jun 1867, bapt. 12 Jun 1867 (Baptism, **St. Michan Parish (RC)**)

    ▪ James Patrick Holland – b. 1 Mar 1870, bapt. 11 Mar 1870 (Baptism, **St. Michan Parish (RC)**)

    ▪ Mary Anne Holland – b. 3 May 1873, bapt. 14 May 1873 (Baptism, **St. Michan Parish (RC)**)

Elizabeth Harris (daughter):

  Residence - 63 Dominick Street - May 16, 1867

John Holland, son of James Holland & Catherine Unknown (son-in-law):

  Residence - 63 Dominick Street - May 16, 1867

  63 Upper Dominick Street - June 12, 1867

  May 14, 1873

  23 Upper Dorset - March 11, 1870

- Thomas Harris & Bridget Unknown

  o Thomas Harris & Mary Jane Fullam – 15 Jul 1875 (Marriage, **St. Andrew Parish (RC)**)

    ▪ William Harris – b. 1876, bapt. 1876 (Baptism, **St. Andrew Parish (RC)**)

    ▪ Mary Ellen Harris – b. 1878, bapt. 1878 (Baptism, **St. Andrew Parish (RC)**)

    ▪ Valentine Thomas Harris – b. 1884, bapt. 1884 (Baptism, **St. Andrew Parish (RC)**)

Thomas Harris (son):

  Residence - 8 Erne Place - July 15, 1875

  1876

  20 Sandwith Place - 1878

  12 Clarence Place - 1884

Hurst

Mary Jane Fullam, daughter of Valentine Fullam & Ellen Unknown (daughter-in-law):

Residence - 16 Erne Street - July 15, 1875

- Thomas Harris & Bridget Wilson

  o John Harris – bapt. 26 Apr 1839 (Baptism, St. Catherine Parish (RC))

- Thomas Harris & Catherine Brown – Feb 1790 (Marriage, Kilmurry Parish (RC))

- Thomas Harris & Catherine Daly

  o Mary Harris – bapt. 23 Dec 1851(Baptism, Ballinhassig Parish (RC))

- Thomas Harris & Catherine Fitzgerald

  o Michael Harris – b. 12 Sep 1819, bapt. 12 Sep 1819 (Baptism, Tralee Parish (RC))

  o Thomas Harris – b. 13 Jan 1823, bapt. 13 Jan 1823 (Baptism, Tralee Parish (RC))

  o William Harris – b. 12 Apr 1830, bapt. 12 Apr 1830 (Baptism, Tralee Parish (RC))

Thomas Harris (father):

Residence - Cloghers - September 12, 1819

January 13, 1823

April 12, 1830

- Thomas Harris & Catherine Meck

  o Unknown Harris – bapt. Jan 1847 (Baptism, St. Michan Parish (RC))

- Thomas Harris & Catherine Sullivan – 4 Oct 1822 (Marriage, Timoleague & Barryroe Parish(RC))

  o Honora Harris – bapt. 15 Jul 1823 (Baptism, Lislee, Abbeymahon, & Donoughmore (Barryroe) Parish (RC))

  o Mary Harris – bapt. 25 Sep 1825 (Baptism, Lislee, Abbeymahon, & Donoughmore (Barryroe) Parish (RC))

  o William Harris – bapt. 10 Feb 1829 (Baptism, Lislee, Abbeymahon, & Donoughmore (Barryroe) Parish (RC))

Harris Surname Ireland: 1600s to 1900s

Thomas Harris (father):

Residence - Lislevane - July 15, 1823

September 25, 1825

February 10, 1829

- Thomas Harris & Debora Allen

  o Elizabeth Harris – bapt. 18 Oct 1800 (Baptism, **Cork - SS. Peter & Paul Parish** (RC))

Thomas Harris (father):

Residence - Patrick Street - October 18, 1800

- Thomas Harris & Deborah Harris

  o Margaret Harris – bapt. 20 Apr 1752 (Baptism, **St. Patrick Parish**)

- Thomas Harris & Elizabeth Harris

  o William Harris – bapt. 31 May 1737 (Baptism, **St. Catherine Parish**)

- Thomas Harris & Elizabeth Harris

  o Thomas Harris – bapt. 31 May 1744 (Baptism, **St. Paul Parish**)

- Thomas Harris & Elizabeth Harris

  o Mary Harris – b. 1748, bapt. 1748 (Baptism, **St. Andrew Parish** (RC))

- Thomas Harris & Elizabeth Harris

  o Thomas Harris – b. 15 Jan 1876, bapt. 18 Feb 1876 (Baptism, **St. Mary Parish**)

Thomas Harris (father):

Residence - 12 Upper Dorset Street - February 18, 1876

Occupation - Coach Man - February 18, 1876

- Thomas Harris & Elizabeth Quigley

  o Thomas Harris – bapt. 1777 (Baptism, **SS. Michael & John Parish** (RC))

  o Lawrence Harris – bapt. 1778 (Baptism, **SS. Michael & John Parish** (RC))

- Thomas Harris & Elizabeth Unknown

  o Robert Harris – bapt. 20 Jul 1712 (Baptism, **Carlow Parish**)

Hurst

- Thomas Harris & Elizabeth Unknown

  - Sarah Harris – bapt. 3 Aug 1735 (Marriage, **St. Nicholas Without Parish**)

Thomas Harris (father):

Residence - Frans Street - August 3, 1735

- Thomas Harris & Elizabeth Unknown

  - Anne Harris – bapt. 1781 (Baptism, **St. Andrew Parish** (RC))

- Thomas Harris & Elizabeth Jane Harris

  - Charles James Harris – b. 2 Oct 1893, bapt. 17 Dec 1893 (Baptism, **St. George Parish**)

Thomas Harris (father):

Residence - 27 Parnel Terrace - December 17, 1893

Occupation - Builder - December 17, 1893

- Thomas Harris & Ellen Crowly

  - John Harris – bapt. 27 Mar 1817 (Baptism, **Kinsale Parish** (RC))

- Thomas Harris & Ellen McCarthy

  - Catherine Harris – bapt. 15 Apr 1849 (Baptism, **Douglas Parish** (RC))

Thomas Harris (father):

Residence - Ballyduhig - April 15, 1849

- Thomas Harris & Frances Unknown

  - Hugh Harris – bapt. 21 Feb 1758 (Baptism, **St. Catherine Parish**)

- Thomas Harris, bur. 28 May 1685 (Burial, **St. Michan Parish**), & Hannah Harris

Thomas Harris (husband):

Occupation - Mealman - before May 28, 1685

Harris Surname Ireland: 1600s to 1900s

- Thomas Harris & Hannah Stewart – 3 Dec 1792 (Marriage, **St. Michan Parish**)

  o Elizabeth Harris – b. 1803, bapt. 28 Feb 1803 (Baptism, **St. Catherine Parish**)

  o Robert Joseph Harris – bapt. 6 Mar 1803 (Baptism, **St. Catherine Parish**)

  o Mary Hannah Harris – bapt. 3 May 1805 (Baptism, **St. Catherine Parish**)

  o James Charles Harris – b. 1807, bapt. 1 May 1807 (Baptism, **St. Catherine Parish**)

  o Jane Isabel Harris – b. 1810, bapt. Jan 1810 (Baptism, **St. Catherine Parish**)

  o Hannah Mary Harris – b. 1811, bapt. Dec 1811 (Baptism, **St. Catherine Parish**)

  o William Henry Harris – b. 1813, bapt. 30 Apr 1813 (Baptism, **St. Catherine Parish**)

  o Frederick Harris – b. 9 Jul 1815, bapt. Aug 1815 (Baptism, **St. Catherine Parish**)

Thomas Harris (father):

Residence - St. Michan's Parish - December 3, 1792

Cork Street - February 28, 1803

45 Cork Street - March 6, 1803

Queen Street - May 3, 1805

May 1, 1807

James Street - August 1815

Hannah Stewart (mother):

Residence - St. Michan's Parish - December 3, 1792

- Thomas Harris & Hannah Warren – 22 Sep 1860 (Marriage, **Cork - South Parish (RC)**)

  o Catherine Harris – bapt. 1 Jul 1861 (Baptism, **Cork - South Parish (RC)**)

Hurst

- Thomas Harris & Harriet Harris

  o Mary Harris – bapt. 26 Nov 1802 (Baptism, **St. Mark Parish**), bur. 26 Sep 1803 (Burial, **St. Mark Parish**)

The church register entry reads as follows:

"**September 26: A child of Capt. Harris**"

  o Anne Mary Harris – bapt. 21 Jun 1804 (Baptism, **St. Mark Parish**)

  o Emily Isabel Harris – bapt. 30 May 1809 (Baptism, **St. Mark Parish**)

  o Mary Adela Harris – bapt. 16 Dec 1810 (Baptism, **St. Mark Parish**)

  o Thomas Harris – bapt. 16 Dec 1810 (Baptism, **St. Mark Parish**)

Mary Adela Harris and Thomas Harris are Twins.

Thomas Harris (father):

Residence - 60 Townsend Street - November 26, 1802

Townsend Street - June 21, 1804

May 30, 1809

December 16, 1810

Military Rank - Captain - November 23, 1802

- Thomas Harris & Helen Ellen Mulcahy – 8 Feb 1876 (Marriage, **Cork - South Parish (RC)**)

  o Elizabeth Harris – b. 7 Nov 1876, bapt. 19 Nov 1876 (Baptism, **Cork - South Parish (RC)**)

  o James Patrick Harris – b. 26 Mar 1878, bapt. 28 Mar 1878 (Baptism, **Cork - South Parish (RC)**)

  o Mary Harris – b. 27 May 1879, bapt. 27 May 1879 (Baptism, **Cork - South Parish (RC)**)

Thomas Harris (father):

Residence - 46 Tower Street - March 28, 1878

47 Tower Street - May 27, 1879

Harris Surname Ireland: 1600s to 1900s

- Thomas Harris & Honora O'Leary – 18 Nov 1800 (Marriage, **Bandon Parish (RC)**)

  - Samuel Harris – bapt. 12 Jul 1804 (Baptism, **Bandon Parish (RC)**)

  - James Harris – bapt. 9 Oct 1806 (Baptism, **Bandon Parish (RC)**)

  - John Harris – bapt. 18 Apr 1818 (Baptism, **Bandon Parish (RC)**)

  - Robert Harris – bapt. 18 Nov 1820 (Baptism, **Bandon Parish (RC)**)

- Thomas Harris & Jane Harris

  - Anne Harris – bapt. 12 Apr 1724 (Baptism, **St. Catherine Parish**)

- Thomas Harris & Jane Unknown

  - Susanna Harris – bapt. 10 May 1705 (Baptism, **St. Catherine Parish**)

- Thomas Harris & Jane Unknown

  - Thomas Harris – b. 18 Jan 1837, bapt. 15 Feb 1837 (Baptism, **St. James Parish**)

Thomas Harris (father):

Residence - Richmond Barracks - February 15, 1837

Occupation - Late Private 46th Regiment - February 15, 1837

- Thomas Harris & Jane Unknown

  - Elizabeth Harris – b. 2 Jun 1839, bapt. 21 Jul 1839 (Baptism, **St. Peter Parish**)

Thomas Harris (father):

Residence - Aungier Street - July 21, 1839

- Thomas Harris & Madge Unknown

  - Emma Harris – b. 1833, bapt. 1833 (Baptism, **Rathfarnham Parish (RC)**)

- Thomas Harris & Margaret Cahill

  - Sarah Harris – bapt. 27 Jul 1854 (Baptism, **Cork - SS. Peter & Paul Parish (RC)**)

  - Helen Harris – bapt. 19 Oct 1856 (Baptism, **Cork - SS. Peter & Paul Parish (RC)**)

Hurst

- Thomas Harris & Margaret Coughlan

  - Harold Harris – bapt. 26 Sep 1833 (Baptism, **Innishannon Parish (RC)**)

  - Unknown Harris – bapt. 30 Apr 1835 (Baptism, **Innishannon Parish (RC)**)

  - William Harris – bapt. 17 Jul 1837 (Baptism, **Kinsale Parish (RC)**)

  - Eleanor Harris – bapt. 15 Oct 1839 (Baptism, **Clontead Parish(RC)**)

  - John Harris – bapt. 24 Apr 1842 (Baptism, **Kinsale Parish (RC)**)

  - Jeremiah Harris – bapt. 30 Jun 1844 (Baptism, **Kinsale Parish (RC)**)

  - Margaret Harris – bapt. 15 Apr 1849 (Baptism, **Kinsale Parish (RC)**)

Thomas Harris (father):

Residence - SH Castle - July 17, 1837

Horse Hill - April 24, 1842

Dunderrow - June 30, 1844

White Castle - April 15, 1849

- Thomas Harris & Margaret Fitzgerald – 31 Aug 1829 (Marriage, **Ballymacelligott & Ballyseedy Parish**)

- Thomas Harris & Margaret Gorman (G o r m a n) – 31 Jul 1789 (Marriage, **St. Andrew Parish (RC)**)

- Thomas Harris & Margaret Harris

  - Mary Harris – bapt. 16 Oct 1687 (Baptism, **St. Michan Parish**)

Thomas Harris (father):

Occupation - Victular - October 16, 1687

- Thomas Harris & Margaret Murphy

  - John Harris & Margaret Howlett – 25 Jun 1871 (Marriage, **Rathmines Parish (RC)**)

John Harris (son):

Residence - Hanover Street - June 25, 1871

Margaret Howlett, daughter of James Howlett & Anne Maher (daughter-in-law).

Harris Surname Ireland: 1600s to 1900s

- Thomas Harris & Margaret Payne – 27 Feb 1808 (Marriage, **Carlow Parish**)

Thomas Harris (father):

Military Service - Carlow Militia - February 27, 1808

- Thomas Harris & Margaret Riordan

  o Francis Harris – bapt. 26 Jan 1837 (Baptism, **Cork - SS. Peter & Paul Parish** (RC))

  o Philip Harris – bapt. 9 May 1839 (Baptism, **Cork - SS. Peter & Paul Parish** (RC))

  o John Harris – bapt. 2 Mar 1841 (Baptism, **Cork - South Parish** (RC))

- Thomas Harris & Margaret Unknown

  o Anne Harris – bapt. 13 Oct 1776 (Baptism, **St. Catherine Parish**)

Thomas Harris (father):

Residence - Dolphin's Barn - October 13, 1776

- Thomas Harris & Margaret Unknown

  o George Harris – bapt. 23 Mar 1818 (Baptism, **Carlow Parish**)

  o Thomas Harris – bapt. 11 May 1820 (Baptism, **Carlow Parish**)

  o Amelia Harris – bapt. 22 Sep 1822 (Baptism, **Carlow Parish**)

  o Richard Harris – bapt. 22 Sep 1822 (Baptism, **Carlow Parish**)

- Thomas Harris & Margaret Unknown

  o Mary Harris – b. 1853, bapt. 1853 (Baptism, **St. Andrew Parish** (RC))

- Thomas Harris & Margaret Unknown

  o Mary Anne Harris & John McCarthy – 23 Jan 1872 (Marriage, **St. Catherine Parish** (RC))

Mary Anne Harris (daughter):

Residence - 24 South Earl Street - January 23, 1872

John McCarthy, son of Charles McCarthy & Bridget Unknown (son-in-law):

Residence - Limerick - January 23, 1872

Hurst

- Thomas Harris & Margaret Unknown

  o Catherine Harris – bapt. 20 Oct 1746 (Baptism, **St. Mary, Pro Cathedral Parish** (RC))

- Thomas Harris & Martha Harris

  o Martha Harris – bapt. 30 Dec 1741 (Baptism, **St. Mark Parish**)

Thomas Harris (father):

Residence - George's Street - December 30, 1741

- Thomas Harris & Martha Unknown

  o John Harris – b. 29 May 1814, bapt. 28 Aug 1814 (Baptism, **St. Nicholas Without Parish**)

Thomas Harris (father):

Residence - New Street - August 28, 1814

- Thomas Harris & Mary Brien

  o Mary Harris – bapt. 21 Dec 1843 (Baptism, **Kilmacabea Parish** (RC))

  o Joan Harris – bapt. 4 May 1850 (Baptism, **Kilmacabea Parish** (RC))

- Thomas Harris & Mary Carr – 1840 (Marriage, **St. Nicholas Parish** (RC))

  o Thomas Harris – bapt. 16 Jun 1841 (Baptism, **St. Nicholas Parish** (RC))

- Thomas Harris & Mary Casey – 26 Oct 1858 (Marriage, **Kinsale Parish** (RC))

  o Thomas Harris – bapt. 27 Apr 1859 (Baptism, **Kinsale Parish** (RC))

  o Francis Harris – b. 2 Jan 1861, bapt. 3 Jan 1861 (Baptism, **Kinsale Parish** (RC))

  o Bridget Harris – b. 4 Feb 1866, bapt. 5 Feb 1866 (Baptism, **Kinsale Parish** (RC))

  o Margaret Harris – b. 1 Aug 1868, bapt. 9 Aug 1868 (Baptism, **Kinsale Parish** (RC))

  o Joan Harris – b. 28 Feb 1871, bapt. 5 Mar 1871 (Baptism, **Kinsale Parish** (RC))

  o Elizabeth Harris – b. 19 Apr 1873, bapt. 20 April 1873 (Baptism, **Kinsale Parish** (RC))

  o Richard Harris – b. 26 Jul 1875, bapt. 30 Jul 1875 (Baptism, **Kinsale Parish** (RC))

Harris Surname Ireland: 1600s to 1900s

Thomas Harris (father):

    Residence - Barrack Street - April 27, 1859

                                January 3, 1861

                                February 5, 1866

                                August 9, 1868

                                March 5, 1871

                                April 20, 1873

                                July 30, 1875

- Thomas Harris & Mary Coates – 25 Oct 1826 (Marriage, St. James Parish)

  o John Eyre Harris & Frances Evans – 19 Aug 1856 (Marriage, Clontarf Parish)

Signatures:

Signatures (Marriage):

John Eyre Harris (son):

    Residence - Strandville Avenue Clontarf - August 19, 1856

    Occupation - Contractor - August 19, 1856

Francis Evans, daughter of George William Evans (daughter-in-law)

    Residence - Strandville Avenue Clontarf - August 19, 1856

Hurst

Wedding Witnesses:

W. H. Harris

Signature:

o Mary Harris & Samuel Martin – 16 Feb 1857 (Marriage, **St. Andrew Parish**)

Signatures:

Mary Harris (daughter):

> Residence - Strand Ville Avenue Clontarf - February 16, 1857

Samuel Martin, Son of John Martin (son-in-law):

> Residence - No 7 College Green - February 16, 1857

> Occupation - Merchant - February 16, 1857

John Martin (father):

> Occupation - Farmer

Wedding Witnesses:

William Henry Harris & John Eyre Harris

Signatures:

Harris Surname Ireland: 1600s to 1900s

○ William Henry Harris & Leticia Wilson – 28 Sep 1861 (Marriage, **St. Thomas Parish**)

Signatures:

Signatures (Marriage):

▪ Leticia Frances Harris – b. 19 Dec 1865, bapt. 24 Jan 1867 (Baptism, **St. Mary Parish**)

William Henry Harris (son):

Residence - 100 Middle Abbey Street - September 28, 1861

100 Abbey Street - January 24, 1867

Occupation - Glass Merchant - September 28, 1861

January 24, 1867

Leticia Wilson, daughter of John Wilson (daughter-in-law):

Residence - 73 Seville Place - September 28, 1861

John Wilson (father):

Occupation - REVN Officer

Hurst

Wedding Witnesses:

John E. Harris

Signature:

Thomas Harris (father):

Residence - St. Mary's Parish - October 25, 1826

Occupation - Gentleman - October 25, 1826

Gentleman

Merchant

Mary Coates (mother):

Residence - St. James Parish - October 25, 1826

- Thomas Harris & Mary Crowly

  - Elizabeth Harris – bapt. 4 Mar 1821 (Baptism, Kinsale Parish (RC))

  - John Harris – bapt. 8 May 1823 (Baptism, Kinsale Parish (RC))

  - Emanuel Harris – bapt. 27 Dec 1824 (Baptism, Kinsale Parish (RC))

- Thomas Harris & Mary Dignam – 18 Nov 1838 (Marriage, St. Mary, Pro Cathedral Parish

  (RC))

  - Margaret Harris – b. 15 May 1854, bapt. 17 May 1854 (Baptism, St. Mary, Pro Cathedral

    Parish (RC))

Thomas Harris (father):

Residence - 16 Bolton Street - May 17, 1854

- Thomas Harris & Mary Donahy

  - Mary Harris – bapt. 15 Aug 1819 (Baptism, Cork - South Parish (RC))

- Thomas Harris & Mary Donovan – 17 Jun 1821 (Marriage, Rossalettiri & Kilkeraunmor

  (Roscarbery & Lissevard) Parish (RC))

Harris Surname Ireland: 1600s to 1900s

- Thomas Harris & Mary Grady – 16 Jul 1844 (Marriage, **Cork - SS. Peter & Paul Parish** (RC))

- Thomas Harris & Mary Griffin

  o Catherine Harris – b. 21 Oct 1802, bapt. 21 Oct 1802 (Baptism, **Tralee Parish** (RC))

Thomas Harris (father):

Residence - Tralee - October 21, 1802

- Thomas Harris & Mary Harney (H a r n e y)

  o Bernard Lawrence Harris – bapt. 19 Aug 1849 (Baptism, **St. Nicholas Parish** (RC))

- Thomas Harris & Mary Harris

  o John Harris – bapt. 3 Aug 1724 (Baptism, **St. Luke Parish**)

Thomas Harris (father):

Occupation - Weaver - August 3, 1724

- Thomas Harris & Mary Harris

  o Mary Harris – bapt. 11 Feb 1776 (Baptism, **St. Luke Parish**)

Thomas Harris (father):

Residence - Skinner's Alley - February 11, 1776

Occupation - Sawer - February 11, 1776

- Thomas Harris & Mary Lawton

  o Anne Harris – bapt. 22 Jul 1821 (Baptism, **Cork - South Parish** (RC))

- Thomas Harris & Mary Mooney

  o John Harris – bapt. 20 Apr 1845 (Baptism, **St. Nicholas Parish** (RC))

Hurst

- Thomas Harris & Mary Sullivan – 7 Sep 1789 (Marriage, **Tralee Parish** (RC))

  o John Harris – b. 11 Aug 1790, bapt. 11 Aug 1790 (Baptism, **Tralee Parish** (RC))

  o Catherine Harris – b. 10 Jun 1792, bapt. 10 Jun 1792 (Baptism, **Tralee Parish** (RC))

  o Elizabeth Harris – b. 20 Nov 1794, bapt. 20 Nov 1794 (Baptism, **Tralee Parish** (RC))

  o Mary Harris – b. 1 May 1798, bapt. 1 May 1798 (Baptism, **Tralee Parish** (RC))

  o Thomas Harris – b. 6 Oct 1801, bapt. 6 Oct 1801 (Baptism, **Tralee Parish** (RC))

  o Catherine Harris – b. 1 Nov 1802, bapt. 1 Nov 1802 (Baptism, **Tralee Parish** (RC))

Thomas Harris (father):

Residence - Tralee - September 7, 1789

June 10, 1792

November 20, 1794

May 1, 1798

October 6, 1801

November 1, 1802

- Thomas Harris & Mary Unknown, bur. 7 Dec 1702 (Burial, **Carlow Parish**)

  o Sarah Harris – bapt. 24 Jan 1699 (Baptism, **Carlow Parish**)

- Thomas Harris & Mary Unknown

  o Samuel Harris – bapt. 1783 (Baptism, **St. Andrew Parish** (RC))

- Thomas Harris & Mary Unknown

  o Mary Harris – bapt. 5 Jul 1837 (Baptism, **St. Mary, Pro Cathedral Parish** (RC))

  o Joseph Peter Harris – bapt. 11 Apr 1841 (Baptism, **St. Mary, Pro Cathedral Parish**

  (RC))

- Thomas Harris & Mary Unknown

  o Hannah Harris – b. 8 Dec 1840, bapt. 10 Feb 1841 (Baptism, **St. Peter Parish**)

Thomas Harris (father):

Residence - 37 Lower Charlemont Street - February 10, 1841

Occupation - Private Gentleman - February 10, 1841

Harris Surname Ireland: 1600s to 1900s

- Thomas Harris & Mary Unknown

  ○ Mary Harris – bapt. 1843 (Baptism, **St. Andrew Parish** (RC))

- Thomas Harris & Mary Unknown

  ○ John Harris & Mary Carroll – 20 Sep 1868 (Marriage, **St. Catherine Parish** (RC))

    ▪ John Joseph Harris – b. 21 Aug 1870, bapt. 22 Aug 1870 (Baptism, **St. Nicholas Parish** (RC))

    ▪ Mary Anne Harris – b. 6 Jan 1875, bapt. 8 Jan 1875 (Baptism, **St. Nicholas Parish** (RC))

    ▪ William Joseph Harris – b. 27 Apr 1877, bapt. 30 Apr 1877 (Baptism, **St. Nicholas Parish** (RC))

    ▪ Michael Harris – b. 1 Oct 1879, bapt. 6 Oct 1879 (Baptism, **St. Nicholas Parish** (RC))

John Harris (son):

Residence - 27 Meath Street - September 20, 1868

19 Coombe - August 22, 1870

January 8, 1875

April 30, 1877

October 6, 1879

Mary Carroll, daughter of Thomas Carroll & Bridget Unknown (daughter-in-law):

Residence - 7 Meath Street - September 20, 1868

- Thomas Harris & Mary Unknown

  ○ Francis Harris & Catherine Bermingham (B e r m i n g h a m) – 20 Jun 1873 (Marriage, **St. Nicholas Parish** (RC))

Francis Harris (son):

Residence - 76 Bride Street - June 20, 1873

Catherine Bermingham, daughter of Thomas Bermingham & Mary Unknown (daughter-in-law):

Residence - 76 Bride Street - June 20, 1873

Hurst

- Thomas Harris & Mary Anne Warren

  o Rose Harris – bapt. 1 Sep 1817 (Baptism, **Cork - South Parish** (RC))

- Thomas Harris & Maud Unknown, bur. 20 Nov 1668 (Burial, **St. John Parish**)

  o Thomas Harris – bur. 11 Oct 1667 (Burial, **St. John Parish**)

- Thomas Harris & Sally Richeson

  o Mary Harris – bapt. 4 Jun 1820 (Baptism, **Caharagh Parish** (RC))

- Thomas Harris & Sarah Harris

  o John Harris – bur. 30 Jan 1726 (Burial, **St. Luke Parish**)

John Harris (son):

Cause of Death - from teeth

- Thomas Harris & Sarah Agnes Harris

  o Thomas John Harris – b. 26 Nov 1888, bapt. 24 Feb 1889 (Baptism, **St. Peter Parish**)

Thomas Harris (father):

Residence - Proud's Lane - February 24, 1889

Occupation - Builder - February 24, 1889

- Thomas Harris & Susan Browne – 9 Sep 1843 (Marriage, **Kilmichael Parish** (RC))

- Thomas Harris & Susanna Harris

  o Thomas Harris – bapt. 24 Jul 1789 (Baptism, **St. Mary Parish**)

Thomas Harris (father):

Residence - Liffey Street - July 24, 1789

- Thomas Harris & Unknown

  o Thomas Harris – bapt. 28 Jan 1638 (Baptism, **St. John Parish**)

  o Thomas Harris – bapt. 28 Jan 1639 (Baptism, **St. John Parish**)

- Thomas Harris & Unknown

  o Wilt Harris – bapt. 10 Oct 1688 (Baptism, **St. John Parish**)

Harris Surname Ireland: 1600s to 1900s

- Thomas Harris & Unknown

  o Mary Harris – bapt. 6 Jun 1699 (Baptism, **St. Catherine Parish**)

- Thomas Harris & Unknown

  o John Harris – bapt. 9 Dec 1700 (Baptism, **St. Catherine Parish**)

- Thomas Harris & Unknown

  o Lawrence Harris – bapt. 23 Sep 1744 (Baptism, **St. Mary, Pro Cathedral Parish (RC)**)

- Thomas Harris & Unknown

  o Harold Harris – bapt. 30 Nov 1790 (Baptism, **Kilmurry Parish (RC)**)

- Thomas Harris & Unknown

  o Michael Harris & Margaret Deady – 27 Feb 1849 (Marriage, **Tralee Parish**)

Signatures:

- John Harris – b. 19 May 1850, bapt. 19 May 1850 (Baptism, **Tralee Parish (RC)**)

Michael Harris (son):

Residence - Tralee - February 27, 1849

Occupation - Laborer - February 27, 1849

Margaret Deady, daughter of John Deady (daughter-in-law):

Residence - Tralee - February 27, 1849

Relationship Status at Marriage - minor age

John Deady (father):

Occupation - Laborer

Thomas Harris (father):

Occupation - Weaver

Hurst

- Thomas Harris & Unknown

  - Elizabeth Harris Cranston & John Beahan – 25 Jul 1859 (Marriage, **St. Catherine Parish**)

Signatures:

Elizabeth Harris (daughter):

    Residence - 95 Cork Street - July 25, 1859

    Relationship Status at Marriage - widow

John Beahan, son of Maurice Beahan (son-in-law):

    Residence - 95 Cork Street - July 25, 1859

    Occupation - Writing Clerk - July 25, 1859

Maurice Beahan (father):

    Occupation - Farmer

Thomas Harris (father):

    Occupation - Stucco Plasterer

- Thomas Harris & Unknown

  - Catherine Harris Lyons & Richard Colclough – 2 Oct 1865 (Marriage, **St. Peter Parish**)

Signatures:

Harris Surname Ireland: 1600s to 1900s

Catherine Harris (daughter):

Residence - 5 Lower Camden Street - October 2, 1865

Relationship Status at Marriage - widow

Richard Colclough, son of William Colclough (son-in-law):

Residence - 30 Wexford Street - October 2, 1865

Occupation - Coach Painter - October 2, 1865

Relationship Status at Marriage - widow

William Colclough (father):

Occupation - Farmer

Thomas Harris (father):

Occupation - Farmer

- o   Jane Harris Manning & James Lynham – 30 Jul 1866 (Marriage, **St. Bride Parish**)

Signatures:

Jane Harris (daughter):

Residence - Bride Street - July 30, 1866

Relationship Status at Marriage - widow

James Lynham, son of Patrick Lynham (son-in-law):

Residence - Bride Street - July 30, 1866

Occupation - Servant - July 30, 1866

Patrick Lynham (father):

Occupation - Gardener

Thomas Harris (father):

Occupation - Farmer

Hurst

- Thomas Harris & Unknown

Signatures:

○ John William Harris & Fanny Isabel Carroll – 26 Sep 1868 (Marriage, **St. Stephen Parish**)

Signatures:

John William Harris (son):

    Residence - 54 Fitzwilliam Square - September 26, 1868

    Occupation - Barrister at Law - September 26, 1868

Fanny Isabel Carroll, daughter of William Hales Carroll (daughter-in-law):

    Residence - 11 Harcourt Street - September 26, 1868

William Hales Carroll (father):

Signature:

    Occupation - Solicitor

Thomas Harris (father):

Occupation - Q C

Wedding Witnesses:

W. Hales Carroll & Thomas Harris

Signatures:

○ Henrietta Mary Harris & Thomas O'Grady Ussher – 14 Jan 1869 (Marriage, **St. Stephen**

Parish)

Signatures:

▪ Thomas Harris Ussher – b. 30 Sep 1877, bapt. 22 Oct 1877 (Baptism, **St. Stephen Parish**)

Henrietta Mary Harris (daughter):

Residence - 54 Fitzwilliam Square - January 14, 1869

Thomas O'Grady Ussher, son of Christopher Musgrave Ussher (son-in-law):

Residence - Camphire Villierstown, Co. Waterford - January 14, 1869

54 Fitzwilliam Square - October 22, 1877

Occupation - Esquire - January 14, 1869

October 22, 1877

Christopher Musgrave Ussher (father):

Occupation - Esquire

Thomas Harris (father):

Occupation - Barrister at Law

Hurst

Wedding Witnesses:

Thomas Harris & A. E. Ussher

Signatures:

- Thomas Harris & Unknown

  o John Harris & Charlotte Thomas – 18 Sep 1877 (Marriage, **St. Stephen Parish**)

Signatures:

John Harris (son):

    Residence - Mallow, Co. Cork - September 18, 1877

    Occupation - Late Captain 35th Regiment - September 18, 1877

Charlotte Thomas, daughter of Richard Thomas (daughter-in-law):

    Residence - 74 Lower Mount Street - September 18, 1877

            Ruthpearm, Co. Cork - September 18, 1877

Richard Thomas (father):

    Occupation - Esquire

Thomas Harris (father):

    Occupation - Esquire

Harris Surname Ireland: 1600s to 1900s

- Thomas Harris & Unknown

  o Thomas Harris & Jane McCreedy – 9 Nov 1878 (Marriage, **Dromod & Prior Parish**)

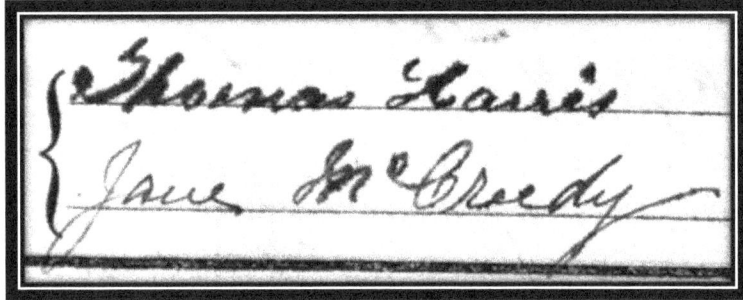

Signatures:

- Elizabeth Jane Harris – b. 4 Oct 1879, bapt. Nov 1879 (Baptism, **Dromod & Prior Parish**)

- Lucy Harris – b. 15 Nov 1880, bapt. 16 Jan 1881 (Baptism, **Dromod & Prior Parish**)

- Catherine Harris – b. 6 Apr 1884, bapt. 30 Oct 1885 (Baptism, **Cahir Parish**)

- Mary Anne Harris – b. 2 Oct 1885, bapt. 30 Oct 1885 (Baptism, **Cahir Parish**)

- Jane Harris – b. 23 Jan 1887, bapt. 11 Feb 1887 (Baptism, **Cahir Parish**)

- Joseph Harris – b. 10 Jun 1889, bapt. 11 Jun 1889 (Baptism, **Cahir Parish**), bur. 13 Jun 1891 (Burial, **Kilcolman Parish**)

Joseph Harris (son of Thomas Harris & Jane McCreedy):

Residence - Coastguard Station - June 13, 1891

Age at Death - 2 years

- William Harris – b. 30 Mar 1891, bapt. 17 May 1891 (Baptism, **Killorglin Parish**)

- James Harris – b. 22 Jul 1893, bapt. 27 Aug 1893 (Baptism, **Killorglin Parish**)

- Margaret Harris – b. 6 Apr 1895, bapt. 19 May 1895 (Baptism, **Killorglin Parish**)

Hurst

Thomas Harris (son):

Residence - Ballinskelligs - November 9, 1878

November 1879

January 16, 1881

Kells Coast Guard Station - October 30, 1885

February 11, 1887

June 11, 1889

Cromane - May 17, 1891

Coast Guard Station - August 27, 1893

May 19, 1895

Occupation - Coast Guard - November 9, 1878

November 1879

January 16, 1881

October 30, 1885

February 11, 1887

June 11, 1889

May 17, 1891

August 27, 1893

May 19, 1895

Jane McCreedy, daughter of John McCreedy (daughter-in-law):

Residence - Ballinskelligs - November 9, 1878

John McCreedy (father):

Occupation - Retired Coast Guard

- Thomas Harris & Unknown

  o Elizabeth Harris & John Grannan – 28 Dec 1884 (Marriage, St. Andrew Parish (RC))

Elizabeth Harris (daughter):

Residence - 10 Moss Street - December 28, 1884

John Grannan, son of Michael Grannan (son-in-law):

Residence - 10 Moss Street - December 28, 1864

Harris Surname Ireland: 1600s to 1900s

- Thomas Harris & Unknown

Signature:

- o Elizabeth Anne Harris & Joseph Noblett – 1 Jul 1890 (Marriage, **St. George Parish**)

Signatures:

Elizabeth Anne Harris (daughter):

    Residence - Castlerea, Co. Roscommon - July 1, 1890

Joseph Noblett, son of Joseph Noblett (son-in-law):

    Residence - 40 St. Patrick's Road - July 1, 1890

    Occupation - Commercial Clerk - July 1, 1890

Joseph Noblett (father):

    Occupation - Farmer

Thomas Harris (father):

    Occupation - Farmer

Wedding Witnesses:

Thomas Harris & Edward Johnston

Signatures:

Hurst

- Timothy Harris & Margaret Coghlan

  - John Harris – bapt. 2 Feb 1802 (Baptism, **Cork - South Parish** (RC))

  - Michael Harris – bapt. Feb 1804 (Baptism, **Cork - South Parish** (RC))

  - Jane Harris – bapt. Dec 1804 (Baptism, **Cork - South Parish** (RC))

  - Daniel Harris – bapt. 28 Oct 1806 (Baptism, **Cork - South Parish** (RC))

  - James Harris – bapt. 16 Apr 1808 (Baptism, **Cork - South Parish** (RC))

  - Ellen Harris – bapt. 27 Jul 1810 (Baptism, **Cork - South Parish** (RC))

  - Timothy Harris –bapt. 1 Apr 1814 (Baptism, **Cork - South Parish** (RC))

  - Mary Harris – bapt. 26 Apr 1816 (Baptism, **Cork - South Parish** (RC))

Timothy Harris (father):

Residence - Weight Lane - February 2, 1802

Old Wighouse Lane - February 1804

December of 1804

Cat Lane - October 28, 1806

April 16, 1808

July 27, 1810

- Timothy Harris & Margaret Reardon

  - Elizabeth Harris – bapt. 18 Apr 1831 (Baptism, **Cork - South Parish** (RC))

- Timothy Harris & Mary McCarthy – 20 Nov 1826 (Marriage, **Cork - South Parish** (RC))

- Unknown Harris & Anne Unknown

  - James Harris – bapt. 1870 (Baptism, **Clondalkin Parish** (RC))

Unknown Harris (father):

Residence - Clondalkin - 1870

- Unknown Harris & Gobinet Rourke

  - Michael Harris – b. 27 Nov 1837, bapt. 27 Nov 1837 (Baptism, **Killorglin Parish** (RC))

Unknown Harris (father):

Residence - Killorglin - November 27, 1837

Harris Surname Ireland: 1600s to 1900s

- Unknown Harris & Louisa Unknown

  - Catherine Harris – bapt. 1857 (Baptism, **St. Andrew Parish** (RC))

- Unknown Harris & Mary Harris

  - Daniel Harris – bapt. 8 Jul 1817 (Baptism, **Kilnaughtin Parish**)

  - John Harris – bapt. 10 Nov 1822 (Baptism, **Kilnaughtin Parish**)

Mary Harris (mother):

> Residence - Ballydonoghue - July 8, 1817

> > Doonard - November 10, 1822

Both of her children were illegitimate.

- Unknown Harris & Sarah Warren

  - Mary Harris – bapt. 10 Jun 1803 (Baptism, **Cork - South Parish** (RC))

- Unknown Harris & Unknown

  - Emily Harris – b. 3 Dec 1886, bapt. 3 Dec 1886 (Baptism, **Killarney Parish**)

Unknown Harris (father):

> Residence - Barracks Killarney - December 3, 1886

> Occupation - Private Soldier - December 3, 1886

- Unknown Harris & Unknown

  - Mary - - Harris – b. 5 Oct Unclear (Baptism, **St. Stephen Parish**)

Unknown Harris (father):

> Residence - 63 Upper - - Street - October 5th

> Occupation - Civil Servant - October 5th

Hurst

- Valentine Harris & Catherine Early

  - Catherine Harris & Joseph Dunne – 21 Feb 1886 (Marriage, **St. Mary, Haddington Road Parish** (RC))

    - Valentine Dunne – b. 30 May 1886, bapt. 31 May 1886 (Baptism, **St. Mary, Haddington Road Parish** (RC))

Catherine Harris (daughter):

Residence - 17 Turner's Cottages - February 21, 1886

Joseph Dunne, son of Jeremiah Dunne & Margaret Unknown (son-in-law):

Residence - 111 Brunswick Street - February 21, 1886

16 Turner's Cottages - May 31, 1886

  - Valentine Harris & Bridget Kinsella – 24 Jul 1898 (Marriage, **Harrington Street Parish** (RC))

    - Valentine Harris – b. 7 May 1899, bapt. 8 May 1899 (Baptism, **St. Mary, Haddington Road Parish** (RC))

    - George Harris – b. 25 Jan 1904, bapt. 1 Feb 1904 (Baptism, **St. Mary, Haddington Road Parish** (RC))

    - James Harris – b. 13 Jan 1905, bapt. 23 Jan 1905 (Baptism, **St. Mary, Haddington Road Parish** (RC))

Valentine Harris (son):

Residence - 13 Saofort Avenue - July 24, 1898

51 Shelbourne Road - May 8, 1899

53 Shelbourne Road - February 1, 1904

January 23, 1905

Bridget Kinsella, daughter of John Kinsella & Catherine Byrne (daughter-in-law):

Residence - St. Victoria Street - July 24, 1898

Harris Surname Ireland: 1600s to 1900s

- o Mary Anne Harris – bapt. 1860 (Baptism, **St. Mary, Haddington Road Parish** (RC)) &
  Peter Keogh – 15 Feb 1885 (Marriage, **St. Mary, Haddington Road Parish** (RC))

Mary Anne Harris (daughter):

Residence - 17 Turner's Cottages - February 15, 1885

Peter Keogh, son of Peter Keogh & Winifred Unknown (son-in-law):

Residence - 10 Turner's Cottages - February 15, 1885

- o Elizabeth Harris – bapt. 1863 (Baptism, **St. Mary, Haddington Road Parish** (RC)) &
  James Ennis – 25 Sep 1887 (Marriage, **St. Mary, Haddington Road Parish** (RC))

  - ▪ James Joseph Ennis – b. 25 May 1888, bapt. 28 May 1888 (Baptism, **St. Mary,**
    Haddington Road Parish (RC))

Elizabeth Harris (daughter):

Residence - 17 Turner's Cottages - September 25, 1887

James Ennis, son of James Ennis & Catherine Unknown (son-in-law):

Residence - 6 Donnybrook - September 25, 1887

                  17 Turner's Cottages - May 28, 1888

- o George Harris – b. 22 Jun 1880, bapt. 28 Jun 1880 (Baptism, **St. Mary, Haddington Road**
  Parish (RC))

Valentine Harris (father):

Residence - 17 Turner's Cottage Shelbourne Road - June 28, 1880

Hurst

- Valentine Harris & Catherine Gannon – 18 Aug 1858 (Marriage, St. Mary, Haddington Road Parish (RC))

  o Valentine Harris – b. 1866, bapt. 1866 (Baptism, St. Mary, Haddington Road Parish (RC))

  o James Harris – b. 1869, bapt. 1869 (Baptism, St. Mary, Haddington Road Parish (RC))

  o Sarah Harris – b. 1871, bapt. 1871 (Baptism, St. Mary, Haddington Road Parish (RC))

  o Jane Harris – b. 1872, bapt. 1872 (Baptism, St. Mary, Haddington Road Parish (RC))

  o Valentine Harris – b. 1873, bapt. 1873 (Baptism, St. Mary, Haddington Road Parish (RC))

  o John Harris – b. 1876, bapt. 1876 (Baptism, St. Mary, Haddington Road Parish (RC))

- W. William Harris & Mary Unknown

  o Sarah Harris – b. 20 Oct 1812, bapt. 29 Oct 1812 (Baptism, Dunleckney Parish), bur. 3 Sep 1842 (Burial, Dunleckney Parish)

  o Ellen Harris – b. 7 Mar 1815, bapt. 19 Mar 1815 (Baptism, Dunleckney Parish)

  o Elizabeth Harris – b. 6 Mar 1818, bapt. 8 Mar 1818 (Baptism, Dunleckney Parish)

  o Mary Harris – b. 4 Apr 1821, bapt. 7 Apr 1821 (Baptism, Dunleckney Parish)

- Walt Harris & Elizabeth Blackwell – 1 Dec 1670 (Marriage, St. Michael Parish)

- Walter Harris & Anne Mahoney

  o Augustine John Harris – b. 6 Dec 1874, bapt. 9 Dec 1874 (Baptism, St. Catherine Parish (RC))

  o Walter Edward Harris – b. 13 Oct 1876, bapt. Oct 1876 (Baptism, St. Catherine Parish (RC))

Walter Harris (father):

Residence - 3 New Row - October 1876

December 9, 1874

Harris Surname Ireland: 1600s to 1900s

- Walter Harris & Elizabeth Ware – 22 Sep 1725 (Marriage, **St. Anne Parish**)

- Walter Harris & Jane Coleman – 28 Apr 1787 (Marriage, **St. Bride Parish**)

- Walter Harris & Juliana Donovan

  - Sarah Harris – bapt. 2 Nov 1814 (Baptism, **Cork - South Parish** (RC))

- Walter Harris & Mary Brennan

  - Anne Eilleen Harris – b. 10 Dec 1891, bapt. 13 Dec 1891 (Baptism, **St. Joseph Parish** (RC))

Walter Harris (father):

Residence - America - December 13, 1891

- Walter Harris & Unknown

  - Eleanor Harris – bapt. 11 Oct 1686 (Baptism, **St. Michan Parish**)

  - Edey Harris – bapt. 24 Jul 1687 (Baptism, **St. Michan Parish**)

The church register entry for each child reads as follows:

"Bapt. A parish child Ellinor, an orphan, who was let at Mr. Walter Harris, his door."

"Bapt. Edey an orphan, who was left at Mr. Walter Harris, his doore."

- Walter Harris & Unknown

  - Walter Harris – bur. 16 Nov 1692 (Burial, **St. Michan Parish**)

The church register entry reads as follows:

"Walter, son of Walter Harris, gent, and his wife [blank], in the first vault on the

left hand of the second entrance, under the body of the church."

Hurst

- Walter Edward Harris & Jane Harris

  - Frederick William Harris – b. 14 Sep 1878, bapt. 17 Nov 1878 (Baptism, **St. Peter Parish**)

  - Septimus Robert Harris – b. 9 Nov 1879, bapt. 25 Nov 1879 (Baptism, **Cahir Parish**)

Walter Edward Harris (father):

Residence - 35 Lombard St West - November 17, 1878

Caherciveen - November 25, 1879

Occupation - Accountant - November 17, 1878

Assistant National Bank - November 25, 1879

- Waltin Harris & Anne Mahoney

  - Anne Agnes Harris – b. 1891, bapt. 1891 (Baptism, **St. Andrew Parish** (RC))

Waltin Harris (father):

Residence - 16 Queens Street - 1891

- William Harris & Alice Power – 25 Sep 1803 (Marriage, **St. Catherine Parish** (RC))

- William Harris & Anne Airs

  - Catherine Harris – bapt. 22 Jun 1796 (Baptism, **Cork - South Parish** (RC))

- William Harris & Anne Boyle – 30 May 1842 (Marriage, **St. Andrew Parish** (RC))

- William Harris & Anne Harris

  - Elizabeth Harris – bapt. 8 Sep 1744 (Baptism, **St. Luke Parish**)

  - Anne Harris – bapt. 19 May 1746 (Baptism, **St. Luke Parish**)

  - Richard Harris – bapt. 10 Jul 1748 (Baptism, **St. Luke Parish**)

  - William Harris – bapt. 11 Jul 1756 (Baptism, **St. Luke Parish**)

Harris Surname Ireland: 1600s to 1900s

- William Harris & Anne Harris

  - Elizabeth Harris – bapt. 18 Apr 1775 (Baptism, **St. Luke Parish**)

  - Anne Harris – bapt. 18 Jun 1779 (Baptism, **St. Luke Parish**)

  - Anne Harris – bapt. 10 Sep 1780 (Baptism, **St. Luke Parish**)

  - William Harris – bapt. 8 Jun 1783 (Baptism, **St. Luke Parish**)

  - John Harris – bapt. 4 Dec 1785 (Baptism, **St. Luke Parish**)

William Harris (father):

Residence - Skinner's Alley - April 18, 1775

   June 18, 1779

   September 10, 1780

   June 8, 1783

   December 4, 1785

Occupation - Silk Weaver - April 18, 1775

   June 18, 1779

   September 10, 1780

   June 8, 1783

Weaver - December 4, 1785

- William Harris & Anne Harris

  - William Harris – b. 22 Feb 1843, bapt. 19 Mar 1843 (Baptism, **Kilnaughtin Parish**)

- William Harris & Anne McArdle

  - George J. Harris – b. 22 May 1892, bapt. 25 May 1892 (Baptism, **St. Mary, Pro Cathedral Parish** (RC))

  - David Harris – b. 28 Sep 1893, bapt. 29 Sep 1893 (Baptism, **St. Mary, Pro Cathedral Parish** (RC))

  - Thomas Victor Harris – b. 17 Sep 1894, bapt. 21 Sep 1894 (Baptism, **St. Mary, Pro Cathedral Parish** (RC))

Hurst

- ○ Walter Joseph Harris – b. 9 Feb 1896, bapt. 12 Feb 1896 (Baptism, **St. Mary, Pro Cathedral Parish** (RC))

- ○ Margaret Anne Harris – b. 24 Jul 1897, bapt. 28 Jul 1897 (Baptism, **St. Mary, Pro Cathedral Parish** (RC))

William Harris (father):

Residence - **52 Jervis Street** - May 25, 1892

September 29, 1893

137 Upper Abbey Street - September 21, 1894

2 Great Britain Street - February 12, 1896

2 Britain Street - July 28, 1897

- William Harris & Anne Unknown

  - ○ John Harris – bapt. 8 Oct 1753 (Baptism, **St. John Parish**)

- William Harris & Anne Unknown

  - ○ Nathaniel Harris – bapt. 10 Jun 1754 (Baptism, **St. Werburgh Parish**)

William Harris (father):

Residence - **Silver Court** - June 10, 1754

- William Harris & Anne Unknown

  - ○ Bridget Harris – bapt. 20 Jan 1762 (Baptism, **St. Michan Parish** (RC))

- William Harris & Anne Unknown

  - ○ Hannah Harris – bapt. 22 Sep 1776 (Baptism, **St. Catherine Parish**)

  - ○ Elizabeth Harris – bapt. 19 Apr 1778 (Baptism, **St. Catherine Parish**)

William Harris (father):

Residence - **Meath Street** - September 22, 1776

April 19, 1778

Harris Surname Ireland: 1600s to 1900s

- William Harris & Anne Unknown

  o Thomas Harris – b. 11 Jul 1821, bapt. 15 Unclear 1821 (Baptism, **St. Catherine Parish**)

  o Robert Harris – b. 14 Sep 1822, bapt. 22 Unclear 1822 (Baptism, **St. Catherine Parish**)

William Harris (father):

Residence - Spitalfields - July 11, 1821

Fra's Street - September 14, 1822

- William Harris & Anne Unknown

  o Ellen Harris – bapt. 1834 (Baptism, **St. Andrew Parish** (RC))

  o Sarah Harris – bapt. 1834 (Baptism, **St. Andrew Parish** (RC))

  o John Harris – bapt. 1835 (Baptism, **St. Andrew Parish** (RC))

  o Walter Harris – bapt. 1838 (Baptism, **St. Andrew Parish** (RC))

  o Mary Harris – bapt. 1839 (Baptism, **St. Andrew Parish** (RC))

  o Michael Harris – bapt. 1842 (Baptism, **St. Andrew Parish** (RC))

  o Sarah Harris – bapt. 1845 (Baptism, **St. Andrew Parish** (RC))

- William Harris & Anne Unknown

  o Michael Harris & Margaret Doody – 23 Oct 1870 (Marriage, **St. Andrew Parish** (RC))

    ▪ Mary Anne Harris – b. 1871, bapt. 1871 (Baptism, **St. Andrew Parish** (RC))

    ▪ William Harris – b. 1873, bapt. 1873 (Baptism, **St. Andrew Parish** (RC))

    ▪ Margaret Harris – b. 1875, bapt. 1875 (Baptism, **St. Andrew Parish** (RC))

    ▪ Anne Harris – b. 1878, bapt. 1878 (Baptism, **St. Andrew Parish** (RC))

    ▪ Mary Harris – b. 1880, bapt. 1880 (Baptism, **St. Andrew Parish** (RC))

    ▪ John Harris – b. 1881, bapt. 1881 (Baptism, **St. Andrew Parish** (RC))

Hurst

Michael Harris (son):

>Residence - Tug-Boat - October 23, 1870
>
>>8 Sir John's Quay - 1871
>>
>>1875
>>
>>5 Creighton Street - 1878
>>
>>1880
>>
>>1881

Margaret Doody, daughter of Christopher Doody (daughter-in-law):

>Residence - 8 Sir John's Quay - October 23, 1870

- William Harris & Anne Susanna Harris

  - Arthur Harris – b. 29 Sep 1888, bapt. 24 Oct 1888 (Baptism, **Portobello Barracks Parish**)

William Harris (father):

>Residence - Portobello Barracks - October 24, 1888
>
>Occupation - Corporal Royal Artillery - October 24, 1888

- William Harris & Bridget Harris

  - Edward Harris – bapt. 19 Jan1735 (Baptism, **St. Luke Parish**)

  - William Harris – bapt. 6 Nov 1738 (Baptism, **St. Mary Parish**)

- William Harris & Bridget Harris

  - Anne Harris – bapt. 23 Nov 1766 (Baptism, **St. Luke Parish**)

  - William Harris – bapt. 31 Jul 1768 (Baptism, **St. Luke Parish**)

  - William Harris – bapt. 5 May 1771 (Baptism, **St. Luke Parish**)

  - Joseph Harris – bapt. 31 Jan 1773 (Baptism, **St. Luke Parish**)

William Harris (father):

>Residence - Three Nunn Alley - November 23, 1766
>
>>The Poddle - July 31, 1768
>>
>>May 5, 1771
>>
>>Truck Street - January 31, 1773

Harris Surname Ireland: 1600s to 1900s

Occupation - Hosier - November 23, 1766

July 31, 1768

May 5, 1771

January 31, 1773

- William Harris & Bridget Quinn

  o John Harris – bapt. 2 Mar 1808 (Baptism, St. Catherine Parish (RC))

- William Harris & Bridget Unknown

  o Anne Harris – bapt. 15 Nov 1789 (Baptism, St. Audoen Parish (RC))

  o Sarah Harris – bapt. 9 Jun 1792 (Baptism, St. Audoen Parish (RC))

  o Elizabeth Harris – bapt. 13 Oct 1793 (Baptism, St. Audoen Parish (RC))

- William Harris & Caroline Unknown

  o William Harris – bapt. 1857 (Baptism, St. Mary, Haddington Road Parish (RC))

- William Harris & Catherine Crowly

  o Catherine Harris – bapt. 28 Jan 1856 (Baptism, Aughadown Parish (RC))

William Harris (father):

Residence - Roringwater - January 28, 1856

- William Harris & Catherine Connolly

  o Helen Harris – b. 1 Nov 1840, bapt. 1 Nov 1840 (Baptism, Kenmare Parish (RC))

  o William Harris – bapt. 1 Oct 1842 (Baptism, Schull East Parish (RC))

  o John Harris – bapt. 8 Jun 1845 (Baptism, Schull East Parish (RC))

  o Elizabeth Harris – bapt. 22 Aug 1847 (Baptism, Schull West Parish (RC))

  o Benjamin Harris – bapt. 11 Sep 1853 (Baptism, Schull East Parish (RC))

  o Timothy Harris – bapt. 4 Dec 1859 (Baptism, Schull East Parish (RC))

Hurst

- William Harris & Catherine Cournane (C o u r n a n e) – 12 Jan 1811 (Marriage, **Tralee Parish (RC)**)

  - Henry Harris – b. 26 Nov 1811, bapt. 26 Nov 1811 (Baptism, **Tralee Parish** (RC))

  - Mary Harris – b. 9 Mar 1816, bapt. 9 Mar 1816 (Baptism, **Tralee Parish** (RC))

  - William Harris – b. 9 Mar 1820, bapt. 9 Mar 1820 (Baptism, **Tralee Parish** (RC))

  - Margaret Harris – b. 21 Feb 1825, bapt. 21 Feb 1825 (Baptism, **Tralee Parish** (RC))

  - Catherine Harris – b. 24 Mar 1828, bapt. 24 Mar 1828 (Baptism, **Tralee Parish** (RC))

William Harris (father):

Residence - Tralee - January 12, 1811

> **November 26, 1811**
>
> **March 9, 1816**
>
> **March 9, 1820**
>
> **February 21, 1825**
>
> **March 24, 1828**

- William Harris & Catherine Coveny – 16 Feb 1847 (Marriage, **Innishannon Parish** (RC))

  - Richard Harris – bapt. 7 Jan 1848 (Baptism, **Innishannon Parish** (RC))

  - John Harris – bapt. 29 May 1849 (Baptism, **Innishannon Parish** (RC))

  - Honora Harris – bapt. 1 Jan 1852 (Baptism, **Innishannon Parish** (RC))

  - Henry Harris – bapt. 10 Feb 1854 (Baptism, **Innishannon Parish** (RC))

  - Joan Harris – bapt. 7 Jan 1856 (Baptism, **Innishannon Parish** (RC))

  - Julia Harris – bapt. 23 Jan 1858 (Baptism, **Innishannon Parish** (RC))

- William Harris & Catherine Downes

  - Edward Harris, bapt. 1864 (Baptism, **St. Mary, Haddington Road Parish** (RC)) & Catherine D'Arcy – 1 May 1898 (Marriage, **St. Mary, Donnybrook Parish** (RC))

    - Catherine Harris – b. 14 Sep 1898, bapt. 19 Sep 1898 (Baptism, **St. Mary, Donnybrook Parish** (RC))

Harris Surname Ireland: 1600s to 1900s

Edward Harris (son):

    Residence - 31 Ballsbridge Terrace - May 1, 1898

        16 Brooklawn - September 19, 1898

Catherine D'Arcy, daughter of Michael D'Arcy & Catherine Keely

(daughter-in-law):

    Residence - 11 Church Lane - May 1, 1898

- Catherine Harris – b. 1874, bapt. 1874 (Baptism, St. Mary, Haddington Road Parish (RC))

- Michael Harris – b. 1874, bapt. 1874 (Baptism, St. Mary, Haddington Road Parish (RC)) & Mary Griffin – 20 Jan 1902 (Marriage, St. Mary, Donnybrook Parish (RC))

  - William Harris – b. 1902, bapt. 1902 (Baptism, St. Andrew Parish (RC))

  - Catherine Harris – b. 6 Sep 1906, bapt. 19 Sep 1906 (Baptism, Rathmines Parish (RC))

Michael Harris (son):

    Residence - 6 Belmont Court - January 20, 1902

        Holles Street Hospital - 1902

        9 Chelmsford Lane - September 19, 1906

Mary Griffin, daughter of Michael Griffin & Catherine Shea (daughter-in-law):

    Residence - 6 Belmont Court - January 20, 1902

- William Harris & Catherine Doyle

  - Elizabeth Harris & Peter Dowling – 18 Apr 1898 (Marriage, St. Mary, Pro Cathedral Parish (RC))

    - Ellen Dowling – b. 28 Oct 1898, bapt. 4 Nov 1898 (Baptism, St. Mary, Pro Cathedral Parish (RC))

    - Catherine Dowling – b. 31 Jan 1900, bapt. 2 Feb 1900 (Baptism, St. Mary, Pro Cathedral Parish (RC))

Hurst

Elizabeth Harris (daughter):

Residence - 132 Summer Hill - April 18, 1898

Peter Dowling, son of John Dowling & Ellen Kenna (son-in-law):

Residence - 132 Summer Hill - April 18, 1898

17 North Cumberland Street - November 4, 1898

25 Summer Hill - February 2, 1900

- William Harris & Catherine Dunnes

  o Mary Anne Harris – bapt. 1859 (Baptism, St. Mary, Haddington Road Parish (RC))

  o Esther Harris – bapt. 1861 (Baptism, St. Mary, Haddington Road Parish (RC))

- William Harris & Catherine Harris

  o Anne Harris – bapt. 11 Jul 1773 (Baptism, St. Mary Parish)

William Harris (father):

Residence - Britain Street - July 11, 1773

- William Harris & Catherine Harris

  o Margaret Harris – b. 4 Aug 1824, bapt. 8 Sep 1824 (Baptism, Tralee Parish)

  o Catherine Harris – bapt. 3 Apr 1828 (Baptism, Tralee Parish)

- William Harris & Catherine Hegarty

  o Unknown Harris – bapt. 4 May 1835 (Baptism, Innishannon Parish (RC))

- William Harris & Catherine McCarthy

  o James Harris – b. 8 Jun 1856, bapt. 8 Jun 1856 (Baptism, Abbeydorney Parish (RC))

  o Mary Harris – b. 26 Jul 1858, bapt. 26 Jul 1858 (Baptism, Abbeydorney Parish (RC))

William Harris (father):

Residence - Ardrahan - June 8, 1856

July 26, 1858

Harris Surname Ireland: 1600s to 1900s

- William Harris & Catherine Mahony

  - Joseph Harris – bapt. 1 Feb 1863 (Baptism, **Schull East Parish** (RC))

  - Honora Harris – bapt. Apr 1865 (Baptism, **Schull East Parish** (RC))

  - Margaret Harris – bapt. 3 Apr 1867 (Baptism, **Schull East Parish** (RC))

- William Harris & Charlotte Blair

  - John Harris – bapt. Oct 1828 (Baptism, **SS. Michael & John Parish** (RC))

- William Harris & Charlotte Harris

  - Thomas Harris & Winifred Doherty – 9 Mar 1902 (Marriage, **St. Mary, Pro Cathedral Parish** (RC))

Thomas Harris (son):
  Residence - 64 Montgomery Street - March 9, 1902
Winifred Doherty, daughter of John Doherty & Catherine Conner (daughter-in-law):
  Residence - 64 Montgomery Street - March 9, 1902

- William Harris & Dorothy Unknown

  - Elias Harris – bapt. 1726 (Baptism, **St. Werburgh Parish**)

William Harris (father):
  Residence - Copper Alley - 1726

- William Harris & Eleanor Harris, bur. 16 May 1677 (Burial, **St. Michan Parish**)

Eleanor Harris (wife):
  Residence - Stony Bater
  Cause of Death - being burnt

- William Harris & Eleanor Harris

  - Anne Harris – bapt. 19 Apr 1789 (Baptism, **Kilnaughtin Parish**)

- William Harris & Eleanor Unknown

  - Joseph Harris – bapt. 5 Feb 1764 (Baptism, **St. Audoen Parish**)

Hurst

- William Harris & Eleanor Unknown

  - John Harris – bapt. 8 Nov 1772 (Baptism, **St. Mary, Pro Cathedral Parish** (RC))

  - Mary Harris – bapt. 13 Dec 1783 (Baptism, **St. Mary, Pro Cathedral Parish** (RC))

- William Harris & Elizabeth Good – Jul 1794 (Marriage, **St. Nicholas Parish** (RC))

  - Alice Harris – bapt. 11 Jun 1797 (Baptism, **SS. Michael & John Parish** (RC))

- William Harris & Elizabeth Harris

  - Joseph Harris – bapt. 3 Jun 1744 (Baptism, **St. Patrick Parish**)

  - Benjamin Harris – bapt. 9 Nov 1746 (Baptism, **St. Patrick Parish**)

  - Anne Harris – bapt. 12 Feb 1748 (Baptism, **St. Patrick Parish**)

- William Harris & Elizabeth Harris

  - Esther Margaret Harris – bapt. 21 Jan 1857 (Baptism, **Tralee Parish**) & Archibald Wunperis

    – 11 Jan 1882 (Marriage, **Tralee Parish**)

Signatures:

Esther Margaret Harris (daughter):

   Residence - Tralee - January 11, 1882

Archibald Wunperis, son of George Wunperis (son-in-law):

   Residence - Tralee - January 11, 1882

   Occupation - Sergeant 48th Regiment - January 11, 1882

George Wunperis (father):

   Occupation - Shoemaker

William Harris (father):

   Occupation - Army Pensioner

Harris Surname Ireland: 1600s to 1900s

Wedding Witnesses:

Samuel Harris & Mary A. Fetherston

Signatures:

- o Elizabeth Harris – bapt. 31 Jul 1860 (Baptism, **Tralee Parish**)

- o Elizabeth Anne Harris – bapt. 17 Jul 1862 (Baptism, **Tralee Parish**)

- o Jane Harris – b. 20 Jul 1864, bapt. 17 Aug 1864 (Baptism, **Tralee Parish**)

- o Samuel Harris & Mary Anne Fetherston – 5 Feb 1884 (Marriage, **Tralee Parish**)

Signatures:

Signatures (Marriage):

Hurst

- Elizabeth May Harris – b. 19 Nov 1884, bapt. 7 Dec 1884 (Baptism, **Tralee Parish**)

- Esther Frances Harris – b. 30 May 1886, bapt. 15 Jun 1886 (Baptism, **Tralee Parish**)

- Gladys Mary Harris – b. 22 Sep 1887, bapt. 13 Oct 1887 (Baptism, **Tralee Parish**)

- Robert Fetherston Harris – b. 6 Oct 1891, bapt. 25 Oct 1891 (Baptism, **Tralee Parish**)

Samuel Harris (son):

Residence - Tralee - February 5, 1884

December 7, 1884

June 15, 1886

October 13, 1887

October 25, 1891

Occupation - Solicitor's Clerk - February 5, 1884

June 15, 1886

October 13, 1887

Law Clerk - December 7, 1884

Clerk - October 25, 1891

Mary Anne Fetherston, daughter of Robert Fetherston (daughter-in-law):

Residence - Tralee - February 5, 1884

Robert Fetherston (father):

Occupation - Accountant

William Harris (father):

Occupation - Army Pensioner

Wedding Witnesses:

Robert Houston Fetherston & Richard Harris

Signatures:

Harris Surname Ireland: 1600s to 1900s

William Harris (father):

Residence - Tralee - January 21, 1857

Oak Park Lodge, Tralee - July 31, 1860

July 17, 1862

August 17, 1864

Occupation - Pensioner - January 21, 1857

July 31, 1860

July 17, 1862

August 17, 1864

- William Harris & Elizabeth Harris

  - Georgina Harris – b. 27 Jun 1884, bapt. 15 Nov 1896 (Baptism, **St. Peter Parish**)

William Harris (father):

Residence - **55 Dawson Street** - November 15, 1896

Occupation - Gentleman - November 15, 1896

- William Harris & Elizabeth Nolan

  - Thomas Harris – b. 25 Jul 1867, bapt. 29 Jul 1867 (Baptism, **SS. Michael & John Parish** (RC))

William Harris (father):

Residence - **15 Crampton Court** - July 29, 1867

- William Harris & Elizabeth O'Reilly

  - Mary Teresa Harris – b. 1901, bapt. 1901 (Baptism, **St. Andrew Parish** (RC))

William Harris (father):

Residence - **10 Nassau Place** - 1901

- William Harris & Elizabeth Pridue

  - Jane Harris – b. 5 Feb 1812, bapt. 23 Sep 1812 (Baptism, **St. Catherine Parish** (RC))

- William Harris & Elizabeth Scanlon

  - William Harris – bapt. 29 Jan 1833 (Baptism, **St. Catherine Parish** (RC))

Hurst

- William Harris & Elizabeth Unknown

  o Ellen Harris – b. 28 Feb 1734, bapt. 28 Feb 1734 (Baptism, **Killiney Parish**)

William Harris (father):

Residence - Killiney - February 28, 1734

- William Harris & Elizabeth Unknown

  o William Harris – bapt. 3 Sep 1809 (Baptism, **Tullow Parish**)

- William Harris & Ellen Cazalett – 2 Sep 1839 (Marriage, **St. John Parish**)

- William Harris & Ellen Fitzgerald – 17 Jan 1826 (Marriage, **Tralee Parish** (RC))

  o Mary Harris – b. 22 Mar 1829, bapt. 22 Mar 1829 (Baptism, **Tralee Parish** (RC))

  o Robert Harris – b. 24 Apr 1831, bapt. 24 Apr 1831 (Baptism, **Tralee Parish** (RC))

William Harris (father):

Residence - Blennerville - March 22, 1829

April 24, 1831

Ellen Fitzgerald (mother):

Residence - Blennerville - January 17, 1826

- William Harris & Ellen Geraghty

  o Martha Harris – bapt. 9 Dec 1830 (Baptism, **St. Nicholas Parish** (RC))

  o Henrietta Harris – bapt. 19 Dec 1832 (Baptism, **St. Nicholas Parish** (RC))

  o Bridget Harris – bapt. 19 Dec 1832 (Baptism, **St. Nicholas Parish** (RC))

  o Mary Harris – bapt. 20 Oct 1834 (Baptism, **St. Nicholas Parish** (RC))

Henrietta Harris & Bridget Harris are Twins.

- William Harris & Ellen Harris

  o Christine Harris – b. 17 Dec 1867, bapt. 5 Jan 1867 (Baptism, **St. Barnabas Parish**)

William Harris (father):

Residence - 25 Lower Oriel Street - January 5, 1867

Occupation - Foreman Printer - January 5, 1867

Harris Surname Ireland: 1600s to 1900s

- William Harris & Ellen Murphy – 6 Mar 1859 (Marriage, **Innishannon Parish** (RC))

- William Harris & Ellen Neville

  - William Harris – bapt. 15 Apr 1808 (Baptism, **Cork - South Parish** (RC))

- William Harris & Ellen Riordan – 4 Nov 1827 (Marriage, **Cork - South Parish** (RC))

- William Harris & Esther Kane – Unclear (Marriage, **Rathfarnham Parish** (RC))

  - Mary Harris – b. 1818, bapt. 1818 (Baptism, **Rathfarnham Parish** (RC))

  - Catherine Harris – b. 1820, bapt. 1820 (Baptism, **Rathfarnham Parish** (RC))

  - William Harris – b. 1822, bapt. 1822 (Baptism, **Rathfarnham Parish** (RC))

  - Elizabeth Harris – b. 1824, bapt. 1824 (Baptism, **Rathfarnham Parish** (RC))

  - Judith Harris – b. 1826, bapt. 1826 (Baptism, **Rathfarnham Parish** (RC))

  - Bridget Harris – b. 1828, bapt. 1828 (Baptism, **Rathfarnham Parish** (RC))

  - John Harris – b. 1832, bapt. 1832 (Baptism, **Rathfarnham Parish** (RC))

  - John Harris – b. 1836, bapt. 1836 (Baptism, **Rathfarnham Parish** (RC))

- William Harris & Hannah Buttler

  - Martin Harris – b. 20 Oct 1874, bapt. 22 Oct 1874 (Baptism, **Cork - South Parish** (RC))

- William Harris & Jane Harris

  - William Harris – bapt. 23 Aug 1704 (Baptism, **St. Mary Parish**)

William Harris (father):

Occupation - Servingman - August 23, 1704

- William Harris & Jane Mangam – 3 Apr 1842 (Marriage, **SS. Michael & John Parish** (RC))

Hurst

- William Harris & Jane Minns – 25 Dec 1803 (Marriage, St. Werburgh Parish)

  o Anne Harris – bapt. 20 Oct 1804 (Baptism, St. Werburgh Parish)

  o William Harris – bapt. 16 Nov 1806 (Baptism, St. Werburgh Parish)

  o Margaret Harris – bapt. 26 Mar 1809 (Baptism, St. Werburgh Parish)

William Harris (father):

Residence - Pembroke Court - October 20, 1804

21 Wood Street - November 16, 1806

15 Copper Alley - March 26, 1809

- William Harris & Jane Thompson

  o Thomas Harris – b. 1859, bapt. 24 Feb 1894 (Baptism, St. Mary, Pro Cathedral Parish

  (RC))

William Harris (father):

Residence - Worcester, England - February 24, 1894

- William Harris & Jane Unknown

  o Anne Harris – bapt. 9 Mar 1746 (Baptism, St. Michan Parish (RC))

  o Mary Harris – bapt. 26 May 1751 (Baptism, St. Michan Parish (RC))

- William Harris & Jane Unknown

  o Anne Harris – bapt. 23 Sep 1764 (Baptism, St. Peter Parish)

- William Harris & Jane Unknown

  o Mary Anne Harris – b. 1813, bapt. May 1813 (Baptism, St. Catherine Parish)

- William Harris & Jane Unknown

  o John Harris – bapt. 16 Feb 1843 (Baptism, SS. Michael & John Parish (RC))

  o William Harris – bapt. Dec 1845 (Baptism, SS. Michael & John Parish (RC))

Harris Surname Ireland: 1600s to 1900s

- William Harris & Joan Callaghan

  - John Harris – bapt. 4 Jan 1849 (Baptism, **Innishannon Parish** (RC))

  - Richard Harris – bapt. 10 Jul 1851 (Baptism, **Innishannon Parish** (RC))

  - Henry Harris – bapt. 14 Nov 1854 (Baptism, **Innishannon Parish** (RC))

  - James Harris – bapt. 18 Jul 1856 (Baptism, **Innishannon Parish** (RC))

  - Frank Harris – bapt. 28 Feb 1858 (Baptism, **Innishannon Parish** (RC))

- William Harris & Joan Donovan – 18 Oct 1842 (Marriage, **Ballinhassig Parish** (RC))

  - Margaret Harris – bapt. 29 Dec 1843 (Baptism, **Innishannon Parish** (RC))

  - Mary Harris – bapt. 29 Jul 1846 (Baptism, **Innishannon Parish** (RC))

- William Harris & Joan Sullivan – 10 Aug 1835 (Marriage, **Cork - South Parish** (RC))

  - John Harris – bapt. 21 May 1836 (Baptism, **Cork - South Parish** (RC))

  - Bartholomew Harris – bapt. 7 Sep 1837 (Baptism, **Cork - South Parish** (RC))

  - John Harris – bapt. 15 Jun 1839 (Baptism, **Cork - South Parish** (RC))

  - William Harris – bapt. 20 Jul 1841 (Baptism, **Cork - South Parish** (RC))

  - William Harris – bapt. 10 Jun 1843 (Baptism, **Cork - South Parish** (RC))

  - Richard Harris – bapt. 20 Jul 1845 (Baptism, **Cork - South Parish** (RC))

  - Mary Harris – bapt. 14 Jun 1848 (Baptism, **Cork - South Parish** (RC))

  - Margaret Harris – bapt. 27 Feb 1853 (Baptism, **Cork - South Parish** (RC))

  - William Harris – bapt. 3 Feb 1856 (Baptism, **Cork - South Parish** (RC))

  - Bridget Harris – bapt. 6 Feb 1860 (Baptism, **Cork - South Parish** (RC))

- William Harris & Jane Kelly – 3 Mar 1878 (Marriage, **Kilmurry, Moviddy, Kilbonane, & Cannavee Parish** (RC))

Hurst

- William Harris & Julia Murphy – 18 Aug 1807 (Marriage, **Cork – South Parish** (RC))

  o Edward Harris – bapt. 5 Jun 1808 (Baptism, **Cork – South Parish** (RC))

  o Mary Harris – bapt. 6 May 1811 (Baptism, **Cork – South Parish** (RC))

William Harris (father):

Residence – Bishop's Town – August 18, 1807

Hospital Lane – June 5, 1808

Julia Murphy (mother):

Residence – Bishop's Town – August 18, 1807

- William Harris & Julia Walsh

  o Nelly Harris – bapt. 18 Jan 1852 (Baptism, **Ballinhassig Parish** (RC))

  o Thomas Harris – bapt. Mar 1854 (Baptism, **Ballinhassig Parish** (RC))

  o Richard Harris – bapt. 17 Nov 1855 (Baptism, **Cork – South Parish** (RC))

  o William Harris – bapt. 29 Mar 1858 (Baptism, **Cork – South Parish** (RC))

  o John Harris – bapt. 30 mar 1860 (Baptism, **Cork – South Parish** (RC))

- William Harris & Laura Anne Harris

  o Eva Harris – b. 15 Mar 1897, bapt. 25 Apr 1897 (Baptism, **St. Barnabas Parish**)

  o Ruth Evelyn Harris – b. 18 Oct 1899, bapt. 12 Nov 1899 (Baptism, **St. Barnabas Parish**)

William Harris (father):

Residence – 4 Emerald Street – April 25, 1897

3 Emerald Street – November 12, 1889

Occupation – Tailor – April 25, 1897

November 12, 1889

- William Harris & Margaret Buckley

  o Unknown Harris – bapt. 22 Apr 1809 (Baptism, **Kilmurry Parish** (RC))

The baptismal register is torn where the child's name was recorded; parents are listed as Wm Harris and Margaret Buckley.

Harris Surname Ireland: 1600s to 1900s

- William Harris & Margaret Harris

  o Charles Harris – bapt. 14 Oct 1834 (Baptism, **St. Mary, Pro Cathedral Parish (RC)**)

  o John Margaret Harris – bapt. 7 Nov 1836 (Baptism, **St. Mary, Pro Cathedral Parish (RC)**)

- William Harris & Margaret McGuirk

  o Mary Esther Harris – b. 31 Mar 1871, bapt. 17 Apr 1871 (Baptism, **St. Mary, Pro Cathedral Parish (RC)**)

William Harris (father):

Residence - 25 Britain Street - April 17, 1871

- William Harris & Margaret Sheerin

  o Alice Evelyn Harris – b. 15 Feb 1900, bapt. 16 Feb 1900 (Baptism, **St. Mary, Pro Cathedral Parish (RC)**)

William Harris (father):

Residence - 29 Richmond Place - February 16, 1900

- William Harris & Margaret Unknown

  o Thomas William Harris – bapt. 27 Jan 1831 (Baptism, **St. Mary, Pro Cathedral Parish (RC)**)

- William Harris & Martha Harris

  o Martha Harris – bapt. 9 Oct 1743 (Baptism, **St. Luke Parish**)

- William Harris & Mary Burke

  o James Harris – bapt. 11 Aug 1808 (Baptism, **Kilmurry Parish (RC)**)

  o Ellen Harris – bapt. 18 Jun 1812 (Baptism, **Kilmurry Parish (RC)**)

  o Richard Harris – bapt. 16 Apr 1815 (Baptism, **Kilmurry Parish (RC)**)

Hurst

- William Harris & Mary Carroll

  o William Harris – bapt. 1833 (Baptism, **St. Mary, Haddington Road Parish** (RC))

  o Mary Anne Harris – bapt. 11 Jul 1838 (Baptism, **St. Michan Parish** (RC))

- William Harris & Mary Connor

  o Mary Ellen Harris – bapt. 16 Oct 1872 (Baptism, **Cork - South Parish** (RC))

  o John Harris – b. 19 Jun 1878, bapt. 24 Jun 1878 (Baptism, **Cork - South Parish** (RC))

William Harris (father):

Residence - Schat Abbey - June 24, 1878

- William Harris & Mary Harris

  o Anne Harris – bapt. 5 Jul 1778 (Baptism, **St. Mary Parish**)

William Harris (father):

Residence - Liffey Street - July 5. 1778

- William Harris & Mary Harris

  o Mary Harris – bapt. 12 Feb 1786 (Baptism, **Kilnaughtin Parish**)

- William Harris & Mary Harris

  o Bridget Harris – bapt. 4 Sep 1812 (Baptism, **Kilnaughtin Parish**)

  o Ellen Harris – bapt. 3 Aug 1815 (Baptism, **Kilnaughtin Parish**)

  o William Harris – bapt. 24 Oct 1817 (Baptism, **Kilnaughtin Parish**), bur. 26 Mar 1824

  (Burial, **Kilnaughtin Parish**)

  o Thomas William Harris – bapt. 19 May 1822 (Baptism, **Kilnaughtin Parish**)

  o Isaac Harris – bapt. 5 Dec 1824 (Baptism, **Kilnaughtin Parish**)

William Harris (father):

Residence - Ballydonoghoe - September 4, 1812

August 3, 1815

December 5, 1824

Doonard - October 24, 1817

May 19, 1822

Harris Surname Ireland: 1600s to 1900s

- William Harris & Mary Harris

  o Catherine Harris – bapt. 28 Jan 1828 (Baptism, **St. Mary, Pro Cathedral Parish** (RC))

  o Jane Harris – bapt. 30 Dec 1835 (Baptism, **St. Mary, Pro Cathedral Parish** (RC))

William Harris (father):

Residence - King Street - January 28, 1828

- William Harris & Mary Harris

  o Joseph William Harris – bapt. 14 Jul 1850 (Baptism, **Arbour Hill Barracks Parish**)

William Harris (father):

Residence - Ship Street - July 14, 1850

Occupation - Private 40th - July 14, 1850

- William Harris & Mary Harris

  o George Harris – b. 9 Jan 1862, bapt. 6 Feb 1862 (Baptism, **Killehenney Parish**) (Baptism,

    Lisselton Parish)

William Harris (father):

Residence - Ballybunion - February 6, 1862

Occupation - Gentleman - February 6, 1862

- William Harris & Mary Harris

  o Alexander Joseph Harris – b. 9 Mar 1877, bapt. 13 May 1877 (Baptism, **Arbour Hill**

    Barracks Parish)

William Harris (father):

Residence - Royal Barracks - May 13, 1877

Occupation - Master Tailor 6th Dragoons - May 13, 1877

- William Harris & Mary Hennessy

  o Jane Harris – bapt. 17 Apr 1846 (Baptism, **Cork - SS. Peter & Paul Parish** (RC))

Hurst

- William Harris & Mary McNally

  - Mary Sarah Harris – b. 30 Jul 1872, bapt. 20 Aug 1872 (Baptism, **St. Michan Parish** (RC))

  - William James Harris – b. 22 Oct 1877, bapt. 31 Oct 1877 (Baptism, **St. Michan Parish** (RC))

  - John Patrick Harris – b. 9 Jan 1888, bapt. 18 Jan 1888 (Baptism, **St. Mary, Pro Cathedral Parish** (RC))

William Harris (father):

Residence - 63 Bolton Street - August 20, 1872

62 Bolton Street - October 31, 1877

11 Jervis Street - January 18, 1888

- William Harris & Mary Newport – 20 Jun 1851 (Marriage, **St. Andrew Parish** (RC))

- William Harris & Mary O'Neill

  - William Harris – bapt. 6 Aug 1833 (Baptism, **St. Michan Parish** (RC))

  - Mary Jane Harris – bapt. 1 Mar 1837 (Baptism, **St. Michan Parish** (RC))

- William Harris & Mary Unknown

  - Mary Harris – bapt. 7 Jun 1778 (Baptism, **St. Catherine Parish**)

William Harris (father):

Residence - Meath Street - June 7, 1778

- William Harris & Mary Unknown

  - Susanna Harris – bapt. 8 Jul 1798 (Baptism, **St. Werburgh Parish**)

  - Margaret Harris – bapt. 16 Apr 1800 (Baptism, **St. Werburgh Parish**)

  - William Harris – bapt. 27 Mar 1803 (Baptism, **St. Werburgh Parish**)

William Harris (father):

Residence - Pembroke Court - July 8, 1798

Castle Street - April 16, 1800

Copper Alley - March 27, 1803

Harris Surname Ireland: 1600s to 1900s

- William Harris & Mary Unknown

  o John Harris – bapt. 22 Sep 1868 (Baptism, **Cork - South Parish** (RC))

- William Harris & Mary Unknown

  o George Harris & Margaret Ward – 27 Sep 1862 (Marriage, **St. Michan Parish** (RC))

    ▪ George Harris – b. 21 Sep 1865, bapt. 25 Sep 1865 (Baptism, **St. Mary, Pro Cathedral Parish** (RC))

    ▪ Catherine Harris – b. 2 Dec 1872, bapt. 6 Dec 1872 (Baptism**, St. Mary, Pro Cathedral Parish** (RC))

George Harris (son):

Residence - 31 Moore Street - September 27, 1862

21 Green Street - September 25, 1865

Britain Lane - December 6, 1872

Margaret Ward, daughter of John Ward & Esther Unknown (daughter-in-law):

Residence - 10 Anne Street - September 27, 1862

- William Harris & Mary Wright

  o William John Harris – b. 26 Sep 1873, bapt. 6 Oct 1873 (Baptism, **St. Michan Parish** (RC))

William Harris (father):

Residence - 31 Greek Street - October 6, 1873

- William Harris & Mary Anne Unknown

  o Mary Anne Harris – bapt. 5 Oct 1774 (Baptism, **St. Werburgh Parish**)

William Harris (father):

Residence - Bride Street - October 5, 1774

Hurst

- William Harris & Mary Margaret Johnson

  - John Harris – bapt. 29 Jan 1839 (Baptism, **Cork - SS. Peter & Paul Parish** (RC))

  - James Harris – bapt. 8 Sep 1842 (Baptism, **Cork - SS. Peter & Paul Parish** (RC))

  - Mary Anne Harris – bapt. 26 Mar 1844 (Baptism, **Cork - SS. Peter & Paul Parish** (RC))

  - Elizabeth Harris – bapt. 28 Nov 1845 (Baptism, **Cork - SS. Peter & Paul Parish** (RC))

- William Harris & Nel Fowlow – 20 Dec 1837 (Marriage, **Schull West Parish** (RC))

- William Harris & Rebecca Harris

  - Henry Matthew Harris – b. 29 Apr 1870, bapt. 12 Jul 1870 (Baptism, **St. Peter Parish**)

  - William James Harris – b. 29 Apr 1870, bapt. 12 Jul 1870 (Baptism, **St. Peter Parish**)

  - Joseph Harris – b. 30 Sep 1871, bapt. 7 Dec 1871 (Baptism, **St. Peter Parish**)

  - Ellen Harris – b. 1873, bapt. 18 Jun 1873 (Baptism, **St. Peter Parish**)

William Harris (father):

Residence - 18 Bishop Street - July 12, 1870

6 Hackett's Court - December 7, 1871

6 Upper Mercer Street - June 18, 1873

Occupation - Porter - July 12, 1870

December 7, 1871

Laborer - June 18, 1873

- William Harris & Rosanna Gayner

  - Mary Jane Harris – b. 1861, bapt. 1861 (Baptism, **St. Andrew Parish** (RC))

William Harris (father):

Residence - 8 Aston Quay - 1861

- William Harris & Rosanna Gaynor

  - Rebecca Harris – b. 11 Dec 1880, bapt. 20 Dec 1880 (Baptism, **St. Mary, Pro Cathedral Parish** (RC))

  - Elizabeth Harris & Thomas Cleary – 30 May 1897 (Marriage, **St. Mary, Pro Cathedral Parish** (RC))

Harris Surname Ireland: 1600s to 1900s

Elizabeth Harris (daughter):

Residence - 57 Jervis Street - May 30, 1897

Thomas Cleary, son of Edward Cleary & Elizabeth Reddington (son-in-law):

Residence - 107 Capel Street - May 30, 1897

William Harris (father):

Residence - 90 Great Britain Street - December 20, 1880

- William Harris & Rosanna Unknown

  o Mary Anne Harris – b. 13 Jun 1862, bapt. 18 Jun 1862 (Baptism, **St. Michan Parish (RC)**)

William Harris (father):

Residence - 125 Dorset Street - June 18, 1862

- William Harris & Rose Chasney

  o Ellen Harris – bapt. 18 Jul 1825 (Baptism, **St. Catherine Parish (RC)**)

- William Harris & Sarah Harris

  o Thomas Harris – b. 21 Jan 1814, bapt. 6 Feb 1814 (Baptism, **St. Luke Parish**)

- William Harris & Sarah Harris

  o Florence Harris – b. 15 Apr 1881, bapt. 22 May 1881 (Baptism, **St. Barnabas Parish**)

William Harris (father):

Residence - 5 Preston Street - May 22, 1881

Occupation - Printer - May 22, 1881

- William Harris & Sarah Nowland – 19 Oct 1702 (Marriage, **St. Nicholas Without Parish**)

- William Harris & Sarah Unknown

  o Robert Harris – bapt. 17 Sep 1723 (Baptism, **St. Werburgh Parish**)

  o Elizabeth Harris – bapt. 13 Feb 1726 (Baptism, **St. Werburgh Parish**)

William Harris (father):

Residence - Castle Street - September 17, 1723

February 13, 1726

Hurst

- William Harris & Sarah Unknown

  - Sarah Harris – b. 1810, bapt. Mar 1810 (Baptism, **St. Catherine Parish**)

- William Harris & Sarah Unknown

  - George Harris – b. 16 Aug 1842, bapt. 18 Sep 1842 (Baptism, **Dunleckney Parish**)

William Harris (father):

Residence - Bagenalstown - September 18, 1842

Occupation - Stonecutter - September 18, 1842

- William Harris & Teresa Griffith – 2 Feb 1842 (Marriage, **St. Catherine Parish**)

William Harris (husband):

Residence - Parish - February 2, 1842

- William Harris & Unknown

  - Ursilla Harris – bapt. 10 Feb 1638 (Baptism, **St. Michan Parish**)

- William Harris & Unknown

  - Adam Harris – bapt. 27 Apr 1662 (Baptism, **St. John Parish**)

  - Mary Harris – bur. 15 Jul 1663 (Burial, **St. John Parish**)

- William Harris & Unknown

  - Elizabeth Harris – bapt. 13 Jan 1692 (Baptism, **St. Patrick Parish**)

- William Harris & Unknown

  - Peter Harris (1st Marriage) & Mary Sims, d. Before 23 Jul 1878 – 24 Apr 1849 (Marriage, Tralee Parish)

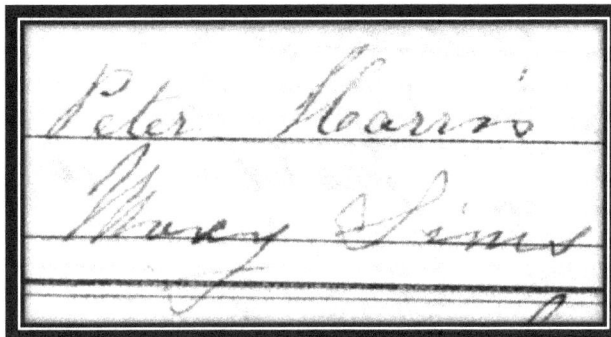

Signatures:

  - William John Harris – bapt. 15 Sep 1850 (Baptism, Tralee Parish)

Peter Harris (son):

  Residence - Tralee - April 24, 1849

  September 15, 1850

  Occupation - Cabinet Maker - April 24, 1849

  September 15, 1850

Mary Sims, daughter of John Sims (daughter-in-law):

  Residence - Tralee - April 24, 1849

John Sims (father):

  Occupation - Parish Clerk

William Harris (father):

  Occupation - Cabinet Maker

Hurst

- o   Peter Harris (2nd Marriage) & Mary Anne Williams – 23 Jul 1878 (Marriage, **Tralee Parish**)

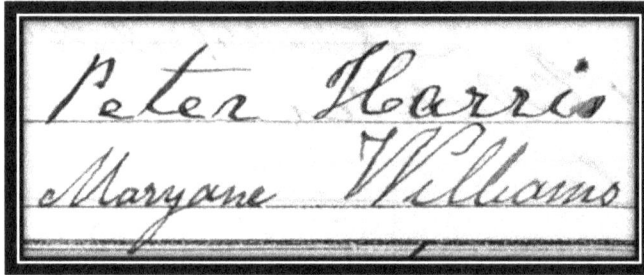

Signatures:

Peter Harris (son):

    Residence - Tralee - July 23, 1878

    Occupation - Cabinet Maker - July 23, 1878

    Relationship Status at Marriage - widow

Mary Anne Williams, daughter of Francis Williams (daughter-in-law):

    Residence - Tralee - July 23, 1878

    Occupation - Servant - July 23, 1878

Francis Williams (father):

    Occupation - Weaver

William Harris (father):

    Occupation - Cabinet Maker

- o   Richard Harris – bapt. 6 Mar 1829 (Baptism, **Tralee Parish**)

William Harris (father):

    Residence - Tralee - March 6, 1829

    Occupation - Cabinet Maker - March 6, 1829

Harris Surname Ireland: 1600s to 1900s

- William Harris & Unknown

  o Unknown Harris, d. Before 27 Dec 1855 & Bridget Hood (1st Marriage), b. 1825

- Bridget Hood Harris (2nd Marriage), b. 1825 & Patrick Suite, b. 1827 – 27 Dec 1855 (Marriage,

  Dunleckney Parish)

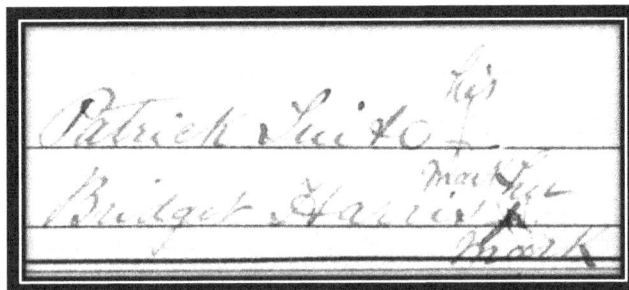

Signatures:

Bridget Hood Harris (daughter-in-law):

    Residence - Bagenalstown, Dunleckney Parish - December 27, 1855

    Occupation - Servant - December 27, 1855

Patrick Suite, the son of Michael Suite (son-in-law):

    Residence - Bagenalstown, Dunleckney Parish - December 27, 1855

    Occupation - Brogue Maker - December 27, 1855

William Harris (father-in-law to Bridget Hood Harris):

    Occupation - Laborer

Hurst

- William Harris & Unknown

  o Edward Harris & Mary Drennan – 7 Feb 1846 (Marriage, **St. Paul Parish**)

Signatures:

Edward Harris (son):

 Residence - Royal Barracks - February 7, 1846

 Occupation - Soldier 41st Regiment - February 7, 1846

Mary Drennan, daughter of John Drennan (daughter-in-law):

 Residence - 167 St Kingstone - February 7, 1846

John Drennan (father):

 Occupation - Clerk

William Harris (father):

 Occupation - Laborer

  o George Harris & Mary Anne Bourke – 1 Feb 1859 (Marriage, **St. Peter Parish**)

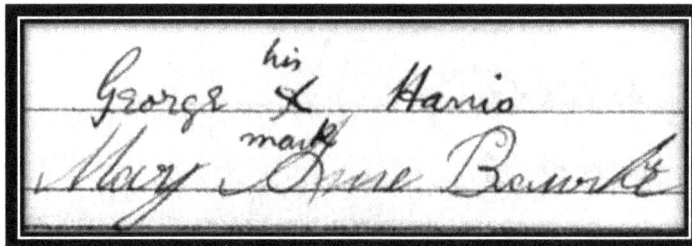

Signatures:

George Harris (son):

 Residence - Portobello Barracks - February 1, 1859

 Occupation - Driver in Royal Artillery - February 1, 1859

Mary Anne Bourke, daughter of Tobias Bourke (daughter-in-law):

 Residence - 18 Leinster Square - February 1, 1859

Harris Surname Ireland: 1600s to 1900s

Tobias Bourke (father):

    Occupation - Gardener

William Harris (father):

    Occupation - Laborer

- William Harris & Unknown

Signature:

    o   Jane Harriet Harris (1st Marriage) & John Thompson, d. Before 12 Apr 1864 – 20 Apr 1850

    (Marriage, St. Peter Parish)

Signatures:

Jane Harriet Harris (daughter):

    Residence - Sandymount, Parish of Donnybrook - April 20, 1850

John Thompson, son of William Thompson (son-in-law):

    Residence - 16 Lower Camden Street - April 20, 1850

    Occupation - Gentleman - April 20, 1850

William Thompson (father):

    Occupation - Esquire

William Harris (father):

    Occupation - Lieutenant in Army

Hurst

Wedding Witnesses:

William Harris

Signature:

- o Jane Harriet Harris Thompson (2nd Marriage) & George Mooney – 12 Apr 1864 (Marriage, St. Peter Parish)

Signatures:

Jane Harriet Harris Thompson (daughter):

Residence - 7 Pembroke Lodge Sandymount - April 12, 1864

Relationship Status at Marriage - widow

George Mooney, son of Gerald Mooney (son-in-law):

Residence - 31 Pleasant Street - April 12, 1864

Occupation - School Master - April 12, 1864

Relationship Status at Marriage - widow

Gerald Mooney (father):

Occupation - Hatter

William Harris (father):

Occupation - Lieut in the Army

Wedding Witnesses:

Thomas Mooney

Signature:

* William Harris & Unknown

  o Mary Harris & John Dargan – 30 Dec 1867 (Marriage, **St. Luke Parish**)

Signatures:

Mary Harris (daughter):

    Residence - 4 Verschoyle's Court - December 30, 1867

John Dargan, son of John Dargan (son-in-law):

    Residence - 4 Verschoyle's Court - December 30, 1867

    Occupation - Chairmaker - December 30, 1867

    Relationship Status at Marriage - widow

John Dargan (father):

    Occupation - Chair maker

William Harris (father):

    Occupation - Chair Maker

Hurst

- William Harris & Unknown

  o Jonathan Harris & Margaret Small – 30 Apr 1872 (Marriage, St. George Parish)

Signatures:

Jonathan Harris (son):

Residence - Bishop Auckland Durham, England - April 30, 1872

Occupation - Draper - April 30, 1872

Margaret Small, daughter of James Small (daughter-in-law):

Residence - 39 North Summer Street - April 30, 1872

James Small (father):

Signature:

Occupation - Shop Keeper

William Harris (father):

Occupation - Farmer

Wedding Witnesses:

James Small

Signature:

- William Harris & Unknown

  - George Harris & Mary Stretton – 8 Aug 1878 (Marriage, **Tralee Parish**)

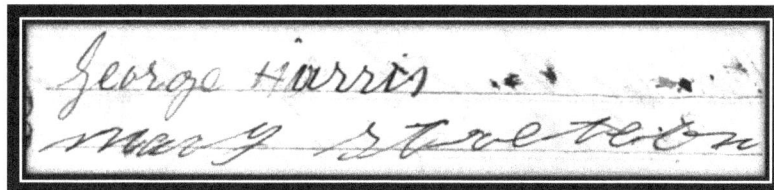

Signatures:

- Mary Ellen Harris – b. 15 May 1881, bapt. 29 May 1881 (Baptism, **Tralee Parish (RC)**)

George Harris (son):

Residence - Tralee Barracks - August 8, 1878

Boherbee - May 29, 1881

Occupation - Private 103rd Regiment - August 8, 1878

Mary Stretton, daughter of Patrick Stretton (daughter-in-law):

Residence - Ballymullin Ratherss - August 8, 1878

Occupation - Cook - August 8, 1878

Patrick Stretton (father):

Occupation - Laborer

William Harris (father):

Occupation - Laborer

Hurst

- William Harris & Unknown

  o John Harris & Elizabeth Gordon – 7 Dec 1880 (Marriage, **St. Peter Parish**)

Signatures:

- Joseph Samuel Harris – b. 21 Apr 1881, bapt. 15 May 1881 (Baptism, **St. Peter Parish**)

John Harris (son):

Residence - 10 Camden Buildings Camden Street - December 7, 1880

10 Camden Buildings - May 15, 1881

Occupation - Laborer - December 7, 1880

Dealer - May 15, 1881

Elizabeth Gordon, daughter of Joseph Gordon (daughter-in-law):

Residence - 10 Camden Buildings Camden Street - December 7, 1880

Relationship Status at Marriage - minor age

Joseph Gordon (father):

Signature:

Occupation - Butler

William Harris (father):

Occupation - Laborer

Wedding Witnesses:

Joseph Gordon

Signature:

- William Harris & Unknown

  o Ellen Mary Harris & James Smith – 15 Sep 1883 (Marriage, **St. Peter Parish**)

Signatures:

Ellen Mary Harris (daughter):

   Residence - Portobello Barracks - September 15, 1883

James Smith, son of William Smith (son-in-law):

   Residence - Portobello Barracks - September 15, 1883

   Occupation - Sergeant - September 15, 1883

William Smith (father):

   Occupation - Builder

William Harris (father):

   Occupation - Butter Buyer

Hurst

- William Carver Harris & Mary Catherine Harris

  - Henry Harris – b. 11 Sep 1864, bapt. 9 Oct 1864 (Baptism, **Kilnaughtin Parish**)

  - Edward Harris – b. 28 Sep 1868, bapt. 29 Oct 1868 (Baptism, **Kilnaughtin Parish**)

William Carver Harris (father):

Residence - Tullylaige Glin - October 9, 1864

October 29, 1868

Occupation - Farmer - October 9, 1864

October 29, 1868

- William Deanes Harris & Anne Buttler

  - William Thomas Harris – bapt. 26 Apr 1872 (Baptism, **Cork - South Parish** (RC))

- William James Harris & Bridget McGouran

  - Esther Harris – b. 14 Apr 1897, bapt. 19 Apr 1897 (Baptism, **St. Mary, Pro Cathedral Parish** (RC))

  - Bridget Harris – b. 11 Nov 1898, bapt. 14 Nov 1898 (Baptism, **St. Mary, Pro Cathedral Parish** (RC))

  - George Harris – b. 20 Jul 1900, bapt. 23 Jul 1900 (Baptism, **St. Mary, Pro Cathedral Parish** (RC))

William James Harris (father):

Residence - 33 Mabbot Street - April 19, 1897

12 Mabbot Street - November 14, 1898

54 Mabbot Street - July 23, 1900

- William John Harris & Elizabeth Unknown

  - Jessie Harris – b. 24 Aug 1878, bapt. 8 Sep 1878 (Baptism, **Killorglin Parish**)

  - Maud Mary Harris – b. 11 Nov 1881, bapt. 19 Dec 1881 (Baptism, **Killorglin Parish**)

  - George John Harris – b. 2 Dec 1885, bapt. 10 Jan 1886 (Baptism, **Killorglin Parish**)

  - Elizabeth Harris – b. 3 Feb 1888, bapt. 4 Mar 1888 (Baptism, **Killorglin Parish**)

  - Louisa Harris – b. 6 Sep 1890, bapt. 21 Sep 1891 (Baptism, **Killorglin Parish**)

Harris Surname Ireland: 1600s to 1900s

William John Harris (father):

    Residence - Cromane - September 8, 1878

                    December 19, 1881

                    January 10, 1886

                    March 4, 1888

                    September 21, 1891

    Occupation - Coast Guard - September 8, 1878

                    December 19, 1881

                    January 10, 1886

                    March 4, 1888

                    September 21, 1891

- William John Harris & Emily Harris
  - Ada Emily Harris – b. 2 Aug 1875, bapt. 2 Jan 1876 (Baptism, Tralee Parish)

William John Harris (father):

    Residence - Tralee - January 2, 1876

    Occupation - Solicitor's Clerk - January 2, 1876

- William Prettie Harris & Unknown
  - George Crofts Harris & Julia Mary Heard – 26 May 1870 (Marriage, St. Peter Parish)

Signatures:

Hurst

George Crofts Harris (son):

Residence - Spettlefields Battesant, Co. Cork- May 26, 1870

Occupation - Esquire - May 26, 1870

Relationship Status at Marriage - widow

Julia Mary Heard, daughter of Edward Heard (daughter-in-law):

Residence - 50 Leinster Road - May 26, 1870

Edward Heard (father):

Signature:

Occupation - M D

William Prettie Harris (father):

Occupation - Esquire

Wedding Witnesses:

Edward Heard & Richard Harris

Signatures:

- William Wallace Harris & Caroline Frances Sydney Arthur – 20 Apr 1843 (Marriage, **St. Peter Parish**)

  o Francis William Fitzgerald Harris – b. 6 Jun 1847, bapt. 2 Jul 1847 (Baptism, **St. George Parish**)

Signature:

  o Reginald Thomas Harris – b. 5 Apr 1861, bapt. 29 May 1861 (Baptism, **St. George Parish**) & Frances Hendy Reede – 2 Jun 1897 (Marriage, **St. George Parish**)

Signatures:

Reginald Thomas Harris (son):

Residence - 24 Mountjoy Square - June 2, 1897

Occupation - Barrister at Law - June 2, 1897

Frances Hendy Reede, daughter of Thomas Picton Reede (daughter-in-law):

Residence - 4 Gardiners Place - June 2, 1897

Thomas Picton Reede (father):

Occupation - Solicitor

William Wallace Harris (father):

Occupation - Barrister at Law

Hurst

Wedding Witnesses:

F. W. Fitzgerald Harris

Signature:

William Wallace Harris (father):

Residence - Parish of Ashfort, Tynan, Armagh - April 20, 1843

No 19 Upper Rutland Street - July 2, 1847

26 Eccles Street - May 29, 1861

Occupation - Esquire - April 20, 1843

Barrister at Law - July 2, 1847

May 29, 1861

Caroline Frances Sidney Arthur (daughter-in-law):

Residence - 49 Lower Mount Street - April 20, 1843

Relationship Status at Marriage - widow

- William Wallace Harris & Gertrude Mary Harris

  o Doris Gertrude Harris – b. 24 Sep 1899, bapt. 24 Oct 1899 (Baptism, **Glasnevin Parish**)

William Wallace Harris (father):

Residence - No 1 Churchill Villas Glasnevin - October 24, 1899

Occupation - Solicitor - October 24, 1899

- William Wellesley Harris & Unknown

  o David John Wellesley Pole Harris & Sophia Conroy – 11 Jul 1864 (Marriage, **St. Thomas Parish**)

Signatures:

  - Anne Elizabeth Lavinia Harris – b. 22 May 1865, bapt. 9 Jun 1865 (Baptism, **St. Mary Parish**)

  - William Wellesley Harris, b. 22 Aug 1866, bapt. 6 Sep 1866 (Baptism, **St. Mary Parish**) & Jessie Kerr – 23 Dec 1897 (Marriage, **North Strand Parish**)

Signature:

Signatures (Marriage):

  - David John Wellesley Harris – b. 9 May 1899, bapt. 18 Jun 1899 (Baptism, **North Strand Parish**)

Hurst

William Wellesley Harris (son):

    Residence - 59 North Strand Road - December 23, 1897

                              June 18, 1899

    Occupation - Commercial Traveller - December 23, 1897

                              June 18, 1899

Jessie Kerr, daughter of William Kerr (daughter-in-law):

    Residence - 70 Talbot Street - December 23, 1897

William Kerr (father):

    Occupation - Sanitary Engineer

David John Wellesley Pole Harris (father):

    Occupation - Commercial Traveller

Wedding Witnesses:

James Howard Kerr & David Charles Harris

Signatures:

    ▪ Sarah Frances Harris, b. 28 Jun 1868, bapt. 29 Jul 1868 (Baptism, **Rotunda Chapel**

        Parish) & Richard Dalton Seymour – 12 Aug 1896 (Marriage, **North Strand Parish**)

Signatures:

Sarah Frances Harris (daughter):

    Residence - 7 Waterloo Avenue - August 12, 1896

Richard Dalton Seymour, son of William George Seymour (son-in-law):

    Residence - 94 North Strand Road - August 12, 1896

    Occupation - Commercial Manager - August 12, 1896

Harris Surname Ireland: 1600s to 1900s

William George Seymour (father):

   Occupation - Commercial Manager

David John Wellesley Pole Harris (father):

   Occupation - Commercial [Traveller]

Wedding Witnesses:

David C. Harris & William Wellesley Harris

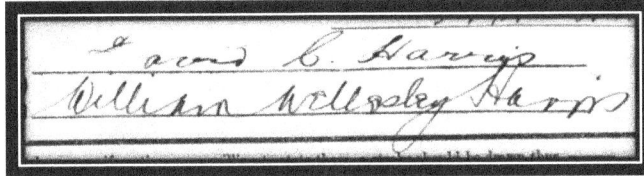

Signatures:

- ▪ Frederick David Harris, b. 13 Sep 1871, bapt. 8 Oct 1871 (Baptism, **St. Barnabas Parish**)

   & Julia Adelaide Verschoyle Lord

  - • David John Wellesley Harris – b. 18 Oct 1896, bapt. 8 Nov 1896 (Baptism, **North**

     Strand Parish)

  - • William Wellesley Harris – b. 1898 Cork, Ireland

  - • George Frederick Harris – b. 9 Feb 1900, bapt. 3 Jun 1900 (Baptism, **North Strand**

     Parish)

Frederick David Harris (son):

   Residence - 3 Fairview Avenue - November 8, 1896

      26 Hardwick Street - June 3, 1900

   Occupation - Commercial Traveller - November 8, 1896

                                                  June 3, 1900

Hurst

George Frederick Harris

born February 9, 1900

baptized June 3, 1900

Photo taken in Sydney, Cape Breton Co., Nova Scotia circa 1920s

Hurst

- Salesbury Harris – b. 21 Dec 1872, bapt. 5 Jan 1873 (Baptism, **St. Barnabas Parish**)

- David Charles Harris – b. 11 Oct 1877, bapt. 2 Dec 1877 (Baptism, **St. Barnabas Parish**)

Signatures:

David John Wellesley Pole Harris (father):

   Residence - 84 Amiens Street - July 11, 1864

            7 Lower Buckingham Street - June 9, 1865

            95 Summer Hill - September 6, 1866

            Harold's Cross - 29 Jul 1868

            15 Upper Buckingham Street - October 8, 1871

            58 Charleville Avenue - January 5, 1873

            13 Berkeley Road - December 2, 1877

   Occupation - Merchant - July 11, 1864

            Commercial Traveller

            Commercial Traveller - June 9, 1865

                 September 6, 1866

            Commission Agent - 29 Jul 1868

            Druggist - October 8, 1871

               January 5, 1873

            Chemist & Druggist - December 2, 1877

Sophia Conroy, daughter of Malachi Conroy (daughter-in-law):

   Residence- 1 Waterloo Terrace North Strand - July 11, 1864

The surname Conroy is also written as Conry.

Malachi Conroy (father):

   Occupation - Gentleman

William Wellesley Harris (father):

Occupation - Clergyman

Wedding Witnesses:

Henry Joseph Harris

Signature:

     o   Henry Joseph Harris & Catherine Conroy – 3 Mar 1864 (Marriage, **St. Thomas Parish**)

Signature:

Signatures (Marriage):

Henry Joseph Harris (son):

Residence - **55** Lower Dominick Street - March 3, 1864

Occupation - Agent - March 3, 1864

Catherine Conroy, daughter of Malachi Conroy (daughter-in-law):

Residence - 1 Waterloo Terrace - March 3, 1864

She is the sister of Sophia Conroy.

Malachi Conroy (father):

Occupation - Esquire

William Wellesley Harris (father):

Occupation - Clergyman

Hurst

- William Fitzharris & Margaret Steward

  - Winifred Fitzharris – bapt. 13 Feb 1782 (Baptism, **St. Catherine Parish** (RC))

- Xpheri Harris & Mary Unknown

  - James Harris – bapt. 1762 (Baptism, **St. Andrew Parish** (RC))

  - Anne Harris – bapt. 1774 (Baptism, **St. Andrew Parish** (RC))

Individual Births/Baptisms

- Anne M. Harris – bapt. Jun 1821 (Baptism, **St. Mark Parish**)

Anne M. Harris (child):

> **Residence - Townsend Street - June 1821**

- Catherine Harris – bapt. 8 Jun 1757 (Baptism, **St. Catherine Parish (RC)**)

- Charles Harris – bapt. 8 Oct 1734 (Baptism, **St. Mary Parish**)

- Elizabeth Harris – bapt. Apr 1824 (Baptism, **St. Mark Parish**)

Elizabeth Harris (child):

> **Residence - Townsend Street - April 1824**

- Emily Harris – bapt. Apr 1824 (Baptism, **St. Mark Parish**)

Emily Harris (child):

> **Residence - Townsend Street - April 1824**

- George Harris – bapt. 31 Mar 1711 (Baptism, **St. Patrick Parish**)

The church register entry is as follows:

> **"Students of Ye College Presented by Ye Revd. Mr. Mat: French Catechist of Ye College and then confirmed."**

- Julia Catherine Harris – b. 30 Jun 1880, bapt. 6 Jul 1880 (Baptism, **St. Audoen Parish (RC)**)

- Sergeant Harris – bapt. 1850 (Baptisms, **Chapelizod Parish (RC)**)

Sergeant Harris (child):

> **Residence - Knockmaroon - 1850**

Individual Burials

- Abigail Harris – bur. 23 Jun 1700 (Burial, **St. Nicholas Without Parish**)

Abigail Harris (deceased):

  Residence - Ffordhams Alley - Before June 23, 1700

- Abigail Harris – bur. 28 Apr 1730 (Burial, **St. Luke Parish**)

- Abigail Harris – b. 1763, bur. 20 May 1829 (Burial, **Dunleckney Parish**)

- Abraham Harris – bur. 30 Jun 1747 (Burial, **St. Paul Parish**)

- Ada Elizabeth Harris – b. Feb 1852, d. 7 Sep 1852, bur. 1852 (Burial, **St. Anne Parish**)

- Agnes Harris – b. 1824, bur. 11 Feb 1833 (Burial, **St. Mark Parish**)

Agnes Harris (deceased):

  Residence - City Quay - Before February 11, 1833

- Alicia Harris – b. 1776, bur. 15 Apr 1846 (Burial, **St. Peter Parish**)

Alicia Harris (deceased):

  Residence - Cuffe Street - Before April 15, 1846

- Allex Harris – bur. 26 Sep 1743 (Burial, **St. Paul Parish**)

- Amelia Harris – b. 1817, d. 25 Jun 1836 (Burial, **St. Peter Parish**)

Amelia Harris (deceased):

  Residence - Mercer's Hospital - June 25, 1836

  Burial - St. Kevin's Cemetery

- Andrew Harris – bur. 9 Jul 1809 (Burial, **St. Peter Parish**)

Andrew Harris (deceased):

  Residence - Kevin Street - Before July 9, 1809

Harris Surname Ireland: 1600s to 1900s

- Anne Harris – bur. Aug 1699 (Burial, **St. Nicholas Without Parish**)

Anne Harris (deceased):

  Residence - PATR Street - Before August 1699

- Anne Harris – bur. 21 Nov 1718 (Burial, **St. Catherine Parish**)

- Anne Harris – bur. Mar 1736 (Burial, **St. Nicholas Without Parish**)

Anne Harris (deceased):

  Residence - St. Anne's Parish - Before March 1736

- Anne Harris – bur. 25 Sep 1748 (Burial, **St. James Parish**)

Anne Harris (deceased):

  Residence - James Street - Before September 25, 1748

- Anne Harris – bur. 8 Sep 1784 (Burial, **St. Peter Parish**)

Anne Harris (deceased):

  Residence - Leeson Street - Before September 8, 1784

- Anne Harris – bur. 26 Aug 1788 (Burial, **St. Paul Parish**)

- Anne Harris – bur. 31 Aug 1795 (Burial, **Glasnevin Parish**)

Anne Harris (deceased):

  Residence - Meath Street - Before August 31, 1795

- Anne Harris – bur. 18 Sep 1804 (Burial, **St. Paul Parish**)

- Anne Harris – bur. 18 Dec 1808 (Burial, **St. Luke Parish**)

Anne Harris (deceased):

  Residence - Still Court - Before December 18, 1808

- Anne Harris – bur. 16 May 1810 (Burial, **St. Paul Parish**)

- Anne Harris – b. 1754, bur. 1 May 1811 (Burial, **St. Luke Parish**)

Anne Harris (deceased):

  Residence - Spitles Field, St. Nicholas Without Parish - Before May 1, 1811

- Anne Harris – bur. 15 Nov Unclear (Burial, **Aghold Parish**)

Hurst

- Anthony Harris – bur. 25 Feb 1701 (Burial, **St. Nicholas Within Parish**) (Burial, **St. Nicholas Without Parish**)

- Arthur Harris – bur. 7 Nov 1698 (Burial, **St. Michan Parish**)

Arthur Harris (deceased):

  Relationship Status at Burial - bachelor

- Bartholomew Harris – bur. 27 Sep 1737 (Burial, **St. Peter Parish**)

- Bridget Harris – b. 1761, bur. 6 Apr 1817 (Burial, **St. Peter Parish**)

- Bridget Harris – b. 1807, bur. 5 Aug 1843 (Burial, **St. Luke Parish**)

Bridget Harris (deceased):

  Residence - Cork Street - Before August 5, 1843

- C. Harris – b. 1821, bur. 26 Sep 1839 (Burial, **St. George Parish**)

C. Harris (deceased):

  Residence - 18 Portland Place - Before September 26, 1839

  Cause of Death - fever

- Catherine Harris – bur. 31 Aug 1733 (Burial, **St. Audoen Parish**)

Catherine Harris (deceased):

  Residence - Purcell's Court - Before August 31, 1733

- Catherine Harris – b. 1701, bur. 3 Nov 1741 (Burial, **St. Werburgh Parish**)

Catherine Harris (deceased):

  Residence - Alm's House - Before November 3, 1741

- Catherine Harris – bur. 9 May 1787 (Burial, **St. Luke Parish**)

Catherine Harris (deceased):

  Residence - Skinner's Alley - Before May 9, 1787

  Cause of Death - old age

Harris Surname Ireland: 1600s to 1900s

- Catherine Harris – b. 1838, bur. 16 Feb 1843 (Burial, **St. Peter Parish**)

Catherine Harris (deceased):

Residence - Charlotte Street - Before February 16, 1843

Age at Death - 5 years

Burial - St. Kevin's Cemetery

- Charles Harris – b. 1876, d. 16 Feb 1879, bur. 1879 (Burial, **St. James Parish**)

Charles Harris (deceased):

Residence - 78 Prussia Street - February 16, 1879

Age at Death - 3 years

- Charlotte Harris – b. 1810, d. 30 Jun 1825, bur. 1825 (Burial, **Chapelizod Parish**)

- Clarissa Harris – b. Dec 1869, d. 11 Mar 1870, bur. 12 Mar 1870 (Burial, **Arbour Hill Barracks Parish**)

Clarissa Harris (deceased):

Residence - Royal Barrack - March 11, 1870

She was the Child of a member of the 30th Regiment.

- Coldstream Hunt Harris – b. 1825, bur. 4 Apr 1850 (Burial, **Carlow Parish**)

Coldstream Hunt Harris (deceased):

Residence - Carlow Barracks - Before April 4, 1850

- David Harris – d. 18 Jan 1813, bur. 1813 (Burial, **Chapelizod Parish**)

- Diana Harris – bur. 26 Aug 1745 (Burial, **St. John Parish**)

- Edward Harris – bur. 6 Nov 1689 (Burial, **St. Audoen Parish**)

- Edward Harris – bur. 8 Apr 1690 (Burial, **St. Catherine Parish**)

- Edward Harris – bur. 20 Feb 1732 (Burial, **St. Audoen Parish**)

Edward Harris (deceased):

Residence - Glib - Before February 20, 1732

- Edward Harris – bur. 19 Sep 1765 (Burial, **St. James Parish**)

Hurst

Edward Harris (deceased):

Residence - Britain Street - Before September 19, 1765

- Edward Harris – bur. 28 Jan 1785 (Burial, **St. James Parish**)

Edward Harris (deceased):

Residence - Watling Street - Before January 28, 1785

- Edward Henry Harris – b. Feb 1845, d. 16 Dec 1845, bur. 1845 (Burial, **St. Anne Parish**)

- Eleanor Harris – bur. 8 Dec 1686 (Burial, **St. Michan Parish**)

The church register entry reads as follows:

"**Ellinor Harris, orphan at Nurs Wth Margery Jackson.**"

- Eleanor Harris – bur. 25 Nov 1689 (Burial, **St. Catherine Parish**)

- Eleanor Harris – bur. 10 Jul 1767 (Burial, **St. Peter Parish**)

- Elizabeth Harris – bur. 7 Jan 1680 (Burial, **St. Catherine Parish**)

- Elizabeth Harris – bur. 27 Oct 1691 (Burial, **St. Michan Parish**)

The church register entry reads as follows:

"**Elizabeth Harris, virgin.**"

- Elizabeth Harris – bur. 22 Feb 1706 (Burial, **Carlow Parish**)

- Elizabeth Harris – bur. 30 May 1713 (Burial, **St. Catherine Parish**)

- Elizabeth Harris – bur. 1725 (Burial, **St. Luke Parish**)

- Elizabeth Harris – bur. 8 Nov 1742 (Burial, **St. James Parish**)

Elizabeth Harris (deceased):

Residence - Temple Barr - Before November 8, 1742

- Elizabeth Harris – bur. 13 Feb 1746 (Burial, **St. Paul Parish**)

- Elizabeth Harris – bur. 11 Mar 1748 (Burial, **St. Audoen Parish**)

- Elizabeth Harris – bur. 11 Mar 1749 (Burial, **St. Audoen Parish**)

- Elizabeth Harris – bur. 8 Apr 1770 (Burial, **St. James Parish**)

Elizabeth Harris (deceased):

Residence - Little Green - Before. April 8, 1770

Harris Surname Ireland: 1600s to 1900s

- Elizabeth Harris – bur. 16 Apr 1784 (Burial, **Aghold Parish**)

- Elizabeth Harris – bur. 3 Jun 1787 (Burial, **St. Catherine Parish**)

Elizabeth Harris (deceased):

> **Residence - Marrowbone Lane - Before June 3, 1787**

- Elizabeth Harris – bur. 25 Jan 1800 (Burial, **St James Parish**)

Elizabeth Harris (deceased):

> **Residence - Thomas Street - Before January 25, 1800**

- Elizabeth Harris – bur. 20 Sep 1801 (Burial, **St. Peter Parish**)

Elizabeth Harris (deceased):

> **Residence - Longford Lane - Before September 20, 1801**

- Elizabeth Harris – bur. 21 Feb 1809 (Burial, **St. Paul Parish**)

- Elizabeth Harris – b. 1754, bur. 5 Mar 1814 (Burial, **St. Peter Parish**)

- Elizabeth Harris – b. May 1838, bur. 12 Sep 1838 (Burial, **St. Peter Parish**)

Elizabeth Harris (deceased):

> **Residence - Charlemont Street - Before September 12, 1838**
>
> **Age at Death - 5 months**
>
> **Place of Burial - St Peter's Cemetery**

- Elizabeth Harris – bur. 28 May 1848 (Burial, **Dunleckney Parish**)

- Elizabeth Harris – b. 1804, bur. 22 Jan 1869 (Burial, **Dunleckney Parish**)

Elizabeth Harris (deceased):

> **Residence - Bagenalstown - Before January 22, 1869**

- Ellen Harris – b. Jan 1831, bur. 29 Jun 1831 (Burial, **St. Catherine Parish**)

Ellen Harris (deceased):

> **Age at Death - 6 months**

- Ellen Harris – b. 1838, bur. 29 Mar 1840 (Burial, **St. Mark Parish**)

Ellen Harris (deceased):

> **Residence - Moss Street - Before March 29, 1840**
>
> **Age at Death - 2 years**

Hurst

- Emma Margaret Harris – b. 1851, d. 21 Jan 1856, bur. 22 Jan 1856 (Burial, **Arbour Hill Barracks Parish**)

Emma Margaret Harris (deceased):

    Cause of Death - scalded by accident - January 21, 1856

She was the daughter of a member of the 44th Foot.

- Frances Harris – bur. 12 May 1794 (Burial, **St. Catherine Parish**)

Frances Harris (deceased):

    Residence - Thomas Street - Before May 12, 1794

- Frances Harris – b. 1791, d. 21 Mar 1815 (Burial, **St. Peter Parish**)

- Frances Harris – b. 1811, d. 14 Nov 1872, bur. 1872 (Burial, **St. Catherine Parish**) (Burial, **St. Catherine Parish** (RC))

Frances Harris (deceased):

    Residence - 61 Summer Hill - Before November 14, 1872

- Francis Harris – bur. 12 Apr 1665 (Burial, **St. John Parish**)

Francis Harris (deceased):

    Occupation - Stranger - April 12, 1665

- Francis Harris – b. 1654, bur. 20 Oct 1707 (Burial, **St. Werburgh Parish**)

Francis Harris (deceased):

    Residence - Copper Alley - Before October 20, 1707

    Cause of Death - kild (Probably abbreviated form of killed)

- Francis Harris – bur. 10 Aug 1741 (Burial, **St. Paul Parish**)

- Francis Harris – b. 1754, bur. 8 Apr 1831 (Burial, **St. Mark Parish**)

Francis Harris (deceased):

    Residence - Magennis Court - Before April 8, 1831

- George Harris – bur. 30 Dec 1744 (Burial, **St. James Parish**)

George Harris (deceased):

    Residence - Dolphin's Barn - Before December 30, 1744

- George Harris – bur. 30 Mar 1774 (Burial, **St. Peter Parish**)

Harris Surname Ireland: 1600s to 1900s

- George Harris – b. 1816, bur. 4 Feb 1817 (Burial, **St. Catherine Parish**)

George Harris (deceased):

  Residence - Queen Street - Before February 4, 1817

  Age at Death - 1 year

- George Harris – b. 1821, d. 1 Sep 1837, bur. 1837 (Burial, **Chapelizod Parish**)

George Harris (deceased):

  Residence - Parliament Street Dublin - Before September 1, 1837

- George Harris – b. Feb 1835. d. 28 Aug 1856, bur. 30 Aug 1856 (Burial, **Arbour Hill Barracks Parish**)

George Harris (deceased):

  Occupation - Private 3rd Dragoons - August 28, 1856

  Cause of Death - fever

- George Harris – b. 1799, d. 13 May 1857, bur. 1857 (Burial, **Clondalkin Parish**)

George Harris (deceased):

  Residence - Cheeverstown - Before May 13, 1857

- George Harris – b. 1864, d. 10 Oct 1865, bur. 1865 (Burial, **St. James Parish**)

George Harris (deceased):

  Residence - South Dublin Union - Before October 10, 1865

  Age at Death - 1 year

- George W. Harris – b. Sep1850, d. 6 Jan 1852, bur. 7 Jan 1852 (Burial, **Arbour Hill Barracks Parish**)

George W. Harris (deceased):

  Cause of Death - convulsions - January 6, 1852

He was the son of a member of the 40th Regiment.

- H. Jane Harris – b. 1827, bur. 22 Apr 1828 (Burial, **St. Catherine Parish**)

- Henry Harris – bur. 1 Apr 1699 (Burial, **St. Michan Parish**)

- Henry Harris – bur. 20 Oct 1700 (Burial, **St. Catherine Parish**)

Hurst

- Henry Matthew Harris – b. May 1874, bur. 5 Oct 1874 (Burial, **St. Peter Parish**)

Henry Matthew Harris (deceased):

Residence - Hacket's Court - Before October 5, 1874

Age at Death - 4 years and 5 months

- Isaac Harris – bur. 28 Oct 1787 (Burial, **Kilnaughtin Parish**)

- Isabel Harris – bur. 28 Jun 1821 (Burial, **St. Luke Parish**)

- Jabath Harris – bur. 16 Apr 1775 (Burial, **St. Paul Parish**)

- James Harris – bur. 5 Jul 1700 (Burial, **St. Nicholas Without Parish**)

James Harris (deceased):

Residence - Fordhams Alley - Before July 5, 1700

- James Harris – bur. 13 Jun 1707 (Burial, **St. Catherine Parish**)

- James Harris – bur. 15 Feb 1735 (Burial, **Dingle Parish**)

James Harris (deceased):

Residence - Marhin - Before February 15, 1735

- James Harris – bur. 11 Jan 1737 (Burial, **St. Mary Parish**)

- James Harris – bur. 9 Oct 1773 (Burial, **St. James Parish**)

James Harris (deceased):

Residence - Barrack Street - Before October 9, 1773

- James Harris – bur. 4 Feb 1801 (Burial, **St. Paul Parish**)

- James Harris – b. 1825, bur. 3 Jul 1825 (Burial, **St. Catherine Parish**)

James Harris (deceased):

Residence - Meath Street - Before July 3, 1825

Age at Death - 3 weeks

- James Harris – bur. 5 Apr 1831 (Burial, **St. Catherine Parish**)

James Harris (deceased):

Residence - Braithwaite Street - Before April 5, 1831

Harris Surname Ireland: 1600s to 1900s

- James Harris – b. 1812, bur. 12 May 1831 (Burial, **Dingle Parish**)

James Harris (deceased):

    Residence - Dingle - Before May 12, 1831

- James Harris – bur. 15 May 1832 (Burial, **St. Nicholas Without Parish**)

James Harris (deceased):

    Residence - Long Lane - Before May 15, 1832

- James Harris – b. 1792, bur. 12 Jan 1836 (Burial, **St. Mark Parish**)

James Harris (deceased):

    Residence - Swords Street Dublin - Before January 12, 1836

- James Joseph Harris – b. Mar 1846, bur. 22 Sep 1846 (Burial, **St. Mark Parish**)

James Joseph Harris (deceased):

    Residence - 38 George's Quay - Before September 22, 1846

    Age at Death - 7 months

- Jane Harris – bur. 16 Oct 1642 (Burial, **St. John Parish**)

- Jane Harris – bur. 27 Jun 1685 (Burial, **St. Catherine Parish**)

- Jane Harris – bur. 27 Sep 1685 (Burial, **St. Catherine Parish**)

- Jane Harris – bur. 25 May 1688 (Burial, **St. Nicholas Without Parish**)

- Jane Harris – bur. 11 Oct 1693 (Burial, **St. Michan Parish**)

Jane Harris (deceased):

    Relationship Status at Burial - widow

- Jane Harris – bur. 18 Jan 1699 (Burial, **St. Peter Parish**)

Jane Harris (deceased):

    Residence - King Street - Before January 18, 1699

- Jane Harris – bur. 4 Feb 1699 (Burial, **St. Peter Parish**)

Jane Harris (deceased):

    Residence - New Street - Before February 4, 1699

Hurst

- Jane Harris – bur. 18 Aug 1700 (Burial, **St. Catherine Parish**)

- Jane Harris – bur. 16 Apr 1703 (Burial, **St. Nicholas Without Parish**)

Jane Harris (deceased):

    Residence - Hey Street - Before April 16, 1700

- Jane Harris – bur. 22 May 1703 (Burial, **St. Catherine Parish**)

- Jane Harris – bur. 20 Mar 1709 (Burial, **St. Nicholas Without Parish**)

Jane Harris (deceased):

    Residence - Skinner's Alley - Before March 20, 1709

- Jane Harris – bur. 9 Jan 1719 (Burial, **St. Paul Parish**)

- Jane Harris – bur. 26 Oct 1720 (Burial, **St. Peter Parish**)

- Jane Harris – bur. 4 Apr 1722 (Burial, **St. Peter Parish**)

- Jane Harris – bur. 15 Feb 1733 (Burial, **St. Catherine Parish**)

- Jane Harris – bur. 13 Aug 1749 (Burial, **St. Paul Parish**)

- Jane Harris – bur. 30 Mar 1794 (Burial, **St. Catherine Parish**)

Jane Harris (deceased):

    Residence - Marlborough Street - Before March 30, 1794

- Jane Harris – bur. 16 Jan 1801 (Burial, **St. Mark Parish**)

- Jane Harris – bur. 29 Sep 1812 (Burial, **St. Catherine Parish**)

Jane Harris (deceased):

    Residence - Pimlico - Before September 29, 1812

- Jane Harris – b. 1851, d. 14 Oct 1859, bur. 1859 (Burial, **Clondalkin Parish**)

Jane Harris (deceased):

    Residence - Cheeverstown - Before October 14, 1859

- Jo Harris – bur. 18 Jun 1721 (Burial, **St. Nicholas Without Parish**)

Jo Harris (deceased):

    Residence - St. Catherines - Before June 18, 1821

Harris Surname Ireland: 1600s to 1900s

- Job Harris – b. 1837, d. 6 Jun 1868, bur. 10 Jun 1868 (Burial, **Arbour Hill Barracks Parish**)

Job Harris (deceased):

    Residence - Beggars Bush Barracks - Before June 6, 1868

    Occupation - Private Coldstream Guards - June 6, 1868

- John Harris – bur. 26 May 1628 (Burial, **St. John Parish**)

- John Harris – bur. 1 Oct 1642 (Burial, **St. John Parish**)

- John Harris – bur. 7 Oct 1651 (Burial, **St. John Parish**)

- John Harris – bur. 7 Nov 1689 (Burial, **St. Catherine Parish**)

- John Harris – bur. 28 Sep 1697 (Burial, **St. Catherine Parish**)

- John Harris – bur. 19 Feb 1699 (Burial, **St. Catherine Parish**)

- John Harris – bur. 3 Nov 1699 (Burial, **St. Catherine Parish**)

- John Harris – bur. 5 Nov 1700 (Burial, **St. Catherine Parish**)

- John Harris – bur. Apr 1701 (Burial, **St. Nicholas Without Parish**)

John Harris (deceased):

    Residence - PATR Street - Before April 1701

- John Harris – bur. 5 Oct 1701 (Burial, **St. Catherine Parish**)

- John Harris – bur. 8 Oct 1701 (Burial, **St. John Parish**)

- John Harris – bur. 29 Oct 1701 (Burial, **St. Catherine Parish**)

- John Harris – bur. 10 Nov 1701 (Burial, **St. Catherine Parish**)

- John Harris – bur. 23 Dec 1703 (Burial, **St. Catherine Parish**)

- John Harris – bur. 17 Aug 1704 (Burial, **St. Catherine Parish**)

- John Harris – bur. 6 Sep 1705 (Burial, **St. Catherine Parish**)

- John Harris – bur. 1 Jun 1706 (Burial, **St. Catherine Parish**)

- John Harris – bur. 13 Apr 1707 (Burial, **St. Catherine Parish**)

Hurst

- John Harris – b. 1668, bur. 1 Nov 1709 (Burial, **St. Werburgh Parish**)

John Harris (deceased):

    Residence - Crean Leane - Before November 1, 1709

    Cause of Death - flux

- John Harris – bur. 22 Jul 1713 (Burial, **St. Catherine Parish**)

- John Harris – bur. 10 May 1716 (Burial, **St. Paul Parish**)

- John Harris – bur. 9 Sep 1717 (Burial, **St. Catherine Parish**)

- John Harris – bur. 2 Apr 1724 (Burial, **St. Mary Parish**)

- John Harris – bur. 14 Dec 1727 (Burial, **St. Paul Parish**)

- John Harris – bur. 27 May 1729 (Burial, **St. Audoen Parish**)

John Harris (deceased):

    Residence - Corn Market - Before May 27. 1729

- John Harris – b. 1670, bur. 4 Apr 1730 (Burial, **St. Werburgh Parish**)

John Harris (deceased):

    Residence - Gun Alley - Before April 4, 1730

    Cause of Death - fever

- John Harris – bur. 11 May 1732 (Burial, **St. Paul Parish**)

- John Harris – bur. 27 Dec 1735 (Burial, **St. Nicholas Without Parish**)

John Harris (deceased):

    Residence - Swift's Alley - Before December 27, 1735

- John Harris – bur. 21 Feb 1737 (Burial, **St. Catherine Parish**)

- John Harris – bur. 5 Jun 1741 (Burial, **St. Paul Parish**)

- John Harris – bur. 11 Mar 1761 (Burial, **St. James Parish**)

- John Harris – bur. 21 Jul 1763 (Burial, **St. James Parish**)

John Harris (deceased):

    Residence - Thomas Court - Before July 21, 1763

- John Harris – bur. 9 Apr 1769 (Burial, **St. James Parish**)

John Harris (deceased):

> **Residence - Cooke Street - Before April 9, 1769**

- John Harris – bur. 2 Jun 1807 (Burial, **St. Paul Parish**)

- John Harris – bur. 18 Feb 1813 (Burial, **St. Paul Parish**)

- John Harris – b. 1781, bur. 21 Nov 1817 (Burial, **St. Mark Parish**)

John Harris (deceased):

> **Military Rank - Captain - November 21, 1817**

- John Harris – b. 1751, bur. 19 Nov 1824 (Burial, **St. Audoen Parish**)

- John Harris – b. 1754, bur. 19 Nov 1824 (Burial, **St. Audoen Parish**)

- John Harris – bur. 13 Feb 1825 (Burial, **Aghold Parish**)

John Harris (deceased):

> **Residence - Coolkenno - Before February 13, 1825**

- John Harris – b. 1790, bur. 22 Dec 1827 (Burial, **Glasnevin Parish**)

John Harris (deceased):

> **Residence - Dublin - Before December 22, 1827**

- John Harris – b. 1784, bur. 15 Mar 1828 (Burial, **St. Catherine Parish**)

- John Harris – b. 1772, bur. 3 Mar 1832 (Burial, **St. Werburgh Parish**)

- John Harris – b. 29 May 1842, bur. 3 Apr 1842 (Burial, **St. Peter Parish**)

John Harris (deceased):

> **Residence - Rathmines - Before April 3, 1842**
>
> **Age at Death - 6 days**
>
> **Place of Burial - St. Peter Cemetery**

- John Harris – b. 1824, bur. 18 Apr 1844 (Burial, **St. Paul Parish**)

John Harris (deceased):

> **Residence - Alborough House Barracks - Before April 18, 1844**
>
> **Occupation - Drummer 24th Regiment - April 18, 1844**

Hurst

- John Harris – b. Jul 1847, bur. 4 Oct 1847 (Burial, **St. George Parish**)

John Harris (deceased):

Residence - 4 Gardiners Lane - Before October 4, 1847

Age at Death - 4 months

- John Harris – bur. 18 Mar 1848 (Burial, **Carlow Parish**)

John Harris (deceased):

Occupation - Prisoner in the jail of Carlow - Before March 18, 1848

- John Harris – b. 1825, d. 7 Jun 1849, bur. 7 Jun 1849 (Burial, **Arbour Hill Barracks Parish**)

John Harris (deceased):

Occupation - Private in the 2nd Regiment - June 7, 1849

Cause of Death - cholera

- John Harris – b. 1846, bur. 16 Sep 1866 (Burial, **Arbour Hill Barracks Parish**)

John Harris (deceased):

Residence - Richmond Barracks - Before September 16, 1866

Occupation - 3rd Buffs Private - September 16, 1866

- John Harris – b. 1780, bur. 15 Mar 1870 (Burial, **Kilnaughtin Parish**)

John Harris (deceased):

Residence - Tarbert - Before March 15, 1870

- Jonathan Harris – bur. 2 Aug 1700 (Burial, **St. Catherine Parish**)

- Joseph Harris – bur. 29 Jan 1683 (Burial, **St. Peter Parish**)

- Joseph Harris – bur. 24 Dec 1768 (Burial, **St. James Parish**)

Joseph Harris (deceased):

Residence - Little Green - Before December 24, 1768

- Joseph Harris – bur. 27 Jul 1776 (Burial, **St. Paul Parish**)

- Joseph Harris – bur. 23 Oct 1805 (Burial, **Glasnevin Parish**)

- Joseph Harris – bur. 30 Jan 1814 (Burial, **St. Paul Parish**)

- Joseph Harris – bur. 17 Dec 1817 (Burial, **St. Paul Parish**)

- Joshua Harris – bur. 23 Apr 1714 (Burial, **St. Catherine Parish**)

Harris Surname Ireland: 1600s to 1900s

- Joshua Harris – bur. 4 Aug 1716 (Burial, **St. Paul Parish**)

- Judith Harris – bur. 4 Mar 1746 (Burial, **St. Paul Parish**)

- Judith Harris – bur. 4 Jan 1807 (Burial, **Glasnevin Parish**)

- Leticia Harris – bur. 2 Sep 1647 (Burial, **St. John Parish**)

- Leticia Harris – bur. 11 Feb 1762 (Burial, **St. Paul Parish**)

- Leticia Frances Harris – b. 1865, d. 4 Nov 1876, bur. 1876 (Burial, **St. Catherine Parish**)

    (Burial, **St. Catherine Parish** (RC))

Leticia Frances Harris (deceased):

   Residence - 100 Abbey Street - November 4, 1876

   Age at Death - 11 years

- M. Harris – bur. 14 Apr 1811 (Burial, **Glasnevin Parish**)

M. Harris (deceased):

   Residence - Dublin - Before April 14, 1811

- Margaret Harris – bur. 3 Aug 1685 (Burial, **St. Catherine Parish**)

- Margaret Harris – bur. Jan 1699 (Burial, **St. Nicholas Without Parish**)

Margaret Harris (deceased):

   Residence - Francis Street - Before January 1699

- Margaret Harris – bur. 23 Aug 1706 (Burial, **St. Catherine Parish**)

- Margaret Harris – bur. 2 May 1772 (Burial, **St. James Parish**)

Margaret Harris (deceased):

   Residence - Dolphin's Barn - Before May 2, 1772

- Margaret Harris – bur. 2 Jun 1827 (Burial, **St. Werburgh Parish**)

Listed under the following heading in the church register:

   "As a confirmation held by his grace William, Lord Arch Bishop of 'Dublin in Saint Werburghs Church on the Second Day of June 1827, the following young persons were presented and confirmed."

Hurst

- Margaret Harris – b. 1813, bur. 14 Jul 1833 (Burial, **St. Werburgh Parish**)

- Mark Harris – bur. 25 Mar 1761 (Burial, **St. Paul Parish**)

- Martha Harris – bur. 4 Apr 1814 (Burial, **St. Paul Parish**)

- Mary Harris – bur. 17 Jun 1681 (Burial, **St. Michan Parish**)

The church register entry reads as follows:

"Mary Harris, a child, Y^t that was left on Y^E Parish."

- Mary Harris – bur. 30 Aug 1685 (Burial, **St. Catherine Parish**)

- Mary Harris – bur. 30 Apr 1693 (Burial, **St. Audoen Parish**)

Mary Harris (deceased):

Relationship Status at Death - widow

- Mary Harris – bur. 2 Jan 1698 (Burial, **St. Peter Parish**)

Mary Harris (deceased):

Residence - Butter Lane - Before January 2, 1698

- Mary Harris – bur. 28 Jul 1699 (Burial, **St. Catherine Parish**)

- Mary Harris – bur. 5 Sep 1700 (Burial, **St. Catherine Parish**)

- Mary Harris – bur. 2 Apr 1702 (Burial, **St. Catherine Parish**)

- Mary Harris – bur. 22 Apr 1702 (Burial, **St. Catherine Parish**)

- Mary Harris – bur. 18 Aug 1703 (Burial, **St. Catherine Parish**)

- Mary Harris – bur. 12 Dec 1705 (Burial, **St. Catherine Parish**)

- Mary Harris – bur. 28 May 1706 (Burial, **St. Nicholas Without Parish**)

Mary Harris (deceased):

Residence - New Market - Before May 28, 1706

- Mary Harris – bur. 24 Dec 1707 (Burial, **St. Catherine Parish**)

- Mary Harris – bur. 19 Sep 1712 (Burial, **St. Catherine Parish**)

- Mary Harris – bur. 7 May 1719 (Burial, **St. Nicholas Without Parish**)

Mary Harris (deceased):

    Residence - Stony Batter - Before May 7, 1719

- Mary Harris – bur. 3 May 1728 (Burial, **St. Paul Parish**)

- Mary Harris – bur. 2 Jan 1729 (Burial, **St. Paul Parish**)

- Mary Harris – bur. 10 Jan 1729 (Burial, **St. Paul Parish**)

- Mary Harris – bur. 11 Jan 1730 (Burial, **St. Nicholas Without Parish**)

Mary Harris (deceased):

    Residence - Hanover Lane - Before January 11, 1730

- Mary Harris – bur. 19 Mar 1738 (Burial, **St. Peter Parish**)

- Mary Harris – bur. 21 Mar 1740 (Burial, **St. Paul Parish**)

- Mary Harris – bur. 9 Dec 1740 (Burial, **St. Mark Parish**)

- Mary Harris – bur. 27 May 1741 (Burial, **St. Paul Parish**)

- Mary Harris – bur. 28 Jun 1741 (Burial, **St. Paul Parish**)

- Mary Harris – bur. 13 Sep 1748 (Burial, **St. Paul Parish**)

- Mary Harris – bur. 21 Jan 1758 (Burial, **St. Mark Parish**)

- Mary Harris – bur. 2 Dec 1773 (Burial, **St. Paul Parish**)

- Mary Harris – bur. 20 Jul 1810 (Burial, **St. Catherine Parish**)

Mary Harris (deceased):

    Residence - Marrowbone Lane - Before July 20, 1810

- Mary Harris – bur. 2 Nov 1816 (Burial, **St. Mary Parish**)

Mary Harris (deceased):

    Residence - Cole's Lane - Before November 2, 1816

- Mary Harris – b. 1783, bur. 26 Jan 1819 (Burial, **St. Peter Parish**)

Mary Harris (deceased):

    Residence - Anne's Court - Before January 26, 1819

Hurst

- Mary Harris – bur. Jul 1834 (Burial, **Tralee Parish**)

Mary Harris (deceased):

> **Residence - Tralee - Before July 1834**

- Mary Harris – b. 1830, bur. 8 Dec 1834 (Burial, **St. Peter Parish**)

Mary Harris (deceased):

> **Residence - Longford Street - Before December 8, 1834**
>
> **Age at Death - 4 years**
>
> **Place of Burial - St. Kevin Cemetery**

- Mary Harris – b. 1756, bur. 1 Feb 1840 (Burial, **St. Mark Parish**)

Mary Harris (deceased):

> **Residence - Kings Town - Before February 1, 1840**

- Mary Harris – bur. 8 Nov 1840 (Burial, **St. Matthew Parish**)

Mary Harris (deceased):

> **Residence - Sandmount - Before November 8, 1840**

- Mary Harris – b. 1845, bur. 14 Sep 1847 (Burial, **St. George Parish**)

Mary Harris (deceased):

> **Residence - 4 Gardiners Lane - Before September 14, 1847**

- Mary Harris – b. 1778, d. 1 Oct 1854, bur. 1854 (Burial, **St. James Parish**)

Mary Harris (deceased):

> **Residence - South Dublin Union - October 1, 1854**

- Mary Harris – b. 1786, bur. 23 Jan 1873 (Burial, **Clontarf Parish**)

Mary Harris (deceased):

> **Residence - Clontarf - Before January 23, 1873**

- Mary Anne Harris – b. 1819, bur. 7 Jan 1850 (Burial, **St. Matthew Parish**)

Mary Anne Harris (deceased):

> **Residence - Pigeon House - Before January 7, 1850**

- Mary Anne Harris – b. May 1848, d. 6 Nov 1854, bur. 7 Nov 1854 (Burial, **Arbour Hill Barracks Parish**)

Mary Anne Harris (deceased):

Cause of Death - water on the brain - November 6, 1854

She was the daughter of a member of the 44th Regiment.

- Mary Anne Harris – b. 1847, d. 1 Nov 1860, bur. 1860 (Burial, **Clondalkin Parish**)

Mary Anne Harris (deceased):

Residence - Cheeverstown - November 1, 1860

- Mary Anne Harris – b. 1808, d. 7 Mar 1883, bur. 1883 (Burial, **St. Catherine Parish**) (Burial, **St. Catherine Parish** (RC))

Mary Anne Harris (deceased):

Residence - 3 Fairview Avenue - March 7, 1883

- Mary S. Harris – b. Jun 1874, bur. 29 Dec 1874 (Burial, **St. George Parish**)

Mary S. Harris (deceased):

Residence - 24 O'Connell Street - Before December 29, 1874

Age at Death - 6 months

- Matilda Harris – b. 1820, bur. 27 Apr 1832 (Burial, **St. George Parish**)

Matilda Harris (deceased):

Residence - Claremount School - Before April 27, 1832

- Michael Harris – bur. 18 Aug 1764 (Burial, **Aghold Parish**)

Michael Harris (deceased):

Residence - Dublin - Before August 18, 1764

Occupation - Work House - August 18, 1764

- Michael Harris – b. 1827, bur. 8 May 1831 (Burial, **St. Catherine Parish**)

Michael Harris (deceased):

Residence - Pool Street - Before May 8, 1831

Age at Death - 4 years

Hurst

- Michael Harris – b. 1759, d. 1 May 1843, bur. 1843 (Burial, **St. Anne Parish**)

    o Unknown Harris (Male)

    o Unknown Harris (Male)

    o Walter Harris – b. 1764, d. 15 Jan 1810 bur. 1810 (Burial, **St. Anne Parish**)

Walter Harris (deceased):

Occupation - Brevet Major 5th Fusileers - January 15, 1810

Michael Harris (deceased):

Residence - Upper Merrion Street - May 1, 1843

Church Register Entry reads as follows:

"Michal Harris Upr Merrion St

Died May 1st 1843 age 84

Also His Third son Walter Harris

Brevet Major 5 Fusileers

Died January 15, 1810 age 46"

- Michael Harris – b. 1828, bur. 22 May 1858 (Burial, **St. Luke Parish**)

Michael Harris (deceased):

Residence - James Street - Before May 22, 1858

- Nancy Harris – d. 18 Nov 1832, bur. 1832 (Burial, **Clondalkin Parish**)

Nancy Harris (deceased):

Residence - Clondalkin - Before November 18, 1832

- Nathaniel Harris – bur. 21 Jan 1746 (Burial, **St. James Parish**)

Nathaniel Harris (deceased):

Residence - James Street - Before January 21, 1746

- Oliver Harris – bur. 30 Sep 1713 (Burial, **St. John Parish**)

- Patrick Harris – bur. 21 Mar 1777 (Burial, **St. James Parish**)

Patrick Harris (deceased):

Residence - Plunkett Street - Before March 21, 1777

Harris Surname Ireland: 1600s to 1900s

- Patrick Harris – b. 1785, bur. 20 May 1821 (Burial, **St. Peter Parish**)

Patrick Harris (deceased):

> **Residence - Aungier Street - Before May 20, 1821**

> **Place of Burial - St. Kevin Church Yard Cemetery**

- Peter Harris – bur. 17 Mar 1797 (Burial, **St. Peter Parish**)

Peter Harris (deceased):

> **Residence - Goat Alley - Before March 17, 1797**

- Rebecca Harris – bur. 14 Jul 1704 (Burial, **St. Catherine Parish**)

- Rebecca Harris – bur. 15 Jan 1719 (Burial, **St. Nicholas Without Parish**)

Rebecca Harris (deceased):

> **Residence - New Street - Before January 15, 1719**

- Rhodia Harris – b. 1826, d. 12 Feb 1831, bur. 1831 (Burial, **Chapelizod Parish**)

- Richard Harris – bur. 23 Feb 1639 (Burial, **St. John Parish**)

- Richard Harris – bur. 23 Feb 1777 (Burial, **St. James Parish**)

Richard Harris (deceased):

> **Residence - Summons Street - Before February 23, 1777**

- Richard Harris – bur. 20 Feb 1788 (Burial, **St. Luke Parish**)

Richard Harris (deceased):

> **Residence - New Market - Before February 20, 1788**

> **Cause of Death - decay**

- Richard Harris – b. 1773, bur. 25 Aug 1831 (Burial, **St. Mary Parish**)

Richard Harris (deceased):

> **Residence - Stafford Street - Before August 25, 1831**

- Robert Harris – bur. 23 Feb 1703 (Burial, **St. John Parish**)

- Robert Harris – bur. 18 Mar 1704 (Burial, **St. Catherine Parish**)

Hurst

- Robert Harris – b. Nov 1835, bur. 19 Feb 1836 (Burial, **St. Matthew Parish**)

Robert Harris (deceased):

    Residence - Sandymount - Before February 19, 1836

    Age at Death - 4 months

- Roger Harris – bur. 30 Aug 1693 (Burial, **St. Nicholas Without Parish**)

- Roger Harris – bur. 3 Feb 1703 (Burial, **St. Catherine Parish**)

- Rose Harris – bur. 1 Jan 1715 (Burial, **St. Audoen Parish**)

- Ruth Harris – bur. 19 Aug 1711 (Burial, **St. Werburgh Parish**)

Ruth Harris (deceased):

    Residence - Leasey Hall - Before August 19, 1711

    Age at Death - infant

- Samuel Harris – bur. 12 Sep 1701 (Burial, **St. Catherine Parish**)

- Samuel Harris – bur. 4 Apr 1706 (Burial, **St. Catherine Parish**)

- Samuel Harris – bur. 9 Feb 1716 (Burial, **St. Nicholas Without Parish**)

Samuell Harris (deceased):

    Residence - Struck Flat - Before February 9, 1716

- Samuel Harris – b. 1755, d. 6 Sep 1816, bur. 1816 (Burial, **Chapelizod Parish**)

Samuel Harris (deceased):

    Residence - City of Dublin - September 6, 1816

- Samuel Harris – d. 19 Mar 1883, bur. 1883 (Burial, **St James Parish**)

Samuel Harris (deceased):

    Residence - South Dublin Union - March 19, 1883

- Samuel Harris – bur. 5 Feb 1796 (Burial, **St. Paul Parish**)

- Sarah Harris – bur. 24 May 1678 (Burial, **St. Peter Parish**)

- Sarah Harris – bur. 11 Jun 1700 (Burial, **St. Nicholas Without Parish**)

Sarah Harris (deceased):

    Residence - Ffordhams Alley - Before June 11, 1700

- Sarah Harris – bur. 24 Aug 1701 (Burial, **St. Catherine Parish**)

- Sarah Harris – bur. 3 Sep 1702 (Burial, **St. Catherine Parish**)

- Sarah Harris – bur. 1 Dec 1702 (Burial, **St. Catherine Parish**)

- Sarah Harris – bur. 14 Jan 1703 (Burial, **St. Catherine Parish**)

- Sarah Harris – bur. 19 Sep 1703 (Burial, **St. Catherine Parish**)

- Sarah Harris – bur. 17 Apr 1704 (Burial, **St. Catherine Parish**)

- Sarah Harris – bur. 22 Jun 1704 (Burial, **St. Catherine Parish**)

- Sarah Harris – bur. 2 Jan 1706 (Burial, **St. Catherine Parish**)

- Sarah Harris – bur. 30 Mar 1706 (Burial, **St. Catherine Parish**)

- Sarah Harris – bur. 2 Jul 1732 (Burial, **St. Paul Parish**)

- Sarah Harris – bur. 22 Jul 1765 (Burial, **St. James Parish**)

Sarah Harris (deceased):

Residence - Martin's Lane - Before July 22, 1765

- Sarah Harris – bur. 2 May 1784 (Burial, **St. Peter Parish**)

Sarah Harris (deceased):

Residence - Charlotte Street - Before May 2, 1784

- Sarah Harris – b. 1769, bur. 21 Mar 1814 (Burial, **St. Catherine Parish**)

Sarah Harris (deceased):

Residence - Vicars Street - Before March 21, 1814

- Sarah Harris – b. 1817, bur. 5 Oct 1846 (Burial, **St. Mark Parish**)

Sarah Harris (deceased):

Residence - George's Quay - Before October 5, 1846

- Sarah Harris – b. 1795, d. 16 Sep 1870, bur. 1870 (Burial, **St. James Parish**)

Sarah Harris (deceased):

Residence - South Dublin Union - September 16, 1870

Hurst

- Sarah Rebecca Harris – b. Mar 1841, bur. 19 Jun 1841 (Burial, **St. Mary Parish**)

Sarah Rebecca Harris (deceased):

    Residence - Portobello Barracks - Before June 19, 1841

    Age at Death - 4 months

- Sisly Harris – bur. 8 Mar 1751 (Burial, **St. Audoen Parish**)

- Susan Elizabeth Harris – b. 1829, bur. 7 Jun 1830 (Burial, **St. Matthew Parish**)

Susan Elizabeth Harris (deceased):

    Residence - Sandymount - Before June 7, 1830

    Age at Death - 1 year

- Susanna Harris – bur. 20 Sep 1738 (Burial, **St. Paul Parish**)

- Susanna Harris – bur. 9 Oct 1777 (Burial, **St. Peter Parish**)

Susanna Harris (deceased):

    Residence - Kevin's Port - Before October 9, 1777

- Thady Harris – bur. 18 May 1703 (Burial, **St. Catherine Parish**)

- Thomas Harris – bur. 18 Nov 1639 (Burial, **St. Michan Parish**)

- Thomas Harris – bur. 12 Jun 1687 (Burial, **St. Catherine Parish**)

- Thomas Harris – bur. 13 Sep 1699 (Burial, **St. Nicholas Without Parish**)

Thomas Harris (deceased):

    Residence - PATR Street - Before September 13 1699

- Thomas Harris – bur. 20 Aug 1700 (Burial, **St. Catherine Parish**)

- Thomas Harris – bur. 29 Jul 1701 (Burial, **St. Catherine Parish**)

- Thomas Harris – bur. 31 May 1702 (Burial, **St. Catherine Parish**)

- Thomas Harris – bur. 11 Jan 1704 (Burial, **St. Catherine Parish**)

- Thomas Harris – bur. Before 1709 (Burial, **Carlow Parish**)

- Thomas Harris – bur. 16 Mar 1712 (Burial, **St. Catherine Parish**)

- Thomas Harris – bur. 17 Oct 1726 (Burial, **St. Paul Parish**)

- Thomas Harris – bur. 31 May 1741 (Burial, **St. Paul Parish**)

- Thomas Harris – bur. 4 Jan 1747 (Burial, **St. Mark Parish**)

The church register entry reads as follows:

> "January 4: Bur Thos Harris A Child".

- Thomas Harris – bur. 27 Feb 1753 (Burial, **St. Audoen Parish**)

- Thomas Harris – bur. 27 May 1795 (Burial, **Glasnevin Parish**)

- Thomas Harris – bur. 25 Mar 1796 (Burial, **Glasnevin Parish**)

Thomas Harris (deceased):

> Residence - **Drumcondra** - Before March 25, 1796

- Thomas Harris – b. 1769, bur. 30 May 1817 (Burial, **St. Peter Parish**)

- Thomas Harris – b. 1794, bur. 6 Feb 1842 (Burial, **St. Catherine Parish**)

Thomas Harris (deceased):

> Residence - **Charlemont Street** - Before February 6, 1842

- Thomas Harris – b. 1790, bur. 3 Feb 1843 (Burial, **St. Luke Parish**)

Thomas Harris (deceased):

> Residence - **New Row** - Before February 3, 1843

- Thomas Harris – bur. 24 May 1809 (Burial, **St. Mark Parish**)

- Thomas Harris – b. 1791, bur. 2 Jun 1836 (Burial, **St. Paul Parish**)

- Thomas Harris – d. 5 Sep 1849, bur. 5 Sep 1849 (Burial, **Arbour Hill Barracks Parish**)

Thomas Harris (deceased):

> Cause of Death - cholera

His father was a member of the 1st Royal Regiment.

- Thomas Stephen Harris – b. 1873, d. 6 Dec 1875, bur. 1875 (Burial, **St James Parish**)

Thomas Stephen Harris (deceased):

> Residence - **13 Pembroke Quay** - December 6, 1875
>
> Age at Death - **2 years**

Hurst

- Thomas Tippen Harris – b. 1803, bur. 17 Mar 1841 (Burial, **St. Mark Parish**)

Thomas Tippen Harris (deceased):

Residence - Sussex Parade Kingstown - Before March 17, 1841

- Townly Harris – bur. 17 May 1700 (Burial, **St. Catherine Parish**)

- Trustrem Harris – bur. 8 Dec 1712 (Burial, **St. John Parish**)

- Unknown Harris – bur. 1 Mar 1681 (Burial, **St. Nicholas Without Parish**)

- Unknown Harris – bur. 1 Jul 1695 (Burial, **St. Nicholas Without Parish**)

Unknown Harris (deceased):

Residence - Fordoms Alley - Before July 1, 1695

- Unknown Harris – bur. Aug 1699 (Burial, **St. Nicholas Without Parish**)

Unknown Harris (deceased):

Residence - PATR Street - Before August 1699

- Unknown Harris – bur. 29 Feb 1704 (Burial, **St. Nicholas Without Parish**)

Unknown Harris (deceased):

Residence - Lilis Lane - Before February 29, 1704

- Unknown Harris – bur. 16 Mar 1713 (Burial, **St. Nicholas Without Parish**)

Unknown Harris (deceased):

Residence - New Roe - Before March 16, 1713

- Unknown Harris – bur. 31 Oct 1715 (Burial, **St. Peter Parish**)

Unknown Harris (deceased):

Residence - Kevin's Street - Before October 15, 1715

- Unknown Harris – bur. 29 May 1722 (Burial, **St. Nicholas Without Parish**)

- Unknown Harris – bur. 29 Jun 1723 (Burial, **St. Nicholas Without Parish**)

Unknown Harris (deceased):

Residence - New Street - Before June 29, 1723

- Unknown Harris – bur. 19 Jan 1726 (Burial, **St. John Parish**)

- Unknown Harris – bur. 11 Jun 1728 (Burial, **St. John Parish**)

Harris Surname Ireland: 1600s to 1900s

- Unknown Harris – bur. 9 Mar 1733 (Burial, **St. John Parish**)

- Unknown Harris – bur. 23 May 1735 (Burial, **St. John Parish**)

- Unknown Harris – bur. 1 Dec 1772 (Burial, **St. Nicholas Without Parish**)

Unknown Harris (deceased):

   Residence - Ormond Street - Before December 1, 1772

- Unknown Harris – bur. 10 Mar 1777 (Burial, **St. James Parish**)

Unknown Harris (deceased):

   Residence - Dirty Lane - Before March 10, 1777

- Unknown Harris – bur. 8 Jun 1789 (Burial, **St. Nicholas Without Parish**)

Unknown Harris (deceased):

   Residence - Meeting House Yard - Before June 8, 1789

- Unknown Harris – bur. 13 Jun 1793 (Burial, **St. James Parish**)

Unknown Harris (deceased):

   Residence - Gravel Walk - Before June 13, 1793

- Unknown Harris – bur. 1796 (Burial, **St. John Parish**)

- Unknown Harris – b. 1735, bur. 10 Mar 1808 (Burial, **Kilnaughtin Parish**)

- Unknown Harris, Child – bur. 28 Jun 1783 (Burial, **St. Mary Parish**)

Unknown Child Harris (deceased):

   Residence - Caple Street - Before June 28, 1783

- Unknown Harris, Child – bur. 11 Jan 1784 (Burial, **St. Mary Parish**)

Unknown Child Harris (deceased):

   Residence - Caple Street - Before January 11, 1784

- Unknown Harris, Ladie – bur. 27 Mar 1637 (Burial, **St. John Parish**)

- Unknown Harris, Mr. – bur. 31 Dec 1785 (Burial, **St. Mary Parish**)

Unknown Harris, Mr. (deceased):

   Residence - Mary Street - Before December 31, 1785

- Unknown Harris, Mrs. – bur. 23 Aug 1696 (Burial, **St. John Parish**)

Hurst

- Widow Harris – bur. 10 Dec 1770 (Burial, **St. Catherine Parish**)

- William Harris – bur. 28 Aug 1639 (Burial, **St. Michan Parish**)

- William Harris – bur. 2 Jul 1703 (Burial, **St. Nicholas Without Parish**)

William Harris (deceased):

    Residence - Marks Alley - Before July 2, 1703

- William Harris – bur. 4 Dec 1728 (Burial, **St. Paul Parish**)

- William Harris – bur. 23 Nov 1734 (Burial, **St. Catherine Parish**)

- William Harris – bur. 8 Feb 1735 (Burial, **Dingle Parish**)

William Harris (deceased):

    Residence - Marhin - Before February 8, 1735

- William Harris – bur. 27 Apr 1744 (Burial, **St. Paul Parish**)

- William Harris – bur. 9 Feb 1746 (Burial, **St. Paul Parish**)

- William Harris – bur. 9 Mar 1746 (Burial, **St. Paul Parish**)

- William Harris – bur. 26 Aug 1746 (Burial, **St. Paul Parish**)

- William Harris – bur. 21 Sep 1757 (Burial, **St. John Parish**)

- William Harris – bur. 5 Feb 1773 (Burial, **St. Peter Parish**)

- William Harris – bur. 15 Jan 1776 (Burial, **St. Paul Parish**)

- William Harris – bur. 26 Jun 1784 (Burial, **St. Peter Parish**)

William Harris (deceased):

    Residence - Head Stone - Before June 26, 1784

- William Harris – d. 4 Oct 1784, bur. 1784 (Burial, **Clondalkin Parish**)

William Harris (deceased):

    Residence - Clondalkin - October 4, 1784

- William Harris – bur. 22 Jul 1788 (Burial, **St. James Parish**)

William Harris (deceased):

    Residence - Dolphin's Barn - Before July 22, 1788

Harris Surname Ireland: 1600s to 1900s

- William Harris – bur. 28 Feb 1796 (Burial, **Glasnevin Parish**)

William Harris (deceased):

  Residence - New Market - Before February 28, 1796

- William Harris – bur. 11 Sep 1796 (Burial, **St. Peter Parish**)

William Harris (deceased):

  Residence - Charlemont Street - Before September 11, 1796

- William Harris – bur. 20 Oct 1807 (Burial, **St. Paul Parish**)

- William Harris – b. 1756, bur. 27 Jan 1816 (Burial, **St. Luke Parish**)

William Harris (deceased):

  Residence - Mill Street - Before January 27, 1816

- William Harris – b. 1804, bur. 27 Sep 1826 (Burial, **St. Mary Parish**)

William Harris (deceased):

  Residence - Jervis Street - Before September 27, 1826

- William Harris – b. 1797, bur. 30 Mar 1827 (Burial, **Glasnevin Parish**)

William Harris (deceased):

  Residence - Westmoreland Street - Before March 30, 1827

- William Harris – bur. 13 Jun 1831 (Burial, **Dunleckney Parish**)

- William Harris – bur. 24 Jul 1832 (Burial, **Tralee Parish**)

William Harris (deceased):

  Residence - Tralee - Before July 24, 1832

- William Harris – b. Feb 1833, bur. 29 Oct 1833 (Burial, **St. Catherine Parish**)

William Harris (deceased):

  Residence - Talbot Inn Yard - Before October 29, 1833

  Age at Death - 9 months

- William Harris – bur. 14 Jan 1844 (Burial, **St. Matthew Parish**)

William Harris (deceased):

  Residence - Beggars Bush Barracks 52nd - Before January 14, 1844

Hurst

- William Harris – b. 1814, bur. 27 Mar 1846 (Burial, **St. Catherine Parish**)

William Harris (deceased):

    Residence - Harold's Cross - Before March 27, 1846

- William Harris – b. 1788, bur. 12 Mar 1851 (Burial, **St. Paul Parish**)

William Harris (deceased):

    Residence - Cannon Street - Before March 12, 1851

- William Harris – b. Sep 1835, d. 10 Feb 1854, bur. 13 Feb 1854 (Burial, **Arbour Hill Barracks Parish**)

William Harris (deceased):

    Occupation - Private 63rd Regiment - February 13, 1854

    Cause of Death - colarrh chronie

- William Harris – b. 1835, d. 7 Feb 1856, bur. 8 Feb 1856 (Burial, **Arbour Hill Barracks Parish**)

William Harris (deceased):

    Occupation - Private Royal Cumberland - February 7, 1856

    Cause of Death - small pox

- William Henry Harris – b. 1834, d. 31 Oct 1891, bur. 1891 (Burial, **St. Catherine Parish**) (Burial, **St. Catherine Parish** (RC))

William Henry Harris (deceased):

    Residence - Strandville Clontarf - October 31, 1891

Individual Marriages

- Abigail Harris & John McCarthy

  - Elizabeth McCarthy – bapt. 18 Jan 1818 (Baptism, **Cork - South Parish** (RC))

  - James McCarthy – bapt. 13 Jun 1819 (Baptism, **Cork - South Parish** (RC))

  - M. Anne McCarthy – bapt. 30 Dec 1821 (Baptism, **Cork - South Parish** (RC))

- Alice Harris & Edward Fitzgerald

  - William Fitzgerald – bapt. 25 Feb 1798 (Baptism, **Cork - SS. Peter & Paul Parish** (RC))

  - John Fitzgerald – bapt. 22 Apr 1802 (Baptism, **Cork - South Parish** (RC))

  - Ellen Fitzgerald – bapt. 13 Jun 1803 (Baptism, **Cork - South Parish** (RC))

Edward Fitzgerald (father):

Residence - Millers Street - February 25, 1798

Margaret Street - April 22, 1802

Dunbar Street - June 13, 1803

The mother's name was written as Ally Harrish in the baptismal register for February 25, 1798.

- Alice Harris & Timothy Cronan

  - Anne Cronan – bapt. 1 Sep 1799 (Baptism, **SS. Michael & John Parish** (RC))

  - Edward Cronan – bapt. Oct 1801 (Baptism, **SS. Michael & John Parish** (RC))

  - Francis Cronan – bapt. 9 Oct 1803 (Baptism, **SS. Michael & John Parish** (RC))

- Alicia Harris & David Dillon – 17 Jun 1792 (Marriage, **St. Andrew Parish** (RC))

- Alicia Harris & Lawrence Fitzgerald – 25 Jan 1797 (Marriage, **St. Andrew Parish** (RC))

Hurst

- Alicia Harris & Michael Cleary – Date Unclear (Marriage, **St. Peter Parish**)

Alicia Harris (wife):

    Residence - Stephen Street

Michael Cleary (husband):

    Residence - Stephen Street

- Alicia Harris & Patrick McGee – 1 May 1808 (Marriage, **St. Andrew Parish (RC)**)

- Amelia Harris & John Faley

  - John Houison Faley – bapt. 28 Aug 1837 (Baptism, **St. James Parish (RC)**)

- Anastasia Harris & Nicholas Stafford – 20 Dec 1749 (Marriage, **St. Michan Parish (RC)**)

- Anne Harris & Andrew Williams – 27 Sep 1799 (Marriage, **St. Andrew Parish (RC)**)

- Anne Harris & Dennis Gallaher – 24 Feb 1846 (Marriage, **St. Catherine Parish (RC)**)

- Anne Harris & Edward Casey – 11 Jun 1812 (Marriage, **St. Nicholas Without Parish**)

- Anne Harris & Edward McLoughlin – 24 Aug 1796 (Marriage, **St. Andrew Parish (RC)**)

- Anne Harris & George Combs – 23 May 1811 (Marriage, **St. Andrew Parish (RC)**)

- Anne Harris & George Millar

  - John Patrick Millar – b. 29 Jul 1890, bapt. 6 Aug 1890 (Baptism, **St. Mary, Pro Cathedral Parish (RC)**)

George Millar (father):

    Residence - 107 Marlboro Street - August 6, 1890

- Anne Harris & Gulielmo Chriswill

  - Thomas Chriswill – bapt. Jul 1816 (Baptism, **St. Nicholas Parish (RC)**)

- Anne Harris & Gulielmo O'Brien – 3 Nov 1776 (Marriage, **St. Andrew Parish (RC)**)

- Anne Harris & Henry O'Brien

  - Henry O'Brien – b. 15 Aug 1902, bapt. 27 Aug 1902 (Baptism, **St. Joseph Parish (RC)**)

Henry O'Brien (father):

    Residence - Kimmage - August 27, 1902

Harris Surname Ireland: 1600s to 1900s

- Anne Harris & Henry Shanahan

  - Henry Michael Shanahan – b. 15 Jul 1874, bapt. 8 Aug 1874 (Baptism, **Cork - South Parish (RC)**)

  - William Shanahan – b. 15 Apr 1876, bapt. 10 May 1876 (Baptism, **Cork - South Parish (RC)**)

  - Edward Shanahan – b. 9 Sep 1877, bapt. 1 Oct 1877 (Baptism, **Cork - South Parish (RC)**)

- Anne Harris & James Dooner

  - Patrick Dooner – b. 1859, bapt. 1859 (Baptism, **St. Andrew Parish (RC)**)

  - Mary Anne Dooner – b. 1861, bapt. 1861 (Baptism, **St. Andrew Parish (RC)**)

  - Thomas Dooner – b. 1865, bapt. 1865 (Baptism, **St. Andrew Parish (RC)**)

  - Francis Dooner – b. 1867, bapt. 1867 (Baptism, **St. Andrew Parish (RC)**)

  - Bridget Dooner – b. 1869, bapt. 1869 (Baptism, **St. Andrew Parish (RC)**)

  - Joseph Dooner – b. 1870, bapt. 1870 (Baptism, **St. Andrew Parish (RC)**)

  - John Dooner & Anne Connor – 3 Oct 1883 (Marriage, **St. Mary, Pro Cathedral Parish (RC)**)

John Dooner (son):
   Residence - 9 Little Strand Street - October 3, 1883
Anne Connor, daughter of George Connor & Susan Felshion (daughter-in-law):
   Residence - 9 Little Strand Street - October 3, 1883
James Dooner (father):
   Residence - 4 Stephen's Place - 1859

   5 Stephen's Place - 1861

   12 Power's Court - 1865

   11 Verschoyle Court - 1867

   1870

   11 Power's Court - 1869

Hurst

- Anne Harris & James Hugins – 18 Oct 1744 (Marriage, **St. Audoen Parish**)

- Anne Harris & James Hyland – 28 Jul 1839 (Marriage, **St. James Parish** (RC))

- Anne Harris & John Moore

  o James Moore – bapt. 25 Sep 1856 (Baptism, **St. Catherine Parish** (RC))

- Anne Harris & Matthew Corrigan – 23 May 1745 (Marriage, **St. Andrew Parish** (RC))

- Anne Harris & Michael Mullen

  o John Mullen – bapt. 18 Oct 1765 (Baptism, **St. Michan Parish** (RC))

- Anne Harris & Michael Toole – 29 May 1808 (Marriage, **St. Mary, Pro Cathedral Parish** (RC))

- Anne Harris & Patrick Flood

  o Patrick Flood – b. 1 Jul 1864, bapt. 11 Jul 1864 (Baptism, **St. Nicholas Parish** (RC))

Patrick Flood (father):

   Residence - 42 Cuff Street - July 11, 1864

- Anne Harris & Robert O' Mealy

  o John O' Mealy – bapt. 13 Apr 1834 (Baptism, **St. James Parish** (RC))

- Anne Harris & Stephen Williams – 1 Dec 1691 (Marriage, **St. Catherine Parish**)

- Anne Harris & Stephen Wray

  o Stephen Wray – bapt. Jun 1810 (Baptism, **Cork - South Parish** (RC))

  o Rowland Wray – bapt. 24 Mar 1817 (Baptism, **Cork - South Parish** (RC))

Stephen Wray (father):

   Residence - Bandon Road - June 1810

- Anne Harris & Thomas Duffy – 14 Apr 1817 (Marriage, **St. Mary, Pro Cathedral Parish** (RC))

- Anne Harris & Thomas Hinch – Sep 1764 (Marriage, **Aghold Parish**)

- Anne Harris & Thomas Reddin – 6 Mar 1791 (Marriage, **St. Catherine Parish** (RC))

Harris Surname Ireland: 1600s to 1900s

- Anne Harris & William Blake

  - Ellen Blake Blake – b. 26 Dec 1891, bapt. 28 Dec 1891 (Baptism, **Rathmines Parish** (RC))

William Blake (father):

Residence - Mrs. Maghers Yard Mount View Harold's Cross - December 28, 1891

- Anne Harris & William Criswell

  - Mary Criswell – bapt. Apr 1823 (Baptism, **St. Catherine Parish** (RC))

  - Catherine Criswell – bapt. 16 Mar 1830 (Baptism, **St. Nicholas Parish** (RC))

  - Thomas Criswell – bapt. 4 May 1832 (Baptism, **St. Nicholas Parish** (RC))

- Anne Jane Harris & Thomas McEneany

  - George Thomas McEneany – b. 7 Nov 1875, bapt. 19 Nov 1875 (Baptism, **St. Mary, Pro Cathedral Parish** (RC))

Thomas McEneany (father):

Residence - 34 Upper Rutland Street - November 19, 1875

- Anne Nancy Harris & Michael Moriarty

  - Mary Moriarty – b. 4 May 1848, bapt. 4 May 1848 (Baptism, **Sneem Parish** (RC))

  - Thomas Moriarty – b. 1 Nov 1857, bapt. 1 Nov 1857 (Baptism, **Sneem Parish** (RC))

  - Anne Moriarty – b. 13 May 1860, bapt. 13 May 1860 (Baptism, **Sneem Parish** (RC))

Michael Moriarty (father):

Residence - Goaleenachorha - May 4, 1848

November 1, 1857

May 13, 1860

- Anne Rebecca Harris & Patrick McCoen

  - Anne McCoen – bapt. 1778 (Baptism, **SS. Michael & John Parish** (RC))

- Ball Harris & Jerry Shaghnessy

  - Timothy Shaghnessy – bapt. 9 Jul 1796 (Baptism, **Kilmurry Parish** (RC))

Hurst

- Barbara Harris & William Rogers – 12 Dec 1835 (Marriage, St. Peter Parish)

Barbara Harris (wife):

   Residence - 9 Cavendish Row, St. George - December 12, 1835

   Occupation - Spinster - December 12, 1835

William Rogers (husband):

   Residence - 28 Holles Street - December 12, 1835

   Occupation - Servant - December 12, 1835

- Biddy Harris & Richard Fitzgerald – 3 Feb 1839 (Marriage, Innishannon Parish (RC))

- Bridget Harris & Christopher Donohoe – 21 Apr 1834 (Marriage, St. Andrew Parish (RC))

- Bridget Harris & Daniel Sullivan – 12 Feb 1882 (Marriage, Glenbeigh/Glencar Parish (RC))

   o John Sullivan – b. 10 Jun 1885, bapt. 14 Jun 1885 (Baptism, Glenbeigh/Glencar Parish (RC))

   o Margaret Sullivan – b. 20 Oct 1886, bapt. 24 Oct 1886 (Baptism, Glenbeigh/Glencar Parish (RC))

   o Mary Sullivan – b. 28 Apr 1888, bapt. 2 May 1888 (Baptism, Glenbeigh/Glencar Parish (RC))

   o Bridget Sullivan – b. 7 Feb 1890, bapt. 11 Feb 1890 (Baptism, Glenbeigh/Glencar Parish (RC))

   o Joan Sullivan – b. 25 Apr 1891, bapt. 26 Apr 1891 (Baptism, Glenbeigh/Glencar Parish (RC))

   o Dennis Sullivan – b. 20 Feb 1893, bapt. 25 Feb 1893 (Baptism, Glenbeigh/Glencar Parish (RC))

   o Daniel Sullivan – b. 7 Sep 1894, bapt. 9 Sep 1894 (Baptism, Glenbeigh/Glencar Parish (RC))

Harris Surname Ireland: 1600s to 1900s

Bridget Harris (wife):

Residence - Drom - February 12, 1882

Daniel Sullivan (husband):

Residence - Curraheen - February 12, 1882

June 14, 1885

October 24, 1886

May 2, 1888

February 11, 1890

April 26, 1891

February 25, 1893

September 9, 1894

- Bridget Harris & Dominick Cunningham

  o Enoch Cunningham – bapt. 21 Apr 1839 (Baptism, Cork - SS. Peter & Paul Parish (RC))

  o Teresa Cunningham – bapt. 16 May 1841 (Baptism, Cork - SS. Peter & Paul Parish (RC))

  o Henry Cunningham – bapt. 8 Jan 1845 (Baptism, Cork - SS. Peter & Paul Parish (RC))

  o Agatha Cunningham – bapt. 28 Sep 1846 (Baptism, Cork - SS. Peter & Paul Parish (RC))

  o Jessey Cunningham – bapt. 23 Nov 1850 (Baptism, Cork - South Parish (RC))

- Bridget Harris & Eaton Purcell

  o Patrick Purcell – bapt. 21 Mar 1829 (Baptism, Cork - South Parish (RC))

- Bridget Harris & Edward Coghlan – 30 Oct 1837 (Marriage, Cork - South Parish (RC))

- Bridget Harris & George Bradley

  o Honora Bradley & Daniel Mahony – 18 Dec 1875 (Marriage, Dromod Parish (RC))

Honora Bradley (daughter):

Residence - Waterville - December 18, 1875

Daniel Mahony, son of Timothy Mahony & Margaret McCarthy (son-in-law):

Residence - Waterville - December 18, 1875

Hurst

- Bridget Harris & George Lightholder

    o   James Lightholder – bapt. 23 Aug 1816 (Baptism, **St. Michan Parish** (RC))

- Bridget Harris & Henry McDonnell

    o   John McDonnell – bapt. 7 Feb 1849 (Baptism, **St. Nicholas Parish** (RC))

- Bridget Harris & James Cahill

    o   Catharine Cahill – bapt. 28 Nov 1845 (Baptism, **St. Catherine Parish** (RC))

- Bridget Harris & James Cavanagh

    o   Elizabeth Cavanagh – bapt. 1832 (Baptism, **St. Mary, Haddington Road Parish** (RC))

- Bridget Harris & James Morrison

    o   Mary A. Morrison – bapt. 24 Nov 1867 (Baptism, **Cork - South Parish** (RC))

- Bridget Harris & James Waldron – 20 Jun 1853 (Marriage, **St. Mary, Pro Cathedral Parish** (RC))

    o   John Waldron – b. 20 May 1854, bapt. 22 May 1854 (Baptism, **St. Mary, Pro Cathedral Parish** (RC))

    o   Patrick Waldron – b. 23 Feb 1856, bapt. 25 Feb 1856 (Baptism, **St. Mary, Pro Cathedral Parish** (RC))

    o   Mary Anne Waldron – b. 21 Dec 1857, bapt. 28 Dec 1857 (Baptism, **St. Mary, Pro Cathedral Parish** (RC))

    o   James Waldron – b. 22 Jul 1859, bapt. 29 Jul 1859 (Baptism, **St. Mary, Pro Cathedral Parish** (RC))

    o   Joseph Waldron – b. 19 Jun 1865, bapt. 19 Jun 1865 (Baptism, **St. Lawrence Parish** (RC))

    o   Peter Aloysius Waldron – b. 21 Jun 1875, bapt. 24 Jun 1875 (Baptism, **St. Lawrence Parish** (RC))

Harris Surname Ireland: 1600s to 1900s

James Waldron (father):

> Residence - 6 Bolton Street - May 22, 1854

> Bolton Street - February 25, 1856

> 1 Bolton Street - December 28, 1857

> July 29, 1859

> 6 Upper Sheriff Street - June 19, 1865

> 22 Upper Sheriff Street - June 24, 1875

- Bridget Harris & John Finigan – 17 Nov 1790 (Marriage, **St. Andrew Parish** (RC))

- Bridget Harris & John Mahony

    o Bridget Mahony – b. 25 Sep 1854, bapt. 25 Sep 1854 (Baptism, **Caherciveen Parish** (RC))

John Mahony (father):

> Residence - **Srugreana** - September 25, 1854

- Bridget Harris & Michael Lyne

    o Michael Lyne – b. 22 Dec 1856, bapt. 22 Dec 1856 (Baptism, **Glenbeigh/Glencar Parish** (RC))

    o Michael Lyne – b. 22 Apr 1860, bapt. 22 Apr 1860 (Baptism, **Glenbeigh/Glencar Parish** (RC))

Michael Lyne (father):

> Residence - Rossbeigh - December 22, 1856

- Bridget Harris & Michael Shea

    o John Shea – b. 18 Jun 1873, bapt. 18 Jun 1873 (Baptism, **Glenbeigh/Glencar Parish** (RC))

Michael Shea (father):

> Residence - **Treangarriv** - June 18, 1873

Hurst

- Bridget Harris & Patrick McDonnell – 10 Apr 1807 (Marriage, Tralee Parish)

Bridget Harris (wife):

Residence - Gaol of Tralee - April 10, 1807

Patrick McDonnell (husband):

Residence - Gaol of Tralee - April 10, 1807

- Bridget Harris & Patrick Riordan – 25 Mar 1868 (Marriage, Glenbeigh/Glencar Parish (RC))

  o Ellen Riordan – b. 1 Dec 1868, bapt. 1 Dec 1868 (Baptism, Glenbeigh/Glencar Parish

  (RC))

  o Bridget Riordan – b. 29 Jun 1871, bapt. 29 Jun 1871 (Baptism, Glenbeigh/Glencar Parish

  (RC))

  o Julia Riordan – b. 28 May 1874, bapt. 28 May 1874 (Baptism, Glenbeigh/Glencar Parish

  (RC))

Bridget Harris (mother):

Residence - Drom - March 25, 1868

Patrick Riordan (father):

Residence - Drom - December 1, 1868

June 29, 1871

May 28, 1874

- Bridget Harris & Peter Groves

  o Mary Groves & Hugh Nolan – 30 Aug 1896 (Marriage, St. Mary, Pro Cathedral Parish

  (RC))

Mary Groves (daughter):

Residence - 41 Britain Street - August 30, 1896

Hugh Nolan, son of Miles Nolan & Catherine Hendrick (son-in-law):

Residence - 44 Bridge Forest - August 30, 1896

- Bridget Harris & Peter Keegan

    o James Keegan – b. 23 Mar 1891, bapt. 31 Mar 1891 (Baptism, **Harrington Street Parish (RC)**)

Peter Keegan (father):

Residence - 107 Lower Clanbrassil Street - March 31, 1891

- Bridget Harris & Richard Fitzgerald

    o Richard Fitzgerald – bapt. 16 Dec 1839 (Baptism, **Ballinhassig Parish** (RC))

    o Elizabeth Fitzgerald – bapt. May 1841 (Baptism, **Ballinhassig Parish** (RC))

    o Richard Fitzgerald – bapt. 20 Jun 1843 (Baptism, **Ballinhassig Parish** (RC))

    o Julia Fitzgerald – bapt. 29 Nov 1845 (Baptism, **Ballinhassig Parish** (RC))

    o John Fitzgerald –bapt. Nov 1847 (Baptism, **Ballinhassig Parish** (RC))

    o Honora Fitzgerald – bapt. Jun 1851(Baptism, **Ballinhassig Parish** (RC))

    o Mary Fitzgerald – bapt. Feb 1854 (Baptism, **Ballinhassig Parish** (RC))

    o James Fitzgerald – bapt. Feb 1856 (Baptism, **Ballinhassig Parish** (RC))

    o Joan Fitzgerald – bapt. 7 Jan 1858 (Baptism, **Ballinhassig Parish** (RC))

    o Bridget Fitzgerald – bapt. 26 Sep 1863 (Baptism, **Ballinhassig Parish** (RC))

- Bridget Harris & Samuel Beats

    o Edward Beats – bapt. 1777 (Baptism, **SS. Michael & John Parish** (RC))

- Bridget Harris & Thomas Barens

    o Mary Anne Barens – b. 28 Mar 1865, bapt. 31 Mar 1865 (Baptism, **St. Michan Parish** (RC))

Thomas Barens (father):

Residence - 4 Beresford Street - March 31, 1865

Hurst

- Catherine Harris & Abel Millar – 20 Jul 1813 (Marriage, **Kilnaughtin Parish**)

- Catherine Harris & Archibald Vickery – 23 Mar 1807 (Marriage, **Cork - South Parish** (RC))

- Catherine Harris & Charles McCarthy – 14 Jun 1810 (Marriage, **Cork - South Parish** (RC))

  o Charles McCarthy – bapt. 23 Oct 1820 (Baptism, **Cork - South Parish** (RC))

Catherine Harris (mother):

Residence - Cove Street - June 14, 1810

- Catherine Harris & Con O'Neill – 23 Oct 1779 (Marriage, **Clondalkin Parish** (RC))

  o Mary O'Neill – bapt. 1780 (Baptism, **Clondalkin Parish** (RC))

  o Charles O'Neill – bapt. 1784 (Baptism, **Clondalkin Parish** (RC))

  o Mary O'Neill – bapt. 1786 (Baptism, **Clondalkin Parish** (RC))

  o Charles O'Neill – bapt. 1788 (Baptism, **Clondalkin Parish** (RC))

  o John O'Neill – bapt. 1791 (Baptism, **Clondalkin Parish** (RC))

- Catherine Harris & Cornelius (C o r n e l i u s) Denahy

  o Thomas Denahy – bapt. 22 Feb 1845 (Baptism, **Cork - South Parish** (RC))

- Catherine Harris & Daniel Casey – 12 Feb 1793 (Marriage, **Kilmurry Parish** (RC))

  o Jane Casey – bapt. 5 Oct 1795 (Baptism, **Bandon Parish** (RC))

  o Timothy Casey – bapt. 3 May 1803 (Baptism, **Bandon Parish** (RC))

  o Margaret Casey – bapt. 23 Oct 1805 (Baptism, **Bandon Parish** (RC))

- Catherine Harris & Daniel Carthy – 27 Nov 1830 (Marriage, **Ballinhassig Parish** (RC))

Harris Surname Ireland: 1600s to 1900s

- Catherine Harris & Daniel Mullins

  o Henry Mullins – bapt. 17 Jul 1833 (Baptism, **Cork - South Parish** (RC))

  o Daniel Mullins – bapt. 12 Aug 1838 (Baptism, **Cork - South Parish** (RC))

  o Timothy Mullins – bapt. 11 Jun 1842 (Baptism, **Cork - South Parish** (RC))

- Catherine Harris & Dennis Whelan

  o Patrick Whelan – b. 1867, bapt. 1867 (Baptism, **St. Mary, Haddington Road Parish** (RC))

  o Ellen Whelan & Thomas Doyle – 11 Jun 1898 (Marriage, **St. Mary, Pro Cathedral Parish** (RC))

Ellen Whelan (daughter):

Residence - 38 Lower Abbey Street - June 11, 1898

Thomas Doyle, son of John Doyle & Elizabeth Brady (son-in-law):

Residence - Ringsend - June 11, 1898

- Catherine Harris & Dermot (D e r m o t) O'Sullivan – 15 Nov 1840 (Marriage, **Tralee Parish** (RC))

Catherine Harris (wife):

Residence - Tralee - November 15, 1840

Dermot O'Sullivan (husband):

Residence - Tralee - November 15, 1840

Hurst

- Catherine Harris & Dionysius Whelan

  - Mary Catherine Whelan – b. 14 Mar 1862, bapt. 21 Mar 1862 (Baptism, St. Lawrence Parish (RC))

  - Michael James Whelan – b. 14 Jan 1875, bapt. 18 Jan 1875 (Baptism, St. Lawrence Parish (RC))

Dionysius Whelan (father):

Residence - 8 Florence Place - March 21, 1862

2 Mayor Street - January 18, 1875

- Catherine Harris & Edward Doyle – 29 Jul 1866 (Marriage, St. Mary, Haddington Road Parish (RC))

- Catherine Harris & Edward O'Halloran – 7 Feb 1875 (Marriage, Cork - South Parish (RC))

  - Margaret Mary O'Halloran – b. 29 Oct 1876, bapt. 30 Oct 1876 (Baptism, Cork - South Parish (RC))

  - Hannah Ellen O'Halloran – b.14 Nov 1879, bapt. 16 Nov 1879 (Baptism, Cork - South Parish (RC))

Edward O'Halloran (father):

Residence - 6 Pickett's Lane - November 16, 1879

- Catherine Harris & Francis Norton

  - Margaret Norton – bapt. 18 Feb 1826 (Baptism, Cork - South Parish (RC))

- Catherine Harris & Gerald Aherne (A h e r n e)

  - Henry Charles Aherne – b. 8 Dec 1883, bapt. 8 Dec 1883 (Baptism, Dingle Parish (RC))

  - Elizabeth Aherne – b. 8 Feb 1886, bapt. 11 Feb 1886 (Baptism, Dingle Parish (RC))

  - Teresa Anne Aherne – b. 13 Jan 1888, bapt. 15 Jan 1888 (Baptism, Dingle Parish (RC))

Harris Surname Ireland: 1600s to 1900s

Gerald Aherne (father):

Residence - Coast Guard Station- December 8, 1883

February 11, 1886

Dingle - January 15, 1888

- Catherine Harris & Hayes Cross

  o Philip Cross – bapt. 14 Nov 1829 (Baptism, **Clonakilty Parish** (RC))

  o Ellen Cross – bapt. 24 Jan 1837 (Baptism, **Clonakilty Parish** (RC))

  o Mary Cross – bapt. 17 Nov 1838 (Baptism, **Clonakilty Parish** (RC))

Catherine Harris (mother):

Residence - Grellagh - November 14, 1829

January 24, 1837

November 17, 1838

Hayes Cross (father):

Residence - Grellagh - November 14, 1829

January 24, 1837

November 17, 1838

- Catherine Harris & Henry Lynch – 24 Oct 1839 (Marriage, **Kinsale Parish** (RC))

Henry Lynch (husband):

Residence - B Gate - October 24, 1839

- Catherine Harris & Henry Scadel

  o Jane Scadel – bapt. 20 Mar 1823 (Baptism, **Cork - South Parish** (RC))

  o Henry Scadel – bapt. 5 Jul 1824 (Baptism, **Cork - South Parish** (RC))

- Catherine Harris & James Curren

  o Mary Curren – bapt. 18 Apr 1820 (Baptism, **Cork - South Parish** (RC))

Hurst

- Catherine Harris & Hugh Condren

  - Margaret Mary Condren – b. 20 Nov 1896, bapt. 30 Nov 1896 (Baptism, **St. Mary, Pro Cathedral Parish** (RC))

Hugh Condren (father):

Residence - 24 Marlboro Street - November 30, 1896

- Catherine Harris & James Donohoe – 10 Aug 1872 (Marriage, **Innishannon Parish** (RC))

  - Jane Donohoe – bapt. 3 Apr 1873 (Baptism, **Innishannon Parish** (RC))

- Catherine Harris & James Swan

  - Patrick James Swan – b. 10 Dec 1875, bapt. 29 Dec 1875 (Baptism, **St. Mary, Pro Cathedral Parish** (RC))

  - Patrick Thomas Swan – b. 13 Feb 1877, bapt. 19 Mar 1877 (Baptism, **St. Mary, Pro Cathedral Parish** (RC))

James Swan (father):

Residence - 52 Lower Dominick Street - December 29, 1875

Lower Dominick Street - March 19, 1877

- Catherine Harris & Jeremiah Collins

  - James Collins – bapt. 6 Aug 1796 (Baptism, **Bandon Parish** (RC))

  - Dionysius Collins – bapt. 25 Apr 1799 (Baptism, **Bandon Parish** (RC))

  - Joan Collins – bapt. 17 Nov 1816 (Baptism, **Rossalettiri & Kilkeraunmor (Roscarbery & Lissevard) Parish** (RC))

- Catherine Harris & Jeremiah Keohane

  - Catherine Keohane – bapt. 19 Nov 1870 (Baptism, **Timoleague Parish** (RC))

Jeremiah Keohane (father):

Residence - Carrig - November 19, 1870

Harris Surname Ireland: 1600s to 1900s

- Catherine Harris & Jerry Connolly – 16 Feb 1831 (Marriage, **Innishannon Parish** (RC))

  - Patrick Connolly – bapt. 25 May 1834 (Baptism, **Enniskeane Parish** (RC))

  - Mary Connolly – bapt. 29 Mar 1837 (Baptism, **Innishannon Parish** (RC))

  - Catherine Connolly & John Daly – 6 Jun 1865 (Marriage, **Douglas & Ballygarvan Parrish** (RC))

    - Joan Daly – bapt. 30 Sep 1866 (Baptism, **Carrigaline & Templebrigid Parish** (RC))

    - Margaret Daly – bapt. 7 Jun 1868 (Baptism, **Carrigaline & Templebrigid Parish** (RC))

    - Charles Daly – bapt. 2 Mar 1870 (Baptism, **Carrigaline & Templebrigid Parish** (RC))

    - Mary Daly – bapt. 10 Nov 1872 (Baptism, **Carrigaline & Templebrigid Parish** (RC))

    - Honora Daly – bapt. Oct 1874 (Baptism, **Carrigaline & Templebrigid Parish** (RC))

    - Catherine Daly – bapt. Sep 1876 (Baptism, **Carrigaline & Templebrigid Parish** (RC))

- Catherine Harris & John Connor

  - Jane Sarah Connor – bapt. Nov 1780 (Baptism, **Cork - SS. Peter & Paul Parish** (RC))

  - Jane Connor – bapt. 1 Jan 1786 (Baptism, **Cork - SS. Peter & Paul Parish** (RC))

  - Sarah Drs Connor – bapt. 1 Jan 1786 (Baptism, **Cork - SS. Peter & Paul Parish** (RC))

- Catherine Harris & John Harrowfield

  - Catherine Harrowfield – bapt. 13 Dec 1824 (Baptism, **St. Catherine Parish** (RC))

Hurst

- Catherine Harris & John Keleagher

  - Mary Keleagher – bapt. 7 Jul 1791 (Baptism, **Cork - South Parish** (RC))

  - John Keleagher – bapt. 14 Apr 1798 (Baptism, **Cork - South Parish** (RC))

  - James Keleagher – bapt. 8 May 1800 (Baptism, **Cork - South Parish** (RC))

  - Judith Keleagher – bapt. 28 Oct 1805 (Baptism, **Cork - South Parish** (RC))

  - William Keleagher – bapt. 18 Jul 1808 (Baptism, **Cork - South Parish** (RC))

John Keleagher (father):

Residence - Bishopstown - July 18, 1808

- Catherine Harris & John McCarthy – 22 Oct 1831 (Marriage, **Innishannon Parish** (RC))

- Catherine Harris & John Moriarty

  - Catherine Moriarty – 22 Jun 1879, bapt. 22 Jun 1879 (Baptism, **Glenbeigh/Glencar Parish** (RC))

John Moriarty (father):

Residence - Drom - June 22, 1879

- Catherine Harris & John Morrissey

  - William Morrissey – bapt. 5 Feb 1830 (Baptism, **St. Catherine Parish** (RC))

  - Patrick Morrissey – bapt. 5 Apr 1831 (Baptism, **St. Catherine Parish** (RC))

  - Mary Morrissey – bapt. 13 Jun 1834 (Baptism, **St. Catherine Parish** (RC))

- Catherine Harris & John Parkins

  - Patrick John Parkins – b. 21 Jun 1879, bapt. 24 Jun 1879 (Baptism, **St. James Parish** (RC))

John Parkins (father):

Residence - 14 Watling Street - June 24, 1879

Harris Surname Ireland: 1600s to 1900s

- Catherine Harris & John Patt – 12 Feb 1874 (Marriage, **Listowel Parish** (RC))

  - Richard Patt – b. 25 Nov 1874, bapt. 25 Nov 1874 (Baptism, **Listowel Parish** (RC))

  - Michael Patt – b. 8 Mar 1876, bapt. 8 Mar 1876 (Baptism, **Listowel Parish** (RC))

  - John Patt – b. 18 Aug 1878, bapt. 18 Aug 1878 (Baptism, **Listowel Parish** (RC))

  - Mary Patt – b. 18 Sep 1881, bapt. 18 Sep 1881 (Baptism, **Listowel Parish** (RC))

  - Frances Patt – b. 22 Apr 1883, bapt. 22 Apr 1883 (Baptism, **Listowel Parish** (RC))

  - Catherine Mary Patt – b. 5 Apr 1885, bapt. 5 Apr 1885 (Baptism, **Listowel Parish** (RC))

  - Alice Patt – b. 17 Jul 1887, bapt. 17 Jul 1887 (Baptism, **Listowel Parish** (RC))

Catherine Harris (mother):

Residence - Listowel - February 12, 1874

John Patt (father):

Residence - Listowel - February 12, 1874

November 25, 1874

March 8, 1876

August 18, 1878

September 18, 1881

April 22, 1883

April 5, 1885

July 17, 1887

- Catherine Harris & John Shaw

  - Susan Shaw – bapt. 19 Jul 1804 (Baptism, **Cork - South Parish** (RC))

John Shaw (father):

Residence - Croft - July 19, 1804

- Catherine Harris & John Wren

  - Margaret Wren – b. 1 Aug 1828, bapt. 1 Aug 1828 (Baptism, **Milltown Parish** (RC))

John Wren (father):

Residence - Milltown - August 1, 1828

Hurst

- Catherine Harris & Luke Sherlock

  o Peter Sherlock – b. 17 Aug 1860, bapt. 24 Aug 1860 (Baptism, **St. Mary, Pro Cathedral Parish** (RC))

  o Francis Sherlock & Mary Murphy – 3 Mar 1889 (Marriage, **St. Mary, Pro Cathedral Parish** (RC))

Francis Sherlock (son):

Residence - 48 Lower Dominick Street - March 3, 1889

Mary Murphy, daughter of John Murphy & Rose M. Parlan (daughter-in-law):

Residence - Gresham Hotel - March 3, 1889

Luke Sherlock (father):

Residence - 5 Great Britain Street - August 24, 1860

- Catherine Harris & Marth Driscol

  o Elizabeth Driscol – bapt. 5 Aug 1822 (Baptism, **Rath & the Islands (Cape & Sherkin) Parish** (RC))

- Catherine Harris & Matthew Connolly – 18 Feb 1844 (Marriage, **St. James Parish** (RC))

- Catherine Harris & Maurice Walsh

  o Timothy Walsh – b. 12 Mar 1843, bapt. 12 Mar 1843 (Baptism, **Dromtariffe Parish** (RC))

Maurice Walsh (father):

Residence - Coolclogh - March 12, 1843

- Catherine Harris & Michael Coghlan

  o Daniel Coghlan – bapt. 20 Mar 1826 (Baptism, **Courcy's Country or Ballinspittal Parish** (RC))

- Catherine Harris & Michael Dnohy – 19 Oct 1855 (Marriage, **Kinsale Parish** (RC))

- Catherine Harris & Michael Shea

  o Margaret Shea – b. 15 Oct 1868, bapt. 15 Oct 1868 (Baptism, **Glenbeigh/Glencar Parish** (RC))

- o Michael Shea – b. 17 Nov 1870, bapt. 17 Nov 1870 (Baptism, **Glenbeigh/Glencar Parish (RC)**)

- o Mary Shea – b. 20 Jul 1874, bapt. 20 Jul 1874 (Baptism, **Glenbeigh/Glencar Parish (RC)**)

- o James Shea – b. 13 Nov 1876, bapt. 13 Nov 1876 (Baptism, **Glenbeigh/Glencar Parish (RC)**)

Michael Shea (father):

Residence - Treangarriv - October 15, 1868

November 17, 1870

July 20, 1874

November 13, 1876

- Catherine Harris & Patrick Brady – 13 Feb 1831 (Marriage, **St. Michan Parish (RC)**)

- Catherine Harris & Patrick Connell – 1 Aug 1853 (Marriage, **St. James Parish (RC)**)

Patrick Connell (husband):

Occupation - 63rd Regiment - August 1, 1853

- Catherine Harris & Patrick Donovan – 6 Oct 1866 (Marriage, **Cork - South Parish (RC)**)

- o Dennis Donovan – bapt. 20 Jan 1868 (Baptism, **Cork - South Parish (RC)**)

- o Patrick Joseph Donovan – bapt. 16 Apr 1872 (Baptism, **Cork - South Parish (RC)**)

- o James Donovan – b. 3 Sep 1874, bapt. 4 Sep 1874 (Baptism, **Cork - South Parish (RC)**)

- o Elizabeth Donovan – b. 13 Apr 1877, bapt. 15 Apr 1877 (Baptism, **Cork - South Parish (RC)**)

- o Honora Donovan – b. 3 Feb 1880, bapt. 5 Feb 1880 (Baptism, **Cork - South Parish (RC)**)

Patrick Donovan (father):

Residence - Quarry Road - February 5, 1880

- Catherine Harris & Patrick Hevey – 18 Sep 1796 (Marriage, **St. Andrew Parish (RC)**)

Hurst

- Catherine Harris & Peter Cullen

  - Mary Josephine Cullen – b. 8 Mar 1875, bapt. 19 Mar 1875 (Baptism, **St. Mary, Pro Cathedral Parish** (RC))

  - Michael Peter Cullen – b. 13 Sep 1876, bapt. 25 Sep 1876 (Baptism, **SS. Michael & John Parish** (RC))

Peter Cullen (father):

Residence - 36 Lower Liffey Street - March 19, 1875

64 Aungier Street - September 25, 1876

- Catherine Harris & Peter Durnan (D u r n a n)

  - Francis Joseph Durnan – b. 4 May 1869, bapt. 12 May 1869 (Baptism, **St. Mary, Pro Cathedral Parish** (RC))

  - Mary Agnes Durnan – b. 1878, bapt. 1878 (Baptism, **St. Andrew Parish** (RC))

Peter Durnan (father):

Residence - 26 Upper Mecklenburgh Street - May 12, 1869

7 Mercer Street - 1878

- Catherine Harris & Samuel Young

  - John Young – b. 10 Jun 1868, bapt. 13 Jun 1868 (Baptism, **Tarbert Parish** (RC))

Samuel Young (father):

Residence - Tarbert - June 13, 1868

- Catherine Harris & Stephan Gilman

  - Mary Gilman – bapt. 22 Dec 1802 (Baptism, **Bandon Parish** (RC))

- Catherine Harris & Thomas Duff – 22 Jan 1789 (Marriage, **St. Michan Parish** (RC))

  - Anne Duff – bapt. 15 Jan 1790 (Baptism, **St. Michan Parish** (RC))

Harris Surname Ireland: 1600s to 1900s

- Catherine Harris & Thomas Gayer

  o Catherine Gayer – b. 9 Nov 1856, bapt. 9 Nov 1856 (Baptism, **Abbeydorney Parish** (RC))

Thomas Gayer (father):

Residence - Ardrahan - November 9, 1856

- Catherine Harris & Thomas Geare – 19 Feb 1840 (Marriage, **Abbeydorney Parish** (RC))

  o Patrick Geare – b. 1 Mar 1841, bapt. 1 Mar 1841 (Baptism, **Causeway Parish** (RC))

  o Michael Geare – b. 16 Oct 1842, bapt. 16 Oct 1842 (Baptism, **Causeway Parish** (RC))

  o Unknown Geare – b. 15 Jun 1844, bapt. 15 Jun 1844 (Baptism, **Causeway Parish** (RC))

  o Thomas Geare – b. 31 May 1847, bapt. 31 May 1847 (Baptism, **Causeway Parish** (RC))

  o Martin Geare – b. 2 Nov 1850, bapt. 2 Nov 1850 (Baptism, **Causeway Parish** (RC))

  o Mary Geare – b. 20 Aug 1862, bapt. 26 Aug 1862 (Baptism, **Abbeydorney Parish** (RC))

Thomas Geare (father):

Residence - Knuckanelheig - March 1, 1841

October 16, 1842

June 15, 1844

May 31, 1847

Lisavadarruch - November 2, 1850

Ardrahan - August 26, 1862

- Catherine Harris & Thomas Henafy

  o Michael Henafy – b. 28 Sep 1812, bapt. 18 Oct 1812 (Baptism, **St. Catherine Parish** (RC))

  o Bridget Henafy – b. 11 Dec 1821, bapt. 16 Dec 1821 (Baptism, **St. Catherine Parish** (RC))

Hurst

- Catherine Harris & Timothy Buckley – 18 Feb 1817 (Marriage, **Kilmurry Parish** (RC))

  - Julia Buckley – bapt. 6 Feb 1818 (Baptism, **Kilmurry Parish** (RC))

  - Catherine Buckley – bapt. 16 Apr 1822 (Baptism, **Kilmurry Parish** (RC))

  - Catherine Buckley – bapt. 1 Jul 1824 (Baptism, **Kilmurry Parish** (RC))

  - Ellen Buckley – bapt. 16 Feb 1827 (Baptism, **Kilmurry, Moviddy, Kilbonane, & Cannavee Parish** (RC))

  - Timothy Buckley – bapt. 8 Apr 1828 (Baptism, **Kilmurry, Moviddy, Kilbonane, & Cannavee Parish** (RC))

  - William Buckley – bapt. 20 Aug 1835 (Baptism, **Kilmurry, Moviddy, Kilbonane, & Cannavee Parish** (RC))

  - Margaret Buckley – bapt. 23 Nov 1838 (Baptism, **Kilmurry, Moviddy, Kilbonane, & Cannavee Parish** (RC))

  - Patrick Buckley – bapt. 23 Nov 1838 (Baptism, **Kilmurry, Moviddy, Kilbonane, & Cannavee Parish** (RC))

  - Honora Buckley – bapt. 15 Apr 1841 (Baptism, **Kilmurry, Moviddy, Kilbonane, & Cannavee Parish** (RC))

Timothy Buckley (father):

Residence - Currabeith - April 16, 1822

July 1, 1824

February 16, 1827

April 8, 1828

Glounneaga - August 20, 1835

- Catherine Harris & Timothy Donoghue – 11 Nov 1806 (Marriage, **Cork - South Parish** (RC))

Catharine Harris (wife):

Residence - Pouladuff - November 11, 1806

Harris Surname Ireland: 1600s to 1900s

- Catherine Harris & William Aherne (A h e r n e) – 20 Jan 1867 (Marriage, **Kinsale Parish (RC)**)

  o William Richard Aherne – b. 8 Oct 1874, bapt. 9 Oct 1874 (Baptism, **Kinsale Parish (RC)**)

William Aherne (father):

Residence - Newman's Mall - October 9, 1874

- Catherine Harris & William Aherne (A h e r n e)

  o Mary Alice Aherne – b. 27 Mar 1891, bapt. 29 Mar 1891 (Baptism, **Castletownbere Parish (RC)**)

William Aherne (father):

Residence - Castletown - March 29, 1891

- Catherine Harris & William Clark

  o Mary Anne Clark – bapt. 9 Feb 1832 (Baptism, **St. Nicholas Parish (RC)**)

- Christian Harris & John Antwisell – 26 Sep 1743 (Marriage, **St. Paul Parish**)

- Christine Harris & Patrick McCormick

  o Harrietta McCormick – b. 10 Aug 1855, bapt. 13 Aug 1855 (Baptism, **St. Nicholas Parish (RC)**)

Patrick McCormick (father):

Residence - 10 Upper Kevin Street - August 13, 1855

- Christine Harrish & John Hawkins

  o Richard Hawkins – b. 4 Feb 1896, bapt. 14 Feb 1896 (Baptism, **St. Mary, Pro Cathedral (RC)**)

John Hawkins (father):

Residence - 62 Lower Dominick Street - February 14, 1896

- Eleanor Harris & John Salmon

  o Ezechiel Salmon – bapt. 30 Mar 1810 (Baptism, **Cork - South Parish (RC)**)

- Eleanor Harris & Lawrence Curren – Jul 1838 (Marriage, **St. Catherine Parish (RC)**)

Hurst

- Eleanor Harris & Richard Doyle

  - Anne Doyle – bapt. 23 Sep 1799 (Baptism, **St. Nicholas Parish** (RC))

- Eleanor Harris & Richard Grattan – 19 Apr 1814 (Marriage, **St. Catherine Parish** (RC))

  - Thomas Grattan – bapt. 31 Jan 1815 (Baptism, **St. Catherine Parish** (RC))

  - Maurice Grattan – bapt. 4 Sep 1816 (Baptism, **St. Catherine Parish** (RC))

  - Francis Augustine Grattan – bapt. 23 Aug 1818 (Baptism, **St. Catherine Parish** (RC))

  - Peter Grattan – bapt. Sep 1820 (Baptism, **St. Catherine Parish** (RC))

  - Michael Grattan – bapt. 18 Aug 1822 (Baptism, **St. Catherine Parish** (RC))

  - John R. Grattan – bapt. 19 Nov 1826 (Baptism, **St. Catherine Parish** (RC))

  - Joseph Grattan – bapt. 20 Sep 1829 (Baptism, **St. Catherine Parish** (RC))

  - John Grattan – bapt. 29 Jan 1832 (Baptism, **St. Catherine Parish** (RC))

- Eleanor Harris & William Whitmore – 1 May 1767 (Marriage, **St. Mark Parish**)

- Elizabeth Harris & Alban Hawley

  - Margaret Hawley – bapt. 24 Sep 1804 (Baptism, **Tracton Abbey Parish** (RC))

  - Mary Hawley – bapt. 1 Mar 1811 (Baptism, **Tracton Abbey Parish** (RC))

  - Alban Hawley – bapt. 12 Jun 1814 (Baptism, **Tracton Abbey Parish** (RC))

- Elizabeth Harris & Augustine Nolan – 1 Feb 1803 (Marriage, **Cork - SS. Peter & Paul Parish** (RC))

Elizabeth Harris (wife):
Residence - Castle Street - February 1, 1803

- Elizabeth Harris & Bernard (B e r n a r d) Powell

  - Enoch Powell – b. 14 Mar 1860, bapt. 23 Oct 1882 (Baptism, **Tralee Parish** (RC))

Bernard Powell (father):
Residence - Staffordshire - October 23, 1882

- Elizabeth Harris & Charles Seaton – 6 Dec 1738 (Marriage, **St. Bride Parish**)

Harris Surname Ireland: 1600s to 1900s

- Elizabeth Harris & Cornelius (C o r n e l i u s) Dinneen

  - Cornelius (C o r n e l i u s) Patrick Dinneen – b. 21 Mar 1869, bapt. 25 Mar 1869 (Baptism, **Kinsale Parish** (RC))

Cornelius Dinneen (father):
Residence - Barracks - March 25, 1869

- Elizabeth Harris & Daniel Byrne (B y r n e)

  - Anne Byrne – bapt. 1829 (Baptism, **Sandyford Parish** (RC))

- Elizabeth Harris & Dennis Byrne (B y r n e) – 16 Jul 1851 (Marriage, **St. Andrew Parish** (RC))

- Elizabeth Harris & Dermot (D e r m o t) Murphy

  - Joan Murphy – b. 25 Dec 1845, bapt. 25 Dec 1845 (Baptism, **Dromtariffe Parish** (RC))

Dermot Murphy (father):
Residence - Lisnacon - December 25, 1845

- Elizabeth Harris & Edward Beatty – 3 Feb 1787 (Marriage, **St. Peter Parish**)

Elizabeth Harris (wife):
Residence - Tanee - February 3. 1787

Edward Beatty (husband):
Residence - Stilorgan - February 3. 1787

- Elizabeth Harris & Edward Blake – 4 Jul 1798 (Marriage, **St. Andrew Parish** (RC))

- Elizabeth Harris & Edward Conway

  - Edward Conway – bapt. 4 Oct 1830 (Baptism, **St. Nicholas Parish** (RC))

- Elizabeth Harris & Edward Martin

  - Thomas Martin & Alicia Parker – 26 Apr 1873 (Marriage, **St. Lawrence Parish** (RC))

Thomas Martin (son):
Residence - 88 Lower Dorset Street - April 26, 1873

Alicia Parker, daughter of Thomas Parker & Elizabeth Cantwell (daughter-in-law):
Residence - 10 North East Anne Street - April 26, 1873

Hurst

- Elizabeth Harris & Edward Wren – 20 Feb 1844 (Marriage, **Tralee Parish** (RC))

  - Patrick Wren – b. 21 Mar 1845, bapt. 21 Mar 1845 (Baptism, **Tralee Parish** (RC))

Elizabeth Harris (mother):

> Residence - Blennerville - February 20, 1844

Edward Wren (father):

> Residence - Blennerville - February 20, 1844

> ### March 21, 1845

- Elizabeth Harris & Feliz Cavanagh – 23 Oct 1854 (Marriage, **St. James Parish** (RC))

- Elizabeth Harris & Francis Martell

  - Mary Martell – b. 14 Feb 1818, bapt. 14 Feb 1818 (Baptism, **Tralee Parish** (RC))

Francis Martell (father):

> Residence - Tralee - February 14, 1818

- Elizabeth Harris & Francis Purcell

  - Peter Purcell – b. 15 Apr 1876, bapt. 19 Apr 1876 (Baptism, **St. Lawrence Parish** (RC))

Francis Purcell (father):

> Residence - 25 Guild Street - April 19, 1876

- Elizabeth Harris & George Kernan (K e r n a n)

  - Mary Anne Kernan – b. 30 Dec 1857, bapt. 6 Jan 1858 (Baptism, **St. Lawrence Parish**

    (RC))

George Kernan (father):

> Residence - 7 Alboro Court - January 6, 1858

- Elizabeth Harris & George Sanson – 29 Jun 1821 (Marriage, **Tralee Parish**)

- Elizabeth Harris & Gulielmo Donahoe – 15 Oct 1838 (Marriage, **St. Nicholas Parish** (RC))

- Elizabeth Harris & Gulielmo McNulty

  - Henry McNulty – b. 28 Apr 1857, bapt. 13 May 1857 (Baptism, **St. Nicholas Parish** (RC))

Gulielmo McNulty (father):

> Residence - 2 Ardee Street - May 13, 1857

Harris Surname Ireland: 1600s to 1900s

- Elizabeth Harris & Hugh Briscoe – 28 Jul 1653 (Marriage, **St. John Parish**)

- Elizabeth Harris & Hugh Lynch

    o Hugh Lynch – bapt. 28 Jan 1771 (Baptism, **St. Catherine Parish** (RC))

    o William Lynch – bapt. 4 Apr 1773 (Baptism, **St. Catherine Parish** (RC))

- Elizabeth Harris & James Burden

    o Margaret Burden – bapt. 1 May 1820 (Baptism, **Cork - South Parish** (RC))

- Elizabeth Harris & James Dillon

    o Gulielmo Dillon – bapt. 30 May 1819 (Baptism, **St. Nicholas Parish** (RC))

- Elizabeth Harris & James Hickey – 15 Apr 1809 (Marriage, **Cork - SS. Peter & Paul Parish** (RC))

Elizabeth Harris (wife):
Residence - Nile Street - April 15, 1809

- Elizabeth Harris & James Keogh

    o Catherine Keogh – b. 1899, bapt. 1899 (Baptism, **St. Andrew Parish** (RC))

James Keogh (father):
Residence - Holles Street Hospital - 1899

- Elizabeth Harris & James Ryder

    o James Ryder & Bridget Green – 7 Feb 1859 (Marriage, **Chapelizod Parish** (RC))

        ▪ Hannah Mary Ryder – bapt. 1861 (Baptism, **Chapelizod Parish** (RC))

James Ryder (son):
Residence - Chapelizod - 1861

- Elizabeth Harris & James Skehan

    o Mary Elizabeth Skehan – b. 17 May 1857, bapt. 25 May 1857 (Baptism, **St. Lawrence Parish** (RC))

James Skehan (father):
Residence - 8 Scallys Cottages Mayor Street - May 25, 1857

Hurst

- Elizabeth Harris & James Ralph Worthington

  - William Ingiram Worthington – b. 1 May 1867, bapt. 21 Jul 1867 (Baptism, St. James Parish)

James Ralph Worthington (father):

Residence - Rossboro House South Circular Road - July 21, 1867

Occupation - Gentleman - July 21, 1867

- Elizabeth Harris & John Barnwell (B a r n w e l l) – 28 Jul 1811 (Marriage, Rathfarnham Parish (RC))

  - William Barnwell – b. 1818, bapt. 1818 (Baptism, Rathfarnham Parish (RC))

- Elizabeth Harris & John Burrows

  - Thomas Burrows – bapt. 30 Nov 1810 (Baptism, Cork - SS. Peter & Paul Parish (RC))

John Burrows (father):

Residence - Clothers Lane - November 30, 1810

- Elizabeth Harris & John Castles

  - Mary Castles – b. 19 Sep 1824, bapt. 19 Sep 1824 (Baptism, Tralee Parish (RC))

John Castles (father):

Residence - Tralee - September 19, 1824

- Elizabeth Harris & John Coffee

  - Ellen Coffee – b. 16 Nov 1827, bapt. 16 Nov 1827 (Baptism, Milltown Parish (RC))

John Coffee (father):

Residence - Castlemaine - November 16, 1827

- Elizabeth Harris & John Deering

  - John Deering – b. 4 May 1873, bapt. 12 May 1873 (Baptism, St. Mary, Pro Cathedral Parish (RC))

John Deering (father):

Residence - 91 Great Britain Street - May 12, 1873

Harris Surname Ireland: 1600s to 1900s

- Elizabeth Harris & John Fitzgerald

  - William Fitzgerald – b. 9 Feb 1842, bapt. 9 Feb 1842 (Baptism, **Tralee Parish (RC)**)

- Elizabeth Harris & John Flynn – 4 Mar 1862 (Marriage, **Ardfert Parish (RC)**)

  - Margaret Flynn – b. 10 Dec 1862, bapt. 14 Dec 1862 (Baptism, **Ardfert Parish (RC)**)

Elizabeth Harris (mother):

Residence - Listrim - March 4, 1862

John Flynn (father):

Residence - Banna - March 4, 1862

Ballinvoher - December 14, 1862

- Elizabeth Harris & John Gale – 1748 (Marriage, **St. Werburgh Parish**)

- Elizabeth Harris & John Greghan

  - Jane Greghan – bapt. 9 Jul 1769 (Baptism, **St. Nicholas Parish (RC)**)

  - John Greghan – bapt. 4 Jun 1774 (Baptism, **St. Nicholas Parish (RC)**)

  - Sarah Greghan – bapt. 13 Aug 1780 (Baptism, **St. Nicholas Parish (RC)**)

- Elizabeth Harris & John Grogan

  - Michael Grogan – b. 15 Aug 1859, bapt. 29 Aug 1859 (Baptism, **St. Mary, Pro Cathedral Parish (RC)**)

  - Teresa Grogan – b. 15 Oct 1864, bapt. 18 Oct 1864 (Baptism, **SS. Michael & John Parish (RC)**)

  - Michael Grogan & Bridget Flynn – 12 May 1891 (Marriage, **Rathmines Parish (RC)**)

Michael Grogan (son):

Residence - 8 Ranelagh Avenue - May 12, 1891

Bridget Flynn, daughter of William Flynn & Bridget Short (daughter-in-law):

Residence - 10 Ranelagh Avenue - May 12, 1891

John Grogan (father):

Residence - Little Britain Street - August 29, 1859

11 Crane Lane - October 18, 1864

Hurst

- Elizabeth Harris & John Hotton

  o Caroline Hotton – bapt. 20 Nov 1826 (Baptism, **Cork - South Parish** (RC))

- Elizabeth Harris & John Hughes

  o Thomas Hughes – bapt. 19 Jan 1793 (Baptism, **St. Michan Parish** (RC))

  o Mary Hughes – bapt. 18 May 1794 (Baptism, **St. Michan Parish** (RC))

- Elizabeth Harris & John Kavanagh

  o Lawrence Kavanagh – b. 1860, bapt. 1860 (Baptism, **St. Andrew Parish** (RC))

John Kavanagh (father):

Residence - 13 Marks Lane - 1860

- Elizabeth Harris & John Kearin

  o Timothy Kearin – b. 31 May 1829, bapt. 31 May 1829 (Baptism, **Milltown Parish** (RC))

John Kearin (father):

Residence - Milltown - May 31, 1829

- Elizabeth Harris & John Mokey

  o Mary Mokey – bapt. 25 Feb 1810 (Baptism, **Cork - South Parish** (RC))

John Mokey (father):

Residence - Tobin Street - February 25, 1810

- Elizabeth Harris & John Mulhall – 19 May 1783 (Marriage, **St. Nicholas Parish** (RC))

- Elizabeth Harris & John Sullivan – 6 Feb 1838 (Marriage, **Kinsale Parish** (RC))

John Sullivan (husband):

Residence - Cork Street - February 6, 1838

- Elizabeth Harris & Josh Hodgins – 26 Feb 1764 (Marriage, **St. Catherine Parish** (RC))

  o Jane Hodgins – bapt. 10 Jun 1770 (Baptism, **St. Catherine Parish** (RC))

  o Thomas Hodgins – bapt. 2 Mar 1773 (Baptism, **St. Catherine Parish** (RC))

  o William Hodgins – bapt. 2 Mar 1773 (Baptism, **St. Catherine Parish** (RC))

Harris Surname Ireland: 1600s to 1900s

- Elizabeth Harris & Mark Byrne (B y r n e)

    o Michael John Byrne – b. 19 Dec 1864, bapt. 30 Dec 1864 (Baptism, **St. Nicholas Parish (RC)**)

    o Margaret Jane Byrne – b. 27 Jan 1867, bapt. 11 Feb 1867 (Baptism, **St. Michan Parish (RC)**)

Mark Byrne (father):

Residence - 2 Camden Villa - December 30, 1864

26 Wellington Street - February 11, 1867

- Elizabeth Harris & Martin Malone

    o Eleanor Malone – bapt. 19 Dec 1773 (Baptism, **St. Catherine Parish (RC)**)

- Elizabeth Harris & Michael Counihan – 25 Apr 1833 (Marriage, **Tralee Parish (RC)**)

Elizabeth Harris (wife):

Residence - Ballard - April 25, 1833

Michael Counihan (husband):

Residence - Ballard - April 25, 1833

- Elizabeth Harris & Michael Lyons

    o James Lyons – bapt. 1 Jul 1792 (Baptism, **Cork - SS. Peter & Paul Parish (RC)**)

    o George Lyons – bapt. 8 Jul 1795 (Baptism, **Cork - South Parish (RC)**)

    o Nelly Lyons – bapt. 28 Jul 1798 (Baptism, **Cork - SS. Peter & Paul Parish (RC)**)

    o Francis Lyons – bapt. 26 Oct 1800 (Baptism, **Cork - South Parish (RC)**)

    o Betty Lyons – bapt. 22 Apr 1803 (Baptism, **Cork - South Parish (RC)**)

Michael Lyons (father):

Residence - Cross Gun Lane - July 1, 1792

Broad Lane - July 28, 1798

Bears Lane - October 26, 1800

Tucky Street - April 22, 1803

Hurst

- Elizabeth Harris & Michael Norton – 4 Sep 1819 (Marriage, **St. Andrew Parish** (RC))

- Elizabeth Harris & Michael Quinn – 27 Jun 1853 (Marriage, **St. Catherine Parish** (RC))

- Elizabeth Harris & Peter Hughes – 6 Dec 1797 (Marriage, **St. Michan Parish** (RC))

- Elizabeth Harris & Richard Connolly

  o Mary Elizabeth Connolly – b. 5 Mar 1879, bapt. 13 Mar 1879 (Baptism, **St. James Parish** (RC))

  o Catherine Mary Connolly – b. 20 Mar 1881, bapt. 29 Mar 1881 (Baptism, **St. James Parish** (RC))

Richard Connolly (father):

Residence - Golden Bridge - March 13, 1879

March 29, 1881

- Elizabeth Harris & Richard O'Donnell

  o Margaret O'Donnell – b. 20 Apr 1824, bapt. 20 Apr 1824 (Baptism, **Ballylongford Parish** (RC))

Richard O'Donnell (father):

Residence - Carrunah - April 20, 1824

- Elizabeth Harris & Roger Callahan – 3 Mar 1764 (Marriage, **St. Andrew Parish**)

- Elizabeth Harris & Stephen Cowen – 31 Jan 1827 (Marriage, **St. Catherine Parish**)

Elizabeth Harris (wife):

Residence - St. Catherine Parish - January 31, 1827

Stephen Cowan (husband):

Residence - St. Andrew's Parish - January 31, 1827

- Elizabeth Harris & Thomas Barry – 25 Jan 1791 (Marriage, **Cork - South Parish** (RC))

Elizabeth Harris (wife):

Residence - Gallows Green - January 25, 1791

Thomas Barry (husband):

Residence - Maypole Road - January 25, 1791

Harris Surname Ireland: 1600s to 1900s

- Elizabeth Harris & Thomas Dwyer

  o John Stephen Dwyer – bapt. 26 Dec 1839 (Baptism, **Cork - South Parish** (RC))

  o Jeremiah Dwyer – bapt. 24 Mar 1844 (Baptism, **Cork - South Parish** (RC))

  o James Dwyer – bapt. 25 Oct 1846 (Baptism, **Cork - South Parish** (RC))

- Elizabeth Harris & Thomas Goffton – 16 Feb 1712 (Marriage, **St. Catherine Parish**)

- Elizabeth Harris & Thomas Heany – 5 May 1739 (Marriage, **St. Bride Parish**)

- Elizabeth Harris & Thomas Hunt

  o Thomas Hunt & Mary Anne Gallagher – 25 Nov 1888 (Marriage, **Rathmines Parish** (RC))

Thomas Hunt (son):

Residence - Portobello Barrack - November 25, 1888

Mary Anne Gallagher, daughter of John Gallagher & Mary McGirvey (daughter-in-law):

Residence - Rathmines - November 25, 1888

- Elizabeth Harris & Thomas Tomson – 20 Dec 1631 (Marriage, **St. John Parish**)

- Elizabeth Harris & Timothy Moynihan – 27 May 1843 (Baptism, **Cork - SS. Peter & Paul Parish** (RC))

- Elizabeth Harris & William Cullen – 30 Jan 1836 (Marriage, **St. Andrew Parish** (RC))

- Elizabeth Harris & William Pembroke

  o William Pembroke – b. 10 Nov 1816, bapt. 10 Nov 1816 (Baptism, **Tralee Parish** (RC))

William Pembroke (father):

Residence - Tralee - November 10, 1816

Hurst

- Elizabeth Williamfolkes Harris & William Leeson – 5 Aug 1865 (Marriage, St. Mark Parish)

Signatures:

Elizabeth Williamfolkes, daughter of William Williamfolkes (wife):

    Residence - 6 Chatham Street - August 5, 1865

    Relationship Status at Marriage -widow

William Leeson, son of Michael Leeson (husband):

    Residence - 58 Sandwith Street - August 5, 1865

    Occupation - Cook & Confectioner - August 5, 1865

Michael Leeson (father):

    Occupation - Stewart

William Williamfolkes (father):

    Occupation - Tarachsman

Due to the quality of the handwriting, it is unclear as to what the actual church register entry states regarding William Williamfolkes occupation.

- Ellen Harris & Bartholomew Stack

  - Francis Stack – b. 3 Dec 1874, bapt. 14 Dec 1874 (Baptism, St. Michan Parish (RC))

  - Joseph Stack – b. 3 Dec 1874, bapt. 14 Dec 1874 (Baptism, St. Michan Parish (RC))

Bartholomew Stack (father):

    Residence - 44 Mary's Place - December 14, 1874

- Ellen Harris & Cornelius (C o r n e l i u s) Mahony

  - Ellen Mahony – bapt. Jan 1791 (Baptism, Kilmurry Parish (RC))

  - Timothy Mahony – bapt. Mar 1796 (Baptism, Kilmurry Parish (RC))

- Ellen Harris & Daniel McCarthy – 9 Jan 1831 (Marriage, **Tralee Parish** (RC))

  o Jane McCarthy – b. 18 Nov 1831, bapt. 18 Nov 1831 (Baptism, **Tralee Parish** (RC))

  o Timothy McCarthy – b. 12 Jan 1834, bapt. 12 Jan 1834 (Baptism, **Tralee Parish** (RC))

  o Elizabeth McCarthy – b. 19 Sep 1836, bapt. 19 Sep 1836 (Baptism, **Tralee Parish** (RC))

  o William McCarthy – b. 5 Dec 1838, bapt. 5 Dec 1838 (Baptism, **Tralee Parish** (RC))

  o Mary McCarthy – b. 18 Dec 1841, bapt. 18 Dec 1841 (Baptism, **Tralee Parish** (RC))

  o Ellen McCarthy – b. 13 Jan 1844, bapt. 13 Jan 1844 (Baptism, **Tralee Parish** (RC))

  o Patrick McCarthy – b. 22 Apr 1850, bapt. 22 Apr 1850 (Baptism, **Tralee Parish** (RC))

Ellen Harris (mother):

　Residence - Blennerville - January 9, 1831

Daniel McCarthy (father):

　Residence - Blennerville - November 18, 1831

　　　　　　January 12, 1834

　　　　　　December 5, 1838

　　　　　　January 13, 1844

　　　Curraheen - September 19, 1836

　　　Curragraig - December 18, 1841

　　　Curragraigue - April 22, 1850

- Ellen Harris & Dennis Murphy – 2 Nov 1817 (Marriage, **Cork – South Parish** (RC))

Ellen Harris (wife):

　Residence - St. Barry's - November 2, 1817

- Ellen Harris & Edward Doyle

  o Elizabeth Doyle – bapt. Sep 1851 (Baptism, **St. Michan Parish** (RC))

- Ellen Harris & Francis Leary

  o Francis Leary – b. 28 Feb 1857, bapt. 28 Feb 1857 (Baptism, **Killarney Parish** (RC))

Francis Leary (father):

　Residence - Killarney - February 1857

Hurst

- Ellen Harris & Garret Hickson – 4 Feb 1711 (Marriage, **Dingle Parish**)

Ellen Harris (wife):

   Residence - Killeiny - February 4, 1711

Garret Hickson (husband):

   Residence - Ardfert - February 4, 1711

- Ellen Harris & George Twiss

   o George Twiss – b. 27 Apr 1842, bapt. 27 Apr 1842 (Baptism, **Glenbeigh/Glencar Parish**

      (RC))

   o Richard Twiss – b. 15 Apr 1846, bapt. 15 Apr 1846 (Baptism, **Glenbeigh/Glencar Parish**

      (RC))

George Twiss (father):

   Residence - Reennanallagane - April 27, 1842

                              April 15, 1846

- Ellen Harris & James Crosbie – 1 Jan 1816 (Marriage, **Cork - SS. Peter & Paul Parish** (RC))

- Ellen Harris & James Higgins

   o Elizabeth Higgins – bapt. 7 Aug 1807 (Baptism, **Cork - South Parish** (RC))

   o Mary Higgins – bapt. 25 Aug 1818 (Baptism, **Cork - South Parish** (RC))

   o Michael Higgins – bapt. 18 Jul 1820 (Baptism, **Cork - South Parish** (RC))

   o John Higgins – bapt. 19 Apr 1824 (Baptism, **Cork - South Parish** (RC))

   o Margaret Higgins – bapt. 15 Jun 1827 (Baptism, **Cork - South Parish** (RC))

James Higgins (father):

   Residence - Broad - August 7, 1807

Harris Surname Ireland: 1600s to 1900s

- Ellen Harris & John Casey

  o Mary Casey – b. 13 Dec 1838, bapt. 13 Dec 1838 (Baptism, **Rathmore Parish** (RC))

  o Mary Casey – b. 5 Oct 1840, bapt. 5 Oct 1840 (Baptism, **Rathmore Parish** (RC))

John Casey (father):

Residence - Gortnagane - December 13, 1838

Knockacullen - October 5, 1840

- Ellen Harris & John Donovan

  o Matthew Donovan – bapt. Jun 1828 (Baptism, **Tracton Abbey Parish** (RC))

- Ellen Harris & John Healy

  o Patrick Healy – b. 1 Jan 1870, bapt. 13 Feb 1870 (Baptism, **Ballymacelligott Parish** (RC))

John Healy (father):

Residence - Gurtbrach - February 13, 1870

- Ellen Harris & John Moynihan – 26 Jan 1845 (Marriage, **Kilmurry, Moviddy, Kilbonane, &**

  Cannavee Parish (RC))

  o Mary Moynihan – bapt. 11 Feb 1846 (Baptism, **Innishannon Parish** (RC))

  o Jerry Moynihan – bapt. 27 Aug 1851 (Baptism, **Innishannon Parish** (RC))

  o John Moynihan – bapt. 6 Nov 1856 (Baptism, **Innishannon Parish** (RC))

- Ellen Harris & John Shaw

  o Michael Shaw – bapt. 1846 (Baptism, **St. Mary, Haddington Road Parish** (RC))

- Ellen Harris & John White – 5 Jan 1824 (Marriage, **Timoleague & Barryroe Parish** (RC))

- Ellen Harris & John Unknown

  o Mary Ellen Unknown – b. 9 Feb 1876, bapt. 10 Feb 1876 (Baptism, **Cork - South Parish**

  (RC))

- Ellen Harris & Joseph Barrett

  o Joseph Barrett – bapt. 17 May 1799 (Baptism, **Bandon Parish** (RC))

Hurst

- Ellen Harris & Lawrence Carran

  o Catherine Carran – bapt. 6 Jul 1849 (Baptism, **St. Catherine Parish (RC)**)

- Ellen Harris & Martin Foley

  o James Foley, b. 18 Jan 1844, bapt. 18 Jan 1844 (Baptism, **Glenbeigh/Glencar Parish (RC)**) & Margaret Mahony – 12 Feb 1865 (Marriage, **Killarney Parish (RC)**)

James Foley (son):

Residence - Killarney - February 12, 1865

Margaret Mahony, daughter of Michael Mahony & Margaret Doherty (daughter-in-law):

Residence - Killarney - February 12, 1865

  o Martin Foley & Margaret Shea – 10 Sep 1876 (Marriage, **Killarney Parish (RC)**)

Martin Foley (son):

Residence - Killarney - September 10, 1876

Margaret Shea, daughter of Daniel Shea & Margaret Coffey (daughter-in-law):

Residence - Killarney - September 10, 1876

   o Patrick Foley & Anne Shea – 17 Oct 1886 (Marriage, **Killarney Parish (RC)**)

Patrick Foley (son):

Residence - Killarney - October 17, 1886

Anne Shea, daughter of Patrick Shea & Mary Grogan (daughter-in-law):

Residence - Middleton - October 17, 1886

   o Jane Foley – b. 18 Apr 1846, bapt. 18 Apr 1846 (Baptism, **Glenbeigh/Glencar Parish (RC)**)

Martin Foley (father):

Residence - Knockbue - January 18, 1844

Drom - April 18, 1846

Harris Surname Ireland: 1600s to 1900s

- Ellen Harris & Martin Kennedy

  o Patrick Kennedy – b. 9 Nov 1897, bapt. 12 Nov 1897 (Baptism, **Killorglin Parish** (RC))

  o Bridget Kennedy – b. 8 Apr 1900, bapt. 8 Apr 1900 (Baptism, **Killorglin Parish** (RC))

Martin Kennedy (father):

Residence - Killorglin - November 12, 1897

April 8, 1900

- Ellen Harris & Maurice Buttimer

  o Jane Buttimer – bapt. 15 Feb 1862 (Baptism, **Kilmichael Parish** (RC))

  o Ellen Buttimer – bapt. 13 Jan 1864 (Baptism, **Kilmichael Parish** (RC))

  o Mary Buttimer – bapt. 15 Apr 1866 (Baptism, **Kilmichael Parish** (RC))

  o Catherine Buttimer – bapt. 3 Oct 1868 (Baptism, **Kilmichael Parish** (RC))

  o Catherine Buttimer – bapt. 28 Mar 1871 (Baptism, **Kilmichael Parish** (RC))

Maurice Buttimer (father):

Residence - Inchinashingane - February 15, 1862

April 15, 1866

March 28, 1871

- Ellen Harris & Patrick Crowly – 28 Jan 1810 (Marriage, **Tralee Parish** (RC))

  o Patrick Crowly – b. 20 Mar 1811, bapt. 20 Mar 1811 (Baptism, **Tralee Parish** (RC))

Patrick Crowly (father):

Residence - Spa - March 20, 1811

Hurst

- Ellen Harris & Patrick Murphy – 23 Jun 1874 (Marriage, **Kilmichael Parish** (RC))

  - Honora Murphy – bapt. 4 Jul 1875 (Baptism, **Kilmichael Parish** (RC))

  - Margaret Murphy – bapt. 5 Aug 1877 (Baptism, **Kilmichael Parish** (RC))

  - Jane Murphy – bapt. 21 Jul 1880 (Baptism, **Kilmichael Parish** (RC))

Patrick Murphy (father):

Residence - Inchinashingane - July 4, 1875

Castleview - August 5, 1877

July 21, 1880

- Ellen Harris & Patrick Riordan

  - Patrick Riordan – b. 16 Apr 1879, bapt. 16 Apr 1879 (Baptism, **Glenbeigh/Glencar Parish** (RC))

Patrick Riordan (father):

Residence - Kilkeehagh - April 16, 1879

- Ellen Harris & Patrick Sheehan – 18 Apr 1880 (Marriage, **Kinsale Parish** (RC))

- Ellen Harris & Patrick Walsh – 25 Jan 1845 (Marriage, **Tralee Parish** (RC))

  - Bartholomew Walsh – b. 12 Apr 1846, bapt. 12 Apr 1846 (Baptism, **Ballybunion Parish** (RC))

  - James Walsh – b. 27 Jul 1847, bapt. 27 Jul 1847 (Baptism, **Ballybunion Parish** (RC))

  - Elizabeth Walsh – b. 29 Oct 1853, bapt. 29 Oct 1853 (Baptism, **Ballybunion Parish** (RC))

  - Catherine Walsh – b. 25 May 1856, bapt. 25 May 1856 (Baptism, **Ballybunion Parish** (RC))

  - William Walsh – b. 20 May 1859, bapt. 20 May 1859 (Baptism, **Ballybunion Parish** (RC))

  - Margaret Walsh – B. 13 Jun 1864, bapt. 13 Jun 1864 (Baptism, **Ballybunion Parish** (RC))

Harris Surname Ireland: 1600s to 1900s

Ellen Harris (mother):

    Residence - Knockanuish - January 25, 1845

Patrick Walsh (father):

    Residence - Knockanish - January 25, 1845

        Laheseragh - July 27, 1847

        Barna - April 12, 1846

            October 29, 1853

            May 25, 1856

            June 13, 1864

        Killibiny - May 20, 1859

- Ellen Harris & Peter Holohan

  - Catherine Holohan – b. 7 Feb 1880, bapt. 10 Feb 1880 (Baptism, **Cork - SS. Peter & Paul Parish** (RC))

- Ellen Harris & Robert Armstrong

  - Mary Armstrong – b. 1860, bapt. 1860 (Baptism, **St. Andrew Parish** (RC))

Robert Armstrong (father):

    Residence - James Street East - 1860

- Ellen Harris & Robert Hoare

  - Ally Hoare – bapt. 7 Sep 1795 (Baptism, **Cork - SS. Peter & Paul Parish** (RC))

  - William Hoare – bapt. 8 Jan 1797 (Baptism, **Cork - SS. Peter & Paul Parish** (RC))

Robert Hoare (father):

    Residence - Coalman's Lane - September 7, 1795

            January 8, 1797

The mother's name was recorded as Nelly Harrish in the church register for January 8, 1797.

- Ellen Harris & Thomas Louth

  - Anne Mary Louth – bapt. 21 Apr 1845 (Baptism, **St. James Parish** (RC))

Hurst

- Ellen Harris & Thomas Sullivan

  - Margaret Sullivan – b. 8 Jan 1874, bapt. 13 Jan 1874 (Baptism, **Tralee Parish** (RC))

Thomas Sullivan (father):
Residence - Derrymore - January 13, 1874

- Ellen Harris & Timothy O'Kelly

  - Mary Anne O'Kelly & Isaac Beverly – 17 Apr 1892 (Marriage, **St. Mary, Pro Cathedral Parish** (RC))

Mary Anne O'Kelly (daughter):
Residence - 191 Great Britain Street - April 17, 1892

Isaac Beverly, son of William Beverly & Elizabeth Burke (son-in-law):
Residence - 15 Green Street - April 17, 1892

- Ellen Harris & Unknown Denahy

  - Patrick Denahy – b. 25 Apr 1867, bapt. 28 Apr 1868 (Baptism, **Killarney Parish** (RC))

Ellen Harris (mother):
Residence - Killarney - April 28, 1868

- Ellen Harris & Unknown Flynn

  - John Flynn – b. 3 Jul 1860, bapt. 8 Jul 1860 (Baptism, **Killarney Parish** (RC))

Ellen Harris (mother):
Residence - Workhouse - July 8, 1860

- Ellen Harris & Unknown Lynch

  - Jeremiah Lynch – b. 4 Oct 1864, bapt. 7 Oct 1864 (Baptism, **Killarney Parish** (RC))

Ellen Harris (mother):
Residence - Killarney - October 7, 1864

- Ellen Harris & William Brien – 25 Apr 1867 (Marriage, **Kinsale Parish** (RC))

- Ellen Harris & William Donovan

  - John Donovan – bapt. 24 Apr 1820 (Baptism, **Kinsale Parish** (RC))

- Ellen Harris & William Murphy – 9 Oct 1797 (Marriage, **Cork - South Parish** (RC))

Harris Surname Ireland: 1600s to 1900s

- Ellen Mary Harris & James Smith

  o May Ellen May Smith – b. 11 May 1885, bapt. 27 May 1885 (Baptism, **Rathmines Parish (RC)**)

James Smith (father):

Residence - Portobello Barrack - May 27, 1885

- Emily Frances Harris & Patrick Driscoll

  o John Edward Driscoll – b. 15 Mar 1888, bapt. 1 Apr 1888 (Baptism, **Caherciveen Parish (RC)**)

  o Gerald Patrick Driscoll – b. 2 Jul 1890, bapt. 13 Jul 1890 (Baptism, **Killorglin Parish** (RC))

  o Charles Harris – b. 27 Sep 1892, bapt. 2 Oct 1892 (Baptism, **Killorglin Parish** (RC))

  o Emily Mary Driscoll – b. 4 Dec 1894, bapt. 9 Dec 1894 (Baptism, **Killorglin Parish** (RC))

  o Alice Frances Driscoll – b. 29 Apr 1896, bapt. 3 May 1896 (Baptism, **Killorglin Parish (RC)**)

  o Elizabeth Driscoll – b. 31 May 1897, bapt. 4 Jun 1897 (Baptism, **Killorglin Parish** (RC))

  o Josephine Elizabeth Driscoll – b. 29 Jul 1899, bapt. 4 Aug 1899 (Baptism, **Killorglin Parish (RC)**)

  o Mary Sophie Driscoll – b. 12 Aug 1900, bapt. 15 Aug 1900 (Baptism, **Caherciveen Parish (RC)**)

  o Laura Driscoll – b. 2 Jan 1902, bapt. 3 Jan 1902 (Baptism, **Caherciveen Parish** (RC))

  o Timothy Driscoll – b. 2 Jan 1902, bapt. 3 Jan 1902 (Baptism, **Caherciveen Parish** (RC))

Hurst

Patrick Driscoll (father):

Residence - Caherciveen - April 1, 1888

August 15, 1900

January 3, 1902

Killorglin - July 13, 1890

October 2, 1892

December 9, 1894

May 3, 1896

June 4, 1897

August 4, 1899

- Emma Harris & Francis Brooks

  - John Brooks – b. 5 Feb 1878, bapt. 11 Feb 1878 (Baptism, St. Lawrence Parish (RC))

  - Mary Catherine Brooks – b. 19 Aug 1879, bapt. 19 Aug 1879 (Baptism, St. Lawrence Parish (RC))

  - Mary Ellen Brooks – b. 1892, bapt. 1892 (Baptism, St. Andrew Parish (RC))

Francis Brooks (father):

Residence - 9 Abercorn Road - February 11, 1878

August 19, 1879

111 Brunswick Street - 1892

- Esther Harris & Philip O'Toole

  - Joseph O'Toole – b. 30 Jan 1827, bapt. 30 Jan 1827 (Baptism, Tralee Parish (RC))

Philip O'Toole (father):

Residence - Tralee - January 30, 1827

- Esther Harris & Thomas Boylan

  - Nicholas Boylan – b. 11 Sep 1868, bapt. 16 Sep 1868 (Baptism, St. Mary, Pro Cathedral Parish (RC))

Thomas Boylan (father):

Residence - 150 Great Britain Street - September 16, 1868

- Frances Annetta Harris & Frederick Geale Monsarrat – 1 Oct 1840 (Marriage, **St. Thomas Parish**)

Signatures:

Wedding Witnesses:

Nicholas W. Monsarrat

Signature:

- Frances Jane Harris & John Maron

    o William Mary Joseph Maron – b. 9 Aug 1878, bapt. 13 Sep 1887 (Baptism, **St. Michan Parish (RC)**)

    o Mary Joseph Patrick Maron – b. 6 May 1880, bapt. 13 Sep 1887 (Baptism, **St. Michan Parish (RC)**)

    o John Mary Joseph Maron – b. 10 Mar 1884, bapt. 13 Sep 1887 (Baptism, **St. Michan Parish (RC)**)

John Maron (father):

   Residence - 76 Mary's Lane - September 13, 1887

- Georgina Harris & Richard Burke

    o Ellen Burke – b. 1864, bapt. 1864 (Baptism, **St. Andrew Parish (RC)**)

Richard Burke (father):

   Residence - No 1 Maguinnis Place - 1864

Hurst

- Grace Harris & Patrick Fortune

  - Ellen Fortune – b. 25 Aug 1813, bapt. 26 Aug 1813 (Baptism, **Clonakilty Parish** (RC))

  - John Fortune – bapt. 26 Sep 1817 (Baptism, **Clonakilty Parish** (RC))

- Hannah Harris & Gulielmo Murphy – 23 Feb 1781 (Marriage, **St. Andrew Parish** (RC))

- Hannah Harris & Gulielmo Unknown

  - Elizabeth Unknown – b. 25 Feb 1858, bapt. Feb 1858 (Baptism, **St. Catherine Parish**

    (RC))

- Hannah Harris & Michael Dinneen – 29 Jan 1881 (Marriage, **Innishannon Parish** (RC))

- Helen Harris & Edward Murphy

  - Henry Murphy – b. 2 Jun 1877, bapt. 12 Jun 1877 (Baptism, **St. Audoen Parish** (RC))

Edward Murphy (father):

    Residence - 50 Cook Street - June 12, 1877

- Helen Harris & John Gibbons

  - Edward Gibbons & Elizabeth Louis – 5 Oct 1873 (Marriage, **Harrington Street Parish**

    (RC))

Edward Gibbons (son):

    Residence - 38 Cuffe Street - October 5, 1873

Elizabeth Louis, daughter of Patrick Louis & Anne Taylor (daughter-in-law):

    Residence - 29 Cuffe Street - October 5, 1873

- Helen Harris & Maurice Kennedy

  - Catherine Kennedy – b. 25 Aug 1896, bapt. 26 Aug 1896 (Baptism, **Glenbeigh/Glencar**

    Parish (RC))

Maurice Kennedy (father):

    Residence - Coolnaharragill - August 26, 1896

Harris Surname Ireland: 1600s to 1900s

- Helen Harris & Peter Driscoll

  o Bridget Driscoll – bapt. 30 Jan 1864 (Baptism, **Skibbereen (Creagh & Sullon) Parish**

  (RC))

Peter Driscoll (father):

Residence - Skibbereen - January 30, 1864

- Helen Harris & Timothy Moriarty

  o John Moriarty & Mary Sullivan – 29 Jan 1870 (Marriage, **Spa Parish (RC)**)

John Moriarty (son):

Residence - Taulaght - January 29, 1870

Mary Sullivan, daughter of Dennis Sullivan & Honora Sullivan (daughter-in-law):

Residence - Taulaght - January 29, 1870

- Honora Harris & Alexander Canning – 25 Jun 1820 (Marriage, **Tralee Parish (RC)**)

  o Jane Canning – b. 15 Apr 1821, bapt. 15 Apr 1821 (Baptism, **Tralee Parish (RC)**)

  o James Canning – b. 4 May 1825, bapt. 4 May 1825 (Baptism, **Tralee Parish (RC)**)

Alexander Canning (father):

Residence - Tralee - June 25, 1820

April 15, 1821

May 4, 1825

- Honora Harris & Daniel O'Murphy – 14 Nov 1826 (Marriage, **Tralee Parish (RC)**)

  o Mary O'Murphy – b. 14 Feb 1830, bapt. 14 Feb 1830 (Baptism, **Tralee Parish (RC)**)

  o Jane O'Murphy – b. 23 Sep 1832, bapt. 23 Sep 1832 (Baptism, **Tralee Parish (RC)**)

  o Daniel O'Murphy – b. 30 Nov 1835, bapt. 30 Nov 1835 (Baptism, **Tralee Parish (RC)**)

Honora Harris (wife):

Residence - Tralee - November 14, 1826

Daniel O'Murphy (father):

Residence - Tralee - February 14, 1830

September 23, 1832

November 30, 1835

Hurst

- Honora Harris & Daniel Sullivan

  o Honora Sullivan – b. 11 Aug 1832, bapt. 11 Aug 1832 (Baptism, **Dromtariffe Parish (RC)**)

Daniel Sullivan (father):

Residence - Lisnacon - August 11, 1832

- Honora Harris & Edward O'Murphy

  o Edward O'Murphy – b. 13 Jul 1828, bapt. 13 Jul 1828 (Baptism, **Tralee Parish** (RC))

Edward O'Murphy (father):

Residence - Tralee - July 13, 1828

- Honora Harris & Francis Rutlege – 10 Mar 1786 (Marriage, **Rathfarnham Parish** (RC))

- Honora Harris & James Hayden

  o Catherine Harris – bapt. Sep 1832 (Baptism, **St. Catherine Parish** (RC))

- Honora Harris & John Daly

  o Mary Daly – b. 27 Aug 1888, bapt. 21 Oct 1888 (Baptism, **Glenbeigh/Glencar Parish (RC)**)

John Daly (father):

Residence - Ross - October 21, 1888

- Honora Harris & Lawrence Regan

  o Ellen Regan – bapt. 14 Dec 1811 (Baptism, **Lislee, Abbeymahon, & Donoughmore (Barryroe) Parish** (RC))

Lawrence Regan (father):

Residence - Currihevern - December 14, 1811

Harris Surname Ireland: 1600s to 1900s

- Honora Harris & Patrick Sullivan – 27 Feb 1892 (Marriage, **Glenbeigh/Glencar Parish (RC)**)

  o John Sullivan – b. 7 Jan 1893, bapt. 8 Jan 1893 (Baptism, **Glenbeigh/Glencar Parish (RC)**)

  o Patrick Sullivan – b. 7 Mar 1895, bapt. 10 Mar 1895 (Baptism, **Glenbeigh/Glencar Parish (RC)**)

  o Dennis Sullivan – b. 2 Apr 1897, bapt. 5 Apr 1897 (Baptism, **Glenbeigh/Glencar Parish (RC)**)

Honora Harris (mother):

Residence - Drom - February 27, 1892

Patrick Sullivan (father):

Residence - Drom - January 8, 1893

March 10, 1895

April 5, 1897

- Honora Harris & Timothy Crowly

  o John Crowly – bapt. 21 Jul 1839 (Baptism, **Desertseges Parish (RC)**)

- Honora Harris & Timothy McCarthy – 29 Apr 1875 (Marriage, **Innishannon Parish (RC)**)

  o Mary McCarthy – bapt. 27 Aug 1876 (Baptism, **Courcy's Country or Ballinspittal Parish (RC)**)

  o Timothy McCarthy – bapt. 6 Jun 1878 (Baptism, **Courcy's Country or Ballinspittal Parish (RC)**)

  o John McCarthy – bapt. 21 Sep 1879 (Baptism, **Courcy's Country or Ballinspittal Parish (RC)**)

Hurst

- Isabel Harris & Thaddeus Finn – Jan 1810 (Marriage, **Ardfield & Rathbarry Parish** (RC))

    o Daniel Finn – bapt. 23 Dec 1810 (Baptism, **Ardfield & Rathbarry Parish** (RC))

    o Mary Finn – bapt. 11 Jul 1812 (Baptism, **Ardfield & Rathbarry Parish** (RC))

    o Patrick Finn – bapt. 30 Mar 1814 (Baptism, **Ardfield & Rathbarry Parish** (RC))

    o John Finn – bapt. Apr 1817 (Baptism, **Ardfield & Rathbarry Parish** (RC))

    o Mary Finn – bapt. 24 Sep 1819 (Baptism, **Ardfield & Rathbarry Parish** (RC))

    o James Finn – bapt. 26 Jul 1823 (Baptism, **Ardfield & Rathbarry Parish** (RC))

    o Timothy Finn – bapt. 26 Nov 1826 (Baptism, **Ardfield & Rathbarry Parish** (RC))

- Jane Harris & Charles Dalton

    o Mary Dalton & John Brown – 7 Feb 1871 (Marriage, **Ballylongford Parish** (RC))

Mary Dalton (daughter):

Residence - Ballinoneen - February 7, 1871

John Brown, son of John Brown & Jane Kane (son-in-law):

Residence - Balladuff - February 7, 1871

- Jane Harris & Cornelius (C o r n e l i u s) Coghlan

    o Ellen Coghlan – bapt. 4 Aug 1818 (Baptism, **Cork - South Parish** (RC))

- Jane Harris & Cornelius (C o r n e l i u s) Donovan – 27 Jan 1833 (Marriage, **Timoleague & Barryroe Parish** (RC))

Jane Harris (wife):

Residence - Lisslee - January 27, 1833

- Jane Harris & David French

    o David French – bapt. 28 Sep 1852 (Baptism, **Cork - SS. Peter & Paul Parish** (RC))

    o Jane French – bapt. 10 Oct 1860 (Baptism, **Cork - South Parish** (RC))

- Jane Harris & Dennis Cronin – 16 Feb 1871 (Marriage, **Kilmichael Parish** (RC))

    o John Cronin – bapt. 7 Dec 1873 (Baptism, **Kilmichael Parish** (RC))

Harris Surname Ireland: 1600s to 1900s

- Jane Harris & John Allen – 8 Jan 1682 (Marriage, **St. Audoen Parish**)

- Jane Harris & John Burke – 1 Feb 1852 (Marriage, **Glenbeigh/Glencar Parish** (RC))

Jane Harris (wife):

> **Residence - Knockbue - February 1, 1852**

- Jane Harris & John Edgar – 24 Feb 1754 (Marriage, **St. Paul Parish**)

- Jane Harris & John Moore

  - Elizabeth Moore – bapt. 20 Aug 1833 (Baptism, **Dunmanway Parish** (RC))

John Moore (father):

> **Residence - Town - August 20, 1833**

- Jane Harris & John Moylan

  - Michael Moylan – bapt. 13 Oct 1868 (Baptism, **Schull East Parish** (RC))

- Jane Harris & John Tidy

  - John William Tidy – b. 10 May 1866, bapt. 2 May 1889 (Baptism, **Rathmines Parish** (RC))

John Tidy (father):

> **Residence - 21 Princes Street Grover End, England - May 2, 1889**

- Jane Harris & John James Watts

  - John James Watts, b. 2 Apr 1871, bapt. 17 Mar 1889 (Baptism, **St. Mary, Haddington Road Parish** (RC)) & Esther McDonnell – 14 Apr 1890 (Marriage, **St. Mary, Donnybrook Parish** (RC))

John James Watts (son):

> **Residence - Carrick Edenderry, Kings Co. - April 14, 1890**

Esther McDonnell, daughter of James McDonnell & Mary Anne Murphy (daughter-in-law):

> **Residence - Lawlor's Cottages, Donnybrook - April 14, 1890**

John James Watts (father):

> **Residence - Plymouth - March 17, 1889**

Hurst

- Jane Harris & Joseph Bolger

  - Margaret Bolger – bapt. 23 Aug 1829 (Baptism, **St. Nicholas Parish** (RC))

- Jane Harris & Martin Murphy

  - Gulielmo Murphy – b. 28 Nov 1858, bapt. 12 Dec 1858 (Baptism, **St. James Parish** (RC))

  - William Murphy – b. 28 Nov 1858, bapt. 12 Dec 1858 (Baptism, **St. James Parish** (RC))

Martin Murphy (father):

Residence - Richmond Barracks - December 12, 1858

Occupation - 14ᵗʰ Regiment - December 12, 1858

- Jane Harris & Matthew Byrne (B y r n e)

  - John Joseph Byrne – b. 30 Mar 1888, bapt. 11 Apr 1888 (Baptism, **St. Mary, Pro Cathedral Parish** (RC))

Matthew Byrne (father):

Residence - 4 Mountjoy Court - April 11, 1888

- Jane Harris & Matthew Caufield

  - James Caufield – bapt. 11 Apr 1770 (Baptism, **St. Catherine Parish** (RC))

  - Anne Caufield – bapt. 23 Jul 1771 (Baptism, **St. Catherine Parish** (RC))

  - Mary Caufield – bapt. 26 Jul 1776 (Baptism, **St. Catherine Parish** (RC))

- Jane Harris & Maurice King – 12 Feb 1868 (Marriage, **Glenbeigh/Glencar Parish** (RC))

Jane Harris (wife):

Residence - Glenbeigh - February 12, 1868

Maurice King (husband):

Residence - Filmore - February 12, 1868

- Jane Harris & Michael Carroll

  - Catherine Carroll – bapt. 4 Mar 1803 (Baptism, **St. Catherine Parish** (RC))

Harris Surname Ireland: 1600s to 1900s

- Jane Harris & Patrick McLaughlin – 5 Jul 1779 (Marriage, St. Catherine Parish (RC))

    o David McLaughlin – bapt. 23 Apr 1780 (Baptism, St. Catherine Parish (RC))

    o James McLaughlin – bapt. 24 Jul 1785 (Baptism, St. Catherine Parish (RC))

    o John McLaughlin – bapt. 18 Jun 1788 (Baptism, St. Catherine Parish (RC))

    o David McLaughlin – bapt. 10 Feb 1791 (Baptism, St. Catherine Parish (RC))

- Jane Harris & Patrick Sullivan

    o Patrick Sullivan – b. 4 Sep 1891, bapt. 6 Sep 1891 (Baptism, Ardfert Parish (RC))

Patrick Sullivan (father):

Residence - Ballyimkin - September 6, 1891

- Jane Harris & Thomas Murray – 10 Jan 1822 (Marriage, St. Mary, Pro Cathedral Parish (RC))

- Jane Harris & William Keating

    o Mary Keating – bapt. 21 Dec 1787 (Baptism, St. Michan Parish (RC))

- Jane Isabel Harris & John Bruce Robinson – 27 Jun 1827 (Marriage, Clontarf Parish)

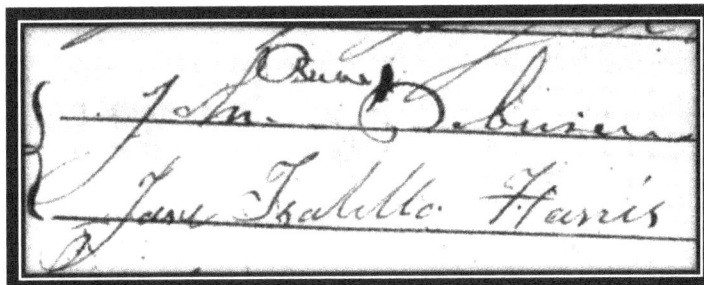

Signatures:

Jane Isabel Harris (wife):

Residence - Clontarf - June 27, 1827

John Bruce Robinson (husband):

Residence - Clontarf - June 27, 1827

Hurst

Wedding Witnesses:

John Harris

Signature:

- Jean Harris & Michael Gallagher – 16 Oct 1754 (Marriage, **St. Catherine Parish** (RC))

- Joan Harris & Patrick Drewery

  - Margaret Drewery – b. 27 Sep 1876, bapt. 27 Sep 1876 (Baptism, **Glenbeigh/Glencar Parish** (RC))

Patrick Drewery (father):

Residence - Drom - September 27, 1876

- Joan Harris & Patrick Fatum

  - Mary Fatum – bapt. 5 Aug 1815 (Baptism, **Clonakilty Parish** (RC))

- Joas Harris & James Scarlott – 30 Jan 1785 (Marriage, **St. Andrew Parish** (RC))

- Joan Harris & Arthur Henessy – 7 Apr 1850 (Marriage, **Dunmanway Parish** (RC))

- Joan Harris & Dennis Finton – 2 Dec 1826 (Marriage, **Innishannon Parish** (RC))

  - Timothy Finton – bapt. Mar 1829 (Baptism, **Ballinhassig Parish** (RC))

  - John Finton – bapt. 22 Mar 1833 (Baptism, **Innishannon Parish** (RC))

  - James Finton – bapt. 7 Jun 1835 (Baptism, **Innishannon Parish** (RC))

  - Dennis Finton – bapt. Nov 1837 (Baptism, **Ballinhassig Parish** (RC))

  - Mary Finton – bapt. 22 Mar 1840 (Baptism, **Ballinhassig Parish** (RC))

  - Patrick Finton – bapt. Mar 1842 (Baptism, **Ballinhassig Parish** (RC))

  - Michael Finton – bapt. 1 Jun 1843 (Baptism, **Ballinhassig Parish** (RC))

Harris Surname Ireland: 1600s to 1900s

- Joan Harris & Dermot (D e r m o t) O'Sughrue

  o James O'Sughrue – b. 6 Nov 1830, bapt. 6 Nov 1830 (Baptism, **Tralee Parish** (RC))

Dermot O'Sughrue (father):

Residence - Caherleheen - November 6, 1830

- Joan Harris & Dionysius Leary

  o Dionysius Leary – bapt. 4 Apr 1805 (Baptism, **Lislee, Abbeymahon, & Donoughmore**

    (Barryroe) Parish (RC))

Dionysius Leary (father):

Residence - Grange - April 4, 1805

- Joan Harris & John Curran

  o Bridget Curran – b. 9 Jan 1892, bapt. 10 Jan 1892 (Baptism, **Dingle Parish** (RC))

John Curran (father):

Residence - Mall - January 10, 1892

- Joan Harris & John Donovan

  o John Donovan – bapt. 2 Dec 1829 (Baptism, **Dunmanway Parish** (RC))

John Donovan (father):

Residence - Cooranig - December 2, 1829

- Joan Harris & John Sullivan

  o Eugene Sullivan – bapt. 8 Mar 1833 (Baptism, **Ballinhassig Parish** (RC))

Hurst

- Joan Harris & Patrick Power

    o Joseph Power – b. 15 Aug 1872, bapt. 23 Aug 1872 (Baptism, **Harrington Street Parish**

    (RC))

    o Patirck Power – b. 25 Jan 1875, bapt. 2 Feb 1875 (Baptism, **Harrington Street Parish**

    (RC))

Patrick Power (father):

Residence - 25 Cuffe Street - August 23, 1872

35 Cuffe Street - February 2, 1875

- Judith Harris & James Moylan

    o Henry Moylan – bapt. 4 Dec 1810 (Baptism, **Bandon Parish** (RC))

- Judith Harris & Walter Morrisson

    o James Morrisson – bapt. 19 Feb 1761 (Baptism, **Cork - South Parish** (RC))

- Julia Harris & James Moylan

    o James Moylan – bapt. 16 Aug 1815 (Baptism, **Kinsale Parish** (RC))

    o John Moylan – bapt. 11 Nov 1821 (Baptism, **Kinsale Parish** (RC))

    o Hannah Moylan – bapt. 27 Mar 1832 (Baptism, **Kinsale Parish** (RC))

Jacob Moylan (father):

Residence - Higher P - March 27, 1832

- Julia Harris & Jeremiah Riordan

    o Mary Riordan – b. 24 Apr 1881, bapt. 24 Apr 1881 (Baptism, **Glenbeigh/Glencar Parish**

    (RC))

Jeremiah Riordan (father):

Residence - Curraheen - April 24, 1881

- Julia Harris & John Hare

  - William Hare – b. 10 Sep 1849, bapt. 10 Sep 1849 (Baptism, **Tralee Parish** (RC))

John Hare (father):

Residence - Ballymullen - September 10, 1849

- Julia Harris & John Hea

  - Catherine Hea – b. 29 Sep 1837, bapt. 29 Sep 1837 (Baptism, **Killorglin Parish** (RC))

John Hea (father):

Residence - Aunagarry - September 29, 1837

- Julia Harris & John Mahony

  - John Mahony – bapt. 18 Nov 1846 (Baptism, **Murragh & Templemartin Parish** (RC))

- Julia Harris & John O'Hayes

  - James O'Hayes – b. 6 Apr 1833, bapt. 6 Apr 1833 (Baptism, **Tralee Parish** (RC))

  - Jane O'Hayes – b. 25 Mar 1835, bapt. 25 Mar 1835 (Baptism, **Tralee Parish** (RC))

  - Bartholomew O'Hayes – b. 21 Oct 1839, bapt. 21 Oct 1839 (Baptism, **Tralee Parish** (RC))

  - John O'Hayes – b. 30 Oct 1841, bapt. 30 Oct 1841 (Baptism, **Tralee Parish** (RC))

  - Mary O'Hayes – b. 21 Jan 1844, bapt. 21 Jan 1844 (Baptism, **Tralee Parish** (RC))

  - Catherine O'Hayes – b. 20 Apr 1848, bapt. 20 Apr 1848 (Baptism, **Tralee Parish** (RC))

John O'Hayes (father):

Residence - Clahane - April 6, 1833

Tralee - March 25, 1835

Ballymullen - October 21, 1839

October 30, 1841

January 21, 1844

April 20, 1848

Hurst

- Julia Harris & Maurice Roache

  - Maurice Roache – b. 19 May 1850, bapt. 19 May 1850 (Baptism, **Glenbeigh/Glencar Parish** (RC))

Maurice Roache (father):

Residence - Knockbue - May 19, 1850

- Julia Harris & Michael Griffin – 1 Feb 1836 (Marriage, **Glenbeigh/Glencar Parish** (RC))

  - Mary Griffin – b. 18 Nov 1843, bapt. 18 Nov 1843 (Baptism, **Glenbeigh/Glencar Parish** (RC))

  - Helen Griffin – b. 1 Jun 1849, bapt. 1 Jun 1849 (Baptism, **Glenbeigh/Glencar Parish** (RC))

  - Catherine Griffin – b. 16 Jul 1851, bapt. 16 Jul 1851 (Baptism, **Glenbeigh/Glencar Parish** (RC))

  - Julia Griffin – b. 27 Jul 1855, bapt. 27 Jul 1855 (Baptism, **Glenbeigh/Glencar Parish** (RC))

Julia Harris (mother):

Residence - Kilnabrack - February 1, 1836

Michael Griffin (father):

Residence - Kilnabrack - November 18, 1843

June 1, 1849

July 16, 1851

Reennanallagane - July 27, 1855

- Julia Harris & Nicholas John O'Griffin – 26 Feb 1846 (Marriage, **Abbeydorney Parish** (RC))

  - Nicholas O'Griffin – b. 6 Jun 1845, bapt. 6 Jun 1845 (Baptism, **Tralee Parish** (RC))

  - Maurice O'Griffin – b. 15 Aug 1846, bapt. 15 Aug 1846 (Baptism, **Tralee Parish** (RC))

  - Jane O'Griffin – b. 20 Aug 1848, bapt. 20 Aug 1848 (Baptism, **Tralee Parish** (RC))

Harris Surname Ireland: 1600s to 1900s

Nicholas John O'Griffin (father):

 Residence - Slieve - June 6, 1845

 Knockanish - August 15, 1846

 Slievenafidoig - August 20, 1848

- Julia Harris & Patrick Riordan

  o Mary Riordan – b. 23 Nov 1876, bapt. 23 Nov 1876 (Baptism, **Glenbeigh/Glencar Parish** (RC))

Patrick Riordan (father):

 Residence - Kilkeehagh - November 23, 1876

- Julia Harris & Patrick Sullivan

  o Michael Sullivan – b. 24 Sep 1888, bapt. 27 Sep 1888 (Baptism, **Killarney Parish** (RC))

Patrick Sullivan (father):

 Residence - Killorglin - September 27, 1888

- Julia Harris & Thomas Forde

  o Catherine Forde – bapt. Mar 1857 (Baptism, **Ballinhassig Parish** (RC))

- Julia Jane Harris & Timothy Foley

  o Joseph Foley – b. 25 Apr 1821, bapt. 25 Apr 1821 (Baptism, **Kenmare Parish** (RC))

  o Timothy Foley – b. 31 May 1823, bapt. 31 May 1823 (Baptism, **Kenmare Parish** (RC))

Timothy Foley (father):

 Residence - Reen - April 25, 1821

 May 31, 1823

Hurst

- Julianna Harris & Abraham Jagoe

  o John Jagoe – bapt. 20 Oct 1816 (Baptism, **Skibbereen (Creagh & Sullon) Parish (RC)**)

  o Patrick Jagoe – bapt. 30 May 1819 (Baptism, **Skibbereen (Creagh & Sullon) Parish (RC)**)

  o William Jagoe – bapt. 18 Nov 1821 (Baptism, **Skibbereen (Creagh & Sullon) Parish (RC)**)

  o Thomas Jagoe – bapt. 25 Jul 1824 (Baptism, **Skibbereen (Creagh & Sullon) Parish (RC)**)

Abraham Jagoe (father):

    Residence - Gortnaclohy - October 20, 1816

                    November 18, 1821

                    July 25, 1824

- Julianna Harris & Richard Donovan

  o Jane Donovan – bapt. 19 Jan 1807 (Baptism, **Lislee, Abbeymahon, & Donoughmore (Barryroe) Parish (RC)**)

Richard Donovan (father):

    Residence - Spuria Lislevane - January 19, 1807

- Lucy Harris & Thomas Browne

  o Esther Browne – bapt. 15 Apr 1805 (Baptism, **St. Catherine Parish (RC)**)

  o Catherine Browne – b. 7 Jan 1810, bapt. 14 Jan 1810 (Baptism, **St. Catherine Parish (RC)**)

  o Edward Browne – bapt. Apr 1811 (Baptism, **St. Catherine Parish (RC)**)

- Ma Harris & Thomas McKenna – 8 Feb 1834 (Marriage, **Annascaul Parish (RC)**)

- Magdalen Harris & Thomas Weyburn – 4 Feb 1749 (Marriage, **St. Catherine Parish (RC)**)

  o Mary Weyburn – bapt. 17 Feb 1771 (Baptism, **St. Catherine Parish (RC)**)

Harris Surname Ireland: 1600s to 1900s

- Margaret Harris & Brien O'Brien

  o Margaret O'Brien – bapt. May 1777 (Baptism, **Cork - South Parish** (RC))

- Margaret Harris & Christopher Southwell – 3 Feb 1781 (Marriage, **St. Andrew Parish** (RC))

- Margaret Harris & Daniel Cahillan

  o Margaret Cahillan – bapt. 5 May 1808 (Baptism, **Lislee, Abbeymahon, & Donoughmore**

  (Barryroe) Parish (RC))

Daniel Cahillan (father):

  Residence - Currihevern - May 5, 1808

- Margaret Harris & Daniel McCarthy

  o Catherine McCarthy – bapt. 17 Nov 1821 (Baptism, **Kinsale Parish** (RC))

- Margaret Harris & Dennis Murphy – 25 Sep 1827 (Marriage, **Cork - South Parish** (RC))

- Margaret Harris & Dennis O'Sullivan – 9 Feb 1839 (Marriage, **Tralee Parish** (RC))

  o Mary O'Sullivan – b. 16 Apr 1840, bapt. 16 Apr 1840 (Baptism, **Tralee Parish** (RC))

  o Jane O'Sullivan – b. 28 Aug 1842, bapt. 28 Aug 1842 (Baptism, **Tralee Parish** (RC))

  o Catherine O'Sullivan – b. 28 May 1845, bapt. 28 May 1845 (Baptism, **Tralee Parish** (RC))

  o Sarah O'Sullivan – b. 11 Sep 1848, bapt. 11 Sep 1848 (Baptism, **Tralee Parish** (RC))

Margaret Harris (mother):

  Residence - Curraheen - February 9, 1839

Dennis O'Sullivan (father):

  Residence - Curraheen - February 9, 1839

  Tralee - April 16, 1840

  August 28, 1842

  May 28, 1845

  September 11, 1848

- Margaret Harris & Hugo Reddy – 2 Nov 1835 (Marriage, **St. Michan Parish** (RC))

Hurst

- Margaret Harris & James Brien

  o John Brien – bapt. 1 May 1859 (Baptism, **Skibbereen (Creagh & Sullon) Parish** (RC))

James Brien (father):

Residence - New Road - May 1, 1859

- Margaret Harris & James McCannon

  o Margaret McCannon – b. 21 Oct 1885, bapt. 16 Nov 1885 (Baptism, **St. Mary, Pro Cathedral Parish** (RC))

James McCannon (father):

Residence - 193 Great Britain Street - November 16, 1885

- Margaret Harris & John Eaton – 29 Jan 1861 (Marriage, **Cork - SS. Peter & Paul Parish** (RC))

  o Henry Eaton – b. 2 June 1861, bapt. 16 Jun 1861 (Baptism, **Cork - SS. Peter & Paul Parish** (RC))

  o Mary Anne Eaton – b. 30 Oct 1862, bapt. 17 Nov 1862 (Baptism, **Cork - SS. Peter & Paul Parish** (RC))

John Eaton (father):

Residence - Cork - January 29, 1861

- Margaret Harris & John Leary – 6 Nov 1853 (Marriage, **Cork - South Parish** (RC))

- Margaret Harris & Matthew Maher – 4 Apr 1802 (Marriage, **SS. Michael & John Parish** (RC))

- Margaret Harris & Michael Corcoran – 25 Jan 1820 (Marriage, **Cork - South Parish** (RC))

  o John Corcoran – bapt. 3 Dec 1820 (Baptism, **Cork - South Parish** (RC))

  o Michael Corcoran – bapt. 8 Jan 1823 (Baptism, **Cork - South Parish** (RC))

Margaret Harris (mother):

Residence - Cat Lane - January 25, 1820

- Margaret Harris & Michael Corcoran

  o Michael Corcoran – b. 1 Nov 1880, bapt. 11 Nov 1880 (Baptism, **Cork - SS. Peter & Paul Parish** (RC))

Harris Surname Ireland: 1600s to 1900s

- Margaret Harris & Michael Daly – 20 Feb 1868 (Marriage, **Firies Parish** (RC))

Michael Daly (husband):

Residence - **Dromore** - February 20, 1868

- Margaret Harris & Michael Dempsey – 13 Sep 1828 (Marriage, **Kinsale Parish** (RC))

   o   Jeremiah Dempsey – bapt. 22 Dec 1830 (Baptism, **Kinsale Parish** (RC))

   o   Patrick Dempsey – bapt. 5 Sep 1832 (Baptism, **Kinsale Parish** (RC))

   o   William Dempsey – bapt. 16 Sep 1834 (Baptism, **Innishannon Parish** (RC))

   o   John Dempsey – bapt. 9 May 1838 (Baptism, **Clontead Parish** (RC))

   o   James Dempsey – bapt. 13 Jul 1840 (Baptism, **Kinsale Parish** (RC))

   o   Dennis Dempsey – bapt. 17 May 1842 (Baptism, **Kinsale Parish** (RC))

   o   Margaret Dempsey – bapt. 23 Jan 1844 (Baptism, **Kinsale Parish** (RC))

Michael Dempsey (father):

Residence - **Ballyregan** - December 22, 1830

September 5, 1832

BK Street - July 13, 1840

May 17, 1842

- Margaret Harris & Michael Flanagan

   o   Thomas Flanagan – bapt. 11 Jul 1813 (Baptism, **St. Michan Parish** (RC))

- Margaret Harris & Michael Fleming – 15 Nov 1807 (Marriage, **SS. Michael & John Parish**

   (RC))

Hurst

- Margaret Harris & Michael Keegan

  - Mary Esther Keegan – b. 12 Apr 1897, bapt. 20 Apr 1897 (Baptism, **Harrington Street Parish** (RC))

  - Margaret Keegan – b. 21 Nov 1898, bapt. 22 Nov 1898 (Baptism, **Harrington Street Parish** (RC))

  - Honora Anne Keegan – b. 26 May 1901, bapt. 31 May 1901 (Baptism, **Harrington Street Parish** (RC))

Michael Keegan (father):

Residence - 119 Lower Clanbrassil Street - April 20, 1897

5 Malpas Street - November 22, 1898

May 31, 1901

- Margaret Harris & Michael Rooney – 23 Jan 1843 (Marriage, **SS. Michael & John Parish** (RC))

  - Mary Rooney – bapt. 24 Jul 1845 (Baptism, **SS. Michael & John Parish** (RC))

- Margaret Harris & Michael Sullivan – 19 May 1829 (Marriage, **Milltown Parish** (RC))

Michael Sullivan (husband):

Residence - Milltown - May 19, 1829

- Margaret Harris & Michael Sullivan

  - John Sullivan – b. 29 Jun 1844, bapt. 29 Jun 1844 (Baptism, **Tuosist Parish** (RC))

Michael Sullivan (father):

Residence - Bunna - June 29, 1844

- Margaret Harris & Michael Walsh

  - Nicholas Walsh – bapt. 23 Jun 1851 (Baptism, **St. James Parish** (RC))

  - Margaret Mary Walsh – bapt. 13 Aug 1855 (Baptism, **St. James Parish** (RC))

Michael Walsh (father):

Residence - Kilmainham - August 13, 1855

Harris Surname Ireland: 1600s to 1900s

- Margaret Harris & Murtagh Buckley – 7 Mar 1859 (Marriage, **Kilgarvan Parish** (RC))

  o Mary Buckley – b. 15 Apr 1860, bapt. 15 Apr 1860 (Baptism, **Kilgarvan Parish** (RC))

Murtagh Buckley (father):

Residence - Clountow - March 7, 1859

April 15, 1860

- Margaret Harris & Oliver William

  o Christopher William – bapt. 31 Mar 1797 (Baptism, **St. Michan Parish** (RC))

- Margaret Harris & Patrick McCarthy

  o Margaret McCarthy – bapt. 14 Jan 1815 (Baptism, **Lislee, Abbeymahon, &**

  Donoughmore (Barryroe) Parish (RC))

Patrick McCarthy (father):

Residence - Lislevane - January 14, 1815

- Margaret Harris & Patrick Moore

  o Jane Moore – bapt. 9 Sep 1856 (Baptism, **St. Catherine Parish** (RC))

  o Thomas Moore – b. 3 Dec 1858, bapt. 7 Dec 1858 (Baptism, **St. Catherine Parish** (RC))

Patrick Moore (father):

Residence - 14 Vicar Street - December 7, 1858

- Margaret Harris & Peter Byrne (B y r n e) – 12 Feb 1804 (Marriage, **SS. Michael & John Parish**

  (RC))

- Margaret Harris & Peter Foley

  o Daniel Foley – bapt. 4 May 1845 (Baptism, **Schull West Parish** (RC))

  o Michael Foley – bapt. Sep 1850 (Baptism, **Skibbereen (Creagh & Sullon) Parish** (RC))

- Margaret Harris & Thomas Davis – 7 Jul 1692 (Marriage, **St. John Parish**)

Hurst

- Margaret Harris & Thomas Evans – 1 Jun 1854 (Marriage, **Castlemaine Parish** (RC))

  - Ellen Evans – b. 17 May 1855, bapt. 17 May 1855 (Baptism, **Castlemaine Parish** (RC))

  - Thomas Evans – b. 30 Apr 1857, bapt. 30 Apr 1857 (Baptism, **Castlemaine Parish** (RC))

  - Mary Evans – b. 29 Jan 1860, bapt. 29 Jan 1860 (Marriage, **Castlemaine Parish** (RC))

Margaret Harris (mother):

Residence - Shanahill - June 1, 1854

May 17, 1855

April 30, 1857

January 29, 1860

- Margaret Harris & Unknown

  - Maud Unknown – b. 16 Dec 1904, bapt. 28 Mar 1905 (Marriage, **Rathmines Parish** (RC))

Margaret Harris (mother):

Residence - 18 Emmet's Street - March 28, 1905

- Margaret Harris & William Aherne (A h e r n e)

  - Michael Aherne – bapt. 8 Sep 1844 (Baptism, **Douglas Parish** (RC))

  - Patrick Aherne – bapt. 31 May 1865 (Baptism, **Cork - South Parish** (RC))

William Aherne (father):

Residence - Ballygarvin - September 8, 1844

- Margaret Harris & William Cartwright

  - Margaret Cartwright – bapt. 3 Feb 1826 (Baptism, **Kinsale Parish** (RC))

- Margaret Harris & William Crossby

  - James Crossby – bapt. 20 Nov 1834 (Baptism, **St. James Parish** (RC))

Harris Surname Ireland: 1600s to 1900s

- Martha Harris & James Hudson

  o Unknown Hudson – b. 9 Feb 1855, bapt. 21 Feb 1855 (Baptism, **St. Nicholas Parish** (RC))

  o Rosanna Hudson – b. 10 May 1865, bapt. 17 May 1865 (Baptism, **St. Nicholas Parish** (RC))

James Hudson (father):
Residence - 12 Ross Lane - February 21, 1855
23 Chancery Lane - May 17, 1865

- Martha Harris & John Benson – 17 May 1797 (Marriage, **Kilnaughtin Parish**)

- Mary Harris & Alfred Stone

  o William Stone – b. 1868, bapt. 1888 (Baptism, **St. Andrew Parish** (RC))

Alfred Stone (father):
Residence - Portabello Brook Premises of PG - 1888

- Mary Harris & Anthony Ophum – 16 Feb 1632 (Marriage, **St. John Parish**)

- Mary Harris & Christian Harman (H a r m a n) – 20 Sep 1766 (Marriage, **St. Anne Parish**)

- Mary Harris & Daniel Counusig

  o Unknown Counusig – bapt. Sep 1823 (Baptism, **Ardfield & Rathbarry Parish** (RC))

- Mary Harris & Daniel Daly

  o Daniel Daly – bapt. 28 Jan 1816 (Baptism, **Rossalettiri & Kilkeraunmor (Roscarbery & Lissevard) Parish** (RC))

- Mary Harris & Daniel Gnaw

  o Daniel Gnaw – b. 18 Aug 1827, bapt. 18 Aug 1827 (Baptism, **Milltown Parish** (RC))

  o Michael Gnaw – b. 23 Aug 1831, bapt. 23 Aug 1831 (Baptism, **Milltown Parish** (RC))

Daniel Gnaw (father):
Residence - Callanafersy - August 18, 1827
August 23, 1831

Hurst

- Mary Harris & Daniel Kerncane (K e r n c a n e) – 14 Jan 1827 (Marriage, **Innishannon Parish (RC)**)

  o Daniel Kerncane – bapt. 15 Jan 1828 (Baptism, **Innishannon Parish** (RC))

  o John Kerncane – bapt. 3 Apr 1831 (Baptism, **Innishannon Parish** (RC))

  o Dennis Kerncane – bapt. Aug 1834 (Baptism, **Ballinhassig Parish** (RC))

- Mary Harris & Daniel Leary

  o John Leary – bapt. 9 Dec 1840 (Baptism, **Bantry Parish** (RC))

- Mary Harris & Daniel Sullivan

  o Jerry Sullivan – bapt. 29 Aug 1803 (Baptism, **Cork - South Parish** (RC))

  o Margaret Sullivan – bapt. 18 Jun 1809 (Baptism, **Cork - South Parish** (RC))

  o Richard Sullivan – bapt. 2 Aug 1812 (Baptism, **Cork - South Parish** (RC))

Daniel Sullivan (father):

Residence - Lamly's Lane - August 29, 1803

Allen's Lane - June 18, 1809

- Mary Harris & Dennis Gorman (G o r m a n)

  o Mary Gorman – bapt. 5 Feb 1843 (Baptism, **Skibbereen (Creagh & Sullon) Parish** (RC))

- Mary Harris & Dennis Murnane (M u r n a n e)

  o Catherine Murnane – b. 1 Oct 1850, bapt. 1 Oct 1850 (Baptism, **Rathmore Parish** (RC))

Dennis Murnane (father):

Residence - Fournase - October 1, 1850

- Mary Harris & Dennis Regan

  o James Regan – b. 23 May 1852, bapt. 23 May 1852 (Baptism, **Rathmore Parish** (RC))

Dennis Regan (father):

Residence - Fournase - May 23, 1852

Harris Surname Ireland: 1600s to 1900s

- Mary Harris & Dennis Riordan

    o Catherine Riordan – b. 25 Oct 1875, bapt. 25 Oct 1875 (Baptism, **Cork - South Parish**

    (RC))

- Mary Harris & Dennis Ryan

    o Jeremiah Ryan – b. 12 May 1854, bapt. 12 May 1854 (Baptism, **Rathmore Parish (RC)**)

    o Ellen Ryan – b. 24 Jul 1856, bapt. 24 Jul 1856 (Baptism, **Rathmore Parish (RC)**)

    o Daniel Ryan – b. 23 May 1858, bapt. 23 May 1858 (Baptism, **Rathmore Parish (RC)**)

    o Mary Ryan – b. 20 May 1860, bapt. 20 May 1860 (Baptism, **Rathmore Parish (RC)**)

Dennis Ryan (father):

Residence - Fournase - May 12, 1854

July 24, 1856

May 23, 1858

May 20, 1860

- Mary Harris & Dionysius McDonald – 19 Aug 1805 (Marriage, **St. Andrew Parish** (RC))

- Mary Harris & Edward Crowly – 6 Jul 1873 (Marriage, **Cork - South Parish** (RC))

    o Edward Crowly – bapt. 15 May 1874 (Baptism, **Cork - South Parish** (RC))

- Mary Harris & Edward Reilly

    o William Reilly – bapt. 8 Mar 1847 (Baptism, **St. Michan Parish** (RC))

    o Catherine Reilly – bapt. 12 Mar 1849 (Baptism, **St. Michan Parish** (RC))

    o Unknown Reilly – bapt. Oct 1850 (Baptism, **St. Michan Parish** (RC))

    o Patrick Reilly – bapt. Mar 1853 (Baptism, **St. Michan Parish** (RC))

Hurst

- Mary Harris & Elisha Lewis Burnam (B u r n a m)

  - Elizabeth Burnam – b. 22 Jan 1859, bapt. 22 Jan 1859 (Baptism, **Tralee Parish** (RC))

  - Jane Burnam – b. 22 Jan 1859, bapt. 22 Jan 1859 (Baptism, **Tralee Parish** (RC))

  - Ellen Burnam – b. 26 Nov 1860, bapt. 2 Dec 1860 (Baptism, **Tralee Parish** (RC))

Elisha Lewis Burnam (father):

Residence - Tralee - January 22, 1859

December 2, 1860

- Mary Harris & Eugene Donovan – 3 Mar 1772 (Marriage, **Cork - SS. Peter & Paul Parish** (RC))

  - Eleanor Donovan – bapt. 4 Jan 1773 (Baptism, **Cork - SS. Peter & Paul Parish** (RC))

- Mary Harris & Eugene Raly

  - Mary Raly – b. 30 Apr 1842, bapt. 30 Apr 1842 (Baptism, **Glenbeigh/Glencar Parish** (RC))

Eugene Raly (father):

Residence - Clohane - April 30, 1842

- Mary Harris & George Carleton – 20 May 1730 (Marriage, **St. Mary Parish**)

- Mary Harris & Henry Smyth

  - Mary Smyth – b. 3 Jan 1862, bapt. 13 Jan 1862 (Baptism, **St. James Parish** (RC))

Henry Smyth (father):

Residence - Golden Bridge - January 13, 1862

- Mary Harris & Henry Willow

  - Ellen Willow – b. 17 Jan 1809, bapt. 17 Jan 1809 (Baptism, **Tralee Parish** (RC))

  - Bridget Willow – b. 2 Oct 1810, bapt. 2 Oct 1810 (Baptism, **Tralee Parish** (RC))

Henry Willow (father):

Residence - Ballinvadarough - January 17, 1809

Ballyanaulorth - October 2, 1810

Harris Surname Ireland: 1600s to 1900s

- Mary Harris & Humphrey Desmond – 9 Feb 1844 (Marriage, **Innishannon Parish** (RC))

- Mary Harris & James Brown

    o Peter Brown – bapt. 27 Apr 1849 (Baptism, **St. Nicholas Parish** (RC))

- Mary Harris & James Egan

    o Catherine Egan – b. 29 Jun 1832, bapt. 29 Jun 1832 (Baptism, **Milltown Parish** (RC))

James Egan (father):

Residence - Lyrby - June 29, 1832

- Mary Harris & James English – 12 Feb 1782 (Marriage, **Cork - South Parish** (RC))

    o Peter English – bapt. 19 Jan 1794 (Baptism, **Cork - South Parish** (RC))

    o James English – bapt. 23 Nov 1803 (Baptism, **Cork - South Parish** (RC))

James English (father):

Residence - Bishop Street - November 23, 1803

- Mary Harris & James Keefe – 12 Feb 1829 (Marriage, **Innishannon Parish** (RC))

    o John Keefe – bapt. Apr 1830 (Baptism, **Ballinhassig Parish** (RC))

    o Julia Keefe – bapt. 25 Aug 1831 (Baptism, **Ballinhassig Parish** (RC))

    o Richard Keefe – bapt. Nov 1833 (Baptism, **Ballinhassig Parish** (RC))

    o Daniel Keefe – bapt. Jun 1836 (Baptism, **Ballinhassig Parish** (RC))

    o Margaret Keefe – bapt. 11 Jan 1840 (Baptism, **Ballinhassig Parish** (RC))

    o Joan Keefe – bapt. 21 Jan 1844 (Baptism, **Ballinhassig Parish** (RC))

    o Patrick Keefe – bapt. Jul 1846 (Baptism, **Ballinhassig Parish** (RC))

Hurst

- Mary Harris & James Quinn

    o John Quinn – bapt. 8 Jan 1822 (Baptism, **Cork - South Parish** (RC))

    o Thomas Quinn – bapt. 5 Feb 1826 (Baptism, **Cork - South Parish** (RC))

    o Margaret Quinn – bapt. 14 Apr 1828 (Baptism, **Cork - South Parish** (RC))

    o Mary Quinn – bapt. 29 Dec 1830 (Baptism, **Cork - South Parish** (RC))

    o Honora Quinn – bapt. Apr 1833 (Baptism, **Cork - South Parish** (RC))

    o Thomas Quinn – bapt. 23 May 1836 (Baptism, **Cork - South Parish** (RC))

    o Bridget Quinn – bapt. 28 Jan 1838 (Baptism, **Cork - South Parish** (RC))

- Mary Harris & James Reilly

    o Gulielmo Reilly – b. 28 Aug 1884, bapt. 2 Sep 1884 (Baptism, **Harrington Street Parish** (RC))

    o James Reilly – b. 30 Aug 1886, bapt. 7 Sep 1886 (Baptism, **Harrington Street Parish** (RC))

    o Thomas Reilly – b. 2 Sep 1888, bapt. 4 Sep 1888 (Baptism, **Harrington Street Parish** (RC))

    o Bridget Reilly – b. 3 Aug 1890, bapt. 5 Aug 1890 (Baptism, **Harrington Street Parish** (RC))

    o George Joseph Reilly – b. 22 Mar 1892, bapt. 29 Mar 1892 (Baptism, **Harrington Street Parish** (RC))

James Reilly (father):

Residence - 2 Orrs Cottages - September 2, 1884

2 Holts Cottages Synge Street - September 7, 1886

September 4, 1888

August 5, 1890

2 Boyds Cottages - March 29, 1892

Harris Surname Ireland: 1600s to 1900s

- Mary Harris & James Riordan

  - James Riordan – b. 13 Apr 1886, bapt. 18 Apr 1886 (Baptism, **Glenbeigh/Glencar Parish (RC)**)

James Riordan (father):

Residence - Kilkeehagh - April 18, 1886

- Mary Harris & James Rooney – 16 May 1819 (Marriage, **St. Andrew Parish** (RC))

- Mary Harris & James Supple – 27 Dec 1808 (Marriage, **St. Catherine Parish** (RC))

- Mary Harris & James Watson – 26 Apr 1786 (Marriage, **St. Mark Parish**)

- Mary Harris & James Wild – 27 Jul 1812 (Marriage, **St. Peter Parish**)

- Mary Harris & James Worthington

  - Anne Worthington – bapt. Dec 1832 (Baptism, **Cork - South Parish** (RC))

  - Catherine Worthington – bapt. Nov 1835 (Baptism, **Cork - South Parish** (RC))

  - Julia Worthington – bapt. 27 Jul 1839 (Baptism, **Cork - South Parish** (RC))

- Mary Harris & Jerry Corbett

  - John Corbett – bapt. 2 Jun 1792 (Baptism, **Cork - South Parish** (RC))

  - Mary Corbett & John Buckley – 8 Apr 1815 (Marriage, **Douglas Parish** (RC))

    - Mary Buckley – bapt. 31 Mar 1816 (Baptism, **Cork - South Parish** (RC))

    - Jane Buckley – bapt. 16 Jan 1819 (Baptism, **Cork - South Parish** (RC))

Mary Corbett (daughter):

Residence - Ballygarvan - April 8, 1815

John Buckley (son-in-law):

Residence - Ballygarvan - April 8, 1815

Hurst

- Mary Harris & John Buckley – 24 Apr 1833 (Marriage, **Dromtariffe Parish** (RC))

  - Patrick Buckley – b. 1 Jan 1834, bapt. 1 Jan 1834 (Baptism, **Boherbue Parish** (RC))

  - Bridget Buckley – b. 24 Jul 1836, bapt. 24 Jul 1836 (Baptism, **Boherbue Parish** (RC))

  - Dermot (D e r m o t) Buckley – b. 18 Dec 1838, bapt. 18 Dec 1838 (Baptism, **Boherbue Parish** (RC))

  - Mary Buckley – b. 16 Nov 1841, bapt. 16 Nov 1841 (Baptism, **Boherbue Parish** (RC))

  - Julie Anne Buckley – b. 1 Jan 1844, bapt. 1 Jan 1844 (Baptism, **Boherbue Parish** (RC))

Margaret Harris (mother):

Residence - Drominagh - April 24, 1833

John Buckley (father):

Residence - Maule - March 1, 1834

July 24, 1836

December 18, 1838

November 16, 1841

January 1, 1844

- Mary Harris & John Carney (C a r n e y)

  - Elizabeth Carney – bapt. 12 May 1807 (Baptism, **St. Catherine Parish** (RC))

  - Mary Anne Carney – bapt. 16 Nov 1813 (Baptism, **St. Catherine Parish** (RC))

- Mary Harris & John Carroll

  - Patrick Carroll – bapt. 26 Feb 1761 (Baptism, **Cork - South Parish** (RC))

- Mary Harris & John Downs

  - James Downs – b. 1 Apr 1801, bapt. 1 Apr 1801 (Baptism, **Tralee Parish** (RC))

- Mary Harris & John Fisher

  - William Fisher – bapt. 27 Jan 1825 (Baptism, **SS. Michael & John Parish** (RC))

Harris Surname Ireland: 1600s to 1900s

- Mary Harris & John Kearney (K e a r n e y)

  o Teresa Kearney – bapt. 25 Apr 1816 (Baptism, St. Catherine Parish (RC))

  o John Kearney – bapt. 3 Jan 1819 (Baptism, St. Catherine Parish (RC))

- Mary Harris & John Kennedy

  o Timothy Kennedy – bapt. 7 Feb 1835 (Baptism, Kilmurry, Moviddy, Kilbonane, & Cannavee Parish (RC))

John Kennedy (father):

Residence - Aherlabeg - February 7, 1835

- Mary Harris & John Kenney

  o Mary Kenney – bapt. 12 Mar 1809 (Baptism, St. Catherine Parish (RC))

- Mary Harris & John Loftus

  o Michael Loftus – b. 2 Oct 1869, bapt. 15 Oct 1869 (Baptism, St. Nicholas Parish (RC))

  o John Joseph Loftus – b. 5 Jul 1875, bapt. 16 Jul 1875 (Baptism, St. Nicholas Parish (RC))

John Loftus (father):

Residence - 4 Plunket Street - October 15, 1869

July 16, 1875

- Mary Harris & John McCabe

  o Frances McCabe – bapt. 8 Oct 1826 (Baptism, Cork - South Parish (RC))

  o William McCabe – bapt. 7 Mar 1829 (Baptism, Cork - South Parish (RC))

Hurst

- Mary Harris & John McCarthy

  - Thomas Peter McCarthy – b. 13 Jul 1876, bapt. Jul 1876 (Baptism, **St. Catherine Parish (RC)**)

  - Charles McCarthy – b. 23 Aug 1878, bapt. Aug 1878 (Baptism, **St. Catherine Parish (RC)**)

  - John McCarthy – b. 14 Jan 1880, bapt. Jan 1880 (Baptism, **St. Catherine Parish (RC)**)

John McCarthy (father):

Residence - 14 Meath Street - June 1876

August 1878

January 1880

- Mary Harris John McDonald

  - Catherine McDonald – bapt. 1 Apr 1858 (Baptism, **Timoleague Parish (RC)**)

  - Catherine McDonald – bapt. 2 Dec 1860 (Baptism, **Timoleague Parish (RC)**)

John McDonald (father):

Residence - Burrane - April 1, 1858

- Mary Harris & John Maguire – 19 Jul 1807 (Marriage, **St. Mary, Pro Cathedral Parish (RC)**)

- Mary Harris & John Moriarty

  - Patrick Moriarty – b. 5 Feb 1877, bapt. 5 Feb 1877 (Baptism, **Glenbeigh/Glencar Parish (RC)**)

  - John Moriarty – b. 7 Apr 1878, bapt. 7 Apr 1878 (Baptism, **Glenbeigh/Glencar Parish (RC)**)

  - Julia Moriarty – b. 27 Mar 1881, bapt. 27 Mar 1881 (Baptism, **Glenbeigh/Glencar Parish (RC)**)

  - Bridget Moriarty – b. 11 Nov 1883, bapt. 11 Nov 1883 (Baptism, **Glenbeigh/Glencar Parish (RC)**)

- o Dennis Moriarty – b. 29 Feb 1888, bapt. 4 Mar 1888 (Baptism, **Glenbeigh/Glencar Parish** (RC))

- o Joan Moriarty – b. 6 Oct 1889, bapt. 6 Oct 1889 (Baptism, **Glenbeigh/Glencar Parish** (RC))

- o Michael Moriarty – b. 1 Aug 1893, bapt. 6 Aug 1893 (Baptism, **Glenbeigh/Glencar Parish** (RC))

- o Thaddeus Moriarty – b. 18 Sep 1895, bapt. 22 Sep 1895 (Baptism, **Glenbeigh/Glencar Parish** (RC))

- o James Moriarty – b. 28 Oct 1897, bapt. 30 Oct 1897 (Baptism, **Glenbeigh/Glencar Parish** (RC))

- o John Moriarty – b. 3 May 1899, bapt. 7 May 1899 (Baptism, **Glenbeigh/Glencar Parish** (RC))

John Moriarty (father):

Residence - Boherbee - March 4, 1888

Drom - February 5, 1877

April 7, 1878

March 27, 1881

November 11, 1883

October 6, 1889

May 7, 1899

Upper Drom - August 6, 1893

September 22, 1895

Knockboy - October 30, 1897

- Mary Harris & John Murphy – 4 Apr 1754 (Marriage, **St. Catherine Parish** (RC))

- Mary Harris & John Murphy – 15 May 1874 (Marriage, **Kilmichael Parish** (RC))

- Mary Harris & John Nicholson – 16 Apr 1860 (Marriage, **Cork - South Parish** (RC))

Hurst

- Mary Harris & John O'Higgins – 27 Jan 1846 (Marriage, **Tralee Parish** (RC))

Mary Harris (wife):

   Residence - Curraheen - January 27, 1846

John O'Higgins (husband):

   Residence - Curraheen - January 27, 1846

- Mary Harris & John O'Neill – 1 Jun 1837 (Marriage, **Kinsale Parish** (RC))

- Mary Harris & John Riordan

  - Daniel Riordan – b. 1 May 1855, bapt. 1 May 1855 (Baptism, **Glenbeigh/Glencar Parish** (RC))

  - John Riordan – b. 25 Feb 1859, bapt. 25 Feb 1859 (Baptism, **Glenbeigh/Glencar Parish** (RC))

  - Mary Riordan – b. 11 Jan 1865, bapt. 11 Jan 1865 (Baptism, **Glenbeigh/Glencar Parish** (RC))

John Riordan (father):

   Residence - Drom - May 1, 1855

                     February 25, 1859

                     January 11, 1865

- Mary Harris & John Splaine – 3 Feb 1838 (Marriage, **Murragh & Templemartin Parish** (RC))

- Mary Harris & Joseph Boodman Blair – 10 Feb 1833 (Marriage, **St. Catherine Parish**)

- Mary Harris & Lawrence Foley – 25 Jan 1838 (Marriage, **Schull West Parish** (RC))

  - Mick Foley – bapt. 26 Sep 1841 (Baptism, **Schull West Parish** (RC))

- Mary Harris & Matthew Keary

  - Bartholomew Keary – bapt. 18 Apr 1845 (Baptism, **Enniskeane Parish** (RC))

Harris Surname Ireland: 1600s to 1900s

- Mary Harris & Matthew Summerlin

  o Matthew Summerlin – bapt. 3 Jul 1803 (Baptism, **Cork - South Parish (RC)**)

Matthew Summerlin (father):

Occupation - 46ᵗʰ Regiment - July 3, 1803

- Mary Harris & Michael Culnane

  o Ellen Culnane – b. 5 Oct 1861, bapt. 10 Oct 1861 (Baptism, **Cork - SS. Peter & Paul Parish (RC)**)

- Mary Harris & Michael Corkran

  o Mary Corkran – bapt. 16 Mar 1825 (Baptism, **Cork - South Parish (RC)**)

- Mary Harris & Michael Grattan

  o Margaret Grattan – bapt. 15 Jan 1808 (Baptism, **St. Catherine Parish (RC)**)

- Mary Harris & Michael Henston

  o Arthur Henston – bapt. 3 Jan 1847 (Baptism, **Cork - South Parish (RC)**)

- Mary Harris & Michael Hoey

  o Jane Hoey – bapt. 28 Nov 1785 (Baptism, **St. Catherine Parish (RC)**)

  o David Hoey – bapt. 2 Mar 1787 (Baptism, **St. Catherine Parish (RC)**)

  o Thomas Hoey – bapt. 16 Apr 1789 (Baptism, **St. Catherine Parish (RC)**)

- Mary Harris & Michael Mitchell

  o Bridget Mitchell – b. 10 Jan 1870, bapt. 18 Jan 1870 (Baptism, **Harrington Street Parish (RC)**)

Michael Mitchell (father):

Residence - 2 Malpas Street - January 18, 1870

Hurst

- Mary Harris & Michael Reynolds

  - M. Anne Reynolds – bapt. 13 Sep 1802 (Baptism, **St. Nicholas Parish** (RC))

  - William Reynolds – bapt. 17 Dec 1804 (Baptism, **SS. Michael & John Parish** (RC))

  - Michael Reynolds – bapt. 29 Nov 1807 (Baptism, **SS. Michael & John Parish** (RC))

- Mary Harris & Miles McCabe – 11 Nov 1773 (Marriage, **St. Nicholas Parish** (RC))

- Mary Harris & Morgan Finelen

  - Anne Finelen – bapt. 27 Feb 1828 (Baptism, **St. Catherine Parish** (RC))

- Mary Harris & Mortimer O'Whelan

  - Patrick O'Whelan – b. 11 Mar 1830, bapt. 11 Mar 1830 (Baptism, **Tralee Parish** (RC))

  - Mary O'Whelan – b. 30 Aug 1836, bapt. 30 Aug 1836 (Baptism, **Tralee Parish** (RC))

Mortimer O'Whelan (father):

Residence - Clashanipooca - March 11, 1830

Ballyroe - August 30, 1836

- Mary Harris & Owen Donovan

  - Bridget Donovan – bapt. 27 Oct 1787 (Baptism, **Cork - SS. Peter & Paul Parish** (RC))

- Mary Harris & Owen Egan

  - Anne Egan – bapt. 8 Aug 1780 (Baptism, **St. Catherine Parish** (RC))

- Mary Harris & Patrick Beggs

  - Anne Beggs – bapt. 22 Nov 1807 (Baptism, **St. Michan Parish** (RC))

  - Margaret Beggs – bapt. 9 Aug 1810 (Baptism, **St. Michan Parish** (RC))

  - Mary Beggs – bapt. 19 Jul 1812 (Baptism, **St. Michan Parish** (RC))

  - Margaret Beggs – bapt. 10 Jul 1814 (Baptism, **St. Michan Parish** (RC))

  - Catherine Beggs – bapt. 26 Dec 1815 (Baptism, **St. Michan Parish** (RC))

  - Joan Beggs – bapt. 29 Mar 1829 (Baptism, **St. Michan Parish** (RC))

Harris Surname Ireland: 1600s to 1900s

- Mary Harris & Patrick Byrne (B y r n e) – 5 Jun 1838 (Marriage, **St. Mary, Pro Cathedral Parish** (RC))

- Mary Harris & Patrick Donnolly – 7 Jan 1745 (Marriage, **SS. Michael & John Parish** (RC))

- Mary Harris & Patrick Gregan

  o Catherine Gregan – b. 28 Nov 1860, bapt. 3 Dec 1860 (Baptism, **St. Mary, Pro Cathedral Parish** (RC))

  o Patrick Stephen Gregan – b. 26 Dec 1862, bapt. 29 Dec 1862 (Baptism, **St. Mary, Pro Cathedral Parish** (RC))

Patrick Gregan (father):

Residence - 10 King's Inns Street - December 3, 1860

12 King's Inns Street - December 29, 1862

- Mary Harris & Patrick Hynes

  o Hannah Hynes – b. 21 Jun 1861, bapt. 24 Jun 1861 (Baptism, **St. Mary, Pro Cathedral Parish** (RC))

  o Edward Hynes – b. 12 May 1867, bapt. 15 May 1867 (Baptism, **St. Michan Parish** (RC))

Patrick Hynes (father):

Residence - 5 Ryder's Row - June 24, 1861

25 Beresford Street - May 15, 1867

471

Hurst

- Mary Harris & Patrick Riordan

  - Bridget Riordan – b. 26 Oct 1873, bapt. 26 Oct 1873 (Baptism, **Glenbeigh/Glencar Parish** (RC))

  - Catherine Riordan – b. 14 Aug 1881, bapt. 14 Aug 1881 (Baptism, **Glenbeigh/Glencar Parish** (RC))

  - Gobinet Riordan – b. 30 Dec 1883, bapt. 30 Dec 1883 (Baptism, **Glenbeigh/Glencar Parish** (RC))

Patrick Riordan (father):

    Residence - Kilkeehagh - October 26, 1873

              August 14, 1881

              December 30, 1883

- Mary Harris & Patrick Sullivan – 25 Sep 1844 (Marriage, **Cork - South Parish** (RC))

  - John Sullivan – bapt. 20 Nov 1845 (Baptism, **Cork - South Parish** (RC))

- Mary Harris & Philip Roach

  - Philip Roach – bapt. 2 May 1848 (Baptism, **St. Catherine Parish** (RC))

- Mary Harris & Philip Rorke – 3 May 1842 (Marriage, **St. Andrew Parish** (RC))

- Mary Harris & Philip Smyth – 28 Feb 1854 (Marriage, **Lucan Parish** (RC))

  - Anne Smyth – bapt. 1858 (Baptism, **Clondalkin Parish** (RC))

  - Mary Jane Smyth – bapt. 1861 (Baptism, **Clondalkin Parish** (RC))

Philip Smyth (father):

    Residence - Lucan - 1858

          1861

- Mary Harris & Robert Piggot – 21 Jun 1770 (Marriage, **Carlow Parish**)

- Mary Harris & Richard Bourke – 17 Sep 1780 (Marriage, **St. Nicholas Parish** (RC))

Harris Surname Ireland: 1600s to 1900s

- Mary Harris & Richard Coursey

    o Ellen Coursey – bapt. 29 Dec 1811 (Baptism, **Lislee, Abbeymahon, & Donoughmore**

    (Barryroe) Parish (RC))

Richard Coursey (father):

Residence - B McCratheen - December 29, 1811

- Mary Harris & Richard King – 6 Jan 1788 (Marriage, **Kilnaughtin Parish**)

- Mary Harris & Richard Splaine

    o Mary Splaine – bapt. 22 Aug 1826 (Baptism, **Kilmurry, Moviddy, Kilbonane, &**

    Cannavee Parish (RC))

Richard Splaine (father):

Residence - B Grolla - August 22, 1826

- Mary Harris & Sylvestor Connor

    o Mary Connor – b. 1779, bapt. 1779 (Baptism, **Rathfarnham Parish** (RC))

    o Catherine Connor – b. 1780, bapt. 1780 (Baptism, **Rathfarnham Parish** (RC))

- Mary Harris & Thaddeus Giles

    o Mary Giles – b. 9 Nov 1836, bapt. 9 Nov 1836 (Baptism, **Milltown Parish** (RC))

Thaddeus Giles (father):

Residence - Castlemaine - November 9, 1836

- Mary Harris & Thomas Broughy

    o Thomas Broughy – b. 24 Dec 1859, bapt. 17 Feb 1860 (Baptism, **St. James Parish** (RC))

Thomas Broughy (father):

Residence - Richmond - February 17, 1860

- Mary Harris & Thomas Cassin – 25 Jan 1789 (Marriage, **St. Michan Parish** (RC))

Hurst

- Mary Harris & Thomas Kelly

  o Thomas Kelly – b. 13 Sep 1859, bapt. 23 Sep 1859 (Baptism, **St. Mary, Pro Cathedral Parish** (RC))

Thomas Kelly (father):

Residence - 39 Capel Street - September 23, 1859

- Mary Harris & Thomas Maguire

  o William Edward Maguire – b. 15 May 1881, bapt. 27 May 1881 (Baptism, **St. Mary, Pro Cathedral Parish** (RC))

  o Thomas Michael Maguire – b. 30 May 1884, bapt. 9 Jun 1884 (Baptism, **St. Mary, Pro Cathedral Parish** (RC))

  o George Maguire – b. 30 Mar 1887, bapt. 6 Apr 1887 (Baptism, **St. Mary, Pro Cathedral Parish** (RC))

Thomas McGuire (father):

Residence - 9 Rutland Place - May 27, 1881

100 Summer Hill - June 9, 1884

April 6, 1887

- Mary Harris & Thomas O'Shea

  o John O'Shea – b. 6 Apr 1833, bapt. 6 Apr 1833 (Baptism, **Tralee Parish** (RC))

Thomas O'Shea (father):

Residence - Tralee - April 6, 1833

- Mary Harris & Timothy Giles

  o Jane Giles – b. 4 Jun 1841, bapt. 4 Jun 1841 (Baptism, **Tralee Parish** (RC))

Timothy Giles (father):

Residence - Tralee - June 4, 1841

Harris Surname Ireland: 1600s to 1900s

- Mary Harris & Unknown Bessler

  o Thomas Patrick Bessler – b. 22 Apr 1891, bapt. 28 Apr 1891 (Baptism, **Harrington Street Parish** (RC))

Unknown Bessler (father):

Residence - 26 Pleasant Street - April 28, 1891

- Mary Harris & Unknown Donovan

  o Patrick Donovan – bapt. 8 May 1848 (Baptism, **Rossalettiri & Kilkeraunmor (Roscarbery & Lissevard) Parish** (RC))

- Mary Harris & Unknown Mahony – 24 Jul 1807 (Marriage, **Ardfield & Rathbarry Parish** (RC))

- Mary Harris & Unknown Mahony

  o Patrick Mahony – b. 28 Feb 1825, bapt. 28 Feb 1825 (Baptism, **Glenbeigh/Glencar Parish** (RC))

- Mary Harris & William Beer

  o Elizabeth Beer – b. 1788, bapt. 1788 (Baptism, **Rathfarnham Parish** (RC))

- Mary Harris & William Forester – 29 Jul 1722 (Marriage, **St. Andrew Parish**)

- Mary Harris & William Henley – 17 Nov 1811 (Marriage, **St. Audoen Parish** (RC))

- Mary Harris & William Mahoney – 18 Feb 1855 (Marriage, **Cork - South Parish** (RC))

  o Timothy Mahoney – bapt. 21 Jun 1856 (Baptism, **Cork - South Parish** (RC))

  o Elizabeth Mahoney – bapt. 23 Jan 1859 (Baptism, **Cork - South Parish** (RC))

  o William Mahoney – bapt. 10 May 1861 (Baptism, **Cork - South Parish** (RC))

Hurst

- Mary Harris & William Stapleton

  - James Stapleton – b. 1847, bapt. 1869 (Baptism, **St. Andrew Parish** (RC))

William Stapleton (father):

Residence - 3 Little Longford Street - 1869

- Mary Anne Harris & Francis McEvoy – 4 Sep 1853 (Marriage, **St. Andrew Parish** (RC))

  - James McEvoy – b. 14 Jun 1854, bapt. 7 Jul 1854 (Baptism, **St. Mary, Pro Cathedral Parish** (RC))

  - Bridget McEvoy – b. 24 Sep 1857, bapt. 2 Oct 1857 (Baptism, **St. Mary, Pro Cathedral Parish** (RC))

  - Catherine McEvoy – b. 1860, bapt. 1860 (Baptism, **St. Andrew Parish** (RC))

Francis McEvoy (father):

Residence - 14 Temple Street - July 7, 1854

2 Horseman's Row - October 2, 1857

3 Sandwith Street -1860

- Mary Anne Harris & George Pike

  - George Pike – b. 17 May 1885, bapt. 20 May 1885 (Baptism, **St. Mary, Pro Cathedral Parish** (RC))

George Pike (father):

Residence - 23 Summer Hill - May 20, 1885

- Mary Anne Harris & George Robinson

  - Elizabeth Mary Joseph Robinson – b. 21 Jun 1875, bapt. 8 Dec 1886 (Baptism, **Rathmines Parish** (RC))

  - Alicia Mary Joseph Robinson – b. May 1876, bapt. 8 Dec 1886 (Baptism, **Rathmines Parish** (RC))

  - Ada Mary Joseph Robinson – b. March 1877, bapt. 8 Dec 1886 (Baptism, **Rathmines Parish** (RC))

Harris Surname Ireland: 1600s to 1900s

George Robinson (father):

Residence - London - December 8, 1886

- Mary Anne Harris & Gulielmo Leary

  - John Leary – b. 19 Jul 1859, bapt. 29 Jul 1859 (Baptism, **St. Mary, Pro Cathedral Parish (RC)**)

  - Gulielmo Andrew Leary – b. 5 Jan 1862, bapt. 15 Jan 1862 (Baptism, **St. Mary, Pro Cathedral Parish (RC)**)

  - Andrew Leary – b. 3 Oct 1863, bapt. 12 Oct 1863 (Baptism, **St. Mary, Pro Cathedral Parish (RC)**)

  - Gulielmo Joseph Leary – b. 10 Aug 1865, bapt. 16 Aug 1865 (Baptism, **St. Mary, Pro Cathedral Parish (RC)**)

Gulielmo Leary (father):

Residence - 9 Horseman's Row - July 29, 1859

10 Horseman's Row - August 16, 1865

Market Place Moore Street - January 15, 1862

3 Market Place - October 12, 1863

- Mary Anne Harris & James Eustace

  - George Eustace – bapt. 1848 (Baptism, **Saggart Parish (RC)**)

  - Patrick Eustace – bapt. 1852 (Baptism, **Saggart Parish (RC)**)

  - Mary Anne Eustace – b. 27 May 1856, bapt. 6 Jun 1856 (Baptism, **St. Nicholas Parish (RC)**)

James Eustace (father):

Residence - 32 Chancery Lane - June 6, 1856

Hurst

- Mary Anne Harris & John Byrne (B y r n e)

  - Francis Byrne – b. 22 Jul 1885, bapt. 24 Jul 1885 (Baptism, **St. Audoen Parish** (RC))

John Byrne (father):

Residence - Bridge Street - July 24, 1885

- Mary Anne Harris & John McCarthy – 30 Nov 1838 (Marriage, **Cork - SS. Peter & Paul Parish** (RC))

  - Mary McCarthy – bapt. 21 Nov 1839 (Baptism, **Cork - SS. Peter & Paul Parish** (RC))

- Mary Anne Harris & John McCarthy

  - Margaret Catherine McCarthy – b. 25 Oct 1874, bapt. 27 Oct 1874 (Baptism, **St. Catherine Parish** (RC))

John McCarthy (father):

Residence - 14 Meath Street - October 27, 1874

- Mary Anne Harris & Joseph Ronan

  - Christopher Ronan – b. 21 Jul 1894, bapt. 10 Aug 1894 (Baptism, **St. Mary, Pro Cathedral Parish** (RC))

Joseph Ronan (father):

Residence - 63 Jervis Street - August 10, 1894

- Mary Anne Harris & Patrick Benn – 8 Nov 1830 (Marriage, **Taney Parish**)

- Mary Anne Harris & Patrick Cleary

  - Mary Anne Cleary – b. 1868, bapt. 1868 (Baptism, **St. Andrew Parish** (RC))

Patrick Cleary (father):

Residence - 10 Aungier Street - 1868

Harris Surname Ireland: 1600s to 1900s

- Mary Anne Harris & Robert Pike

  o Edward Patrick Pike – b. 9 Oct 1871, bapt. 13 Oct 1871 (Baptism, **St. Agatha Parish** (RC))

  o Charlotte Elizabeth Mary Pike – b. 29 May 1873, bapt. 4 Jun 1873 (Baptism, **St. Lawrence Parish** (RC))

  o Hugh Pike – b. 10 Jun 1875, bapt. 16 Jun 1875 (Baptism, **St. Lawrence Parish** (RC))

  o Mary Ellen Pike – b. 1 Oct 1877, bapt. 15 Oct 1877 (Baptism, **St. Lawrence Parish** (RC))

Robert Pike (father):

Residence - 3 Sackdille Garden - October 13, 1871

25 North Court Avenue - June 4, 1873

8 Upper Baggot Street - June 16, 1875

59 Sheriff Street - October 15, 1877

- Mary Anne Harris & Thomas Hanbridge

  o Thomas Peter Hanbridge – bapt. 7 Jul 1845 (Baptism, **St. Nicholas Parish** (RC))

  o Mary Hanbridge – bapt. 28 Nov 1848 (Baptism, **St. Nicholas Parish** (RC))

  o Thomas Hanbridge – bapt. 13 Feb 1850 (Baptism, **St. Nicholas Parish** (RC))

  o Mary Hanbridge – b. 13 Jul 1854, bapt. 17 Jul 1854 (Baptism, **St. Nicholas Parish** (RC))

Thomas Handbidge (father):

Residence - 97 Francis Street - July 17, 1854

- Mary Anne Harris & William Drislane – 7 Nov 1846 (Marriage, **Cork - South Parish** (RC))

- Mary Anne Harris & William Leary

  o John Leary & Catherine Parsons – 18 Apr 1880 (Marriage, **St. Mary, Pro Cathedral Parish** (RC))

John Leary (son):

Residence - 5 Sackville Lane - April 18, 1880

Catherine Parsons, daughter of John Parsons & Rosanna Dunne (daughter-in-law):

Residence - 15 Moore Street - April 18, 1880

Hurst

- ○ Andrew Leary & Elizabeth Williams – 23 Jan 1887 (Marriage, St. Mary, Pro Cathedral Parish (RC))

Andrew Leary (son):

Residence - 12 Moore Street - January 23, 1887

Elizabeth Williams, daughter of Henry Williams & Mary Bradshaw (daughter-in-law):

Residence - 7 Mason Market - January 23, 1887

- Mary Anne Harris & William Wilkinson

  - ○ James Wilkinson – bapt. 5 Nov 1850 (Baptism, Cork - SS. Peter & Paul Parish (RC))

- Mary Ellen Harris & Robert Rickaby

  - ○ Robert Patrick Rickaby – b. 4 Mar 1889, bapt. 11 Mar 1889 (Baptism, St. Mary, Donnybrook Parish (RC))

  - ○ Joseph Rickaby – b. 3 Jan 1891, bapt. 5 Jan 1891 (Baptism, St. Mary, Donnybrook Parish (RC))

  - ○ Samuel Rickaby – b. 19 Mar 1894, bapt. 26 Mar 1894 (Baptism, St. Mary, Donnybrook Parish (RC))

  - ○ Robert Thomas Rickaby – b. 21 Nov 1895, bapt. 25 Nov 1895 (Baptism, St. Mary, Donnybrook Parish (RC))

  - ○ Jane Rickaby – b. 15 Jun 1898, bapt. 20 Jun 1898 (Baptism, St. Mary, Donnybrook Parish (RC))

  - ○ William Rickaby – b. 25 Sep 1900, bapt. 1 Oct 1900 (Baptism, St. Mary, Donnybrook Parish (RC))

Harris Surname Ireland: 1600s to 1900s

Robert Rickaby (father):

    Residence - 1 Tram Cottage - March 11, 1889

        4 Tram Cottages - January 5, 1891

        March 26, 1894

        27 St. Joseph's, Donnybrook - November 25, 1895

        53 Donnybrook - June 20, 1898

        October 1, 1900

- Mary Jane Harris & Charles Duggan – 17 Feb 1863 (Marriage, **Skibbereen & Rath Parish (RC)**)

  - Charles William Duggan – bapt. 25 Dec 1863 (Baptism, **Skibbereen (Creagh & Sullon) Parish** (RC))

  - Jeremiah Duggan – bapt. 3 May 1865 (Baptism, **Skibbereen (Creagh & Sullon) Parish** (RC))

  - Mary Duggan – bapt. 1 Sep 1867 (Baptism, **Cork - South Parish** (RC))

  - Catherine Duggan – bapt. 24 Jan 1871 (Baptism, **Cork - South Parish** (RC))

  - Elizabeth Bridget Duggan – bapt. 3 Feb 1873 (Baptism, **Cork - South Parish** (RC))

Charles Duggan (father):

    Residence - High Street - December 25, 1863

        May 3, 1865

- Mary Jane Harris & John Moylan

  - William John Moylan – bapt. 5 Jul 1864 (Baptism, **Muintervara Parish** (RC))

John Moylan (father):

    Residence - Gurthavalig - July 5, 1864

Hurst

- Mary Magdelin Harris & George Bonaparte

  o Mary Magdelin Bonaparte – bapt. 14 Jun 1835 (Baptism, **St. Mary, Pro Cathedral Parish (RC)**)

  o William Henry Bonaparte – bapt. 18 Sep 1836 (Baptism, **St. Mary, Pro Cathedral Parish (RC)**)

- Mary Magdelin Harris & George Elliot

  o George Elliot – bapt. 24 Apr 1832 (Baptism, **St. Mary, Pro Cathedral Parish (RC)**)

- Mary Margaret Harris & George Frederick William Nuttall – 6 May 1841 (Marriage, **St. George Parish**)

Signatures:

Mary Margaret Harris (wife):

    Residence - Great Charles, St George Parish - May 6, 1841

George Frederick William Nuttall (husband):

    Residence - Telloun Newtown Mount Kennedy, Co. Wicklow, NewCastle -

                          May 6, 1841

    Occupation - Esquire - May 6, 1841

Wedding Witnesses:

John Nuttall, Charles A. Plunkett, [Unclear] Nuttall, & W. H. [Unclear]

Signatures:

Harris Surname Ireland: 1600s to 1900s

- Mary Margaret Harris & James Madden

  - Jeremiah Madden – bapt. 27 Jun 1852 (Baptism, **Douglas & Ballygarvan Parrish** (RC))

  - Kenry Madden – bapt. 24 Feb 1854 (Baptism, **Douglas & Ballygarvan Parrish** (RC))

  - Margaret Madden – bapt. 4 Aug 1860 (Baptism, **Douglas & Ballygarvan Parrish** (RC))

  - John Madden – bapt. 29 Apr 1863 (Baptism, **Douglas & Ballygarvan Parrish** (RC))

  - Bridget Madden – bapt. 3 Feb 1866 (Baptism, **Douglas & Ballygarvan Parrish** (RC))

James Madden (father):

Residence - Kingillee - February 24, 1854

Kilingla - June 27, 1852

- Nancy Harris & Unknown

  - George Unknown – bapt. 23 May 1863 (Baptism, **Schull East Parish** (RC))

- Nane Harris & Patrick Walsh

  - Patrick Walsh – bapt. 22 Jul 1851 (Baptism, **Castlehaven & Myross Parish** (RC))

- Nelly Harris & Cornelius (C o r n e l i u s) Aherne

  - Unknown Aherne – bapt. Mar 1842 (Baptism, **Kilmichael Parish** (RC))

  - Timothy Aherne – bapt. 13 Apr 1844 (Baptism, **Kilmichael Parish** (RC))

  - Jerry Aherne – bapt. 3 May 1846 (Baptism, **Kilmichael Parish** (RC))

  - Con Aherne – bapt. 17 Oct 1848 (Baptism, **Kilmichael Parish** (RC))

Cornelius Aherne (father):

Residence - Carrigboy - March 1842

April 13, 1844

Rea - October 17, 1848

Hurst

- Rachel Harris & Timothy Keeffe – 12 May 1835 (Marriage, **Cork - SS. Peter & Paul Parish (RC)**)

  - Mary Keeffe – bapt. 14 Dec 1837 (Baptism, **Cork - South Parish** (RC))

- Rebecca Harris & Patrick McKean

  - Eleanor McKean – bapt. 25 Jun 1772 (Baptism, **St. Nicholas Parish** (RC))

  - Esther McKean – bapt. 13 Sep 1773 (Baptism, **St. Nicholas Parish** (RC))

  - Nicholas McKean – b. 1785, bapt. 1785 (Baptism, **SS. Michael & John Parish** (RC))

  - Thomas McKean – b. 1789, bapt. 1789 (Baptism, **SS. Michael & John Parish** (RC))

- Roberta Harris & George Adams

  - George Simpson Adams – b. 4 Nov 1885, bapt. 15 Jan 1886 (Baptism, **St. Mary, Pro Cathedral Parish** (RC))

George Adams (father):
Residence - 43 Belvidere Place - January 15, 1886

- Rosanna Harris & James Thompson

  - Isabel Mary Thompson – bapt. 1 Jan 1879 (Baptism, **Rathmines Parish** (RC))

- Rosanna Harris & John William McGlone

  - William James Mary McGlone – b. 15 Jul 1892, bapt. 16 Jul 1892 (Baptism, **St. Mary, Pro Cathedral Parish** (RC))

  - Rosanna Frances McGlone – b. 17 Apr 1894, bapt. 20 Apr 1894 (Baptism, **St. Mary, Pro Cathedral Parish** (RC))

  - Catherine Christine Violet McGlone – b. 8 Apr 1896, bapt. 13 Apr 1896 (Baptism, **St. Mary, Pro Cathedral Parish** (RC))

John William McGlone (father):
Residence - 14 Lower Gardiner Street - 16 July 1892
52 Jervis Street - April 17, 1894
April 13, 1896

Harris Surname Ireland: 1600s to 1900s

- Sally Harris & James Carthy

  - Charles Carthy – bapt. 15 Apr 1814 (Baptism, **Bandon Parish (RC)**)

  - John Carthy – bapt. 26 May 1818 (Baptism, **Desertseges Parish (RC)**)

  - Joan Carthy – bapt. 19 Dec 1820 (Baptism, **Desertseges Parish (RC)**)

  - Ellen Carthy – bapt. 24 Oct 1823 (Baptism, **Desertseges Parish (RC)**)

- Sally Harris & James Cronin

  - Mary Cronin – bapt. 10 Feb 1845 (Baptism, **Courcy's Country or Ballinspittal Parish (RC)**)

- Sarah Harris & Daniel Riordan – 22 May 1803 (Baptism, **Cork - SS. Peter & Paul Parish (RC)**)

  - Daniel Riordan – bapt. 18 Apr 1804 (Baptism, **Cork - South Parish (RC)**)

  - Daniel Riordan – bapt. 30 Apr 1804 (Baptism, **Cork - South Parish (RC)**)

Daniel Riordan (father):

> **Residence - Lying in Hospital - April 18, 1804**
>
> **April 30, 1804**
>
> **Military Service - Cork Militia - May 22, 1803**

- Sarah Harris & Garret Farrell

  - Dennis Farrell – bapt. 15 May 1812 (Baptism, **Clonakilty Parish (RC)**)

- Sarah Harris & John Hanlon – 11 Jun 1854 (Marriage, **Rathmines Parish (RC)**)

  - James Hanlon – b. 23 Aug 1860, bapt. 24 Aug 1860 (Baptism, **St. Catherine Parish (RC)**)

  - John Hanlon – b. 19 Mar 1863, bapt. 27 Mar 1863 (Baptism, **St. Catherine Parish (RC)**)

John Hanlon (father):

> **Residence - 9 Madden's Court - August 24, 1860**
>
> **41 Chambers Street - March 27, 1863**

Hurst

- Sarah Harris & John Jacques

  - Mary Agnes Jacques – b. 1 Apr 1874, bapt. 18 Jul 1895 (Baptism, **St. Agatha Parish** (RC))

John Jacques (father):

Residence - 48 Butain Street - July 18 1895

- Sarah Harris & Joseph Fitzpatrick

  - Elizabeth Fitzpatrick & Michael Darcy – 8 Jan 1882 (Marriage, **St. Mary, Pro Cathedral Parish** (RC))

Elizabeth Fitzpatrick (daughter):

Residence - 28 Lower Gloucester Street - January 8, 1882

Michael Darcy, son of James Darcy & Sarah Unknown (son-in-law):

Residence - 116 Lower Gardiner Street - January 8, 1882

- Sarah Harris & Joseph Levett – 30 Oct 1802 (Marriage, **St. Mary Parish**)

Sarah Harris (wife):

Relationship Status at Marriage - widow

- Sarah Harris & Matthew Shea – 18 Nov 1851 (Marriage, **Tralee Parish** (RC))

  - Mary Shea – b. 13 Oct 1852, bapt. 13 Oct 1852 (Baptism, **Tralee Parish** (RC))

  - Michael Shea – b. 30 Apr 1854, bapt. 30 Apr 1854 (Baptism, **Tralee Parish** (RC))

  - Patrick Shea – b. 16 Mar 1856, bapt. 16 Mar 1856 (Baptism, **Tralee Parish** (RC))

  - Jane Shea – b. 21 Feb 1858, bapt. 29 Feb 1858 (Baptism, **Tralee Parish** (RC))

  - Mary Shea – b. 23 Jan 1863, bapt. 24 Jan 1863 (Baptism, **Tralee Parish** (RC))

  - Honora Shea – b. 19 Apr 1865, bapt. 22 Apr 1865 (Baptism, **Tralee Parish** (RC))

Harris Surname Ireland: 1600s to 1900s

Sarah Harris (mother):

Residence - Curraheen - November 18, 1851

Matthew Shea (father):

Residence - Curraheen - November 18, 1851

October 13, 1852

April 30, 1854

March 16, 1856

February 29, 1858

January 24, 1863

April 22, 1865

- Sarah Harris & Michael Durdon – 30 Aug 1827 (Marriage, **Aghold Parish**)

Sarah Harris (wife):

Residence - Coolkenno - August 30, 1827

Michael Durdon (husband):

Residence - Coolkenno - August 30, 1827

- Sarah Harris & Michael Toole

  ○ Mary A. Toole – b. 27 Jul 1866, bapt. 30 Jul 1866 (Baptism, **Rathmines Parish** (RC))

Michael Toole (father):

Residence - Mount Pleasant - July 30, 1866

- Sarah Harris & Patrick Neill

  ○ George Neill – b. 1859, bapt. 1859 (Baptism, **St. Andrew Parish** (RC))

  ○ Mary Anne Neill – b. 1859, bapt. 1859 (Baptism, **St. Andrew Parish** (RC))

  ○ Joseph Neill – b. 1865, bapt. 1865 (Baptism, **St. Andrew Parish** (RC))

Patrick Neill (father):

Residence - 3 Gloucester Street - 1859

66 Townsend Street - 1865

- Sarah Harris & Richard Gee – 2 Jul 1836 (Marriage, **St. Andrew Parish** (RC))

Hurst

- Sarah Harris & Richard Coleman

    - David Coleman – bapt. 26 Jan 1843 (Baptism, **Desertseges Parish** (RC))

    - Richard Coleman – bapt. 10 Oct 1847 (Baptism, **Timoleague Parish** (RC))

    - Elizabeth Coleman – bapt. 27 May 1851 (Baptism, **Clonakilty Parish** (RC))

    - John Coleman – bapt. 9 Oct 1853 (Baptism, **Clonakilty Parish** (RC))

Sarah Harris (mother):

Residence - George Street - May 27, 1851

Richard Coleman (father):

Residence - George Street - May 27, 1851

- Sarah Harris & Stephen Cullen – 22 May 1836 (Marriage, **St. Andrew Parish** (RC))

    - Margaret Cullen – bapt. 1837 (Baptism, **St. Andrew Parish** (RC))

    - Thomas Arthur Cullen – bapt. 27 Nov 1843 (Baptism, **St. James Parish** (RC))

- Sarah Harris & Thomas Peirce

    - Mary Peirce – b. 1859, bapt. 1859 (Baptism, **St. Andrew Parish** (RC))

    - Sarah Pierce & James Connor – 2 Jul 1882 (Marriage, **St. Mary, Pro Cathedral Parish** (RC))

Sarah Pierce (daughter):

Residence - 10 Taafes Row - July 2, 1882

James Connor, son of Jeremiah Connor & Mary Hall (son-in-law):

Residence - 112 Lower Mecklenburgh Street - July 2, 1882

Thomas Peirce (father):

Residence - 39 Poolbeg Street - 1859

- Sarah Harris & William Eglinton

    - Rosanna Eglinton – b. 26 Jun 1857, bapt. 29 Jun 1857 (Baptism, **St. Michan Parish** (RC))

William Eglinton (father):

Residence - 28 King Street - June 29, 1857

Harris Surname Ireland: 1600s to 1900s

- Sarah Harris & William Haughton – 9 Nov 1806 (Marriage, **St. Werburgh Parish**)

Sarah Harris (wife):

Residence - Golden Lane - November 9, 1806

- Sarah Harris & William Mahon – 3 Dec 1815 (Marriage, **St. Catherine Parish**)

- Sarah Harris & William Mallin – 18 Dec 1815 (Marriage, **St. Catherine Parish**)

Sarah Harris (wife):

Residence - Meath - December 18, 1815

- Susan Harris & Joseph Cross

  o Arthur Cross – b. 22 Jul 1864, bapt. 1868 (Baptism, **St. James Parish** (RC))

  o Ellen Cross, b. 24 May 1874, bapt. 21 May 1897 (Baptism, **St. Mary, Pro Cathedral Parish** (RC)) & Christopher Canavan – 24 May 1897 (Marriage, **St. Mary, Pro Cathedral Parish** (RC))

Ellen Cross (daughter):

Residence - 197 Great Britain Street - May 24, 1897

Christopher Canavan, son of Christopher Canavan & Anne Murphy (son-in-law):

Residence - 17 Denmark Place - May 24, 1897

  o Mary Hannah Cross – bapt. 2 Jul 1898 (Baptism, **St. Mary, Pro Cathedral Parish** (RC))

Joseph Cross (father):

Residence - Wonahampton - 1868

197 Great Britain Street - May 21, 1897

July 2, 1898

- Susan Harris & Michael Riordan

  o Thomas Riordan – bapt. 1827 (Baptism, **Cork - SS. Peter & Paul Parish** (RC))

- Susanna Harris & Michael Reardon

  o Michael Reardon – bapt. 2 Feb 1777 (Baptism, **St. Catherine Parish** (RC))

Hurst

- Teresa Harris & Edward Irwin

  - Catherine Irwin – b. 25 Jun 1885, bapt. 3 Jul 1885 (Baptism, **St. Mary, Pro Cathedral Parish** (RC))

Edward Irwin (father):

  Residence - 3 Dillon's Place - July 3, 1885

- Unknown Harris & James Unknown – 15 Jun 1850 (Marriage, **St. Andrew Parish** (RC))

The writing in the church register entry is very difficult to read. It is hard to accurately list the last name of the groom and the first name of the bride.

- Unknown Harris & John Power

  - William Power – bapt. 31 Jan 1796 (Baptism, **Cork - SS. Peter & Paul Parish** (RC))

John Power (father):

  Residence - Kyrl Quay - January 31, 1796

- Unknown Harris & Michael Shea – 2 Mar 1867 (Marriage, **Glenbeigh/Glencar Parish** (RC))

Unknown Harris (wife):

  Residence - Kilchuae - March 2, 1867

Michael Shea (husband):

  Residence - Treangarriv - March 2, 1867

- Winifred Harris & Thomas Madden

  - John Madden – bapt. 11 May 1770 (Baptism, **St. Nicholas Parish** (RC))

Harris Surname Ireland: 1600s to 1900s

Name Variations

Includes Latin and Abbreviated forms of names found in the original documents.

Abigail = Abigale, Abigall

Anne = Ann, Anna, Annae

Bartholomew = Barth, Bartholmeus, Bartholomeo

Bridget = Birgis, Brigid, Brigida, Bridgit

Catherine = Catharine, Catharina, Catharinae, Catherina, Cath, Cathae, Cathe, Cathn, Kate

Charles = Carolus, Charls, Chas

Christopher = Christoph

Daniel = Danielem, Danielis

Edward = Ed, Edwd

Eleanor = Eleo, Eleonora, Elinor, Ellenor

Elizabeth = Betty, Elisa, Elisabeth, Eliz, Eliza, Elizab, Elizh, Elizth

Ellen = Elena, Ellena

Emily= Emilia

Esther = Essie, Ester

Francis = Fransicum

George = Geo, Georg, Georgius

Grace = Gratiae

Gulielmo = Guil, Guillelmi, Gulielmum, Guillelmus, Gulmi

Harold = Harry

Honor = Hanora, Honora

Harris Surname Ireland: 1600s to 1900s

Hugh = Hew

James = Jacobi, Jacobus, Jas

Jane = Joanna

Jeanne = Jeannae, Joannae

Joan = Johanna, Joney

John = Jno, Joannem, Joannes, Johannis

Joseph = Jos

Leticia = Letitia, Lettice, Letticia

Lewis = Louis

Luke = Lucas

Margaret = Margarita, Margaritae, Margeret, Marget, Margt

Mary = Maria, My

Mary Anne = Marianna, Marianne, Maryanne

Michael = Michaelis, Michl

Patrick = Pat, Patt, Patk, Patricii, Patricius

Peter = Petri, Petrus

Ralph = Ralfe

Richard = Ricardi, Ricardus, Rich, Richd

Robert = Roberti

Rose = Rosa, Rosae

Samuel = Samuelis

Thomas = Thom, Thomae, Thoms, Thos, Ths

Timothy = Timotheus, Timy

Valentine = Val, Valentinae, Valentinus

William = Wil, Will, Willm, Wm

Notes

Notes

Notes

Notes

Notes

Notes

Harris Surname Ireland: 1600s to 1900s

Hurst

Gerald Patrick
  1890 Jul 2 433
John Edward
  1888 Mar 15 433
Josephine Elizabeth
  1899 Jul 29 433
Laura
  1902 Jan 2 433
Mary Sophie
  1900 Aug 12 433
Timothy
  1902 Jan 2 433
Patrick 433
Peter 437
Drislane
William 479
Duff
Baptisms
  Anne
    1790 Jan 15 410
  Thomas 410
Duffey
Catherine 131
Duffy
Baptisms
  Elizabeth
    1899 Apr 14 132
  Owen
    1897 Aug 9 132
Births
  Elizabeth
    1899 Apr 12 132
  Owen
    1897 Aug 7 132
  Eugene 132
  Nicholas 132
  Thomas 392
Duggan
Baptisms
  Catherine
    1871 Jan 24 481
  Charles William
    1863 Dec 25 481
  Elizabeth Bridget
    1873 Feb 3 481
  Jeremiah

  1865 May 3 481
Mary
  1867 Sep 1 481
Charles 481
Dulea
Margaret 120
Duncan
William 256
Dunn
Mary 150
Sarah 55
Dunne
Baptisms
  Valentine
    1886 May 31 302
Births
  Valentine
    1886 May 30 302
  Jeremiah 302
  Joseph 302
  Mary 174, 212
  Rosanna 479
  Thomas 174
Dunnes
Catherine 314
Durdon
Michael 487
Durnan
Baptisms
  Francis Joseph
    1869 May 12 410
  Mary Agnes
    1878 410
Births
  Francis Joseph
    1869 May 4 410
  Mary Agnes
    1878 410
  Peter 410
Dwyer
Baptisms
  James
    1846 Oct 25 423
  Jeremiah
    1844 Mar 24 423
  John Stephen

516

Harris Surname Ireland: 1600s to 1900s

Hurst

Harris Surname Ireland: 1600s to 1900s

Harris Surname Ireland: 1600s to 1900s

Hurst

Hurst

Hurst

John

Hurst

Harris Surname Ireland: 1600s to 1900s

Hurst

Harris Surname Ireland: 1600s to 1900s

Hurst

Harris Surname Ireland: 1600s to 1900s

Harris Surname Ireland: 1600s to 1900s

Hurst

Burials

Hurst

Hurst

Hurst

Hurst

Harris Surname Ireland: 1600s to 1900s

Hurst

K

Hurst

Harris Surname Ireland: 1600s to 1900s

L

M

Hurst

N

Neary
Margaret..24
Michael 24
Neill
Anne..221
Baptism
Joseph
1865 487
Baptisms

Hurst

T

U

Hurst

Y

About The Author

Donovan Hurst graduated from San Diego State University with a Bachelor of Arts in the major field of studies of History and a minor in the field of studies of Anthropology. He is a current member of The General Society of Mayflower Descendants and has been conducting genealogical research for over 10 years tracing back his ancestors to their ancestral homelands in Denmark, England, France, Germany, Ireland, Norway, and Scotland.

.

www.ingramcontent.com/pod-product-compliance
Lightning Source LLC
Chambersburg PA
CBHW080407270326
41929CB00018B/2931